The Legacy of Thatcherism

The Legacy of Thatcherism

Assessing and exploring
Thatcherite social and
economic policies

Edited by
Stephen Farrall and Colin Hay

Published for THE BRITISH ACADEMY
by OXFORD UNIVERSITY PRESS

Oxford University Press, Great Clarendon Street, Oxford OX2 6DP

British Library Cataloguing in Publication Data
Data available

Library of Congress Cataloging in Publication Data
Data available

Typeset by Keystroke, Station Road, Codsall, Wolverhampton
Printed in Great Britain by
TJ International, Padstow, Cornwall
ISBN 978-0-19-726570-3

MIX
Paper from
responsible sources
FSC
www.fsc.org
FSC® C013056

The big question mark over the Thatcher years . . . is how durable the changes will prove to be when circumstances change.

Andrew Gamble, 'Privatisation, Thatcherism
and the British State', *Thatcher's Law* (1989: 18)

No doubt, thirty to forty years hence, we will have a much fuller picture of the events of these years.

Dennis Kavanagh, *Thatcherism* (1987: 2)

Contents

Contents

Notes on contributors

Sarah Childs is Professor of Politics and Gender at the University of Bristol, UK. She has published widely on women, representation and party politics and Parliament over the last decade or so. Key articles on New Labour's women MPs, descriptive and substantive representation, the concept of critical mass, and conservatism, gender and representation, have been published in *Political Studies, Politics and Gender, Government and Parliamentary Affairs and Party Politics*. Her latest book, *Sex, Gender and the Conservative Party: From Iron Lady to Kitten Heels*, with Paul Webb was published in 2012 (Palgrave Macmillan). She is currently researching gender and party regulation, and the UK Parliament as a gendered institution. In 2009–10 she was the gender Special Adviser to the UK Parliament's 'Speaker's Conference' on representation.

Miriam E. David, PhD, AcSS, FRSA is Professor Emerita of Sociology of Education and was, until recently, Professor (2005–10) and Associate Director (Higher Education) of the ESRC's Teaching & Learning Research Programme (2004–9) at the Institute of Education University of London. She is a visiting professor in the Centre for Higher Education & Equity Research (CHEER) in the School of Education and Social Work at the University of Sussex. She was formerly a Professor at London South Bank (1988–97); University of the Arts (1997–99) and Keele University (1999–2005). She has a world-class reputation for her feminist social research on families, gender, social diversity and inequalities across education. She has published 25 books and reports, and 160 articles or chapters, including an intellectual biography in 2003, *Personal and Political: Feminisms, Sociology and Family Lives* (Trentham Books).

Peter Dorey is Professor of British Politics at Cardiff University. He has published extensively on post-1945 Conservative politics, the Labour party, House of Lords reform, trade unionism, and aspects of contemporary public policy, particularly education policy since the 1960s. His 2011 book, *British Conservatism: The Politics and Philosophy of Inequality* (I.B. Tauris), was awarded the annual prize for the best publication on Conservatives and Conservatism in 2011, by the Political Studies Association's specialist group on Conservatives and Conservatism. Peter Dorey is also the co-author, with Mark Garnett and Andrew Denham, of *From Crisis to Coalition: The Conservative Party 1997–2010* (Palgrave Macmillan), also published in 2011. He is currently writing, with Mark Garnett, a book on the Conservative-Liberal Democrat Coalition. In spring 2014, Peter Dorey will be Visiting Professor of Politics at the University of Bordeaux.

Danny Dorling is a professor at the School of Geography and the Environment, University of Oxford. He went to University in Newcastle upon Tyne. He has worked in Newcastle, Bristol, Leeds, Sheffield and New Zealand. With a group of colleagues he helped create the website www.worldmapper.org which shows who has most and least in the world. Much of Danny's work is available open access (see www.dannydorling. org). His work concerns issues of housing, health, employment, education and poverty. His recent books include, co-authored texts *The Atlas of the Real World: Mapping the Way we Live* (Thames & Hudson, 2010) and *Bankrupt Britain: An Atlas of Social Change* (Policy Press, 2011). Recent sole authored books include, *The No-nonsense Guide to Equality* (New Internationalist, 2012), *The Visualization of Social Spatial Structure* (Wiley, 2012), *The Population of the UK* (Sage, 2012); and, in 2013, *Unequal Health, The 32 Stops* and *Population Ten Billion* (Policy Press).

David Downes is Professor Emeritus of Social Administration and a founder member of the Mannheim Centre for Criminology at the London School of Economics. His main contributions to the criminological field have been: a study of delinquency in east London (*The Delinquent Solution*, The Free Press, 1966); a study of the major forms of gambling (main author, *Gambling, Work and Leisure*, Law Book Co. of Australasia, 1976); a text on the sociology of deviant behaviour (with Paul Rock, *Understanding Deviance*, Oxford University Press, sixth edn, 2011); and a comparative study of penal policy in the Netherlands and England (*Contrasts in Tolerance*, Clarendon Press, 1988). With Rod Morgan, he has written the chapter on 'The politics of law and order' in successive editions of the *Oxford Handbook of Criminology* (1994, 1997, 2002, 2007 and 2011). He was editor of the *British Journal of Criminology* 1985–90, and was a founding editor of the Clarendon Studies in Criminology series for Oxford University Press.

Stephen Farrall is Professor of Criminology and Director of the Centre for Criminological Research at the University of Sheffield. Previous monographs of his include: B. Godfrey, D. Cox, and S. Farrall, *Serious Criminals: A Historical Study of Habitual Criminals* (Clarendon Studies in Criminology, Oxford University Press, 2011), and S. Farrall, J. Jackson, and E. Gray, *Social Order and the Fear of Crime in Contemporary Times* (Clarendon Studies in Criminology, Oxford University Press, 2009). He is currently continuing to research the Thatcherite influence on crime with Will Jennings, Colin Hay, and Emily Gray (funded by the ESRC).

Andrew Gamble is Professor of Politics and a Fellow of Queens' College in the University of Cambridge. He is a Fellow of the British Academy and the UK Academy of Social Sciences. His main research interests lie in political economy, political theory and political history. His books include *The Free Economy and the Strong State: The Politics of Thatcherism* (Duke University Press, 1988), *Between Europe and America: the Future of British Politics* (Palgrave Macmillan, 2003) and *The Spectre at the Feast: Capitalist Crisis and the Politics of Recession* (Palgrave Macmillan, 2009). In 2005 he received the Isaiah Berlin Prize from the Political Studies Association for lifetime contribution to political studies.

Colin Hay is Professor of Government and Comparative Public Policy at Sciences Po, Paris and an Affiliate Professor of Political Analysis at the University of Sheffield where he co-founded the Sheffield Political Economy Research Institute. He is the author of a number of books including, most recently, *The Failure of Anglo-Liberal Capitalism* (Palgrave, 2013) and *The Political Economy of European Welfare Capitalism* (Palgrave, 2012, with Daniel Wincott). He is editor or co-editor of the journals *New Political Economy*, *Comparative European Politics* and *British Politics*.

Michael Hill is Emeritus Professor of Social Policy of the University of Newcastle. He has written on many aspects of social policy and the policy process. He is author of *The Public Policy Process* (Pearson, 2012) and *Implementing Public Policy* (with Peter Hupe; Sage, 2008), *Social Policy in the Modern World* (Wiley-Blackwell, 2006) and *Understanding Social Policy* (with Zoë Irving; Wiley-Blackwell, 2009). In 2009 he was given the Social Policy Association's lifetime award.

Peter M. Jackson AcSS, is Research Director for the College of Social Science at the University of Leicester and Professor of Economics and Strategy in its School of Management. For the past forty years Peter has researched topics in the general area of public sector economics and public sector management and has made contributions to the study of public expenditure, local government finance and public sector efficiency. In the 1980s he led the Royal Institute of Public Administration's examination of the first Thatcher government's policies, which resulted in the book *Government Policy Initiatives 1979/80* (RIPA, 1982). He was an adviser to the Scottish Parliament's Finance Committee on the Private Finance Initiative and has regularly provided advice for national and international agencies.

Will Jennings is Reader in Politics at the University of Southampton. He specializes in the quantitative analysis of politics, policy and society (in particular in the application of time-series methods), in relation to fields such as political behaviour, agenda-setting, public policy and criminology. He also specializes in executive politics and the governance of risk in mega-projects.

Ken Jones is Professor of Education at Goldsmiths, University of London. He is the author of *Right Turn* (Radius, 1989), an early attempt to take the measure of Thatcherism's achievements in education. He has also written *Education in Britain* (Policy Press, 2003 – revised edn forthcoming) and co-written *Schooling in Western Europe: The New Order and its Adversaries* (Palgrave, 2007). Both books aim to understand Thatcherism in wider, comparative contexts.

Peter A. Kemp is a professor of public policy in the Blavatnik School of Government at the University of Oxford and a member of the Oxford Institute of Social Policy. His main area of research is housing, particularly housing allowances and private rental housing. He is currently writing a book on the political economy of private renting in Britain since the late nineteenth century. His other projects include research into the impact on private tenants of cuts in housing benefit in the UK and a comparative study of income-related housing allowances in the EU-15 countries. His most recent book (co-authored with Tony Crook) is *Transforming Private Landlords: Housing, Markets and Public Policy* (Wiley-Blackwell, 2011).

Chris Philo completed his education to PhD level at the University of Cambridge, then took a lecturing position at the University of Wales, Lampeter (1989–95), before being appointed to a Chair of Geography at the University of Glasgow. His principal research interest has been 'madness', or the changing geographies, past and present, of 'asylums' and other mental health facilities/services, leading to his substantial, archivally based monograph *The Space Reserved for Insanity* (Mellen Press, 2004). He has also researched many different dimensions to the social geography of 'otherness', 'outsiderness', marginality, exclusion and abandonment, as well as editing volumes such as *Off the Map: The Social Geography of Poverty in the UK* (Child Poverty Action Group, 1995).

Alan Murie is Emeritus Professor of Urban and Regional Studies at the Centre for Urban and Regional Studies at Birmingham University. He was previously Head of the School of Public Policy and Director of the Centre for Urban and Regional Studies at the University of Birmingham and Professor of Planning and Housing at Heriot-Watt University, Edinburgh. He has written widely on housing provision, housing policy and issues related to cities and neighbourhoods throughout the UK and Europe. His research on UK housing has included original work on privatization of public housing and the development of housing policy and problems.

Adrian Sinfield, Professor Emeritus of Social Policy at the University of Edinburgh, has taught and researched on social security, unemployment, poverty, inequality and the social division of welfare. He has been both Chair and President of the Social Policy Association and received its first lifetime achievement award. Co-founder of the Unemployment Unit and chair for its first ten years, he has also been vice-chair of the Child Poverty Action Group for eight years and continues to be a very strong supporter. His publications include: *The Long-term Unemployed* (OECD, 1968), *Which Way for Social Work?* (Fabian Society, 1969), *What Unemployment Means* (Blackwell, 1981); *The Workless State* (co-edited; Martin Robertson, 1981), *Excluding Youth* (co-authored; Edinburgh Bridges Project, 1991), *Comparing Tax Routes to Welfare in Denmark and the United Kingdom* (co-authored; Danish National Institute of Social Research, 1996).

Peter Taylor-Gooby, OBE, FBA, AcSS, FRSA is Professor of Social Policy at the University of Kent, Chair of the British Academy programme on *New Paradigms in Public Policy* and project on *Nudging Citizens towards Localism* and of the HEFCE REF 2014 and RAE 2008 Social Work and Social Policy Panels, and previously President of the British Association for the Advancement of Science's Sociology and Social Policy Section. He directed the ESRC 'Social Contexts and Responses to Risk' and 'Economic Beliefs and Behaviour and the EU Welfare Reform and the Management of Societal Change' and 'Subsidiarity and Convergence' programmes and chaired the HEFCE Social Work and Social Policy RAE 2008 Panel. He is a contributor to Downing Street and Treasury roundtables, Government Office for Science Foresight Reviews, Council of Europe Policy Fora and Blackett Reviews. Recent books include: *New Paradigms in Public Policy* (Oxford University Press and the British Academy, 2013), *Reframing Social Citizenship* (Oxford University Press, 2009), *Risk in Social Science* (with Jens Zinn; Oxford University Press, 2006), *Ideas and the Welfare State Reform in Western Europe* (Palgrave Macmillan, 2005) and *New Risks, New Welfare* (Oxford University Press, 2004). Current research, supported by Leverhulme, ESRC and the EU examines different aspects of citizenship and social cohesion. His current work is mainly on welfare state restructuring and retrenchment, following the Great Recession and is summed up in *The Double Crisis of the Welfare State and What We can do About it* (Palgrave Macmillan, 2013).

Helen Thompson is a Reader in Politics at the University of Cambridge. She is the author of various books on different aspects of international political economy, most recently *China and the Mortgaging of America: Domestic Politics and Economic Interdependence* (Palgrave Macmillan, 2010).

Paul Webb is Professor of Politics at the University of Sussex and editor of the journal *Party Politics*. He is author or editor of numerous publications on British and comparative party politics, including *The Modern British Party System* (Sage, 2000), *Political Parties in Advanced Industrial Societies* (Oxford University Press, 2002, with David Farrell and Ian Holliday), and *Sex, Gender and the Conservative Party* (Palgrave Macmillan, 2012, with Sarah Childs). He was elected to the Academy of Social Sciences in 2010.

Alan Walker, BA, DLitt, Hon. DSocSc (HKBU), FBA, FRSA, AcSS, is Professor of Social Policy and Social Gerontology at the University of Sheffield, UK. He is currently Director of the New Dynamics of Ageing Programme (http://www.newdynamics.group.shef.ac.uk) funded by five UK Research Councils and Social Innovations for an Ageing Population funded by the European Commission. In 2007 he received a Lifetime Achievement Award from the Social Policy Association and the first Outstanding Achievement Award made by the British Society of Gerontology. At the 2011 IAGG European Congress in Bologna, he was awarded the Association's first Medal and Honorary Diploma for Advances in Gerontology and Geriatrics (Social and Behavioural Sciences). In 2013 he became the Economic and Social Research Council's first Impact Champion.

Carol Walker is Professor of Social Policy in the School of Social and Political Sciences at the University of Lincoln. In the period leading up to and during the Thatcher administrations, she was closely involved with local and national welfare rights activity, advising claimants in their dealings with the then Department of Health and Social Security (now Department of Work and Pensions). She undertook a close study of the Supplementary Benefits Review which, though set up by the preceding Labour government, led to the first Social Security Act 1980, introduced in the first Thatcher administration. She then went on to research and publish on the impact of those reforms (*Managing Poverty: The Limits of Social Assistance*, Routledge, 1993) and as part of the Social Security Consortium on the impact of the Social Fund introduced in 1986. She also co-edited, with Alan Walker, two audits of the social impact of the Thatcher administrations (*Britain Divided: The Growth of Social Exclusion in the 1980s and 1990s* and *The Growing Divide: A Social Audit 1979–1987*, both published by the Child Poverty Action Group). More recently her main research focus has been on people with learning disabilities and their families, particularly in older age.

Acknowledgements

We would like to acknowledge both the support of the British Academy in hosting in July 2011 the conference from which this book emerged, and for the diligent and extremely helpful ways in which its staff assisted us during both the arranging of the conference and on the days itself. As Editors we have been delighted with the speed and clarity with which our contributors produced their respective chapters and the insights which they have brought to our own thinking on this matter. In addition to those whose chapters are included herein, we wish to acknowledge the additional contributions made to the debates during the conference itself, namely: Hugh Bochel, John Curtice, Andrew Defty, Stephen Driver, David Faulkner, Richard Heffernan, John Hills, Christopher Hood, Richard Vinen and Peter Williams.

Stephen Farrall
Colin Hay

Foreword

Controversy continues to swirl around Margaret Thatcher and Thatcherism. As a leader she made a greater impact than almost any other British political leader in the twentieth century apart from Churchill. Polls in the USA have shown that the names of only three British Prime Ministers are familiar to the American public – Churchill, Thatcher and Blair. Thatcher looms large in the Conservative pantheon, but like several other key figures in the party's history she succeeded in part because she was an outsider. During her ascendancy there were many critics in her own party who doubted that she was really a Conservative at all. She was a dynamic force of the kind Conservatives have generally resisted. Yet she came to be adored by a large part of the party rank and file – 'her people' as she referred to them. Her career before she became leader was unremarkable, and she won the leadership through a set of accidents and contingencies. Once installed as leader she had to deal with the hostility and scepticism of a large part of her Shadow Cabinet, and she trailed Jim Callaghan in the polls for most of her period as Opposition leader. Yet even in those early years of her leadership there were hints of what was to come. The 'Iron Lady' speech on the new cold war marked her out, as did the encouragement she gave to the radical economic, political and cultural ideas which were fermenting in the Conservative Party in the 1970s. She was a cautious pragmatic politician, generally very good until the end at calculating the political odds and not overreaching, but she was always able at the same time to convey the sense that she wanted to go much further than circumstances allowed. This ability to let 'her people' know that she was 'on their side', that she wanted radical changes and was more frustrated than anyone about the obstacles in the way, won her a devoted following in the party, and helped create the heroic myth around her leadership, which still casts a long shadow over the party.

This notion of Thatcherism, as Colin Hay and Stephen Farrall argue, does not mean that Thatcherism was a fully-worked-out ideological and political project, but emphasizes instead how much of it was improvised. In Peter Riddell's phrase, Thatcherism was a set of instincts which pushed policy in certain directions without ever laying down very detailed blueprints for policy. Thatcherism on this view was a form of statecraft, shaped by agency but also by circumstances and contingencies, hesitations and expediency, its meaning dependent on particular contexts, and often retrospective interpretation. Thatcherism seen in this way is still an engrossing tale, partly because Thatcher was leader and Prime Minister for such a long time, almost sixteen years, but partly because of some of the momentous events and changes which marked these years, culminating in her overthrow by opponents within her own party, still regarded as treason by many Thatcherites, not least by Thatcher herself. Yet as Hay and Farrall point out, there are many other ways of thinking about Thatcherism, and how significant it was for British politics. One view is that the claims for Thatcherism have always been over-blown, and that it was never much more than part of the normal din of politics, with much less real impact on policies. Many of the changes associated with Thatcherism, it is suggested, would have come about anyway; it did not need the *Sturm und Drang* of the Thatcher years. Political parties and their conflicts are eye-catching but do not have very much to do with the long-term evolution of policy.

Hay and Farrall note this view but they develop a different perspective, drawing on the seminal work of Rhodes and Marsh on the implementation of Thatcherite policies, emphasizing how policy does matter, and that a true account of Thatcherism and its significance needs to analyse policy in different sectors, and to be aware of the different times and speeds at which policies developed. This book develops further the editors' innovative 'cascade' theory of policy radicalism, and offers a new way of periodizing Thatcherism, taking into account the Major years as well. The authors of the various chapters are charged with the task of providing an empirically based examination of how policy developed in particular areas from the economy to education, housing and crime, within the general framework the editors set out. The great merit of this approach is that it provides a much more detailed and nuanced assessment of the impact of Thatcherism and of its relative coherence or incoherence over time by placing the emphasis on policy outcomes rather than ideological commitments. The authors assess which policy initiatives and outcomes can properly be labelled Thatcherite, and which have little to do with Thatcherism as such. What emerges is a much fuller picture of both the strengths and the limits of Thatcherism, as well as its complexity and unevenness.

Another intriguing aspect of Thatcherism is that in some areas, including the future of the United Kingdom and Britain's participation in the European Union, many consequences of the policies the Thatcher government pursued were unintended. Many of the problems of funding the welfare state and economic management which governments must now wrestle with stem from the collapse of the full employment economy in the 1980s and the emergence of a very different growth model, based on finance, services, and immigration. Thatcherism also had a profound impact on British political parties, transforming both the Conservative party and the Labour party in irreversible ways, and introducing a very different style of politics.

This book is a major contribution to the study of Thatcherism, and deserves to reignite interest in the Thatcher period and how best to characterize and understand Thatcherism. It rejects the idea that politics does not matter, and that human affairs are shaped only by deep structural forces. But it avoids the opposite trap of asserting that only politics matters, and of endorsing the heroic myth of Thatcher and Thatcherism which has been promulgated by a strange alliance between those most hostile to her legacy and those most in thrall to it.

Andrew Gamble
University of Cambridge
March 2013

PART I
SETTING THE SCENE

1
Interrogating and conceptualizing the legacy of Thatcherism

COLIN HAY AND STEPHEN FARRALL

Too often the analysis of policy looks at the short-term effects of legislation.
(Rhodes and Marsh, 1992: 5)

Looking at Thatcherism afresh

Throughout the 1980s and the early 1990s the pages of academic and popular journals were filled with debate – invariably heated – on the nature, extent, significance and reversibility of Thatcherism. Today the echoes of a once deafening clamour are scarcely audible. Thatcherism has almost disappeared from the lexicon of British political analysis.[1] The inspiration for this volume was the desire to bring together a distinguished array of seasoned commentators on Thatcherism to reflect on the object of these previous analyses with the benefit of hindsight not afforded the protagonists of the time.

We are by no means the first to call for such an assessment (see, for instance, Gamble, 1989; Terrill, 1989; Whitty and Menter, 1989; and more recently Evans, 2006). But we do have certain advantages over our predecessors. For the authors we have assembled in this volume – many of whom contributed to the earlier debates – have had rather longer to

---

[1] And this despite the recent resurgence of interest in Thatcher's period in office – see, for instance, Chessyre (2012), Jackson and Saunders (2012), and Vinen (2009). What also distinguishes this new literature is that it is written largely by historians, confirming perhaps our sense that Thatcherism (in so far as the term is seen as warranted) is considered a phenomenon that is now concluded.

gather their thoughts (and, indeed, empirical evidence) on the legacy of Thatcherism; and they are also an extremely distinguished bunch – we do not have to go it alone in providing the assessment we now feel necessary. Three decades on and as the members of the first generation to grow up in a 'post-consensus' UK make their way in the world, is, we suggest, a particularly apposite moment at which to embark upon such an assessment.

To be clear from the outset, this volume is not about what has come to be known as 'neo-liberalism' – or it is not just about neo-liberalism as an approach to the management of the economy, the distribution of resources and the relationships between people, organizations and institutions. Whilst such a view has undoubtedly proved highly influential since the 1970s in several economically advanced nations (Harvey, 2005), our concern is not principally with the fortune of neo-liberalism in Britain. For Thatcherism is not simply neo-liberalism. Thus, whilst we hope to contribute to the current assessment of the ramifications of neo-liberalism and neo-liberalization (see also, Leys, 2001; Offer, 2006: 297; Taylor, 1990), we do so whilst in part bemoaning the ascendancy of the term neo-liberalism. In our view it has unfortunately crowded out and narrowed the range of the analyses offered of specific political projects such as 'Thatcherism' or 'Reaganomics' or, indeed, those offered by a more general account of the rise of the New Right (see Hay, 1994, 1886; Hayes, 1994; King, 1985). Our focus, both in this introductory and framing chapter and in the collection more widely, is thus on the continued relevance of one of these 'earlier labels' (Larner et al., 2007: 244) – 'Thatcherism'.

Some of the changes in social and economic policies adopted during Thatcher's period in office have been described as being as radical as anything since the creation of the welfare state following the end of the Second World War (Glennester, 1994). And it is clear that whatever we may think of them, the debates around the nature, impact and legacy of Mrs Thatcher's eleven years in office do not seem destined to subside quietly – indeed as we get further *from* her period in office, we need increasingly to *return to* some of the decisions made during her tenure in office to make sense of the present (Gamble, 1996: 19; Hay, 2009; Vinen, 2009). More recent assessments by political scientists of the rise of 'New Labour' (Hay, 1999; Heffernan, 2000) and of the development of the British state in the post-war period (Kerr, 2001; McAnulla, 2006) have had, at some level, to grapple with the period between 1979 and 1990 (and, indeed, 1997). But there are other reasons for returning to the Thatcher years and, as we shall argue, for preferring the term 'Thatcherism' to that of 'neo-liberalism' to describe the period since 1979 in Britain. For 'Thatcherism' – however hard it remains to offer a strict definition – embraced more than just neo-liberal ideas. As has been discussed at length elsewhere, Thatcherism combined both neo-liberal and neo-conservative strands. And it was often at its more radical and consequential when its identified policy targets were firmly in the cross-wires of each set of ideological dispositions (see Hay, 1996: 137; Hayes, 1994 and Levitas, 1986).

Three decades after the first election of a government led by Mrs Thatcher, it is perhaps time to take stock of the concept of 'Thatcherism' and the prominent role it has played in the history of post-war Britain. Most commentators seem to accept that Thatcherism is now a *historic* concept – referring, if not exactly to the period 1979–90, then certainly to events now largely concluded. This allows us a degree of historical perspective that was unavailable to the protagonists in the debates that came to define the term.

Of course, there is much debate about what 'Thatcherism' was, with some, such as Gamble (1989), reminding us that Thatcherism was more noteworthy for its rhetoric than for its achievements (see also Phillips, 1998). Indeed, for some at least, even in areas characterized by significant rhetorical radicalism, such as agricultural policy (Smith, 1991) or criminal justice (Newburn, 2007), little changed after 13 years of Thatcherism (Timmins, 2001). The historian Arthur Marwick suggests that the social forces and social values that brought Thatcher to power will outlast her, but goes on to acknowledge that 'Thatcherism produced an increasingly divided and polarized society' (2003: 337). Gamble (1989) raises questions over the durability of Thatcher's influence, whilst Windsor (2003) claims that her governments have had a more enduring impact on the UK.

Yet we need to tread carefully here; the counterfactuals, as ever, are important. For even if Thatcher had *not* won the May 1979 general election, much of what has subsequently transpired (indeed, much of what we now term Thatcherism) might well have happened anyway. As Bateson (1997) notes, Callaghan's Ruskin College speech in 1976 has been seen as the end of consensus in education policy – although this has not prevented some from pointing to the 1988 Education Reform Act as *the* decisive break from post-war education policy (Jones, 2003). Similarly, the decline of the penal welfare model can be traced back to the 1970s (Garland, 2001). Yet it is difficult not to accept that, as one influential commentator has put it, Thatcher 'did some extraordinary things to her country' (Young, 1993).

Indeed, in so doing she (and the administrations over which she presided) arguably altered the trajectory of the country's development. Even long-term and seemingly enduring path dependencies *can* and arguably *were* altered dramatically. Whichever way one looks at it, the Thatcherite period brought about a fundamental reorganization of central–local government relations (Leys, 2001; Loughlin, 1989: 26) and of the nexus between citizen and state. As such, Thatcher's period in office can be seen as a 'critical juncture' for the UK – an idea supported by the recent resurgence of interest in this period.

The seminar which gave rise to this collection was hosted and largely funded by the British Academy. Held in July 2011, the seminar brought together a range of experts in housing, economics, law and order, education and so on to discuss the enduring legacy of those social and economic policies initiated by the first of the UK's New Right governments (1979–90). Each paper had an invited discussant who responded to its keys messages. A roundtable was also convened at the end of the two-day seminar in order to distil further messages about the enduring legacy of Thatcherism. In this way as the seminar's convenors we sought to develop a multi-disciplinary perspective on radical social and economic change and its consequences. Those invited to speak (including the respondents to each paper) were identified on the basis of their international reputation and the significance of their contribution to our understanding of Thatcherism. Each gave a prepared paper on one aspect of social or economic policy. Although the papers dealt with the experiences of the UK, we anticipate that this collection will be of interest to scholars around the world seeking to explore the impact of similar neo-liberal and neo-conservative policies on their own societies and the citizens who live and work within them – and we have encouraged authors and commentators to make their observations com-paratively where appropriate (in order to sharpen their focus on the UK's experience since the mid-1970s).

What was (or is) Thatcherism?

Thatcherism, in so far as it tends to be defined at all, is typically defined in ideational terms. In many accounts it is, in effect, the implementation in Britain of New Right ideas. Gamble (1989: 5) summarizes the tenets of the New Right as follows: state intervention does not work, alternatives to the market are flawed, government failure is more common than market failure and individual citizens' rights are likely to be violated by anything other than the most minimal of forms of state intervention. As this suggests, core to Thatcherism was a reduced role of the state (Gamble, 1989: 7). This was reflected in the avowed privatization of key services hitherto provided by the state since the late 1940s or early 1950s. Gamble goes on to recount the principal objectives of privatization: greater freedom of choice; greater efficiency; the reduction of the Public Sector Borrowing Requirement; reduction in the costs of public sector pay; the removal of key decisions from the political arena altogether; increased share ownership amongst the citizenry; the promotion of liberalization and competition; an increase in active citizenry and a reduction of state dependency (1989: 11). To this Leys (2001: 3) adds the desire to make the state serve business interests, remodel the former's internal operations to become more like the latter's and to reduce the government's exposure to political pressure from the electorate. Marwick (2003: 241) notes also that Thatcherism expressed overt hostility toward 1960s style 'permissiveness'.

What is also clear from the most recent literature on the subject (e.g. Heffernan, 2000; Kerr, 2001; McAnulla, 2006; see also Hay, 2007) is that the benefits of hindsight have tended to reinforce an often unacknowledged consensus on the enduring significance of Thatcherism. Commentators, it seems, are pretty much united in seeing the election of Thatcher in 1979 as a highly significant moment, even where they see it is an epiphenomenon of broader socio-economic developments. Moreover, even the self-styled 'sceptics' in the literature – unconvinced of the seismic break with the past which the election of Thatcher in 1979 is held to mark (Kerr, 2001; Kerr and Marsh, 1999; Marsh, 2008; Marsh and Hall, 2007) – are nonetheless happy to periodize subsequent developments by reference to, and in terms of, 'Thatcherism'. Indeed, in their typical sensitivity to institutional legacies and path dependencies, they are also among the most willing to attribute to Thatcherism an enduring legacy – emphasizing the extent and significance of the Thatcherite inheritance for later administrations (Kerr, 2001; McAnulla, 1999, 2006).

Yet, despite this growing (if largely unacknowledged) consensus, there are those who still challenge the value of the concept of Thatcherism – if perhaps more implicitly than explicitly. Their analysis tends to be more inductive in character – in that they seek to discern turning points in recent British political history through an empirical mapping of the changing content and focus of the policy agenda. Most notable here is the recent work of John and Jennings (2009), which seeks to identify key shifts in issue salience arising from the content analysis of Queen's speeches. There is much to commend in their approach; but it is important that we interpret their findings carefully. For while it is certainly true that the turning points they identify are not easily reconciled with accounts according Thatcherism a key role, the analysis itself is not nearly as incompatible with such a view as this might seem to imply. If, as most commentators seem to agree, it was the *failure* of the existing regime to deal with the challenging economic circumstances of the mid- to late 1970s that brought Thatcher to power, then we would not expect the advent of Thatcherism to be associated with a dramatic shift in *issue salience*. For, having set out its stall in terms of its capacity to respond to the economic crisis, the Thatcher government's initial policy priorities were always likely to be highly conserved from those which had characterized the outgoing Labour administration. If Thatcherism marked a radical break with the past it was the *content* of policy, not the relative salience of issue domains, that was always most likely to characterize that radicalism. In fact, the kind of turning points that John and Jennings identify are perhaps better seen as moments of inflection – most likely to arise in a context in which a political project is coming to be *consolidated*. For, having responded to the high salience issues which brought it to power in the first place (economic management, the trade unions and so forth), this is the point at which an administration turns its attentions to issues of long-term structural reform (particularly, for the Thatcher government, the reform of the public sector). If we see the early Thatcher years as characterized by a period of consolidation in which the key policy domains associated with the economic crisis of the 1970s were addressed before 'Thatcherite' reforms were rolled out into other policy domains, then such a view is perfectly consistent with the findings of John and Jennings; and it is this *refocusing* of the policy agenda that their methodology leads them to detect. As this perhaps already suggests, there is considerable potential in bringing a more inductive and empirical perspective to bear on the question of the nature, development and, indeed, the very identity of Thatcherism. That is our principal objective in this volume.

But if to proceed to such an analysis, it is important first that we frame – at least in a provisional sense – our object of analysis. As noted above, most analyses of Thatcherism whether they acknowledge this explicitly or not, proceed essentially from an ideational understanding of the term. Thatcherism, if it is anything, is distinctive in ideational terms. Our preference is to borrow and develop Peter Riddell's notion of a 'Thatcherite instinct' (1991) or disposition. By this we refer to an approach to thinking about the problems of governance based upon a reasonably highly conserved set of dispositions: distrust of 'big' government; support for 'traditional values' (however defined); a focus on the 'freeing' of the economy from the control of the state; a reliance on the market as the most efficient mechanism for resource distribution and an associated normative commitment to the sanctity of the individual and individual choice. As such, Thatcherism can be seen to be characterized by a combination of neo-liberal and neo-conservative themes (see also Hayes, 1996), with the Thatcherite instinct itself being strongest where both ideological sources served to point in a common direction, identifying common targets for reform – the Thatcherite instinct, in other words, is strongest where the cross-wires in neo-conservatism's and neo-liberalism's independent targeting devices align. This we depict schematically in Figure 1.1.

This much, we suspect, is not especially contentious – and would seem to have clear parallels in much, at least, of the early work on Thatcherism (certainly that of Andrew Gamble, Stuart Hall, Desmond King and Peter Riddell – all of whom emphasis the flexible synthesis of neo-conservative and neo-liberal themes). That said, it is perhaps important to note the tendency in more recent writing on Thatcherism to ignore neo-conservatism, reducing Thatcherism in effect to neo-liberalism in Britain (see, e.g. Harvey, 2005). But this we see as more of an omission than a matter of contention – there being no literature of which we are aware to challenge the association between Thatcherism and neo-conservatism (or,

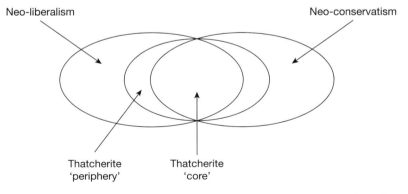

Figure 1.1 The (ideational) content of Thatcherism: mapping the 'Thatcherite instinct'

at least, what was termed neo-conservatism at the time).[2] But if specifying the ideational distinctiveness of Thatcherism is not especially controversial, then the same cannot be said of the questions of implementation and periodization. Here accounts ostensibly diverge wildly; it is to these differences and what we are to make of them that we now turn.

The temporality of Thatcherism

Whatever else it may or may not have done, the literature on Thatcherism has undoubtedly served to encourage a greater degree of reflexivity among political analysts of Britain as to the determinants of political change. Indeed, one might go so far as to suggest that the contested analysis of Thatcherism – precisely because of the extent to which it is contested – has served to heighten, as never before, the sensitivity of analysts of British politics to issues of time and temporality. If this is so, then it is because there is no pair of issues more contentious in the literature on Thatcherism than the temporality it exhibits and the impact of its political desires and designs on the temporality of the British state.

For many authors Thatcherism represents an abrupt, decisive and unprecedented break with the past. This is, perhaps, the standard view of Thatcherism – and is certainly presented in such terms by Kerr and Marsh and other critics of its use (Kerr and Marsh, 1999; Marsh and Rhodes, 1992). It is associated, in particular, with the highly influential early assessments of Thatcherism on both sides of the Atlantic (see, for instance, Gourevitch, 1986; Hall, 1986; Hall and Jacques, 1983; Jenkins, 1988; Kavanagh, 1987; Kavanagh and Morris, 1989; Krieger, 1986). Heffernan's perspective would also seem to fall squarely within this tradition of writing on the subject. Others see far greater elements of continuity, pointing, for instance, to the Treasury's proclivity throughout the post-war period for monetary conservatism, to the correspondingly tenuous nature of its commitment to Keynesianism before 1979 and to the (albeit reluctant) conversion of the Callaghan government to monetarism in 1976 (see, for instance, Kenway, 1998; Morgan, 1992; Tomlinson, 1986). Still others suggest that, despite the radical rhetoric, the first two Thatcher governments were characterized

---

[2] It need scarcely be pointed out that the associations and connotations of this term have changed since the 1980s.

more by pragmatism than by ideological fervour (Marsh and Rhodes, 1992; 1995; Riddell, 1991). In so far as Thatcherism might be seen as radical at all, its radicalism was developed cumulatively and incrementally as its strategic capacity to translate grand visions into substantive policy detail was learned, through experimentation, adaptation to environmental signals, and trial and error. This, in essence, is the view of Kerr (2001).

As this perhaps already serves to indicate, the literature on Thatcherism is fundamentally divided over issues of temporality. This is made very clear if we seek to counterpose schematically, as in Figure 1.2, the range of different opinions on the subject. Here we differentiate, albeit in a somewhat stylized way, between just four of the contending views of the temporality of Thatcherism as a political and economic project that can be identified in the existing literature. Each approach is considered in terms of its assessment of the relative pace of change over time.

Consider each (stylized) view of the temporality of Thatcherism in turn. The first – represented by plot 1 – sees Thatcherism as of no great consequence. Change is incremental and iterative; it may or may not be cumulative. By virtue of holding office alone, consecutive Thatcher governments were in a position to make policy, but they were no more privileged in so doing than any other post-war administration. Consequently, we are wrong to associate Thatcherism (a term which, from this perspective, is perhaps unwarranted) with an intensification of the pace of political and economic change. For such change is, by its very nature, far more glacial than such a characterization would imply. Unremarkably, perhaps, few

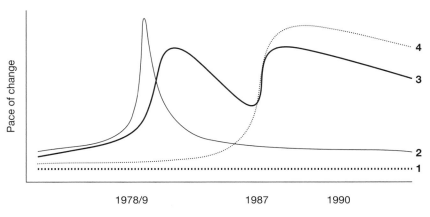

Figure 1.2 The contested temporality of Thatcherism

authors in the debate on Thatcherism articulate such a view. For, if Thatcherism is of no great consequence, there are surely more important tasks than demonstrating to those that may think otherwise that this is so. Interestingly, however, at times Kerr and Marsh, clearly key protagonists in the debate, come close to embracing such a view. The thrust of much of their argument is that, in essence, British political analysts subscribe to far too discontinuous (or punctuated) a view of social and political change. The appeal of the evolutionary perspective, they propose, is precisely that it sensitizes us to the often incremental, sometimes cumulative and invariably glacial character of social and political change. Change is an ongoing feature of social and political systems, but the pace of change varies far less then we tend to assume. Consequently, we are as wrong to see the long period of so-called post-war consensus as one of stasis as we are to see the subsequent period (Thatcherism) as one of a significant quickening in the pace of change.

The danger in this, as in plot 1, is that we 'flat-line' the whole period of historical time we are interested in – holding the magnifying glass, as it were, so far away from the object of analysis that we can no longer discern the changing contours of social and political change at all. Yet it would do some considerable disservice to Kerr and Marsh's perspective to suggest that this is the position to which they ultimately commit themselves. It is certainly a position which, on occasions, they seek to defend (individually and together); but when it comes to the more detailed analysis of the evolution of Thatcherism itself (especially in the work of Kerr), a far more fine-grained temporality emerges.

The second perspective – represented schematically by plot 2 – is that which Kerr and Marsh most explicitly set out to challenge. This they associate with the 'established narrative'. It has a distinctly punctuated conception of social and political change, counterposing relatively enduring periods of self-equilibrating stability (such as the post-war consensus) to more abrupt moments of ideational and institutional transformation (such as Thatcherism). Seen from this perspective, Thatcherism is a decisive intervention made in the context of the pervasive state and economic crisis of the late 1970s. It has served to precipitate a seismic shift in the governing economic and political paradigm, instituting a new period of stability which largely endures to the present day. Kerr casts this as the dominant view of contemporary British history, a view accepted uncritically by the majority of academic analysts despite its worrying similarities with the legitimatory rhetoric of Thatcherism itself (see, especially, Kerr, 2001: 17, 211).

Such a view is nowhere more clearly expressed than in Peter Hall's extremely influential work on the development of British macro-economic policy since the mid-1970s (especially, Hall, 1993). Drawing an analogy with Thomas Kuhn's (1970) seminal distinction between normal and exceptional periods of scientific development, Hall suggests that British macro-economic policy can be periodized in terms of the dominance of, respectively, Keynesian and monetarist paradigms.

The election of the first Thatcher administration in the context of state and economic crisis marks the moment of paradigm shift. Scarcely less committed to such a view is Heffernan, whose indebtedness to Hall's Kuhnian conception of paradigm shifts, and whose broader reliance on historical institutionalism's characteristic 'punctuated equilibrium' approach to institutional change are both quite explicit (Heffernan, 2000: 9–10). Yet just as it is wrong to see Kerr and Marsh's approach as flat-lining the entire post-war period, so it is problematic to suggest that Heffernan's (or, indeed, Hall's) understanding of the temporality of Thatcherism can be encapsulated in plot 2 above.

This brings us to a simple but crucial point, largely unacknowledged in the debates on Thatcherism and responsible, at least in part, for the tendency of agonists and protagonists in such debates simply to talk past one another. Thatcherism, as both Kerr and Marsh and Heffernan note, means a variety of different things to a variety of different authors. Moreover, even where authors may agree on a common framing of their subject matter, they will invariably emphasize different aspects or dimensions of it, and there is no a priori reason to expect those various dimensions or aspects of the phenomenon in question to reveal a common temporality – that is, for them to unfold over time in a similar manner. Consequently, in comparing – as in Figure 1.2 – different accounts of the temporality of Thatcherism we may be in danger of comparing apples and pears. Peter Hall's (1993) punctuated evolutionary model of paradigm shift is a case in point, as is Stuart Hall's (1988) account of Thatcherism in terms of 'authoritarian populism'. For what both accounts share, in addition to the surnames of their authors, is a relative privileging, in the periodization of Thatcherism, of the ideas informing policy rather than the policy itself. Were this privileging reversed, a rather different periodization and temporality would surely be revealed.

As this suggests, accounts of the temporality of Thatcherism which are invariably presented, in the heat of debate, as antagonistic and mutually incompatible may well be reconcilable. There are, for instance, very good reasons for thinking that a periodization of paradigmatic/ideational

13

change is likely to exhibit a far more punctuated temporality than an equivalent periodization of the institutional/policy change to which paradigmatic change may contribute. Indeed, this is the basis for the suggestion that there is in fact a rather greater degree of common ground between Kerr and Marsh, on the one hand, and Hall and Heffernan, on the other, than either seems prepared to acknowledge.

When it comes to periodizing Thatcherism in terms of its substantive impact on the institutions and structures of the state and economy or indeed its policy content, Heffernan's account is, in fact, far closer to plot 3 than plot 2. In both intent and content, Thatcherism was radical from the outset. Grounded in New Right ideology the governments of both Thatcher and Major pursued and enacted a coherent political agenda which was always recognizably ideological in terms of its content (Heffernan, 2000: viii). It was a 'project' driven by conviction, though often struggling to find the most effective means of implementation; it was not a fully fledged 'programme' planned in advance and unleashed in office (2000: 31–7). Consequently, Thatcherism unfolded in an incremental manner and much of the break with the past which it is now rightly seen to mark is a product of the duration of its tenure in office rather than any abrupt transformation that occurred with the election in 1979 (2000: 39–46). Moreover, not all phases in the development of the Thatcherite project were equally radical. As Heffernan explains, fearing electoral defeat in 1983, a more cautious approach was adopted between 1981 and 1983. This was reflected in a somewhat less ambitious programme of reform for the second term and, despite something of a re-radicalization after the 1983 election, for many ardent Thatcherites the period 1983–87 was something of a missed opportunity (2000: 43).

Although perhaps closer to plot 4 than plot 3, Kerr's view of the unfolding of Thatcherism is not so very different. That may seem odd. For, in marked contrast to Heffernan, he is certainly quick to deny the radicalism of the first Thatcher administration, stating that it emerged in 1979 with a strategy which was both 'ill-defined and often incoherent' – though he adds, in parentheses, 'except at a discursive level' (2001: 37). The caveat is important. It suggests that here, as elsewhere, Kerr and Heffernan may well be divided by a common language. For, as Kerr makes very clear, what he means by 'radicalism' in this context is rather different from what one might assume – and it is certainly very different from Heffernan's use of the same term. For Heffernan, the first Thatcher government is radical in the sense that, in his judgement, it was animated consistently by a normative/ideological sense of direction and priority *and* the policies it enacted were compatible with that sense of purpose. Yet for Kerr that is not enough. The first Thatcher government, for him, cannot be judged radical since it lacked a coherent strategy for the translation of its ideological convictions into policy outcomes. In the end, the disagreement is largely semantic. For both authors seem to accept: (1) that the first Thatcher government was animated by an albeit abstract and deeply ideological sense of priority and purpose (an 'instinct' or 'disposition', as we shall term it); (2) that it lacked, in 1979, a programmatic sense of how best to realize politically and embed institutionally such convictions; but (3) that the policies it did pursue were both compatible with and, indeed, driven by its New Right ideological commitment.

In most other respects, their analyses are remarkably similar. Both authors emphasize the rather cautious nature of the Conservative Party's 1983 manifesto and the rather slow unfolding of the Thatcherite project in the mid-1980s. Equally, they both note the far more radical character of the 1987 manifesto and the discernible intensification in the scope and scale of the economic, social and political reform to follow. Moreover, controversial though it undoubtedly is, both authors see the Major and Blair governments as inheritors of the Thatcherite mantle (see also Jenkins, 2007). In so doing they highlight the evolutionary, incremental, and cumulative nature of Thatcherism, drawing attention to the many enduring legacies it bequeaths to the present, not the least of which has been its capacity to circumscribe the realm of feasible policy choice for all credible contenders for political office. For Heffernan, a Thatcherite settlement has replaced the post-war settlement (2000: 178); for Kerr, Thatcherism has emerged as 'Britain's first real post-war settlement' (2001: 216). What is more, though Kerr repeatedly (and rightly) warns of the dangers of overemphasizing the significance of ideas (2001: 12, 21), and is as a consequence far less interested in periodizing Thatcherism in such terms, he would seem to rely, at least implicitly, on an ideational periodization very similar to that offered by Heffernan.

A number of points might here be made. The first, and most obvious, is that the very use of the term Thatcherism to characterize the process of social and political change in the period 1979 to the present day clearly commits Kerr to a periodization rather more abrupt and punctuated than he tends to imply. One does not have to label that which precedes Thatcherism the 'post-war consensus' in order to invoke a dualistic distinction between Thatcherism and that which went before it. Moreover, since Kerr is apparently quite happy to talk about Thatcherism as a state project in the period 1979–87, a period during which he suggests it was unified not by a coherent strategy but only by ideology (2001: 22), one can only assume that the type of periodization Kerr is implicitly engaged in here is an ideational one. And if that is right, then this surely suggests his acknowledgement (albeit tacit) of something of a paradigmatic shift, at the ideational level, occurring around 1979 – a conception almost identical to that rendered rather more explicit by Heffernan (2000: 9–10).

As this suggests – all appearances to the contrary and the appeal to rather different senses of the term 'radical' notwithstanding – there is actually very little that divides these ostensibly alternative accounts, at least in terms of their understanding of the temporality of Thatcherism. What is more, these areas of commonality are rather confirmed by the empirical chapters presented in this volume.

Thatcherism: from an implementation perspective to an impact perspective

If any one collection of essays has inspired our approach to Thatcherism in this collection, then it is surely Marsh and Rhodes's splendid *Implementing Thatcherite Policies* (1992). Though we will ultimately challenge a number of its claims and findings, its approach to Thatcherism is, we think, a significant advance on the earlier literature on which we seek to build. Based on a conference held in January 1991 (some two months after Thatcher herself had stepped down as leader of the Conservative Party and Prime Minister) theirs is a collection with the feel of the end of an era to it.[3] And yet, this collection was ahead of its time in very many ways. Unlike other collections of essays on the topic, the contributors to the Marsh and Rhodes collection gave considerable attention to the issue of the ways in which Thatcherite policies were (or were not) implemented. As they note in their introductory essay (Rhodes and Marsh, 1992: 2–3), the existing literature was deficient in a number of ways. For example, although the first term was well covered, the second term was less well covered and the third term had not (by that stage) had time to be assessed (of course, the

---

[3] John Major, who was to lead the country for almost seven years after Thatcher's demise, has fewer references than the Greater London Council, abolished in 1986, for example.

fourth term was still some way off). Furthermore, few had attempted fully to analyse the extent of policy change, why some ostensible policy target had led to policy innovation and implementation whilst others had not, and why some policy realms had produced the desired outcomes whilst others seemed impermeable to Thatcherite influence – or, indeed, why such variations might exist at all. Reflecting on the literature on Thatcherism which existed at the time, they noted:

> There is an unambiguous tendency to overstate the Thatcher effect because the contributions [in other collections] concentrate upon legislative change rather than upon changes in policy outcomes.
>
> (1992: 3)

To this one could add that, at the time, the policy changes might not yet have had the chance to produce substantive outcomes in terms of the redistribution of tangible goods or access to services – since many of the windows for the assessment of policy changes had been so short. In effect, the insights afforded by a consideration of the *longue durée* were (necessarily) absent. Furthermore, the existing literature on such matters had tended to 'silo' policy domains. Few consider 'knock-on' effects of policy changes in one arena for another policy arena. Our vision for this collection is to produce a more settled judgement, consideration, and appraisal of the Thatcherite 'moment' – and one not just confined to Thatcher's own tenure in office, nor even her party's period of electoral dominance. We focus as much then on the administrations which have come after, and on citizens as the social and economic subjects of Thatcherism. This is no easy task; laws are repealed; policies reviewed and revised; all historical periods have their own cohorts of individuals with their own values, age structures, and experiences; and so on. Yet, we feel that there is still much mileage in the questions which Rhodes and Marsh used as their touchstones (1992: 4–10). We restate them here – updating and supplementing them as appropriate.

The key questions

In order to assess the extent to which there was a policy change along 'Thatcherite' lines, one has first to assess the extent to which there was a discernible 'Thatcherite' policy agenda – a Thatcherite instinct reflected in a systematic way in policy-making. Following this, and assuming that one accepts our argument that something one might credibly call 'Thatcherism' can be said to have existed, one needs to ask the following sorts of questions in order to assess the extent to which there was (and perhaps remains) a shift towards Thatcherite policies:

1   How much policy and substantive change was there during (and immediately after) the Thatcher era? Such a question begs a series of follow-up questions. These include (but are not limited to): When did such changes take place? How were such changes implemented and assessed? At which point (if at all) did such changes cease to be meaningfully attributable to the policies to which they are ascribed? How and why can any changes be attributable to Thatcherism?

2   An equally crucial question concerns the extent to which the policies deemed responsible for any change are themselves part of a distinct policy agenda which was 'Thatcherite' in outlook and sensibility (as opposed to merely connected to legislation passed during the period following 1979). For example, the 1980 Education Act has been seen (along with other Education Acts until 1988) as being essentially incrementalist (McVicar, 1990: 133). Until 1986, education policy was, to all intense and purposes, bipartisan (Tomlinson, 1989: 186). If there had been little radical actions on education until the late 1980s (Scott, 1994: 335), the year 1986 marked a shift in thinking, as 'hard right' approaches came to dominate the government's approach to education and schooling. Indications of this shift in thinking came during the 1987 General Election when it was announced that schools would be allowed to 'opt out' of LEA control completely (Whitty and Menter, 1989: 47). However, it was the 1988 Education Act which was to radically change education in the UK. Thus, for a policy to be labelled 'Thatcherite' it must, at some very basic level speak to, be provoked by, or informed by some version of what we have called the 'Thatcherite instinct' (Hay, 1996; Riddell, 1991), rather than just to have been passed into law after 1979.

3   One must also be able to explain why a particular policy domain experienced the sorts of changes it did, when it did and, allied to this, why some policy domains experienced more change than others. This entails having to grapple with why some domains experienced less (or no) change than one might expect, and also – as we do so in terms of the notion of a policy cascade (Hay and Farrall, 2011) – why some policy domains were nonetheless decisively impacted despite the absence of a sustained Thatcherite offensive.

Such questions force one to consider how policies are 'produced' and to recognize that not all goes as planned during either the legislative process or the rolling-out and implementation of policies. Furthermore, ensuring that the policy has the desired effect in the 'real world' is never easy; unintended, unanticipated and contradictory consequences can (and do) arise and they are difficult to plan for.[4] And yet – as our quote from Rhodes and Marsh at the start of this chapter implies – changes in policies which may take several years to work through to changes in lived experiences are not often the object of much inquiry in social science. Essentially, this boils down to being able to attribute impacts to policy vehicles.

An applied example

Let us try to add some flesh to this skeletal structure. We do this by taking two Acts in two policy areas which were seen as central to the Tory party's electoral strategy in the late 1970s. We review briefly the key policy decisions made, assessing the extent to which these intentions and outcomes can be read as consistent with Thatcherism. The first of these is the 1982 Criminal Justice Act, and the second is the 1980 Housing Act. Both were passed within the first term of office; we see one (the 1980 Housing Act) as central to the aims and stated objectives of Thatcherism, and one (the 1982 Criminal Justice Act) as distinctly un-Thatcherite in that it deviated markedly from the articulated Thatcherite disposition on law and order.

The 1982 Criminal Justice Act was the result of policy reviews going back to 1974 and which were initiated under the previous (Labour) administration (Faulkner, 2001: 110). It was, as such, hardly a new venture. The Act – along with the rest of the criminal justice system – was not a priority for the first or indeed subsequent Thatcher administrations. Indeed, several autobiographies by home secretaries suggest that they were left to get on with the job with little interference from Downing Street (see, for example, Hurd, 2003: 377–8, 395). Again this suggests little by way of a clear or distinctive Thatcherite input. Finally, the 1982 Act in no way produced

---

[4] There is, of course, a more extensive literature (especially in the fields of criminal justice and health) on the opposite of this – namely, policy changes that produce immediate effects in trials but which fail to generate anything like the same effect when rolled out in full.

outcomes that were in any way what one might reasonably expect from a 'Thatcherite' take on criminal justice. Indeed, the Act very much produced outcomes which one might well regard as running counter to a Thatcherite criminal justice instinct; it was essentially liberal in tone. To give a flavour of these, during the first year of the Act's operation (1984–85) imprisonment of young people was reduced by 7 per cent (Windlesham, 1993: 170), whilst the Home Secretary was enabled to release certain categories of prisoners six months early (Windlesham, 1993: 238). Neither of these effects, it need hardly be pointed out, are consistent with a 'tough' approach to crime.

Instead, Thatcher (and other of her key supporters in the Cabinet, such as Norman Tebbit)[5] used TV programmes to speak out on individual sentences, reinforcing the 'authoritarian populist' tones that had paid dividends during the campaign itself and consolidating the party's lead in the polls on the issue (Loader, 2006: 574). As such, despite rhetorical radicalism, there was no legislation on crime (let alone radical legislation) in the first two sessions of Parliament after 1979 (Windlesham, 1993: 152). It was therefore not until the early 1990s that criminal justice policies started to become staunchly infused with New Right thinking. When it came, the transition was abrupt, with a clear departure from the pre-existing consensus within whose terms both parties had sought to limit the size of the prison population (Newburn, 2007: 434).

On the other hand, to suggest that the 1980 Housing Act was Thatcherite would seem to make much more sense. For the aims of the Act (even if they originated in reviews of housing, which pre-dated Thatcher's arrival in Downing Street) chimed very clearly with the ideological aims and spirit of Thatcherism (anti-corporatist, pro-market, inversely redistributive and in keeping with an electoral strategy of mobilizing support amongst the affluent and working 'working class'). Additionally, the Act was followed up with, and supported by, subsequent Acts throughout the 1980s which further extended and incentivized the sale of council housing whilst diminishing local authority assets.

Even so, the 1980 Housing Act was in keeping with the Housing Policy Review (1975–77), which had asserted the desirability of home ownership (Williams, 1992: 161), and, accordingly, public expenditure on housing was trimmed back from 1976, albeit as part of a programme of public spending

---

[5] It should be remembered that Tebbit's famous 'he got on his bike and he looked for work' quote was in response to a suggestion that rioting was a response to unemployment.

cuts following the negotiation with the IMF (Atkinson and Durde, 1990: 118; Murie, 1989: 213; Williams, 1992: 160). Yet the election of the Thatcher government, nevertheless, brought about a dramatic shift in housing policy, with a concerted attempt to extend home ownership (Kemp, 1992: 65; Monk and Kleinman, 1989: 121). This, in turn, was a clear attempt to extend the party's electoral basis into the aspirant working classes and was strongly flagged as such in the election campaign itself (Hay, 1992). The 1980 Housing Act (which introduced the right to buy for council tenants), was key to this process (Atkinson and Durden, 1990: 120; Williams, 1992: 165), and resulted in a rise in home ownership from 55 per cent in 1979 to 64 per cent in 1987 (Monk and Kleinman, 189: 126–7). It was followed by further Acts, couched in a similar vein, between 1984 and 1988 – there was, in short, both innovation and continuity in policy.

What such examples do is to remind us that Thatcherism did not arrive out of nowhere; that is (even in its embryonic form), it spoke to the desires and concerns of many people living in the UK in the middle to late 1970s. In some respect, then, Thatcherism was a response to shifts in social values and relational concerns inasmuch as it was the driver of such matters. As this suggests, deciding 'when' Thatcherism 'started' is no easy matter, since it evolved over a considerable period of time, eventually working its way through a number of policy domains in something approaching a sequential order (see Hay and Farrall, 2011 and Farrall and Hay, 2010). As such, we think it perfectly acceptable to view the economic policies of the Thatcher administrations (i.e. from 1979 until 1990) as being 'Thatcherite' (albeit achieved through different models of economic thought). Similarly, we have no problem with the idea that very little of the criminal justice policy before 1993 can in anyway be thought of as Thatcherite, whilst much of what came after 1993 (and beyond 1997 too for that matter) can be thought of as holding many resonances with the Thatcherite instinct on law and order (especially that which took its inspiration from the neo-conservative strands of Thatcherite thought – see Farrall and Jennings, Chapter 7 in this collection). This should alert us to the fact that Thatcherism was just one of the drivers behind the policies which were pursued after 1979, and that the targeting of the Thatcherite instinct moved from policy domain to policy domain in what might be termed a 'cascading' model of policy radicalism (see Hay and Farrall, 2011).

Problematizing periodization

As we have noted above (see also Hay, 2007), there is some confusion in the literature which seeks to periodize Thatcherism as to what actually such a task entails – what, precisely, is being periodized. Different periodizations arise from attempts to periodize different things, just as much as they do from differences in the interpretation of the empirical record. Indeed, it is our contention that, despite superficial impressions to the contrary, the existing literature is characterized rather more by differences in the criteria by which periodizations are arrived at than by substantive disagreements about the events themselves. In particular, and as we have already argued, it is not difficult to detect a fairly stark contrast in the literature on Thatcherism between those accounts emphasizing the ideas informing policy and those emphasizing the substantive content of the policy implemented. Those, like both Stuart Hall and Peter Hall, who see the distinctiveness of Thatcherism as residing in the ideological break with the past that it marks are far more likely to interpret the same empirical phenomena as evidence of discontinuity than those, like David Marsh and Rod Rhodes, who are more concerned with questions of policy implementation and substantive outcomes. For policy implementation takes time.

The point is that there is no necessary incompatibility between the two accounts (just a difference in analytical focus). Put slightly differently, Thatcherism (if it can usefully be said to exist) is likely to exhibit different temporalities and to give rise to different periodizations depending on the criteria by which such periodizations are gauged.

Our attempt to periodize different policy domains seeks to build explicitly from an acknowledgement of this. We look at the process in and through which ideational change comes to guide policy direction and through which policy comes unevenly to be implemented to yield a combination of intended and unintended outcomes. As such, whilst we attribute to ideas a significant role, we recognize the likelihood of what Marsh and Rhodes usefully term 'implementation gaps' – disparities between the declared intention of policy-makers and the substantive impact of the policy as implemented, arising from difficulties in, or failures of, implementation (Marsh and Rhodes, 1992: 187). To this we would also add the importance of acknowledging the likelihood of 'strategic gaps' – disparities between the rhetorical radicalism of policy presentation and the strategic intention underpinning policy as it comes to be implemented.

There is a clear danger, then, of taking rhetoric at face value (see also Hay, 1996: 152–3).

The above discussion leads us to identify a series of limitations, as we would see it, of the existing literature which seeks to periodize Thatcherism.

1   Through no fault of their own, most existing periodizations are partial and hence inadequate – since they were written at the time and sought to chart a still moving object of analysis.

2   They tend to be characterized by a certain lack of clarity about what is being periodized (and with respect to what criteria that periodization is developed). This, we suggest, has tended on occasions to result in a dialogue of the deaf, as authors mistake differences in the criteria by which periodizing judgements are made for differences of interpretation.

3   There is also something of a tendency to the proliferation of deductive, as opposed to inductive, periodizations. Stylized periodizations too often precede the analysis of the evidence, with it being far from clear how these are informed by a consideration of the historical record – a rare and valuable exception is John and Jennings (2010). For instance, immensely valuable though it undoubtedly is, Jessop et al.'s (1988) periodization of Thatcherism reads to us like a theoretically informed account of the stages through which a project would need to pass in order for it to be said to be coherent, rather than an empirically based account which arises out of a consideration of the development of policy in real time.

4   Relatedly, we tend to see a proliferation of overly holistic periodizations which fail to differentiate between the temporally and strategically uneven process of 'Thatcherization' within different policy domains. From the perspective outlined above, we cannot expect Thatcherism (like any other '-ism') to proceed evenly across policy domains and to develop through a series of stages that are highly conserved in terms of their timing. Thus, it would be unrealistic, naive even, to gauge the radicalism of Thatcherism in terms of its correspondence to such an ideal.

A cascade theory of policy radicalism

The approach adopted in this volume – namely to take a long-term view of policy change – also allows us to chart more fully a number of other aspects of the Thatcherite agenda, which (to varying degrees) have escaped previous considerations. For example, we have been able to assess the ways in which radical policy changes in those areas of policy tackled initially (for example the economy and housing), had both partially anticipated and wholly unanticipated consequences for policy domains such as social security and criminal justice policies. In this way we are able to link together the consequences for radicalism in policy areas which seem disconnected from one another. (Who, for example, would have thought that changes in housing policy would have had such wide-ranging ramifications for the geo-social distribution of crime or the concentration of ethnic minorities?) Only by charting unfolding policies and considering their differential impacts and influences on other policy domains is one able to pull together more thoroughgoing analyses of the outcomes of policy radicalism to break down the siloed nature of too much current thinking.

What such an approach also allows is a more systematic consideration of the temporality of Thatcherism across different policy domains (see Figure 1.3). This we outline schematically here and return to in more detail in the light of the empirical chapters to follow.

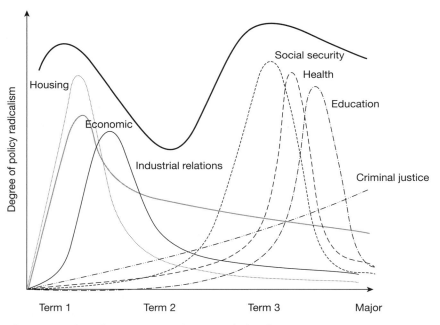

Figure 1.3 A preliminary periodization of Thatcherism

The broad model that we develop might most simply be described as a 'cascade' theory of policy radicalism. It charts the development of Thatcherism through a series of different policy fields and domains. First to be targeted were those policy arenas central to the construction of the crisis demanding immediate action (such as the economy), and those key to the mobilization and consolidation of an electoral base (such as housing). Once reform in these areas was underway, attention increasingly turned to those policy domains not implicated closely with the crisis narrative yet requiring reform in order to bring them into accordance with a Thatcherite instinct (such social security and education). Yet it took a considerable amount of time and effort to translate a rather amorphous and unfocused Thatcherite instinct into a working set of proposals for complex institutional reform in such fields. There was, quite simply, no blueprint for public sector reform – and it would take the best part of two terms for one to be developed. But, from 1987 onwards, we see the unfolding of a radical reform agenda for the entire public sector, with key public services taken on one at a time around highly significant pieces of legislation (such as the Education Reform Act, the NHS Reform Act and the Local Government Finance Act). Finally, if the project were to be consolidated it became increasingly necessary to deal with issues arising as spill-over effects in policy domains such as criminal justice, which were targeted last. Indeed, as Farrall and Jennings (2012) have demonstrated empirically for this very period, increased rates of unemployment and inequality were clearly predated and themselves led directly to increases in crime rates, which in turn led to mounting public concern with crime. It is this rise in both crime and public concern, we contend, which led the government to repoliticize and radicalize 'law and order'. In this respect, we attribute the late radicalization of criminal justice policy not to the unfolding of a pre-planned project but to the perceived need to respond to the spill-over effects arising from the consequences of earlier radicalism in other issues domains (here, principally, economic and education policy).

Overall, then, Thatcherism would appear to have passed through at least five phases:

1   the mobilization of perceptions of a crisis to which it would present itself as the solution linked to the mobilization of an electoral base capable of securing its election

2   the immediate and targeted response to the crisis (involving radicalism in economic policy and industrial relations) and the further consolidation of its electoral base through the extension of home ownership

3   a comparative lull in policy activism during which ideas for the trans-
      lation of a Thatcherite instinct into detailed proposals for profound
      public sector reform were developed (such as the Fowler review of
      social security provision)
4   a second wave of policy radicalism targeting key public services in a
      cascade of reforming legislation
5   consolidation and responses to unanticipated consequences and spill-
      over effects from earlier phases of policy radicalism.

Such a periodization is, of course, necessarily preliminary – designed
more to illustrate our approach to periodization than to be exhaustive or
definitive in its breadth or depth of coverage. It is a periodization, however,
that this volume sets out to test empirically. Each of the substantive
chapters in Part II focuses on a separate policy domain, allowing us to build
up, more inductively than we have been able to do here, an account of
cascading policy radicalism (if any) exhibited by policy developments since
1979.

In so far as such a periodization of Thatcherism proves credible in the
light of the empirical chapter – or, indeed, in so far as an alternative
emerges – it is, we suggest, both realistic and useful to accord to
Thatcherism the status of a singular political project. In other words, if the
analysis of this volume shows that Thatcherism is *periodizable*, then it also
shows that the term deserves the central place it has come to hold in the
analysis of post-war British politics. This is the key question to which we
return in the concluding chapter.

The preceding paragraphs serve to establish the distinctiveness, in the
context of the existing literature, of our approach to periodization. Its key
facets can be summarized as follows:

1   We ought not to expect logical consistency over time in the unfolding
      of events. It is not credible to expect the unfolding of a blueprint
      (established in advance) over time; nor is this what one would need to
      see in order to discern the existence of a strategic project consistently
      implemented. Instead, in order to identify a project that is periodizable
      we need only to be able to discern a strategy and process of strategic
      renewal in the light of contingent events that is *rationalizable* after the
      fact.
2   Some policies inevitably fail – the focus must be on the capacity to
      retain a long-term strategic focus and a sense of initiative in the light
      of such difficulties of implementation.

3 A periodization must be disaggregated in terms of policy domains whilst retaining a sense of the overall picture; it must also be disaggregated in terms of the process from ideational innovation through to implementation and policy effects, whilst again retaining a sense of how these are connected.

4 There must be latitude within the periodization for different things (and different types of things) to be happening in different policy domains at the same time – for instance, radical reform in one area of policy at the same time as consolidation in another; the periodization must reveal the strategy informing the relative sequencing of dynamics in different policy domains (in so far as one can be identified).

This book is divided into three parts. The first part sets the scene for the whole collection and outlines current thinking, and theorizing, on Thatcherism. The second part deals with examples of specific policy domains (namely, the economy, housing, social security, education, families, and crime). Yet each chapter reflects the wider concerns with an attention to inputs from and impacts upon other policy areas, and includes an exploration of cross-cutting themes that do not relate to any one specific policy domain but which are, nevertheless, still crucial for a full understanding of the legacy of this period (and as such we explore issues such as changes in the geographic trajectory of the UK, shifts in attitudes and the rise of inequality). The third and final part pulls together what we can learn from both the impact of Thatcherite social and economic policies and how similar analyses may be applied to other administrations both in the UK and further afield.

References

Atkinson, R. and Durden, P. (1990) 'Housing Policy in the Thatcher Years', in S. Savage and L. Robins (eds) *Public Policy Under Thatcher*. London: Macmillan.

Bateson, C. (1997) 'A Review of the Politics of Education in the "Moment of 1976"', *British Journal of Educational Studies*, 45(4): 363–77.

Marsh, D., Buller, J., Hay, C., Johnston, J., Kerr, P., McAnulla, S., and Watson, M. (eds) (1999) *Postwar British Politics in Perspective*. Cambridge: Polity, pp. 168–88.

Evans, E.J. (2006) *Thatcher and Thatcherism*, 2nd edn. London: Routledge.

Farrall, S. and Hay, C. (2010) 'Not so Tough on Crime? Why weren't the Thatcher Governments more Radical in Reforming the Criminal Justice System?' *British Journal of Criminology*, 50(3): 550–69.

Farrall, S. and Jennings, W. (2012) 'Policy Feedback and the Criminal Justice Agenda: An Analysis of the Economy, Crime Rates, Politics and Public Opinion in Post-war Britain'. *Contemporary British History*, 26(4): 467–88.

Faulkner, D. (2001) *Crime, State and Citizen*. Winchester: Waterside Press.

Gamble, A. (1989) 'Privatization, Thatcherism, and the British State', in A. Gamble and C. Wells (eds) *Thatcher's Law*. Cardiff: GPC Books.

Gamble, A. (1996) 'The Legacy of Thatcherism', in M. Perryman (ed.) *The Blair Agenda*. London: Lawrence & Wishart.

Garland, D. (2001) *The Culture of Control*. Oxford University Press.

Glennerster, H. (1994) 'Health and Social Policy', in D. Kavanagh and A. Seldon (eds) *The Major Effect*. London: Macmillan.

Gourevitch, P. (1986) *Politics in Hard Times: Comparative Responses to International Economic Crises*. Ithaca, NY: Cornell University Press.

Hall, P. (1993) 'Policy Paradigms, Policy Learning and the State', *Comparative Politics*, 25(3): 185–96.

Hall, P.A. (1986) *Governing the Economy: The Politics of State Intervention in Britain and France*. Cambridge: Polity.

Hall, S. (1988) *The Hard Road to Renewal: Thatcherism and the Crisis of the Left*. London: Lawrence & Wishart.

Hall, S. and Jacques, M. (eds) (1983) *The Politics of Thatcherism*. London: Lawrence & Wishart.

Harvey, D. (2005) *A Brief History of Neoliberalism*. Oxford University Press.

Hay, C. (1992) 'Housing Policy in Transition: From the Keynesian Welfare State towards a Thatcherite Settlement', *Capital and Class*, 46, 25–64.

Hay, C. (1996) *Restating Social and Political Change*. Buckingham: Open University Press.

Hay, C. (2007) 'Whatever Happened to Thatcherism?' *Political Studies Review*, 5: 183–201.

Hay, C. (2009) 'The Winter of Discontent Thirty Years On', *Political Quarterly*, 80(4).

Hay, C. and Farrall, S. (2011) 'Establishing the Ontological Status of Thatcherism by Gauging its 'Periodisability': Towards a "Cascade Theory" of Public Policy Radicalism', *British Journal of Politics and International Relations*, 13(4): 439–58.

Hayes, M. (1994) *The New Right in Britain*. London: Pluto Press.

Heffernan, R. (2000) *New Labour and Thatcherism*. Basingstoke: Macmillan.

Hurd, D. (2003) *Memoirs*. London: Abacus.

Jenkins, P. (1988) *The Thatcher Revolution: The Post-Socialist Era*. Cambridge, MA: Harvard University Press.

Jenkins, S. (2007) *Thatcher and Sons*. London: Penguin.

Jessop, B., Bonnett, K., Bromley, S. and Ling, T. (1988) *Thatcherism*. Cambridge: Polity Press.

Jennings, W. and John, P. (2009) 'Punctuations and Turning Points in British Politics: The Policy Agenda of the Queen's Speech, 1940–2005', *British Journal of Political Science*, 40(3), 561–86.

Jones, K. (2003) *Education in Britain: 1944 to the Present*. Cambridge: Polity Press.

Kavanagh, D. (1987) *Thatcherism and British Politics: The End of Consensus?* Oxford: University Press.

Kavanagh, D. and Morris, P. (1989) *Consensus Politics: From Attlee to Thatcher.* Oxford: Blackwell.

King, D.S. (1985) *The New Right.* London: Macmillan.

Kemp, P. (1992) 'Housing', in R.A.W. Rhodes and D. Marsh (eds) *Implementing Thatcherite Policies.* Buckingham: Open University Press.

Kenway, P. (1998) *From Keynesianism to Monetarism: The Evolution of UK Macroeconomic Models.* London: Routledge.

Kerr, P. (2001) *Postwar British Politics: from Conflict to Consensus.* London: Routledge.

Kerr, P. and Marsh, D. (1999) 'Explaining Thatcherism: Towards a Multidimensional Approach', in D. Marsh et al. (eds) *Postwar British Politics in Perspective.* Cambridge: Polity Press.

Krieger, J. (1986) *Reagan, Thatcher and the Politics of Decline.* Cambridge: Polity.

Kuhn, T.S. (1970) *The Structure of Scientific Revolutions.* Chicago, IL: Chicago University Press.

Larner, W., Le Heron, R. and Lewis, R. (2007) 'Co-constituting "After Neoliberalism": Political Projects and Globalizing Governmentalities in Aotearoa/New Zealand', in K. England and K. Ward (eds) *Neoliberalization: States, Networks and Peoples.* Oxford: Blackwell Publishing.

Levitas, R. (1986) 'Introduction: Ideology and the New Right', in R. Levitas (ed.) *The Ideology of the New Right.* Cambridge: Polity Press.

Leys, C. (2001) *Market-Driven Politics.* London: Verso.

Loader, I. (2006) 'Fall of the Platonic Guardians', *British Journal of Criminology*, 46: 561–86.

Loughlin, M. (1989) 'Law, Ideologies, and the Political-Administrative System', in A. Gamble and C. Wells (eds) *Thatcher's Law.* Cardiff: GPC Books.

Marsh, D. (2008) 'Understanding British Government: Analysing Competing Models', *British Journal of Politics and International Relations*, 10(2): 251–68.

Marsh, D. and Hall, M. (2007) 'The British Political Tradition: Explaining the Fate of New Labour's Constitutional Reform Agenda', *British Politics*, 2(2): 215–34.

Marsh, D. and Rhodes, R.A.W. (eds) (1992) *Implementing Thatcherite Policies.* Buckingham: Open University Press.

Marsh, D. and Rhodes, R.A.W. (1995) 'Evaluating Thatcherism', *Politics*, 15(1): 49–54.

Marwick, A. (2003) *British Society Since 1945.* London: Penguin Books.

McAnulla, S. (2006) *British Politics: A Critical Introduction.* London: Continuum.

McVicar, M. (1990) 'Education Policy', in S. Savage and L. Robins (eds) *Public Policy Under Thatcher.* London: Macmillan.

Monk, S. and Kleinman, M. (1989) 'Housing' in P. Brown and R. Sparks (eds) *Beyond Thatcherism.* London: Open University Press.

Morgan, K. (1992) *The People's Peace: British History, 1945–90.* Oxford: Oxford University Press.

Murie, A. (1989) 'Housing and the Environment', in D. Kavanagh and A. Seldon (eds) *The Thatcher Effect.* Oxford: Clarendon Press.

Newburn, T. (2007) 'Tough on Crime: Penal Policy in England and Wales', *Crime and Justice*, 425–70.

Offer, A. (2006) *The Challenge of Affluence*. Oxford: Oxford University Press.

Phillips, L. (1998) 'Hegemony and Political Discourse: The Lasting Impact of Thatcherism', *Sociology* 32(4): 847–67.

Riddell, P. (1991) *The Thatcher Era and Its Legacy*. Oxford: Blackwell.

Rhodes, R.A.W. and Marsh, D. (1992) 'Thatcherism: an Implementation Perspective', in D. Marsh, and R.A.W. Rhodes (eds) *Implementing Thatcherite Policies*. Buckingham: Open University Press.

Scott, P. (1994) 'Education Policy', in D. Kavanagh and A. Seldon (eds) *The Major Effect*. London: Macmillan.

Taylor, I. (ed.) (1990) *The Social Effects of Free Market Policies*. London: Harvester Wheatsheaf.

Terrill, R.J. (1989) 'Margaret Thatcher's Law and Order Agenda', *The American Journal of Comparative Law*, 37: 429–56.

Timmins, N. (2001) *The Five Giants*. London: HarperCollins.

Tomlinson, G. (1989) 'The Schools', in D. Kavanagh and A. Seldon (eds) *The Major Effect*. London: Macmillan.

Vinen, R. (2009) *Thatcher's Britain*. London: Simon & Schuster.

Whitty, G. and Menter, I. (1989) 'Lessons of Thatcherism: Education Policy in England and Wales, 1979–88', in A. Gamble and C. Wells (eds) *Thatcher's Law*. Cardiff: GPC Books.

Windlesham, Lord (1993) *Responses to Crime*, vol. 2. Oxford: Oxford University Press.

Windsor, D. (2003) 'Reprivatising Britain: Thatcherism and its Results', in S. Pugliese (ed.) *The Political Legacy of Margaret Thatcher*. London: Politicos.

Williams, P. (1992) 'Housing', in P. Cloke (ed.) *Policy and Change in Thatcher's Britain*. Oxford: Pergamon Press.

Young, H. (1993) *One of Us*. London: Pan Books.

PART II
SPECIFIC POLICY DOMAINS

2
The Thatcherite economic legacy

HELEN THOMPSON

Governments can leave a legacy in terms of policy outcomes, the ideo-logical parameters of future debate, and the nature of electoral competition between political parties. These legacies can be deliberate achievements or the unintended consequences of decisions taken for other purposes. Assessing the nature of a 'Thatcherite' legacy raises some fundamental issues of analysis, and the question of which governments to consider as 'Thatcherite' is not straightforward. We can draw the line either in November 1990 with Margaret Thatcher's departure as Prime Minister or in May 1997 with the Conservatives' eventual electoral defeat. Moreover, the notion of a legacy focuses immediate analytical attention on the relationship between the 'Thatcherite' governments and their successors, but to analyse the specific impact of these governments we need two other kinds of comparisons: how far was what the 'Thatcherite' governments did a substantial break with their predecessors; and how far was their legacy a singular one or one comparable to governments in other states in the 1980s and 1990s?

Most scholars writing during the Thatcher years argued that there *would* be a very significant Thatcherite economic legacy (see, for example, Gamble, 1988; Jessop, Bonnet, Bromley and Ling, 1988). Those looking back with hindsight have generally accepted this claim and some have argued that this legacy produced a new consensus in UK politics (Heffernan, 2000; Kerr, 2001). In general substantive terms, this legacy is frequently taken to be a neo-liberal economy, a debate about economic policy circumscribed within neo-liberal parameters, and a return to power for Labour at a point when it had accepted both ideologically and practically what the Thatcher governments had done economically. Seen this way, UK politics post-1990 has consolidated a largely unchallenged economic settlement founded during the Thatcher years, and this new consensus superseded the one that emerged after the Second World War around full employment, Keynesian demand management, a mixed economy and, at least since the 1960s, state intervention in industry (Heffernan, 2002).

There are several problems with this narrative in relation to the analytical issues conceptualizing what a 'Thatcherite' legacy entails. First, it assumes a basic continuity in approach from the Conservative governments between 1979 and 1997 when there were significant discontinuities in macro-economic policy between 1979 and 1990, a sharp change in approach in the last month of Thatcher's premiership, and a collapse of that policy six months into the final Conservative government under John Major, which required the construction of an entirely new monetary framework. Given the role disagreements about macro-economic policy played in the end of Thatcher's premiership, the question of when any 'Thatcherite' period ended is particularly vexed. Put differently, was the Major government the 'Thatcherite' heir or did it exist because at least part of the 'Thatcherite' approach had become a political liability to Thatcher and had to be refashioned by her successor? Second, this narrative ignores some of the comparisons required to make claims about an agency-driven legacy. It tends to create a singular past of the period between 1945 and 1979 in macro-economic policy when there was not one. Macro-economic policy from 1945 to 1979 was not driven by the pursuit of full employment using Keynesian demand management but rather managing a succession of exchange rate problems (Brittan, 1983; Bulpitt, 1986: 24–6). Similarly, this narrative tends to downplay parallel shifts in economic policy in other states and the changes in the international economy during the 1980s and 1990s that shaped the choices confronting governments. Consequently, it tends to explain the Thatcher governments in overly domestic terms. Third, temporal issues are further muddled by the use of the term 'neo-liberalism'. Its common parlance began in the 1990s, not the 1980s (see Farrall and Jennings, Chapter 7), and it cannot be used to described a self-conscious project of the Thatcher governments themselves. Its use also once more begs the question of how far there was something deliberately distinctive about the Thatcher governments' economic approach in relation to international economic conditions.

The analysis offered here seeks to avoid these analytical traps and the empirical simplifications they risk generating. It makes distinctions around different periods between 1979 and 1997 and utilizes a comparative framework in relation to the period after 1997, the period before 1979, and other states between 1979 and 1997, in particular France, Italy, Germany and the USA. It also eschews the term neo-liberalism for the language in which economic policy in the 1980s was debated. The discussion is divided into four parts. The first part analyses the structure of the UK economy; the second examines macro-economic policy, broadly divided between the parameters of debate about unemployment and inflation, the components of fiscal policy, and monetary policy and exchange rate management;[1] the third, more briefly, considers some of the political and social consequences of the Conservative governments' economic management; and the fourth part draw some conclusions.

The structure of the UK economy 1979–97

Important changes in the structure of the UK economy were purposefully brought about by the Thatcher governments between 1979 and 1997. The economy the Thatcher government inherited in 1979 had strict capital and exchange controls in place, was 20 per cent owned by the state, and included powerful trade unions that had directly contributed to the demise of the previous two governments. The economy the Major government left behind was characterized by full capital account convertibility, very few state-owned industries, and relatively weak trade unions. In each of these areas, the Thatcher governments pursued radical policies and UK politics since has operated around the new status quo. The Thatcher government abolished all capital and exchange controls in October 1979. It pursued a comprehensive privatization programme from the second term. Between 1980 and 1990 the Thatcher governments passed eight laws placing new restrictions on trade unions in regard to strike action, picketing, internal organization, and the closed shop. By 1997, the political parameters of debate about the economy had shifted such that capital controls, nationalization, and trade union law were not part of the political debate. When Labour returned to power in 1997 it did not consider reform in any of these areas.

However, at least some of these shifts in policy and outcomes were also made elsewhere. The USA had lifted all capital controls in 1974 and by 1990

---

[1] Fiscal policy covers decisions on government expenditure, revenue, and borrowing; monetary policy covers decisions about interest rates and the money supply; and exchange rate management covers the approach of a government to the exchange rate.

all the EU states had too, although some retained the capacity to deploy them temporarily. Trade unions were much weaker in other large developed-country states by both the end of the 1980s and 1998. As Figure 2.1 shows, there was a shift away from unionized employment in the USA, Germany, France and Italy as well as the UK. Although the fall in trade union density in the UK was sharper in both the 1980s and 1990s than that in other four states, the UK began and ended the period with higher trade union density than any of Germany, France or the USA.

Where the UK clearly differed, by 1997, from the three other large EU countries, as Figure 2.2 shows, was in employment protection legislation. However, the time-series data here does not go back far enough to show any specific effect of the three Thatcher governments.

Privatization is more complex because there was only limited commonality in comparable states in having a mixed economy during the post-war period. Neither the USA nor West Germany had significant nationalized industries in 1979. Other states also moved away from them in the 1980s and 1990s. Compared to these other states, the Thatcher government was

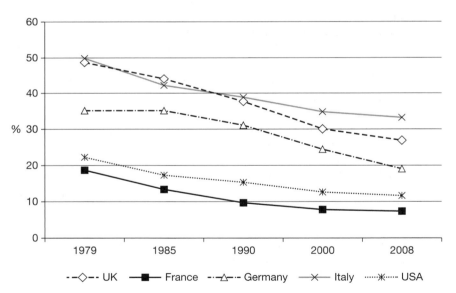

Figure 2.1 Comparative trade union density 1979–2008 measured by the ratio of earners that are trade union members to the total number of earners

Source: OECD Employment and Labour Market Statistics

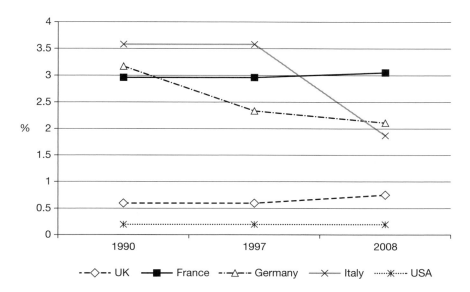

Figure 2.2 Comparative strictness of employment protection legislation by OECD synthetic indicator

Source: OECD Employment and Labour Market Statistics

distinctive in acting first, beginning its privatization programme in 1984. In France, the Chirac government embarked on a similar programme between the second half of 1986 and 1988 but this came after the socialist governments between 1981 and the first half of 1986 had nationalized various enterprises. In Italy, significant privatization only began in 1992.

There was also a significant shift in the UK economy that took place between 1979 and 1997 that cannot be attributed to the intentional agency of the Thatcher government. In 1979 the manufacturing sector constituted 40 per cent of the economy and the service sector 57 per cent whilst in 1997 the manufacturing sector constituted 30 per cent and the service sector 69 per cent. The financial services sector was significantly more important to the UK economy in 1997 than it had been in 1979. Rather than seeking to reverse this, New Labour pushed further the development of financial services as the primary sector of growth in the British economy. As Figure 2.3 shows, although the first Thatcher government presided over this change, a shift away from manufacturing towards services was already evident in the first half of the 1970s (Crafts, 1991; Tomlinson, 1990).

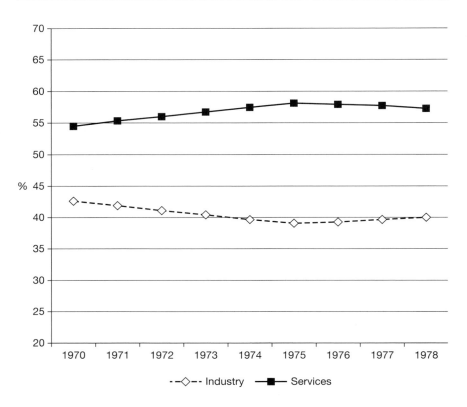

Figure 2.3   Value added in industry and services as a percentage of total in the UK 1970–78

Source OECD Country Statistical Profiles – 2010 edition

Certainly, it was temporarily reversed between 1976 and 1978. Yet the most obvious explanation for this would seem to be the boost to manufacturing export competitiveness provided by sterling's sharp fall in the second half of 1975 and early 1976. This fits with the fact that (as Figure 2.4 shows), the sharp fall in manufacturing output over which the Thatcher government presided occurred between 1979 and 1981 when a very substantial appreciation of sterling took place.

Whilst the first Thatcher government decided upon the monetary policy that produced this appreciation, Thatcher and her first Chancellor, Geoffrey Howe, had not anticipated the consequences for sterling of high interest

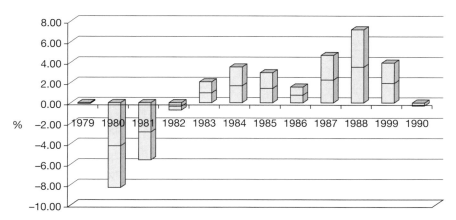

Figure 2.4 Annual percentage growth in UK manufacturing output 1979–90

Source: OECD Main Economic Indicators

rates and had not been looking to weaken the manufacturing sector. Indeed, by early 1981, Thatcher and Howe were so alarmed by the fallout of their initial monetary policy that they abandoned it in March 1981 specifically to secure sterling depreciation and help industry (see Hoskyns, 2000). The change in the sectoral composition of the UK economy during the 1980s was also part of a strong trend among large developed-country states. As Figures 2.5 and 2.6 show, the USA, France, Germany and Italy in the 1980s all had shrinking industrial sectors and rising service sectors.

Within the service economy, the Thatcher and Major governments bequeathed a stronger financial and business services sector than that they inherited. The second Thatcher government used deregulation in the 1986 Financial Services Act to re-launch London as an international financial centre (see Moran, 1990). Comparatively, the Thatcherite legacy here was distinctive in some respects and less so in others. Domestically, the second Thatcher government's encouragement of the financial sector was as much a rejuvenation of an old bias in the UK economy as a new development. The UK has long had an economically significant financial sector. Complaints about a bias towards the financial sector over the manufacturing sector are long-standing and surrounded much of the debate about successive government's management of sterling during the Bretton Woods era (Ingham, 1984). Comparing the UK with other states, by the end of the Conservative period of government (see Figure 2.7), finance and

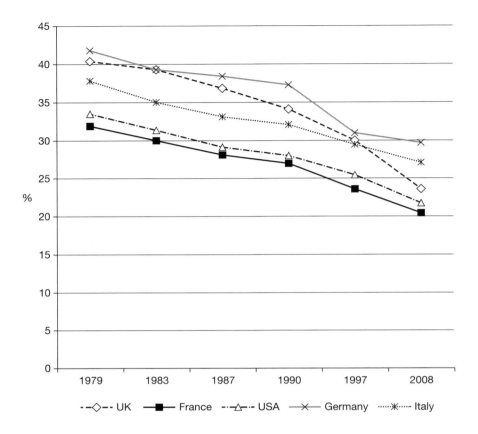

Figure 2.5 Comparative value added by industry as a percentage of the total economy 1979–2008

Source: OECD Country Statistical Profiles, 2010

insurance was more important to the UK economy than it was to any of the French, German or Italian. However, as Figure 2.8 illustrates, if a broader definition of the sector is used – covering finance and insurance, real estate and renting, and business services – it constituted a smaller proportion of value added to the UK economy in 1998 than it did in any of the USA, Germany or France. Moreover, the growth of this sector in relation to the rest of the economy from 1988 to 1998 in the UK was matched by growth in the other four states.

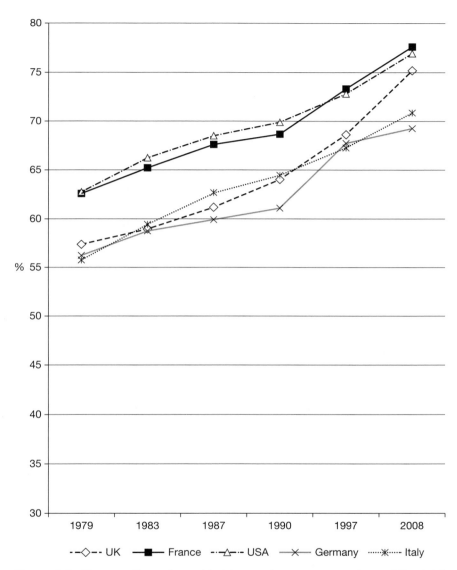

Figure 2.6 Comparative value added by services as a percentage of the total economy 1979–2008

Source: OECD Country Statistical Profiles 2010

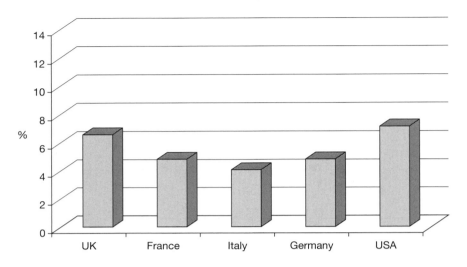

Figure 2.7 Comparative value added by finance and insurance as a percentage of the total economy in 1997

Source: OECD in Figures 2009

Summarizing the UK's trajectory

In sum, the Thatcher governments between 1979 and 1990 both brought about a significant change in the structure of the UK economy and presided over one that had causes that went beyond the policies they pursued. On the first, there is a plausible counter-factual that neither a Conservative government led by Willie Whitelaw nor a Labour government that had called and won an election in the autumn of 1978 would have pursued such radical trade union reform between 1979 and 1983 or abolished capital controls. The absence of these policies would have left the UK not only with a rather different economy in some important respects but would have changed the macro-economic conditions under which the second Thatcher term, which began the privatization programme, took place. Financial liberalization and trade union reform were policy decisions that had profound consequences for the whole scope of economic management and what governments could look to do economically. On the second, the Thatcher government reinforced trends, at first inadvertently over manufacturing and then strategically over the financial sector that grew out of changes in the international economy as developed-country states

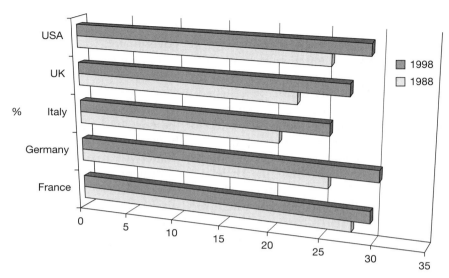

Figure 2.8 Comparative percentage of value added to the total economy by finance, insurance, real estate and renting, and business services 1988 and 1998

Source: OECD in Figures 2000

faced more competition in manufacturing production and the spread of financial liberalization and technological change created opportunities for the growth of financial sectors and business services.

Macro-economic policy

Assessing the legacy of the Thatcher governments in macro-economic policy is rather more complex, not least because there was a significant disjuncture in this policy area between the rhetoric of the Thatcher governments, the actions of the government, the policy outcomes, and the ideological narrative created around the confluence of the three. Consequently, the question needs to be broken down into two separate questions: how far has a Thatcherite ideological narrative about macro-economic policy persisted to set the parameters of policy today; and how far has the practical macro-economic approach pursued by the Thatcher governments endured in any way?

Inflation and unemployment

The ideological rhetoric of the early Thatcher governments was unequivocal: the enemy was inflation and inflation was a monetary phenomenon;
Keynesian demand management could not be used to boost employment;
and the UK economy had to be adjusted to the world as it was. On the
surface, the evidence for a Thatcherite narrative in these terms setting the
parameters for macro-economic policy for the post-1997 period would
seem strong. In 1997 the incoming New Labour government appeared
to accept ideologically and practically that there was a past in macro-
economic policy from before the Thatcher governments to which it could
not return (see Balls, 1998). Indeed, the whole notion of New Labour was
dependent on the idea that there was an old Labour approach to economic
policy that the party had repudiated. As Hay (2004: 40) has argued,
New Labour accepted the assumptions that there is a natural rate of
unemployment, no long-term trade-off between inflation and unemployment, and the futility of macro-economic policy as an instrument of
demand management. This ideological narrative would also seem to have
been accepted by the 2010 Coalition government. Seen in this light, the
Thatcherite ideological legacy in macro-economic policy was a bipartisan
consensus about the ends of policy and their implicit limits, which was
achieved when Labour shifted its stance in this area after the party's defeat
in 1992 (Hay, 1998).

The strength of this narrative is buoyed by the simple fact (see Figure
2.9) that since 1979 unemployment has never once fallen below the level
inherited by the Thatcher government, falling only in 2004 to the same level
as 1979. Moreover, even during the period when official unemployment
fell generally steadily between 1993 and 2004, the number of men economically inactive rose, as illustrated in Figure 2.10. Even more clearly (see
Figure 2.11), inflation has never risen anywhere near the level at which it
peaked during the first Thatcher government, or for that matter in the early
months of the first Major government.

However, the ideological narrative pushed by the Thatcher governments and critics gives a misleading account of what happened to UK
macro-economic policy between 1979 and 1997 and ignores what is
revealed by comparative analysis in relation to the past and other states.
Crucially, the change both in rhetoric and policy comes in 1976 not 1979
(Smith, 1991). It was James Callaghan who stood up and told the Labour
party conference in 1976 that it was not possible for a state to spend its

Figure 2.9 Annual UK unemployment 1979–2009 as percentage of the civilian labour force

Source: OECD Employment and Labour Market Statistics

way out of recession and increase employment with an expansionary fiscal policy. Policy-wise, it was the Labour government, after the sterling crisis that year, that prioritized inflation reduction over short-term growth and employment (see Kenway, 1998). And contrary to its rhetoric, the Thatcher governments' first acts in office added to inflation particularly through an increase in VAT, implementing the public sector pay rises recommended by the Clegg Commission, and adding demand through income tax cuts. In terms of outcomes (as Figures 2.9 and 2.11 show), inflation had been on a generally downward trajectory and unemployment was on a rising trajectory until the last months before the Thatcher government came into office.

If we compare the UK with other states during the period from 1979 to 1997, we see both similarities and differences with the UK experience. The

45

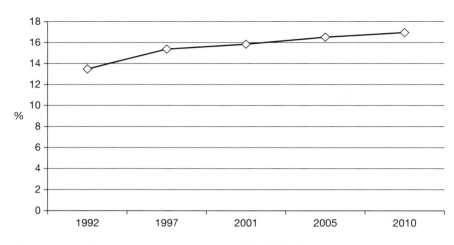

Figure 2.10 Economically inactive men 1992–2010 (The rate for each year is for the period June–August)

Source: NOMIS Official Labour Market Statistics

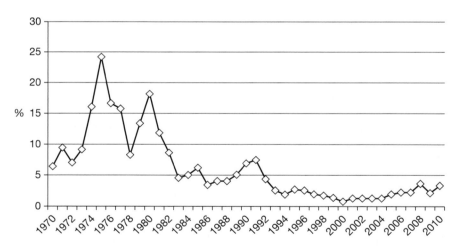

Figure 2.11 UK annual percentage inflation of consumer prices 1970–2010

Source: OECD Main Economic Indicators

UK was not alone in suffering from a steep rise in unemployment between 1979 and 1983, albeit the UK rise was sharper. By 1997, however, UK unemployment was comparatively low (see Figure 2.12). Similarly, UK inflation fell more sharply than in comparable economies between 1979 and 1983. Yet by the end of Thatcher's premiership, it was strikingly high in comparative terms (see Figure 2.13).

In this rise of inflation from 1987 lies the dirty little secret of the Thatcher governments' economic policy. After the first term it was inflationary in comparison to what other developed-country governments were doing such that by 1990 even Italy, an economy notorious for having inflationary problems, was doing better. Contrary to the 'Thatcherite' ideological narrative, the last years of the Thatcher governments did trade off inflation and unemployment, as Figure 2.14 shows.

New Labour's commitment to macro-economic stability and repudiation of demand management as an instrument of unemployment-reduction was

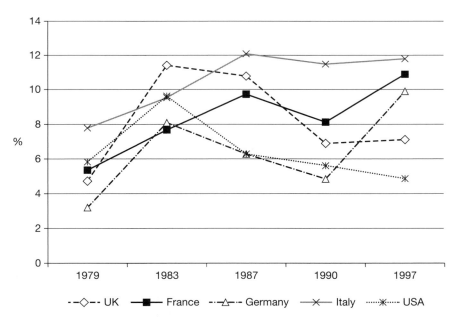

Figure 2.12 Comparative unemployment as a percentage of the civilian labour force 1979–97

Source: OECD Employment and Labour Market Statistics

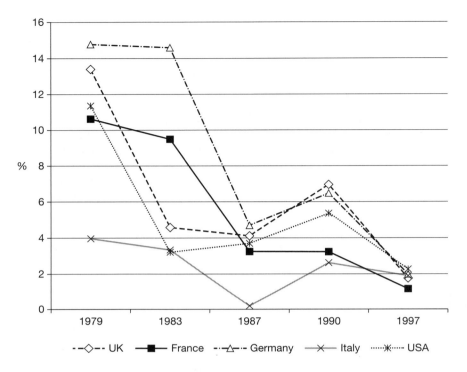

Figure 2.13 Comparative annual inflation rate 1979–97

Source: OECD Main Economic Indicators

a critique of the late Thatcher governments' approach to macro-economic policy not an acceptance of it for reasons that will become clear in the discussion of monetary issues.

Fiscal policy

Breaking down macro-economic policy into its fiscal and monetary dimensions, the Conservative governments from 1979 to 1997 left a limited fiscal legacy. If the Thatcherite ideological aspiration in fiscal policy began with the statement in the Conservative 1979 manifesto that 'the State takes too much of the nation's income; its share must be steadily reduced' the Thatcher governments failed (Conservative Party, 1979). As Figure 2.15 shows, public expenditure as a percentage of GDP rose sharply during the

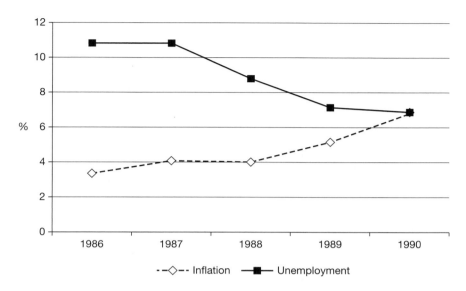

Figure 2.14   Annual percentage rate of UK unemployment and inflation 1986–90

Source: OECD Main Economic Indicators and OECD Employment and Labour Market Statistics

first term, falling back to a level just 1.7 per cent lower in 1990 than it was in 1979. Thereafter it rose above the 1979 level in 1993 and stayed there until 1996, falling only in 1997 significantly below the level that the first Thatcher government had inherited.

Meanwhile neither the Thatcher nor Major governments succeeded in reducing tax revenue as a percentage of GDP. Indeed, as Figure 2.16 illustrates, not once during the years of the Thatcher and Major governments was tax revenue at even the same level as it was in 1979. Standing at 31.9 per cent in 1979, it rose sharply for most of the first term reaching a peak of 38.5 per cent in 1982. In 1990 it stood at 35.5 per cent, in 1997 at 34.3 per cent.

Again, as Figures 2.17 and 2.18 show, there was a prior shift in policy. Public expenditure had risen sharply in the middle of the 1970s and the IMF crisis of 1976 led to the Labour government making significant cuts in public expenditure such that it fell as a proportion of GDP by 4.4 per cent between 1976 and 1978, even though unemployment was rising during this period. This was a sharper fall over a two-year period than was ever procured by the Thatcher governments.

49

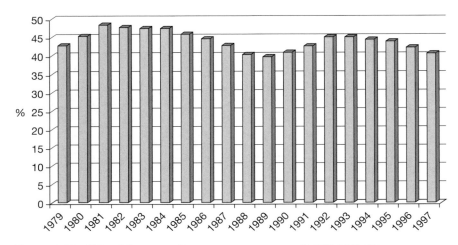

Figure 2.15   UK public expenditure as a percentage of GDP 1979–97

Source: OECD National Account Statistics

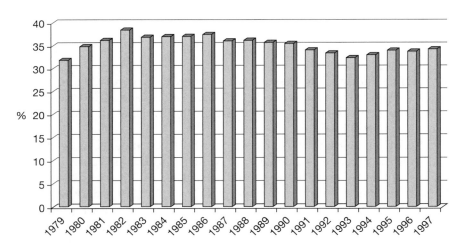

Figure 2.16   UK tax revenue as a percentage of GDP 1979–97

Source: OECD Tax Statistics

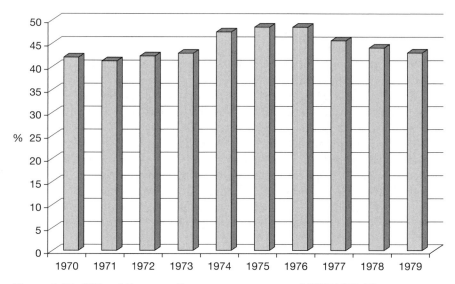

Figure 2.17   UK public expenditure as a percentage of GDP 1970–79

Source: OECD National Account Statistics

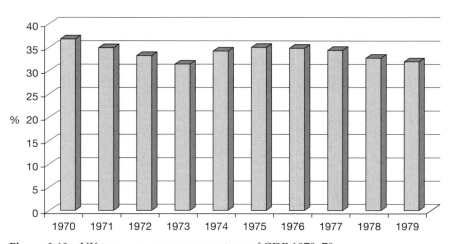

Figure 2.18   UK tax revenue as a percentage of GDP 1970–79

Source: OECD Tax Statistics

Meanwhile, tax revenue as a percentage of GDP had been falling from 1976. Indeed, it was not only the Labour government after the 1976 crisis that succeeded in reducing the overall tax burden where the Thatcher governments failed but the Conservative government led by Edward Heath earlier in the decade too.

Comparatively (Figure 2.19), the UK fits to a considerable extent the same pattern of public expenditure growth and reduction as in other states. The sharp rise in public expenditure during the first years of the first Thatcher government reflected what was happening elsewhere. The fall from its peak after the early 1990s recession was matched by falls in other states. There would appear to be a period of UK exceptionalism during the second half of the period of the Thatcher governments when UK public expenditure fell while it was stable or rising elsewhere. However, since this is also a period where the UK was seeing a sharper fall in unemployment

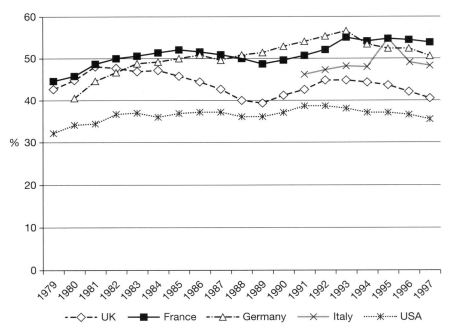

Figure 2.19 Comparative public expenditure as a percentage of GDP 1979–97

Source: OECD National Accounts Statistics

than other economies, that discrepancy can in part be explained by the cyclical level of unemployment-driven welfare state expenditure.

On tax revenue as a proportion of GDP, as Figure 2.20 illustrates, the first Thatcher government presided over an increase comparable only to that in Italy. Moreover, whereas the UK took a lower proportion of GDP in tax revenue than Germany in 1979, in 1990 it was slightly higher. Only between 1990 and 1993 does the direction of the UK position stand out, and this was during a recession that was deeper and longer than those seen elsewhere during those years.

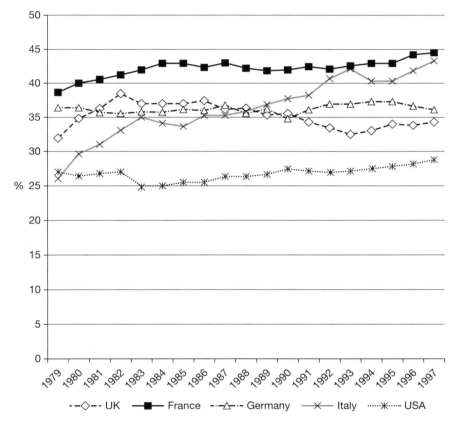

Figure 2.20   Comparative tax revenue as a percentage of GDP 1979–97

Source: OECD Tax Statistics

53

Looking at the policies pursued by Thatcher and Major successors, the legacy of the expressed ideological intent to reduce the financial size of the state did not survive the end of New Labour's first term in office. Whilst there was significant continuity on the overall tax burden (see Figure 2.21), this was not so on public expenditure (Figure 2.22). By 2009, during New Labour's last full year in office, the UK state was spending the equivalent of 51.4 per cent of GDP.

There is a political narrative that ties the 2010 Coalition government to the Thatcher government's ideological rhetoric about state expenditure. This means seeing New Labour as succeeding over time in undoing the Thatcherite aspiration for a retrenched state, and seeing the 2010 Coalition government, or at least its Conservative component, as Thatcher's heir. However, this argument is problematic for several reasons. The 2010 Coalition government said that it aims to reduce expenditure by the end of the Parliament to the level of 2006–7, which would still be more than 1 per cent higher than the level prevailing in 1979. This narrative also ignores the very different situations in regard to state borrowing between 1979 and 2013 and the consequent comparative risks run by the 2010 Coalition government compared to the Thatcher governments in deciding annual

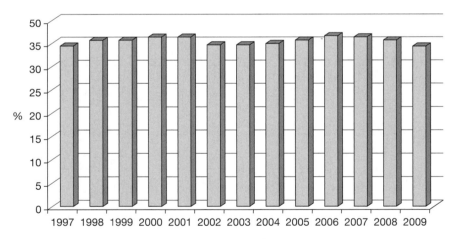

Figure 2.21   UK tax revenue as a percentage of GDP 1997–2009

Source: OECD Tax Statistics

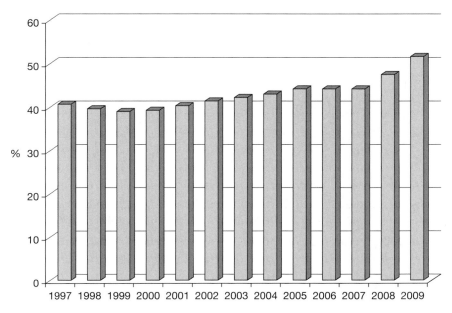

Figure 2.22   UK public expenditure as a percentage of GDP 1997–2009

Source: OECD National Account Statistics

borrowing. Whilst general government new borrowing was 3.8 per cent for 1980–81 and 3.9 per cent in 1996–99, it was 11.4 per cent in 2009–10 (Treasury, *Pocket Data Bank*, 2011a and 2011b).

Nonetheless, as Figures 2.23 and 2.24 show, the Thatcher and Major governments did make a significant change to the composition of taxes towards taxes on goods and services. The corollary was a reduction in the proportion of revenue coming from income, profits and capital gains. This revision began in the first budget in June 1979 when the Chancellor of the Exchequer, Geoffrey Howe, created a single VAT rate of 15 per cent from the previous two bands of 8 per cent and 12.5 per cent, whilst reducing basic rate of income tax from 33 per cent to 30 per cent. In 1991 the Major government raised VAT to 17.5 per cent. This was a change in policy that demarcated the Conservative governments from their predecessors. Whilst there was a slight shift in the direction of taxes on goods and services after the 1976 crisis, it was nothing like as sharp as the increase from 1979.

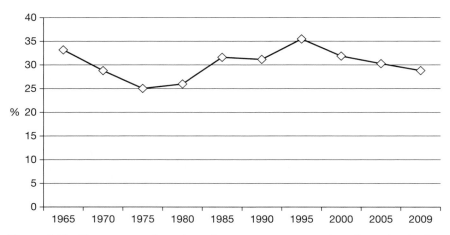

Figure 2.23 Taxes on goods and services as a percentage of total taxation in the UK 1965–2009

Source: OECD Tax Statistics

Comparing the UK with other states in this period, this rise in taxes on goods and services stands out, as Figure 2.25 shows, with these kind of taxes falling in France, Germany and Italy in the first half the 1980s and rising by much less in the USA. In the early 1990s, they rose much more modestly in Germany and the USA and fell in Italy and France. In 1990 and 1997 the UK was taking a higher proportion of revenue from taxes on goods and service than any of these states whereas in 1979 all of Germany, France and Italy had taken more.

However, as Figures 2.23 and 2.24 also show, this shift in the composition of taxes was in significant part reversed by New Labour with both the proportion taken in taxes on goods and services falling and that on income, profit and capital rising after 1997. This happened despite the fact that during the same period policy in Germany and the USA moved in the opposite direction. Although the Thatcher and Major governments succeeded in achieving a change in policy direction, they did not bring Labour into a new bipartisan consensus about the composition of taxes.

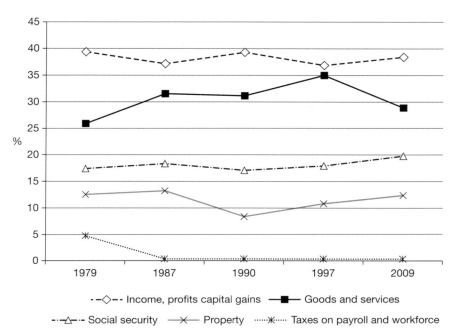

Figure 2.24 Kinds of taxes in the UK as a percentage of the total 1979–2009

Source: OECD Tax Statistics

Macro-economic policy: monetary policy and exchange rate management

On entering office in 1979 the Thatcher government deemed the primary macro-economic problem inflation and made monetary policy directed at money supply targets the centrepiece of an anti-inflationary strategy. The government set targets for the growth of the money supply and then promised to raise interest rates if those targets were not met. This led the government to increase what was then the Minimum Lending Rate from 12 to 17 per cent between May and November 1979. This approach to inflation was formalized into the Medium Term Financial Strategy (MTFS) in the March 1980 budget, which set money supply targets for the following four years, putting a premium on M3 as a broad measure of money. However, money supply targeting proved difficult to operationalize and had severe unintended consequences. By the end of 1980 the growth of the

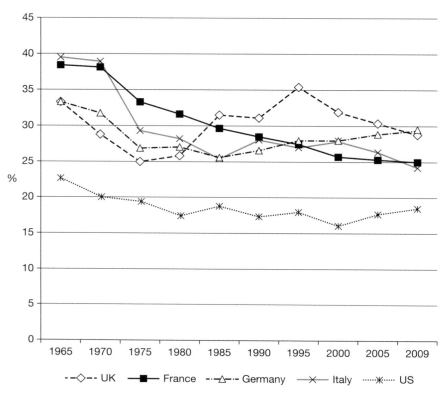

Figure 2.25 Comparative taxes on goods and services as a percentage of total taxes

Source: OECD Tax Statistics

money supply was outstripping the targets, despite the tightness of monetary policy, and the economy was in a deep recession with the manufacturing sector hit particularly hard. In the first quarter of 1981 the Thatcher government reversed its anti-inflationary tactics with the explicit aim of producing sterling depreciation, lower interest rates, and an end to the recession. It substituted fiscal tightening via tax increases and public expenditure cuts for money supply targets. In so doing it redirected monetary policy firmly towards the exchange rate. In immediate outcomes this achieved its purpose. Sterling fell, the economy returned to growth in the second quarter of 1981, and inflation continued to fall. However, the first Thatcher government's problems with sterling were far from over. In September 1981, a bout of sterling weakness led the government to increase interest rates again. For the remainder of the first term, it continued to direct monetary policy towards exchange rate stability and the money supply targets were rendered meaningless in practical terms (see Smith, 1991).

In the face of the facts of policy, it is difficult to characterize a distinct 'Thatcherite' approach to macro-economic policy in the first term. In prioritizing inflation over unemployment, the first Thatcher government made the same choice as its immediate predecessor had done after the IMF crisis. Certainly the MTFS was distinctive as a means in that it operated a largely one-tool approach to inflation and in eschewing an incomes policy the Thatcher government drew a clear line between it and its predecessors. However, the Thatcher government then abandoned the MTFS for the same structural reason the Labour government had moved towards its anti-inflationary approach in the middle of 1976: the exchange rate consequences of a macro-economic policy conceived without regard to external constraints. Whilst Thatcher coined an image of the lady who was not for turning during the recession, the first Thatcher government implemented a significant U-turn in its macro-economic policy in pursuit of growth and different exchange rate outcomes. In reconstructing its approach in 1981 to try to deal with problems generated by sterling, the first Thatcher government trod the same route as UK politicians had done in 1931, 1947, 1966 and 1976.

This reversion to a monetary policy focused on the exchange rate left the Thatcher government by the end of the first term in much the same position as other governments of large EU countries, except that these states had an institutionalized approach by virtue of being inside the Exchange Rate Mechanism (ERM). Comparatively, there is an interesting parallel between the first Thatcher government and President Mitterrand's first 22 months in office in France (May 1981–March 1983). Both had wanted to pursue an independent monetary policy in the sense of it being set to achieve domestic objectives, albeit for different purposes, and both had found that the consequences for the exchange rate of that stance had produced a crisis. Both had responded to that crisis by reversing policy and both had ended up by the summer of 1983 with a macro-economic policy focused around exchange rate stability. They had done so because their original approaches had proved extremely problematic under conditions of open capital flows and the foreign exchange market conditions created by the monetary power of both the USA and West Germany.

Yet the fact that the UK ended the first Thatcher term outside the ERM created the space for a period during which the Thatcher governments pursued a more distinctive approach to monetary policy in comparative terms. During the second and third terms policy veered off in various, and at times incoherent, directions and was marked by severe internal disagreement particularly between Thatcher and her second Chancellor of the Exchequer, Nigel Lawson. There were constant changes in approach between trying to use monetary policy to stimulate more growth and trying to maintain exchange rate stability as an anti-inflationary discipline. From the second half of 1988, the third Thatcher government used the exchange rate to reduce inflation by procuring an appreciation in sterling (Smith, 1993). Part of this muddle arose because the government had reduced its macro-economic toolbox to monetary and fiscal policy by eschewing any more direct approach to wages and credit expansion. It also came from the disagreement between Thatcher and Lawson on the question of whether sterling should join the ERM. Whilst Lawson wanted to give monetary policy a formal external anchor and thus prioritize exchange rate stability as the primary anti-inflationary discipline, Thatcher did not want to lose the discretion that membership would have entailed. Eventually, in October 1990 (after Lawson had left office), Thatcher conceded ERM membership to her third Chancellor, John Major, but without the government having a clear strategy as to how inside the system it would match Germany's monetary policy beyond the short term with the economy having entered recession that summer. Twenty-three months later, in September 1992, the ERM policy collapsed on Black Wednesday (see Thompson, 1996).

The question in assessing any ongoing legacy of the Thatcher governments in monetary policy and exchange rate management is how one views the ERM watershed. Since ERM membership did put the premium in overall macro-economic policy on inflation and since it made monetary policy the first tool of the anti-inflationary discipline it required, it could perhaps be seen in terms of ends as the final manifestation of a 'Thatcherite' approach to macro-economic policy. However, in tying interest rates to an external constraint rather than a domestic target, it was, at the same time, the exact opposite kind of monetary policy from that which the first Thatcher government had originally pursued, and it required other policy instruments to be directed towards price stability too. It also gave UK monetary and exchange rate policy the same framework as its EU counterparts, much against what Thatcher herself had for a long time wanted. In this sense, ERM membership as the final general macro-economic framework established by the Thatcher governments might be best understood as representing the failure of the Thatcher governments over time to identify and pursue any kind of coherent or distinctive policy of their own.

Yet, of course, the legacy of the Thatcher governments from ERM membership was not ultimately an enduring policy stance but a policy failure. Strikingly, it is that policy failure that shapes the practical parameters of overall macro-economic policy today. The primary defining feature of UK macro-policy for the past decade has been non-membership of the euro and the ERM failure was the reason first why the Major government stayed out of the preparations for the euro and why Gordon Brown as Chancellor was so insistent on retaining that position. And it is the context in which the New Labour government in 1997 established a monetary framework based on formal operational independence for the Bank of England and without reference to the exchange rate. Although after sterling's exit from the ERM the Major government had given some de facto autonomy to the Bank of England by publishing the minutes of monthly meetings between the Chancellor and the Governor, New Labour established an entirely new legal framework for monetary policy in the Bank of England Act of 1998, which gave the Monetary Policy Committee responsibility for setting interest rates to meet an inflation target. This monetary framework has been entirely accepted by the Coalition government and reflects a cross-party consensus about monetary policy, which has endured since New Labour's first term in office. This concurrence is in place despite the fact that in substantive terms the policy was, in practice, broken by the time the Coalition government entered office with the Bank ignoring the inflation target to cut interest rates aggressively from the autumn of 2008 and Alastair Darling, the then Labour Chancellor, making explicit that the decision to pursue some quantitative easing in response to the financial crisis was his and not the Bank's.

In assessing the relationship of the three Thatcher governments' approach to monetary policy and the exchange rate to this post-ERM framework there is continuity and discontinuity. At one level the two years of ERM membership through the end of the third Thatcher government and the first 22 months of Major's premiership is the aberration. Until the moment of ERM entry itself, the Thatcher governments did not want to tie the whole of macro-economic policy to the exchange rate. Even Nigel Lawson, who supported earlier ERM membership, did not want to accept that fiscal policy, as well as monetary policy, would have to operate within an external discipline inside the system (Thompson, 1996). Post-ERM policy has similarly eschewed the external framework, tying monetary policy formally to an inflation target and allowing the exchange rate to be largely determined in the foreign exchange markets. In this sense, Thatcher's successors have continued the policy pursued by the Thatcher governments until late 1990 and the Thatcher governments bequeathed a legacy. Yet even here a caveat is in order. Prior to 1979, UK politicians were already less willing than their west European counterparts to tie monetary policy to the exchange rate with the Heath government taking sterling out of the ERM's predecessor, the snake, after just six weeks of membership in 1972 and the Labour government keeping the UK out of the then newly created ERM in 1978.

Nonetheless, there is a clear rupture from the Thatcher period prior to ERM membership to the monetary approach now in place. The formal, legal framework for monetary policy created in 1997 gives UK politicians much less discretion than they had during the Thatcher governments. Even taking account of the relationship between the inflation target and monetary decisions since the autumn of 2008, UK politicians now have significant restrictions on what they can do with monetary policy and do not decide interest rates themselves and that is in sharp contrast to what was true during the Thatcher governments. Put in comparative terms, the UK does have a framework for monetary policy and a stance towards the exchange rate that stands out from comparable European states: the UK has its own currency, an independent monetary policy, and no stated exchange rate policy. This formation can in significant part be explained in terms of the legacy of the Thatcher governments but not in terms of direct policy continuity. The Thatcher governments' monetary and exchange rate legacy was that there was not one in policy terms, and its successors, particularly the New Labour government, had to construct an alternative.

The political and social fallout

In analysing the political legacy of the Conservative governments' approach to economic policy, we need to draw a clear distinction between the two periods 1979–92 and 1993–97. In the first the first three Conservative governments clearly ended the political crises of the 1970s generated by the problems of economic management that beset all the governments in power during that decade. Whilst no government was re-elected after four years in office from 1970 to 1979, the Conservatives were re-elected to office three times and Labour then won the three subsequent elections. The first and second Thatcher governments' eschewal of an incomes policy, pursuit of trade union reform, and defeat of the National Union of Mineworkers ensured that governments thereafter did not fear trade union resistance to their economic policies or have to risk their governing competence in confrontations over wage demands.

Meanwhile, the first Thatcher government demonstrated that high unemployment did not have to be an electoral liability. Whilst Edward Heath had executed a macro-economic U-turn in 1972 because he had thought that unemployment at over a million would bring electoral retribution, the Conservative party won a landslide in 1983 with unemployment over 3 million and did so again with little improvement in the level of joblessness in 1987. The first Thatcher government was able to manage unemployment politically in part because of its geographical distribution in relation to the electoral map and in part because of the Labour party's difficulties in presenting itself as a potential governing party and the breakaway of the Social Democratic Party and the formation of the Alliance. But the first Thatcher government also succeeded politically because the ideological narrative it constructed around macro-economic policy allowed it to present unemployment as the price paid for facing economic reality, however disingenuous that was as an account of what had practically transpired in economic policy over the time in question or the government's own early concerns about the electoral consequences of that outcome. The Thatcher governments appeared to reduce the expectations of many voters about what the state could do in regard to employment. If it were James Callaghan who told UK voters that the era of full employment was over, it was probably the first two Thatcher governments who were responsible for many of them believing that this was true.

Yet for all the electoral rewards the Conservatives reaped from the economy in 1983 and 1987 the final political legacy of the Thatcher governments' economic choices was the disaster of the ERM exit and the termination of the Conservatives' ability to retain power. After September 1992 voters' confidence in the Conservatives' competence collapsed and continued to fall for several years (Sanders, 1996: 206). Meanwhile, Black Wednesday let loose a wave of Euro-scepticism within the parliamentary party and Major's Cabinet that produced an internal civil war, pushed Major into calling a leadership election, and by the end of 1996 had cost the Conservatives their majority in the House of Commons. Even when the Major government succeeded in achieving four years of non-inflationary growth and a fall in unemployment, something which had escaped the

Thatcher governments and their post-war predecessors, there was no political reward for the Conservatives because of what the failure of the ERM policy and its fallout had destroyed. In this context, it is plausible to argue that Labour did not have to become New Labour to win in 1997 and that the shift in its economic policy stance between 1992 and 1997 was redundant in its return to power.

Meanwhile, the social fallout of the Thatcher governments' approach to economic policy centred on a rise in income inequality (see Walker, Chapter 9 in this collection). Whilst income inequality had begun to rise before 1979, it began to grow rapidly from the middle of the 1980s (Goodman and Webb, 1994). In part this rise was the consequence of the uneven geographical spread of the unemployment produced by the early 1980s recession (see Dorling, Chapter 8, in this collection), and which contributed to crime (see Farrall and Jennings, Chapter 7 in this collection). Those parts of the UK which had been largely dependent on the manufacturing sector were irrevocably changed by the sharp fall in capacity produced by the high interest rate and strong sterling policy pursued in the first phase of the first Thatcher government and the burden fell hardest on relatively low-skilled men. As the 1980s wore on and the financial services sector grew, proffering opportunities for extremely high financial rewards to those who worked at the top of it, income inequality was fuelled further.

Although the rise in income inequality was checked in the early 1990s and there was a modest reversal in the middle of the 1990s (Goodman, Johnson and Webb, 1997), high income inequality has become a long-term feature of the UK political economy since the 1980s (Institute of Fiscal Studies, 2011). Crucially, there remains a strong regional variation in unemployment and the numbers of those economically inactive that corresponds strongly with income disparities between regions. Meanwhile, despite various policies devised by the New Labour government directed at the working poor, which led to significant real income growth for those groups, growth in income at the top has ensured that overall income inequality rose through the New Labour years (Institute for Fiscal Studies, 2011). Whilst the 2008 financial crisis and its continuing fallout have certainly politicized one end of this issue through the frequent collective outrage expressed at bankers' remuneration, the changes to the UK economy directly and indirectly brought about by the Thatcher governments make practical action to act radically to transform such outcomes difficult.

Conclusions

The legacy of the Conservative governments between 1979 and 1997 was much clearer on the structure of the economy than macro-economic policy. The UK economy of 1990 and 1997 was substantively different to the one the Thatcher government inherited. Whilst most of these changes were matched by changes in comparable economies, most were also brought about by the deliberate intent of the Thatcher governments. On financial liberalization and trade union reform the Thatcher governments acted early and systematically to change the economy. On the shift away from manufacturing towards services, and the growth of the financial sector within that, the Thatcher government first produced unintended consequences on manufacturing and then reinvigorated what had previously been a strong financial sector and the cumulative effect had a significant economic and social impact on the UK.

There are several reasons why we would expect an enduring legacy once change of this kind had taken place. First, financial liberalization made it much more costly than it would otherwise have been for future governments to reverse course. Opening the UK economy to the ebb and flow of short-term capital movements meant that governments had to maintain credibility in the foreign exchange markets about their economic policies or risk a currency crisis which meant in practice ruling out most approaches likely to be deemed as reverting back to 'left-wing' policies. This would have certainly included renationalization and quite possibly repealing restrictive trade union legislation. Second, undoing privatization would have been expensive and generated lots of practical implementation problems. Third, reversing the changes in the composition of the economy between sectors outcome would have been politically difficult 10 or 20 years later. By the time New Labour was in office, deliberately trying to shrink the financial services sector and pursue a developmental strategy for a reconstructed manufacturing sector would have been a major practical enterprise that, in the short term, would have reduced growth. It would also have been a big political risk to take the most internationally competitive part of an economy on which many other parts of the economy in the south-east feed and pronounce it a problem that required action by shrinking it. Moreover, expanding the manufacturing sector is quite simply difficult, especially since manufacturing production has declined across virtually all developed-country economies. The Coalition government has talked the language of manufacturing renewal (Conservative Party, 2010), but the Coalition government's policies in this area have been ad hoc and a period of fiscal austerity provides inauspicious conditions for such a project. A report in 2010 by the National Endowment for Science, Technology and the Arts analysing four scenarios for the UK economy in the decade to 2020 showed that a broad-based manufacturing renaissance as the way forward would entail levels of growth in manufacturing not seen since before 1945 (Shanmugalingam, Puttick, and Westlake, 2010: executive summary).

In macro-economic policy the Thatcher governments left little policy legacy. They were unable to reduce the fiscal size of the state and New Labour departed company from the Thatcher governments' fiscal stance immediately on the composition of taxes and over time on public expenditure. On monetary matters, the first Thatcher government grappled with the same problems as its predecessor within the same general parameters about prioritizing inflation reduction and like all its post-war predecessors ended up managing sterling. Over time, the policy of the second and third Thatcher governments became incoherent such that the ERM failure was a disaster waiting to happen. Although the first Thatcher government appeared to succeed in reducing the political expectations many voters had of what the state could do in macro-economic policy, this did not stretch to voters tolerating the kind of failure Black Wednesday represented.

In part, the absence of a legacy in macro-economic policy is not surprising. Fiscal policy is set on a year-by-year basis and is operationally easy for future governments to change. Not infrequently macro-economic policy is about crisis management and the first Thatcher government inherited a significant set of economic problems at a time when governments everywhere were struggling to get to grips with the post-Bretton Woods international economy and the dilemmas created by the rapid growth of short-term capital flows. Little that any comparable government was doing between 1979 and 1983 was still in place in 1997 even in Germany, which saw more stability in policy than others.

And yet at the same time there is a significant paradox around the Thatcher governments. Precisely because of the nature of macro-economic policy, most governments do not end up with reputations for having ideologically changed it as the Thatcher governments did. The final irony of seeing an ideological Thatcherite macro-economic legacy stretching forth past 1997 is that the supposed substance of that approach had very little do with where the Thatcher governments took UK policy. If broad 'Thatcherite' macro-economic policy is defined by an ideological commitment to price stability, by the end of the 1980s the UK had the least Thatcherite approach of any EC state. If in specific policy terms a 'Thatcherite' approach is defined by using monetary policy independently of the exchange rate to control the domestic money supply, Thatcher handed over to Major membership of a fixed exchange rate regime in which monetary policy was massively constrained by another state's central bank. And if there was a bipartisan consensus about the ends of macro-economic policy by the time Labour returned to power in 1997, it did not stretch back to include the second and third Thatcher governments. Rather than the Thatcher governments having left a macro-economic legacy, a great deal of UK macro-economic policy since 1993 has been an implicit repudiation of the practice of the Thatcher governments.

References

Balls, E. (1998) 'Open Macroeconomics in an Open Economy', *Scottish Journal of Political Economy*, 45(2): 113–32.

Bulpitt, J. (1986) 'The Discipline of the New Democracy: Mrs Thatcher's Domestic Statecraft', *Political Studies*, 34(1): 19–34.

Brittan, S. (1983) *The Role and Limits of Government*. London: Temple Smith.

Conservative Party (1979) *1979 Manifesto*. London: Conservative Party.

Conservative Party (2010). *A New Economic Model: 8 Benchmarks for Britain*. London: Conservative Party.

Crafts, N.F.R. (1991) 'Economic Growth', in *The British Economy Since 1945*, edited by N.F.R. Crafts and Nicholas Woodward. Oxford: Clarendon Press.

Gamble, A. (1988) *The Free Economy and the Strong State*. Basingstoke: Macmillan.

Goodman, A., Johnson, P. and Webb, S. (1997) *Inequality in the UK*. Oxford: Oxford University Press.

Goodman, A. and Webb, S. (1994) *For Richer, for Poorer: the Changing Distribution of Income for the UK, 1961–91*, Commentary for no. 42. London: Institute for Fiscal Studies.

Institute of Fiscal Studies (2011) *Poverty and Inequality in the UK: 2011*. London: Institute of Fiscal Studies.

Hay, C. (1998) 'That was Then, This is Now: the Revision of Policy in the 'Modernisation' of the British Labour Party 1992–1997', *New Political Science*, 20(1): 7–32.

Hay, C. (2004) 'Credibility, Competitiveness and the Business Cycle in Third Way Political Economy', *New Political Economy*, 9(1): 39–57.

Heffernan, R. (2000) *New Labour and Thatcherism*. Basingstoke: Macmillan.

Heffernan R. (2002) '"The Possible as the Art of Politics": Understanding Consensus Politics', *Political Studies*, 50(3): 742–60.

HM Treasury (2011a) *Pocket Data Bank*, 18 August. London: HM Treasury.

HM Treasury (2011b) *Pocket Data Bank*, 22 October. London: HM Treasury.

Hoskyns, J. (2000) *Just in Time: Inside the Thatcher Revolution*. London: Aurum Press.

Ingham, G. (1984) *Capitalism Divided: the City and Industry in British Social Development*. Basingstoke: Macmillan.

Jessop, B., Bonnet K., Bromley S., and Ling T. (1988) *Thatcherism*. Cambridge: Polity Press.

Kenway, P. (1998) *From Keynesianism to Monetarism: the Evolution of Macro-Economic Models*. London: Routledge.

Kerr, P. (2001) *Postwar British Politics: from Conflict to Consensus*. London: Routledge.

Moran, M. (1990) *The Politics of the Financial Services Revolution: the US, the UK and Japan*. Basingstoke: Macmillan.

Sanders, D. (1996) 'Economic Performance, Management Competence and the Outcome of the Next General Election', *Political Studies*, 44(2): 203–31.

Shanmugalingam, S., Puttick, R., and Westlake S. (2010) *Rebalancing Act, Research Report: June 2010*. London: National Endowment for Science, Technology and the Arts.

Smith, D. (1991) *The Rise and Fall of Monetarism*. Harmondsworth: Penguin.

Smith, D. (1993) *From Boom to Bust: Trial and Error in British Economic Policy*, 2nd revd edn. Harmondsworth: Penguin.

Thompson, H. (1996) *The British Conservative Government and the European Exchange Rate Mechanism*. London: Pinter.

Tomlinson, Jim (1990) *Public Policy and the Economy Since 1900*. Oxford: Clarendon Press.

Commentary

The long run economic consequences of Mrs Thatcher

PETER M. JACKSON

Margaret Thatcher, with a majority of 43 seats, became Prime Minister of the UK on 3 May 1979 and continued in that office for 11 years. The Thatcher revolution which ensued changed the socio-economic landscape of the UK for decades. It influenced the Major government's economic policies and when the 'New Labour' governments of Tony Blair, and subsequently Gordon Brown, came to power they did not reject the economic policy framework of Thatcherism but instead built upon in it. Thatcher's economic legacy is much subtler than her precise policies, which were frequently ill conceived, poorly thought out and driven by ideology and rhetoric rather than sound principles based on a coherent theory supported by empirical evidence.

Helen Thompson, in Chapter 2, 'The Thatcherite economic legacy', does a good job at charting, through a number of aggregate level indices, the changes which followed the introduction of Thatcher's and subsequent governments' policies. Whether or not these changes were the intended consequences of deliberative agency is a moot point which Thompson is right to raise. Also, 'legacy' suggests a long-term enduring impact, which is much more difficult to establish. Policies evolve; policies are, both ex ante and ex post, conditional; as circumstances change our knowledge changes and along with that the appropriateness of the policies adopted change. Rather than focus on the precise detail of policies, which may or may not have been appropriate, and which might have produced unintended consequences, it is suggested in this commentary that Thatcher's economic legacy is that with the election of her government in 1979 there was a distinctive rupture with the past in terms of the framework within which economic policy is considered. Thatcherism was a counter-revolution to the post-war Keynesian revolution and economic policy-making, whilst it has evolved, has not experienced a further counter-revolution which has returned the world to its pre-Thatcher days. Moreover, as a consequence of Thatcherism greater attention is paid to the level of micro-economics. This level is important because it is in the details of micro-economics that behaviours which influence the supply side of the economy and indeed the macro-economic aggregates are to be found.

The UK economic landscape pre-Thatcher

The UK emerged from the Second World War economically weak and heavily in debt. Despite the post-war boom fuelled by pent-up demand UK growth rates were not exceptional relative to other economies. Britain was portrayed as the sick man of Europe and the British disease was diagnosed as resulting from an excessive emphasis on short-termism; low rates of investment; poor productivity; high taxation, at all levels; too large a public sector; strong and militant trade unions and money wage rates that outstripped productivity improvements.

The Heath government of 1970 was elected on a mandate to reduce the size of the public sector and the role of the state; and to reduce public subsidies for the inefficient sectors of private industry. The 1973/74 hike in the world price of oil not only pressed hard on the weak points of the UK economy, it also created the conditions for global 'stagflation' – a set of circumstances which Keynesian economics had ruled out as being impossible. Heath's project failed to break the power of the unions and his financial support for Upper Clyde Shipbuilders and Rolls-Royce signalled a willingness to bail out the private sector rather than to accept the consequential impacts on unemployment. His failure to win the 1974 election, despite the miners' strike and the three-day week, brought about dissent and growing opposition from within the Conservative Party and resulted in Margaret Thatcher's election as leader.

Harold Wilson won the 1974 election but after 11 months handed the prime ministership over to James Callaghan whose government, facing high inflation (25 per cent in 1975) and a weak pound sterling, continued to use variants of the prices and incomes policies of previous governments to combat inflation whilst Denis Healey's 1975 budget increased income tax and VAT and reduced the rate of increase in public spending. The pound began a downward slide and Healey obtained credit from overseas banks, but by September 1976 the pound had fallen to $1.60 (it had been $1.90 in February 1976) and Healey applied to the IMF for $3.9 billion. In return, the IMF imposed conditions of cuts in public spending (£2.5 billion over two years) along with the introduction of a tight monetary policy. The result was a system of planning public spending in cash terms; surplus in the balance of payments and an appreciation of sterling back to $1.90 by 1977 (due in large measure to North Sea oil). Despite improvements in the economic indicators there were deep running currents of disaffection with the government's policy of pay restraint, which exploded in the 1978/79 'winter of discontent'. Support for the Callaghan government fell rapidly (February 1979 Gallup showed a 20 per cent Conservative lead) and on 28 March Callaghan lost a Conservative tabled vote of no confidence by one vote – the SNP, Ulster Unionists and Liberals had voted with the Conservatives.

Changing the rules of the game

The post-war Keynesian democratic consensus which had emerged from 1945 until the late 1970s represented a commitment by successive post-war governments to high employment, low inflation, economic growth, and a sustainable external balance. These economic policy objectives were laid out in the UK's 1944 Employment White Paper and the US 1946 Employment Act. This economic settlement formed an implicit social contract between labour and capital. The consensus was built upon the strong sense of cooperation and partnership that had been experienced during the war. In return for wage moderation and restraint (to deliver low inflation) Labour expected job creation and public services (healthcare, social housing, education and the security provided by the new welfare state). Economic policies focused on the management of aggregate demand mainly through manipulation of public expenditure and taxation along with the management of exchange rates and the use of incomes policies.

In the event, however, the post-war Keynesian demand management policies did not deliver according to expectations. Cooperative solutions are by their nature fragile and depend upon trust and reciprocity. Like all prisoner dilemma games there are incentives for one or both parties to renege on the agreement and to unrelentingly pursue their unbridled self-interests. The alleged cooperative spirit of the war (if it had substance and was not a doe-eyed myth) rapidly decayed over time. Governments were regarded as cynically manipulating the economy in order to achieve short run electoral gains. Government interventions were regarded as a source of instability by creating 'political business cycles'. Unions pursued higher real wages despite low levels of productivity. The unions (correctly) assumed that governments with an eye on the next election would take care of full employment, irrespective of real wage increases and low productivity. The inevitable outcome was inflation, external imbalance, stop–go and government bailing out inefficient private companies.

The first Thatcher government of 1979 essentially ripped up the social contract that supported post-war Keynesian policies. The economic policies of post-war governments were regarded by the Thatcher government to have been ineffective and costly in terms of inflation, efficiency losses and weak economic growth. These were replaced by policies forged within a radically different set of rules – rules that it was believed would be less distortionary in terms of economic behaviour and resource allocation decisions (the stuff of micro-economics). The Thatcher government introduced a strategy of credible threats for those setting wages and prices in the private sector. Get these decisions wrong and you pay the price – as one commentator at the time described it, 'you break it, you own it'.

To make these threats credible and the policies time consistent there could be no weakening of fiscal or monetary policy in the face of rising unemployment. That is, no U-turns – hence the famous Thatcher ('This lady is not for turning') speech to the 1980 Conservative Party conference.

The monetarist turn

The first Thatcher administration embraced monetarism. This is seen clearly in Geoffrey Howe's (February 1980) letter to Edward du Cann, then Chair of the House of Commons Treasury and Civil Service Committee. In that letter Howe declared unambiguously that the government's economic priority was reduction in the rate of inflation. The underlying argument was that inflation acted to reduce economic efficiency and was a disincentive for investment both of which were essential for strengthening the supply side of the economy. Improvements in the supply side would be facilitated through improvements in 'incentives so that hard work pays, success is rewarded, and genuine new jobs are created in an expanding economy' (Conservative Manifesto, 1979). This meant cutting taxes (marginal tax rates) at all levels and the creation of greater 'freedom of choice for the individual by reducing the role of the State', and a reduction in 'the burdens of financing the public sector, so as to leave room for commerce and industry to prosper' (see Chancellor's Budget Statement, *Hansard*, 1979). The government aimed to establish an enterprise culture supported by free markets undistorted by special interests.

A Medium Term Financial Strategy (MTFS) was presented in the Budget Statement 1980, in which the government set out to achieve a substantial reduction in government borrowing over the medium term on the grounds that government borrowing contributes to growth in the money supply, increases in nominal interest rates, and crowding out of private sector investment in capital markets.

These arguments were presented as if they were 'fundamental truths' and yet there was little theoretical or empirical support for them. They were part of an academic debate about whether fiscal policy mattered and which involved Keynesians, post-Keynesians, Chicago monetarists, public choice theorists and rational expectations scholars. These controversies leached into the political rhetoric of the time and became solidified in Thatcher's first set of economic policies. They suited and supported Thatcherism's ideological prejudice against the public sector. The MTFS planned a reduction in public spending by 4 per cent in real terms by 1983/84 and public sector borrowing was planned to fall from 5 per cent of GDP in 1979/80 to 1 per cent by 1983/84.

These policy aims demanded a strong exchange rate and Thompson emphasizes this in her chapter. A strong exchange rate not only places downward pressure on inflation, it also forces industry to moderate costs and improve competitiveness. Just as the unions had to face up to a new reality so too did company decision makers. They could no longer grant excessive pay increases in the expectation that government would reduce the exchange rate and thereby bail them out.

The whole episode was at the time correctly referred to as the 'Thatcher experiment'. It was a journey into the unknown. Not only was a strong theoretical and empirical foundation lacking, there was no sense of what was necessary to achieve the policy objectives. For example, how big did the wage reductions need to be; what changes were necessary for the institutions of pay bargaining; how interest elastic is private sector investment; what is the size of tax disincentive effects – indeed are such effects positive or negative? The government had no strategy for managing large-scale change. Underlying their mindset about the way in which economies work was a naive mechanistic model that adjusted with infinite velocity. Moreover, the ethical consequences of the deindustrialization which followed and the moral implications of economic policy generally were ignored. It was down to the individual to cope with change – there was, it was asserted, no role for collective action.

Thatcherism was emergent and emerged. It was emergent in the sense that it represented a crystallization of ideas that were in circulation during the 1960s and 1970s. Harold Macmillan (1973: 85) reveals in his memoirs that from 1962 he had become disaffected with Keynesian demand management as a means of rectifying wage inflation. James Callaghan, when he was Prime Minister, in his 1976 speech to the Labour Party conference, completely dismissed traditional demand management and thereby delivered a death blow to the post-war Keynesian consensus:

> We used to think that you could spend your way out of a recession, and increase employment by cutting taxes and boosting government spending. I tell you in all candour that that option no longer exists, and that in so far as it ever did exist, it only worked by injecting a bigger dose of inflation into the economy, followed by a higher level of unemployment as the next step.

These words could have been written by Milton Friedman. In fact it is acknowledged that the speech was drafted by Peter Jay, Callaghan's son-in-law and an early convert to monetarism. Similar sentiments were expressed by Sir Douglas Wass (1978) who was then head of the civil service, and in the 1978 Mais lecture delivered by Gordon Richardson, who was Governor of the Bank of England. Thatcher's speech to the Conservative Party's annual conference 1968 revealed early shades of what emerged as Thatcherite economic policy – rolling back the frontiers of the state, tax reductions, stimulating enterprise and the confrontation of inflation with control of the money supply.

What Thatcher and her government did in 1979 was to solidify into their manifesto the various strands of thought that were flying around at the time. As economic history has revealed the implementation of Thatcherism was a learning exercise. Monetary policy was much more difficult to formalize than was originally imagined. Early monetarism gave way, under Nigel Lawson, to pragmatic monetarism. Similar observations can be made of other elements of the 1979 manifesto. Thatcherism emerged through trial and error and 'muddling through'.

If Callaghan had won the 1979 general election would he have implemented a Thatcher-like set of policies and confront the power of the unions and break inflation expectations? It is doubtful. Thatcher's determination, her conviction politics and lack of self-doubt were essential for the counter-revolution that she led as she changed the rules of the macro-economic game. The post-1997 Labour government did not reverse her policies – far from it, they built upon them. Blair and Brown abandoned active fiscal policy, used inflation targeting and liberated the financial services sector.

Micro-economic reforms

Thatcher's economic reforms had a more pronounced micro-economic foundation compared to earlier economic policies. Revitalization of the supply side of the economy required that greater attention be paid to the micro-economics of labour and capital markets. It is at that level that the incentives to shape decisions are to be found. Thus, tax policies were aimed at reducing tax rates and shifting the tax base from direct to indirect taxation in an attempt to create incentives for work effort, saving, and investment. Many government regulations and other forms of red tape were culled in order to liberate markets. There is no better example of the pursuit of micro-economic reform than in the relentless quest for improvements in public sector efficiency at all levels of government. The Thatcher government came to power assuming that the public sector was overstaffed, inefficient, suffered from low productivity, was badly managed, and was unresponsive to the demands of public service users ('consumers'). Sir Derek Rayner, a businessman who had risen through the ranks of Marks and Spencer (eventually becoming CEO and Chairman), had a strong reputation for implementing systems of tight financial control. He had served previously as an adviser to Edward Heath and Mrs Thatcher brought him in to shake up the public sector's system of financial management. An underlying assumption was that if efficiency savings were delivered then levels of service provision could be maintained whilst public spending was being cut. This was the beginning of many rounds of schemes to improve public sector efficiency and the 'managerialization' of the public sector. Legion after legion of consultants have been employed over the past 30 years to introduce one untested managerial practice after another. The language of the public sector has changed but evidence of efficiency improvements are more difficult to find. Once again no subsequent government has sought to reverse the initial Thatcher public sector efficiency reforms or her tax reforms. They have instead built upon them.

Conclusion

Thatcher's economic legacy is clear and is usefully summed up by David Marquand (2008):

> Similar changes took place right across the developed world, from the Antipodes to North America to Western Europe and even, in some degree, to what had once been the Communist bloc, but Thatcher's aggression, willpower and élan gave the British version of the transformation a special flavour that long survived her ejection from office. Since her fall, British politics have been conducted in her monstrous shadow. No serious contender for power seeks to undo her work: the only question is how best to come to terms with it. For better or worse, twenty-first-century Britain is her monument.
>
> (2008: 315)

References

Callaghan, J. (1976) Labour Party conference address, *Report of the 75th Annual Conference of the Labour Party*, Blackpool, 28 September. Published by the Labour Party.

Macmillan, H. (1973) *At the End of the Day 1961–63*. London: Macmillan.

Marquand, D. (2008) *Britain Since 1918: The Strange Career of British Democracy*. London: Weidenfeld & Nicolson.

3
What were the lasting effects of Thatcher's legacy for social security? The burial of Beveridge?

MICHAEL HILL and ALAN WALKER

Introduction

There are alternative ways of delineating the Thatcherite legacy in respect of social security. The most straightforward of these involves simply identifying the specific measures enacted between 1979 and 1991. What we find when we do this is a sustained attack on the benefits available, increasing in intensity across the period. But incrementalism influences legislative changes; the actual legislation does not entirely reflect the rhetoric. Compromises are made and change was more gradual than might be expected. What is then significant is the way in which a combination of changes supported by a sustained cluster of arguments – that poverty is not a problem, that people must do more to help themselves, and that in the long run a successful economy will bring income gains for all – have created an ideological legacy (sustained by her successors, and not only her Conservative ones), which have muted the role concerns about poverty and inequality play on the political agenda.

However, there needs to be another theme in any discussion of the Thatcherite legacy, to question the appropriateness of personalizing a political and ideological change. Particularly in social policy, to talk of the impact of 'Thatcherism' is a British way of identifying an ideological current against the post-Second World War aspiration to establish a welfare state. The UK was not alone in respect of this current.

This chapter starts with the last of those themes before moving on to an examination of specific policy changes. It then continues to a consideration of the wider implications of the Thatcherite onslaught against social security.

Where was the social security system going in 1979?

The history of social security policy in the UK involved the enactment in the 1940s of a relatively weak social insurance model, embodied in the Beveridge Plan. This left a legacy of contributory pensions and benefits typically either supplemented by other income or underpinned by means-tested benefits. Efforts to reform this system in the 1960s and 1970s encountered a continuing tension between a desire to strengthen social insurance entitlements and a recognition that benefits for the very poorest needed to be improved, in a context in which governments were unwilling to budget for really substantial increases. At the same time, low wage levels and inadequate child benefits (then family allowances) meant that many of the working poor secured little more than those dependent on benefits. The 1970s saw, first, the Heath government exploring ways to make means-testing more central to the system particularly through benefits that might be payable to people in work, and then the efforts of Barbara Castle to secure an effective universal contributory second-tier pensions scheme. Then, just before Labour fell from power (in 1979), efforts to strengthen rights to social assistance benefits highlighted the unresolved conflict between social insurance and social assistance, the former representing benefits and pensions paid for by contributions made in employment and the latter the means-tested safety net.

Hence, whilst the Thatcher government engaged in a substantial attack upon the social security system, most appropriately described as 'residual-ization', it is important to raise a counter-factual question. Was further change inevitable, since what was in place was a mixed system of inadequate universalist benefits, supplemented by the better off through private arrangements (particularly in respect of pensions), limited and complex contributory additions and an underpinning social assistance scheme that was year by year becoming more important for the relief of poverty? Of course, that change could have involved a strengthening of universalism but the rising cost of the social security system was seen as strengthening the case for a shift in the direction of residualism. As Donnison (1979: 52) warned in an article published just before Thatcher won power:

> We cannot assume that the social wage or the taxes which finance it will grow – least of all that they will grow in egalitarian ways. 'Middle England' is not ready to be convinced . . . that benign public services will – or should – create a more humane and a more equal society.

Economic and social changes – particularly the decline of large-scale industrial employment and changing patterns of family life – were making the 'breadwinner' based Beveridge model for social security less appropriate in the face of changing 'social risks' (Taylor-Gooby, 2004, see also David, Chapter 6 in this collection). New approaches to social security had been put on the agenda by measures to subsidize the wages and/or relieve the rental costs of households in which there were full-time earners. Comparative studies show that in the last quarter of the twentieth century social security retrenchment was on the agenda in many European countries (Taylor-Gooby, 2001). However, the retrenchment, of the already weak UK system, that was initiated by the Thatcher governments went further and faster than elsewhere in Europe, generating a process of residualization that continues to the present.

An overview of the measures enacted by the Thatcher governments

Given the size of social security expenditure, dominating public expenditure, the arrival of the Thatcher government, committed to public expenditure cuts, implied at least a further weakening of the social security system and, at most, a much more significant move away from universalism. That perspective was clear from 1979 but was made explicit in a 1985 Green Paper:

> The social security system must be consistent with the overall objectives for the economy . . . Social Security . . . is responsible for a major share of the current heavy tax burden on individuals and companies . . . continued growth of this burden could severely damage the prospects for economic growth.
>
> (HMSO, 1985: 2)

In practice change came slowly. Before 1985 what occurred was a sequence of incremental cuts to most aspects of social security: limiting the uprating of benefits, eliminating earnings related additions to short-term insurance benefits and making access to benefits more difficult. Paradoxically, if seen as efforts to cut the size of the social security budget, these measures could be regarded as failures simply because poverty increased significantly across this period and, as a consequence spending rose, a point we will pick up again later. Whilst some of the causes of this increased need and social security spending could be seen as independent of government policy – notably the ageing of the population and the increase in the numbers of single parent families (see David, Chapter 6) – the rise in unemployment (see Thompson, Chapter 2 in this collection) and other measures that reduced earnings (over which the government did have some control) can be shown to have played a crucial role in respect of the rise of the social security budget. On top of this, changes to housing policy had the effect of placing further demands on the social assistance budget (see Murie, Chapter 5, in this collection).

The second phase of reform may be seen as not just a response to the continuing rise of social security but as something more thoroughly ideologically driven, taking policy further away from universalism. The Fowler review of social security (HMSO, 1985) contained an expression of the new ideological thrust of policy. Instead of simply a cuts programme policy pronouncements began to be dressed up in the language of 'welfare reform'. However, since the earlier changes had already cut to the heart of the short-term insurance benefit system it was an attack on Castle's efforts to strengthen insurance pensions that proved to be the central measure in this phase. Meanwhile, as far as other benefits were concerned the administrative implications of policy which put means tests into central roles in public policy became more evident towards the end of Thatcher's period in government. These issues were complicated by growing concerns about the support of housing costs. Beveridge had recognized that basic (low) universal benefits could not cope with varying housing costs. These variations were small in the 1940s but grew, enhancing the case for means-tested additions. The Thatcher governments' approach to housing subsidy then made the housing/social security relationship much more critical.

A more detailed examination of the measures

Pensions

The first measure to affect pensions was a change in uprating rules for social insurance benefits involving calculation on the basis of changes in prices, instead of the previous rule which involved the use of the prices or wages index whichever was higher (The 'earnings link' had been established in Labour's last year in office). While the implications of this seemed slight at the time, the long-run effect was substantial erosion in the value of the basic state pension. That, of course, had the implication of making the impact of the second change to the pension system all the more significant for those dependent on state pensions.

The Social Security Pensions Act of 1975 provided for an earnings related superannuation scheme, known as the State Earnings Related Pension Scheme (SERPS). This measure involved allowing individuals who were already in private schemes adjudged by the government to be adequate to opt out of the state scheme, but provided an enhanced state scheme for all other working people. This was essentially a superannuation scheme in which contributions would determine benefits, with inflation proofing provided by the government. It also included provision to enable enhancement for working women whose periods in employment might be broken by periods of 'family responsibilities'. According to the review of social security policy in the mid-1980s SERPS was deemed to impose excessive burdens on future generations. The government's initial idea was to replace it altogether with individual funded accounts with insurance companies. The latter were not keen to take on this work with large numbers of relatively low-paid workers. Furthermore, the government recognized that heavy short-term costs would be imposed upon the exchequer in as much as it would lose the use of contributions to fund current benefits. Instead, in the end, it was decided to sharply cut the benefits guaranteed under SERPS. Part of this cut involved the weakening of the provisions designed to protect the pensions of married women forced to leave the labour market for a period in order to attend to caring tasks, which had been seen as a great strength of SERPS.

In enacting these changes to SERPS, the government also gave further encouragement to the private pensions industry through tax relief and a National Insurance contribution rebate. They also abolished the requirement that any approved private scheme should be, potentially, at least as good as SERPS. These measures unleashed a massive sales campaign by the private pensions industry. Salespeople exploited fears of the growth of the older population and suggested that the state could not be trusted to deliver in the long run. Not only were individuals encouraged to leave SERPS for worse schemes but in some – subsequently publicized cases – public employees such as teachers and nurses were lured out of their government protected occupational schemes into inferior private insurance schemes (Waine, 1995). Estimates of the scale of this mis-selling scandal vary up to 3 million (Walker, 1991).

Sickness and disability benefits

The change in the uprating rules for insurance benefits mentioned in the last section had an impact upon sickness and invalidity benefits as well. But in this case more fundamental change came in the form of two measures. The first involved the abolition of earnings related additions, an improvement to the Beveridge scheme that had been introduced in the 1960s. The second was the replacement of sickness benefit by statutory sick pay. This measure shifted responsibility for support of short-term sick employees to employers. However, it was complicated by provisions under which benefit support was retained for former insurance contributors who became sick when not in employment and for long-term sick individuals. Its impact was softened for employers by provisions for them to get insurance contributions rebated. Similar changes were made to the maternity benefits scheme. The long-run impact of these changes has been to shift responsibility for support for almost all short terms of sickness entirely away from the state scheme, in effect the privatization of the responsibility for short-term sickness provision. This led on, after the Thatcher years, to a government concern about the cost of the 'invalidity' scheme remaining for the long-term sick and to a further sequence of benefit cuts.

Unemployment benefits

The earnings additions to unemployment benefits were also eliminated. There were also measures that limited benefit availability to under 18s and that prevented recipients of occupational pensions below pension age from claiming unemployment benefit. The most substantial change to the unemployment system was made, however, by Thatcher's successor. The Major government integrated the systems of insurance benefits and means-tested benefits for unemployed people renaming the benefits 'jobseeker's allowance', and making all support means tested after six months' unemployment.

National Insurance (NI) contributions: becoming simply a regressive tax

Although the basic state insurance pension rate was cut, the sickness protection in the Beveridge scheme was largely eliminated and the extent to which individuals could secure insurance benefits if unemployed was severely restricted, there were no cuts to social insurance contributions. Indeed, since the 1960s, with the introduction of earning-related benefits and earnings related contributions, the government has had a substantial income flow which, from the Thatcher changes onwards, is more appropriately seen as a tax than as an insurance contribution.

Moreover, the structure of that 'tax' is regressive. In the model established during the period examined here (there have been some changes since that make the system slightly less regressive) the rate of payment was a percentage of earnings between a very low initial threshold and an upper limit, where the effect was to reduce the percentage of earnings paid by the higher paid.

Significantly, government commentaries on the cost of social security (see for instance, Department of Social Security, 1993) generally pay no attention to NI contributions as an offsetting income, reinforcing the view that they are simply treated as a generic source of government income for all purposes. It is significant that the Cameron government's proposals to supply taxpayers with a statement on how their taxes are spent simply include insurance payments as a 'tax'.

Social assistance (including housing benefit)

If the objective of social security change had been simply to curb the universal benefits and make means testing central to the system it might have been expected that no efforts would have been made to limit the availability of social assistance. This was far from the case. It seems that the Thatcher government wanted to have its cake and eat it on the social security front: to diminish the role of universal insurance benefits by replacing them with selective ones as well as limiting spending as far as possible.

The incoming Thatcher government took on board the case for the reform of the Supplementary Benefit System set out in the review report, which had been presented to the Labour government (Department of Health and Social Security, 1978). It enacted these changes in the Social Security Act 1980. This involved some simplification of the rules relating to entitlement to supplementary benefit, together with extensive codification of the discretionary powers. New rules relating to additional payments to the basic benefits were more restrictive, with grants for clothing replacement being largely eliminated. The initial effect of this change was a marked reduction in single payments to supplementary benefit claimants. It looked, for a year or so, as if the new system had succeeded in reducing both the costs of these additional payments and the heavy demands made upon the administration by individual applications for help. This short-term saving for the government proved to be illusory, as claimants and their advisers subsequently learnt how to extract help from the system, using the structure of rules clarifying entitlement; the demand for single payments rose sharply.

This experience was important, influencing the government's decision in the middle of the 1980s to undertake a further review of the system. That review brought forward a very much more radical restructuring of the supplementary benefit system (Walker, 1993). The 1986 Social Security Act, renamed supplementary benefit 'income support'. It introduced a structure which discriminated very much less elaborately between different categories of claimants, replacing specific additions to individuals' weekly benefits by a uniform structure of premiums, taking into account, for example, whether individuals were disabled or pensioners or the heads of one-parent families. The 1986 Act also abolished entitlements to single payments, except in the special cases of help for maternity needs and funerals (though in this case the benefits were limited and replaced the universal National Insurance-related maternity and death grants). The system of entitlement to single payments was replaced by a discretionary cash-limited 'social fund', providing most of its help (70 per cent) through loans reclaimable from weekly benefits.

The 1980 changes might perhaps be described as a victory for welfare rights. Whilst the Act did involve the elimination of some kinds of discretionary payments it enshrined in regulations rights to many others. In contrast, the 1986 Act can therefore be seen as a backlash against that victory, with rights to additional single payments being largely eliminated.

The 1986 Social Security Act also replaced family income supplement by family credit, and in so doing developed for this benefit a means test rather more compatible with that used for income support and for housing benefit. In other words, it created a situation in which the working poor could expect to get a benefit which, if they had children, would sustain them at an income above the income support level. In this way, the government tried to tackle what is described as the 'unemployment trap' under which it is possible for individuals to be deterred from taking work by the fact that their income situation will be worse than if they remain on benefit.

It is appropriate to include comments on housing benefit in this account of social security change. Although the full implications of housing benefit measures need to be considered in relation to housing policy, the subject of another chapter in this book, they were seen as social security measures (and their costs reflected in social security budgets) and the interactions between these benefits and other ones are important for the issues being explored here. The story of means-tested housing support in the 1980s is one of a hasty legislative decision (in the Social Security and Housing Act 1982), followed by an attempt to make social security savings by cutting housing benefit in 1983. These events led on to the urgent need for second thoughts, with these being embodied in the 1986 Social Security Act. The first Act brought together some aspects of the support for the housing costs of supplementary benefit claimants with the local authority administered rent and rate rebate schemes and rent allowance scheme. Its aim was to eliminate the anomalies about the existence of the various means-tested housing support schemes operating side by side. In practice, some of the anomalies of the previous system were eliminated, but new ones were created (Hill, 1984).

Once housing benefit was established not only did it face administrative problems, it also proved to be very costly in both administrative and benefit terms. The growth in benefit costs was largely attributable to government housing policies, involving pressure upon local authorities to increase rents. Since large proportions of local authority tenants were entitled to housing benefit the effects of these rent increases was to increase sharply the cost of the housing benefit scheme.

When, in 1983, the Secretary of State for Health and Social Security came under pressure from the Treasury to make economies he found it convenient to make most of these in cuts in the value of the housing benefit scheme. Cuts were achieved by steepening the rate at which benefit tapered off as individual incomes rose.

However, this taper steepening intensified another problem, the problem of the 'poverty trap'. The poverty trap is the name given to the phenomenon by which individuals find that as their earned incomes rise they lose benefit income, at rates above the highest income tax rates, because of reductions in means-tested benefits. By the middle 1980s the combination of separate means-tested rules for different benefits had the effect of making the poverty trap a serious problem. In some circumstances individuals found that an increase of a pound in earned income led, after tax and benefit losses, to a reduction in disposable income. The recognition of the problem of the poverty trap made it urgent to establish a system in which the rules operating for the different systems of means-tested benefit were compatible with each other. The 1986 Act did this. But as the government refused, at the same time, to reduce the rates at which benefit entitlement tapered off they merely made the poverty trap effect less erratic. The net effect was to increase rather than diminish the problem. Losses on receipt of another pound in income could be up to 96 pence and in many cases were 80 pence.

At the centre of the reforms to social security associated with Norman Fowler, the 1986 Social Security Act, was the development of a structure with three benefits: income support, family credit and housing benefit all based upon broadly similar principles. Both family credit and housing benefit take income after tax and National Insurance deductions into account, rather than gross income as had been the case in the past. This was thus a modest move towards an integrated tax and benefit system, as envisaged by advocates of negative income tax (see, for example, Minford, 1984). Its main long-run legacy is the system of tax credits introduced by the Blair government after 1997.

Treatment of families

The account of the impact of Thatcherism upon social security so far has placed it squarely in the context of the ideologically driven attack upon public expenditure and the not entirely consistent efforts to replace social insurance by social assistance (Piachaud, 1997; Walker, 1993). However, in any assessment of Thatcherism as a whole other concerns need attention. One of these is the treatment of families, based upon an attitude to family life holding to traditional views of the desirability of marriage.

This was particularly manifest in measures to change the social assistance system. A number of changes bore heavily upon the young, notably the establishment of a low rate of income support making independent living difficult and an expectation of high contributions to family rent costs in the formula for housing benefit calculation, indicating a view that they should remain in and contribute significantly to their family of origin.

However, the most significant development concerned the treatment of single parent families, involving a measure initiated during the Thatcher premiership but actually enacted by the Major government. Ironically, the period of rule by the Thatcher government saw, as of course part of a longer run trend, a rise in the number of single parent households (see Table 3.1).

Table 3.1 Percentages of families with dependent children by family type

	Couple families	Single mothers	Divorced mothers	Separated mothers	Widowed mothers	All lone mothers	Lone fathers
1971	91	1	2	2	2	7	1
1981	88	2	4	2	2	11	1
1986	86	3	6	3	1	13	1
1991	80	7	6	4	1	18	2

Source: Central Statistical Office (1995), table 2.12

While governments can surely not be, at least in any simple way, the progenitors of a social trend like that shown in Table 1, this has not stopped commentators pointing the finger of blame at public policies (see for example, Murray, 1990). More to the point, as far as the 1980s are concerned, there can be a connection between the incidence of single parenthood and the need for single parents to seek benefits inasmuch as there was a lack of employment. However, Charles Murray's (1984) tirade against the single-headed household in the USA was taken up by Conservative politicians in the UK, who began to attribute the growth in single parenthood to the availability of benefits and housing. This stimulated a debate about (a) work opportunities for single parents, and (b) contributions from absent parents. Interestingly, perhaps because of Thatcher's 'family orientation', the first issue was not really taken up until the twenty-first century. But a decision was made to tackle the issue of contributions from absent parents by means of a comprehensive, formula-driven scheme to replace both the assessments made as part of the administration of the existing means-tested benefits and the assessments made by the courts in determining maintenance on the breakdown of a relationship. The word 'replace' in that last sentence should be emphasized. The new legislation has been widely misrepresented as making absent parents pay where they did not do so before. This was not the case; rather the government decided that a new comprehensive and formula-driven approach would do a much better job.

The Major government enacted the Child Support Act in 1991, setting up an agency to administer it. That legislation ran into severe implementation problems. There were four main objections to the new legislation:

- That it was retrospective in effect – agreements, including court settlements, made in the past were overturned (a particular problem here

was the overturning of agreements in which the absent parent relinquished an interest in a house in return for a lower maintenance expectation).
- That where the absent parent had obligations to a second family, these were given relatively low weight in the calculations.
- That the parent with care of the child had nothing to gain from collaborating with the agency if she (it is nearly always she in this situation) was on income support, since everything collected went to reimburse the state; a special problem here was the expectation of co-operation in the supply of information about the father of her child unless there are strong reasons to protect a woman from further indirect dealings with him.
- That the operation of a rigid formula was unfair when there are regular contacts with the absent parent and a variety of connected expenses.

The enforcement of the Act was not helped by the income generation targets imposed on the agency and a programme of work which meant that it started with families on 'income support' and had incentives to tackle the easier cases (that was, the more compliant absent parents). It would go beyond our specific concern here with the Thatcher era other than to note the administration faced by this legislation led on to successive amendments, and eventually to a return to a system not widely dissimilar to that which prevailed before it.

Costs and benefits

Paradoxically, given the way the Thatcher government highlighted the need for social security cuts as a central strategy for realizing its commitment to reducing public expenditure, it was actually the case – as Table 3.2 makes clear – that social security costs rose significantly (in real terms) through the 1980s. The argument that the welfare state was largely impervious to Thatcher's first wave neo-liberal policies places great store on the social spending record (Pierson, 2001). But social security under Thatcher saw simultaneous cuts and rises in spending. The evidence of cutting effort is clear enough, to recap briefly:

- reducing inflation linked increases
- eliminating insurance benefits
- curbing social assistance.

Table 3.2 Expenditure trends (billions)

Year	Insurance	Non-contrib.	Means tested (excl. HB)	Admin. costs and 'other'	Total
1979–80	31.1	9.3	4.3	4.8	49.4
1990–91	36.1	10.9	10.7	5.4	63.1
% increase	16	17	149	13	28

Source: Evans, table 7.3 in Glennerster and Hills (1998)

What then undermined this effort? In a nutshell, the 'demand-led' nature of social security. One such factor outside government control was an increase in numbers of over 65s by over half a million across this period. It has to be noted that pensions form a large element in overall social security expenditure and that a substantial growth in this category of benefit claimants was bound to push up expenditure. A second factor partly out of government control was the increase in single mother headed households, though here (as noted above) economic conditions, upon which government policies had some impact, will have had an influence on family breakdown and hence on the numbers of families needing to seek benefit support.

Thompson (Chapter 2 in this collection) gives more attention to economic policies than is required here, but it is important to identify the significance of high levels of unemployment for the social security budget even if it is beyond our brief to consider the extent to which the finger of blame for this phenomenon should be pointed directly at the government. The Thatcher government engaged in extensive efforts to massage the unemployment statistics to mask the extent to which, having campaigned in 1979 with the slogan 'Labour isn't working', the unemployment problem intensified through most of the period of its rule, only moderating slightly at the end of the 1980s. OECD statistics, using a shared international concept, are thus one of the more reliable indices to use here. The UK rate was 5.6 per cent in 1976, 9.8 per cent in 1981, 11.2 per cent in 1986 and then 8.8 per cent in 1991 (Central Statistical Office, 1995, table 4.25). In terms of the direct impact of this on benefits: £7.1 billion was spent on benefits for unemployed people in 1981–82, £10.6 billion in 1986–87 and £8.1 billion in 1991–92 (Central Statistical Office, 1995, table 8.28, figures calculated on the basis of 1993–94 prices).

Table 3.2 shows the size of the increase in expenditure and the implications of the shift towards means testing, evident in both the expenditure on these benefits and the increase in administrative costs (since these benefits cost more to administer). The increase in means testing under successive Thatcher administrations was not uniform: while among older people there was a decline in the proportion receiving supplementary benefit/income support, it rose sharply among the short-term sick, lone parents and unemployed people (Piachaud, 1997).

These figures, however, do not include Housing Benefit. Here government policies certainly had an impact on the increase in expenditure, since what was going on was a continuation of a process began by the Heath government of shifting social housing costs from general subsidies to properties to specific subsidies to occupiers. However, it is difficult to put a figure on this because two other things that were occurring were

- a shift from a system in which housing costs were hidden in supplementary benefit payments to one where they were manifest in housing benefit payments
- a shift from the subsidy of housing to the subsidy of tenants ('as general subsidies were cut the cost of housing benefit rose by an equivalent amount', Hills, in Glennerster and Hills, 1998: 132).

The later change certainly increased dependency upon means testing.

Impact on people: poverty

The context for the policy changes explored here was a wider onslaught by the Thatcherites against the political concern about poverty, epitomized by a pamphlet by one of her more outspoken junior ministers Rhodes Boyson called *Down with the Poor* (1971). Thus the impact on social security in this period was not only a result of the measures taken to restrict and curtail spending but also the sustained attempt to harden the political context in which discussions of poverty and social security took place. As well as stigmatizing poor people as 'scroungers' and 'cheats' (Thatcher, 1993) efforts to measure poverty and to develop a yardstick to measure the adequacy of benefits were also attacked. However, the government did not go so far as abandoning all efforts to measure incomes. Hence it can be demonstrated (without needing to get into arguments about how to define it) that there was a very significant growth in the numbers of people with incomes so low that there is really very little need to justify the use of word poverty in this context.

Poverty and inequality are discussed by Dorling and by Walker (both this collection) so we will deal only briefly with them here. Goodman and Webb of the Institute of Fiscal Studies examined the changing distribution of income between 1961 and 1991. Their data on the trend in respect of low incomes is set out in Table 3.3. It shows a very substantial growth in the numbers of people with incomes falling well below the national average.

Goodman and Webb (1994) conclude that the increase in income inequality during the 1980s dwarfed the fluctuations in inequality seen in previous decades. They show that whilst inequality declined gradually during much of the 1960s, rose slightly to the early 1970s and then fell back to its lowest point in around 1977, these fluctuations were very modest compared with the changes seen in the 1980s. In sum, between 1979 and 1985 widening inequality was due to many families losing their incomes as unemployment rose; during 1985–90, however, the inequalities were due largely to government policies (Atkinson, 2000: 365). Goodman and Webb (1994: 61) go on to say, 'over the period 1961 to 1991 the incomes of the richest tenth had risen twice as fast as the poorest tenth. Furthermore the incomes of the poorest tenth fell from a peak of £73 per week in 1979 to £61 per week (figures for incomes after housing costs calculated in January 1994 prices).' Throughout the period around half of the pensioner population was in the poorest decile, but their position improved in relative terms. It should of course be noted that the Thatcher governments' changes to pensions had their main impact in the long term. Even those relating to benefit uprating had slight initial effects but significant cumulative effects.

With regard to non-pensioners:

> The emergence of mass unemployment has had a major effect on the income distribution. Families with children now make up more than half of the poorest decile group compared with only around a third three decades ago, with the main reason for this change being the more than eightfold increase in unemployment between the early 1960s and the mid-1980s.
>
> (Goodman and Webb, 1994: 61)

Table 3.3 Numbers of individuals at various levels below national average income (millions)

	1979	1981	1983	1985	1987	1989	1991
Below 40%	1.3	1.4	1.6	1.5	2.8	4.9	5.7
Below 50%	4.5	4.6	4.7	5.9	8.5	10.5	11.4
Below 60%	9.6	10.5	10.5	12.6	14.4	16.1	16.6

Source: Goodman and Webb (1994: 41)

Here then we have to contend with, on the one hand, the interaction between economic policies that had an impact on the growth of poverty and, on the other, social security policies that might have relieved it. Unfortunately, measures such as the abolition of the earnings link for benefit increases and the sustained undermining of the incomes of the unemployed reduced the capacity of the system to offset the impact of the rise in poverty. But we lack a precise examination of the extent to which attacks on benefit levels contributed to the rise of poverty in the Thatcher years. It is however pertinent to note that a comparative analysis using the Luxembourg Income Survey data collected in the UK in 1991 suggested that relative to most of the other countries in the survey the performance of UK benefit policies in the relief of poverty was weak. Compared with an average of 57.9 (and figures for Germany of 46.5 and the Netherlands of 71.8) the UK percentage poverty reduction effect (computed by comparing incomes before and after benefits and taxes) was 39.6 (Bradshaw and Chen, 1997).

The Thatcherite legacy

Before taking stock and reflecting on the legacy of the Thatcher administrations it is worth recalling that the 1979 Conservative Manifesto was actually rather supportive of social security:

> Child benefits are a step in the right direction . . . One-parent families' face much hardship so we will maintain the special addition for them . . . Much has been done in recent years to help the disabled, but there is still a long way to go.
>
> (Quoted in Piachaud, 1997: 73)

There were also promises to reduce the poverty trap and to 'bring more effective help to those in greatest need'. Completely absent were any references to the transformational changes we have discussed in this chapter, including the replacement of the earning link for pensions with price-indexation, the abolition of the earning-related supplements to unemployment, sickness and invalidity benefits and the substitution of means-tested social assistance for contribution based social insurance for several groups of claimants. Yet the pensions indexation switch was one of the first actions taken by the new administration in 1979, in line with its overarching mission to cut public spending. The mild Manifesto reference to those 'in greatest need' can be seen in retrospect as presaging a full-scale attack on social security claimants (other than pensioners). Terms such as 'genuine need' become commonplace as did individualistic, often accusatory, explanations for poverty and unemployment (Walker, 1993). Arguably this rhetorical agenda setting is as important to the story of social security under Thatcher as the more immediately and personally damaging expenditure cuts.

As of 1991 the legacy of Thatcherism was a severely weakened system of social insurance and an increasingly costly social assistance system, whose salience was a clear product of the rise of poverty across the period. The social security policy of the Major government can then be seen as the linear descendant of Thatcherism. It made more cuts to benefits for unemployed people, further undermined insurance benefits for sick and disabled people and took forward what was perhaps the most ideologically driven of all the Thatcherite policies, the measure to try to enhance the contributions of absent fathers.

Since the 1960s, governments had been struggling with the social insurance/social assistance relationship. Thatcher contributed substantially to a resolution in favour of letting assistance dominate. There is no sign of efforts by later governments to reverse the thrust of this. However, when we consider the contemporary importance of in-work benefits in the modern system then Heath's Family Income Supplement may also be seen as a crucial preceding innovation.

While Major explicitly continued the Thatcherite legacy it cannot be said that after 1997 Blair and Brown turned their backs on it. As far as older people are concerned the familiar tension between enhancing social insurance and protecting the poorest re-emerged first in a programme of means-tested support for poor pensioners and then, in the longer run, efforts to try to turn back to something like the goal that Barbara Castle had been aiming at in the 1970s.

In respect of support for housing costs the shift of social housing subsidies directly on to housing benefit generated a situation in which rent increases inflated the benefit budget and produced government cuts which increased the amounts of those costs low income tenants have to pay. The response of the Cameron government on this issue has been particularly draconian in its impact.

Efforts to curb the size of the social security budget also continued with a particular obsession (continuing to this day) with the cost of the one remaining piece of the short term insurance benefit system: invalidity benefit. Otherwise so-called 'welfare reform' carried forward the redirection of policy towards the subsidy of wages through tax credits. 'Work based welfare' became a dominant mantra, in that sense Thatcherism may perhaps be seen as more all pervading than it ever was in the 1990s.

Returning to the introductory comments that the Beveridge settlement, despite the efforts of Labour governments in the 1970s and 1980s, provided the UK with a weak social policy system and that in an era of retrenchment the Thatcher government started earlier and moved faster that other comparable governments it is appropriate to look at comparative data. Table 3.4 does this, using the crude OECD social expenditure statistics for the UK and a group of other countries.

While it is recognized that Esping-Andersen's (1990) placing of the UK with the USA in the 'liberal market' regime category, which was based upon 1980 statistics, used more complicated data than simply expenditure statistics, it is clear that the UK was in relative terms then already a low performer. The subsequent record across the period of rule by Thatcher and her successor shows that initial view of the UK regime to have been reinforced. Esping-Andersen (1990: 26) defines liberal market regimes as ones in 'which means-tested assistance, modest universal transfers, or modest social-insurance plans predominate'. The word 'liberal' in the definition refers to liberal economic ideas which see the free market as the ideal device for allocating life chances, and the primary role for the state being to enhance economic efficiency.

Notwithstanding that the Thatcher and Major governments did not eliminate the tax funded and broadly free National Health Service the fact that they cut out some of the 'universal transfers' in respect of sickness and unemployment benefits and weakened the state pension, arriving certainly at a system in which 'means-tested assistance' dominated, contributed to placing the UK squarely in Esping-Andersen's liberal market category by

Table 3.4 Public Social Expenditure as percentage of GDP

Country	1980	1992	1997	% increase
Sweden	27	30	31	14
Germany	21	25	26	24
France	21	20	29	29
UK	17	20	19	12
USA	13	15	15	13

Source: OECD Statistics

the 1990s. It has been argued that what was developed was a system more sophisticated and more protective of the poor (particularly the working poor) than in many other countries in the 'liberal-market' group, particularly if the reference point for that group is the USA (Mitchell, 1991). On the other hand there was a built in problem about this response (the poverty trap or plateau – on which only 'basic income' advocates have an answer) which Thatcher's successors struggle with to this day. The concerted, if not uniform, switch from insurance to selective benefits began a trend that was to continue and today means that there is little prospect of a restoration of the universal principle in social security (Walker, 2011).

Overall, driven in the first place by a commitment to reduce social security expenditure and then facing the fact that her own economic policies undermined that objective, Thatcher may be seen as taking crucial steps towards the undermining of Beveridge, but it must also be acknowledged that the Beveridge design had weaknesses that were becoming more evident at that time. A distinction is however appropriate here, particularly with the Thatcher legacy in view, between policies for those under pension age and policies for those above it.

In respect of the younger group Thatcher more or less eliminated social insurance, turning the insurance contribution into a tax. Her government did that in the context of high unemployment, with the perverse outcome that, whilst it started out with a commitment to eliminate all the special schemes to provide training for unemployed people, it quickly found it necessary to re-visit that area of policy (Moon and Richardson, 1985). In so doing it was quite slow to move towards repressive measures, compared with later governments, aiming at coercing people into work. In particular it paid little attention to female roles in the job market (See David, this collection). As suggested above it may be that Thatcher was unwilling to consider measures that aimed to coerce single parents into the workforce at a time of high unemployment. It was left to the Blair government to do this, in a context of lower unemployment, though now high unemployment does not seem to inhibit the Cameron government on this issue. In a similar way the initial effect of the changed provisions for support of the sick – employer support in the short run non-means-tested invalidity benefits in the long run – did not imply particularly coercive attitudes towards the latter. In the context of massive job losses amongst the older victims of industrial decline a tolerant attitude to invalidity benefit claims helped to mask the unemployment problem, and allow for a form of premature retirement that in countries such as Germany and France was done explicitly in the form of pre-retirement benefits (Kohli et al., 1991). Again it was left to later governments to see high bills for invalidity benefits as a problem. In these two senses, whilst the Thatcher governments surely implicitly embraced the doctrine 'that work is the best form of welfare' it was left to later governments to do so explicitly.

The story in respect of pensions is rather different. The Beveridge settlement had left the UK with a weak state system, purposely leaving a gap for occupational pensions to fill. Efforts during the 1960s and 1970s to deal with the extent to which that outcome meant that many employees with lower incomes (and persons, particularly women, whose labour market participation was limited) were unprotected culminated in SERPS, introduced by Barbara Castle in 1975. The Thatcher government's changes to the uprating of pensions and weakening of SERPS, taken in combination, largely reversed that gain. What is more, it did so at a time when industrial decline and privatization were actually undermining access to good occupational pensions. But this is then one area where the Blair/Brown Labour governments from 1997 to 2010 made some efforts to recover the position, with the introduction of the State Second Pension and measures to slowly restore the value of the basic pension. In that sense at least Labour were unwilling to be heirs of the Thatcher legacy. However, on this issue it may be too early to draw firm conclusions. A state supported market-based savings scheme for pensions may yield limited gains to counteract the decline of occupation pensions, and the Cameron government is engaged in an attack, based on a report from a former Labour minister, on occupational pensions in the public sector from which many low income workers, particularly female ones, benefit.

Conclusions

In conclusion we come back to the ideological dimension of the Thatcher legacy on social security. Stigma and welfare always go hand in hand and this relationship is especially close in liberal welfare regimes. Thus rhetorical attacks on benefit claimants have figured prominently as a deterrent to others since the nineteenth century Poor Law (Hill, 1972; Deacon, 1996). The Beveridge social security system was crafted, by a liberal, to both encourage work and to minimize accusations that benefits were a free lunch. The Thatcher years, however, represented a huge ratcheting-up of the rhetorical climate surrounding social security and the poor. It is difficult to convey now the strength of this rhetorical onslaught, or 'scrounger-phobia', that was sustained for the whole of Thatcher's premiership (Walker, 1993). Thatcher (1993: 8) herself encapsulated in one sentence what her ministers embellished in hundreds of others:

> Welfare benefits, distributed with little or no consideration of their effects on behaviour, encouraged illegitimacy, facilitated the breakdown of families, and replaced incentives favouring work and self-reliance with perverse encouragement for idleness and cheating.

Earlier she had summarized the broader philosophical position that characterized her approach and which underpinned her governments' social security policies.

> I think we've been through a period where too many people have been given to understand that if they have a problem, it's the government's job to cope with it. 'I have a problem, I'll get a grant'. 'I'm homeless, the government must house me.' They're casting their problems on society. And, you know, there is no such thing as society. There are individual men and women, and there are families. And no government can do anything except through people, and people must look to themselves first. It's our duty to look after ourselves and then, to look after our neighbour. People have got entitlements too much in mind, without obligations. There's no such thing as entitlement, unless someone has first met an obligation.
>
> (Article in *Woman's Own*, 31 October 1987)

The culmination of the rhetorical barrage, towards the end of Thatcher's premiership, was the debate, triggered by the US commentator Charles Murray, about an 'underclass'. Of course this label was just the latest in a long list used to denigrate or 'other' a group of poor people regarded as undeserving, feckless and threatening (MacNicol, 1987). But, to the extent that the Thatcher governments can be seen as implementing aspects of the first wave neo-liberal political project (back then it was called the New Right and included elements of neo-conservatism particularly with regard to the family), the overt aim to restore stigma as an instrument of social policy must be judged a success. As one leading British neo-liberal put it 'Bring back stigma; all is forgiven!' (Green, 1990: 3).

Although this campaign to shape the political and policy climate surrounding social security met with ready amplification in the media, it did not have a demonstrable impact on public attitudes to every aspect of the welfare state. For example, the British Social Attitudes surveys show that, between 1983 and 1993, the proportion of the public saying that the government should raise both taxes and public spending doubled from

30 per cent to 60 per cent (Jowell, 1994, 1996). Moveover, nearly at the close of Thatcher's term of office, only a minority agreed that 'people who get social security don't really deserve any help' (28 per cent, with 45 per cent disagreeing), and 'most people on the dole are fiddling' (31 per cent and 37 per cent respectively). None the less statements, like the ones quoted above, from political leaders accompanying the benefit changes and also campaigns against perceived benefit scroungers (even bus advertisements inviting us to 'shop' others) have contributed to an ideological climate that is still very hostile to social security. That clearly remains a significant aspect of Thatcher's legacy. A sure sign of how far the political agenda on social security has shifted towards the Thatcherite agenda is that the term itself is no longer used in official circles. When ministers speak of social security these days they distinguish between pensions (for the deserving) and the rest which are 'welfare'. Even the surveyors of public attitudes have fallen in line with this agenda (Park et al., 2012). The absence of an Opposition strategy to restore social security to an honourable position in the UK's social policy, the guarantor of income at times of need that Beveridge intended (if not a basic human right as the UN declares it to be), is glaring.

References

Atkinson, A.B. (2000) 'Distribution of Income and Wealth', in A.H. Halsey and J.Webb (eds) *Twentieth-Century British Social Trends*. London: Macmillan.

Boyson, R. (1971) *Down with the Poor*. London: Churchill.

Bradshaw, J. and Chen, J.-R. (1997) 'Poverty in the UK. A Comparison with Nineteen Other Countries', *Benefits*, 18: 13–17.

Central Statistical Office (1995) *Central Statistical Office*. London: HMSO.

Deacon, A. (1976) *In Search of the Scrounger*. London: Bell, pp. 145–76.

Department of Health and Social Security (1978) *Social Assistance: A Review of the Supplementary Benefits Scheme in Great Britain*. London: HMSO.

Department of Social Security (1993) *The Growth of Social Security*. London: HMSO.

Donnison, D. (1979) 'Social policy since Titmuss', *Journal of Social Policy*, 8(2).

Esping-Andersen G. (1990) *Three Worlds of Welfare Capitalism*. Cambridge: Polity Press.

Glennerster, H. and Hills, J. (1998) *The State of Welfare. The Economics of Public Spending*. Oxford: Oxford University Press.

Goodman, A. and Webb, S. (1994) 'For Richer, For Poorer: The Changing Distribution of Income in the UK, 1961–91', *Fiscal Studies*, 15(4): 29–62.

Green, D. (1990) 'Foreword', in D. Green (ed.) *The Emerging British Underclass*. London: IEA.

HMSO (1985) *Reform of Social Security: Programme for Action*. Cmnd. 9691, London.

Hill, M. (1984) 'The Implementation of Housing Benefit', *Journal of Social Policy*, 13(3): 297–320.

Hill, M. (1972) 'Selectivity for the Poor', in P. Townsend and N. Bosanquet, *Labour and Inequality*. London: Fabian Society, pp. 335–45.

Jowell, R., Curtice, J., Brook, L. and Ahrendt, B. (eds) (1994) *British Social Attitudes*. Aldershot: Dartmouth.

Jowell, R., Curtice, J. and Brook, L. (eds) (1996) *British Social Attitudes*, Aldershot: Dartmouth.

Kohli, M. et al. (1991) *Time for Retirement. Comparative Studies of Early Exit from the Labour Force*. Cambridge: Cambridge University Press.

MacNicol, J. (1987) 'In Pursuit of the Underclass', *Journal of Social Policy*, 16(3): 293–318.

Minford, P. (1984) 'State Expenditure: a Study in Waste', *Economic Affairs* (April/ June).

Mitchell, D. (1991) *Income Transfers in Ten Welfare States*. Aldershot: Avebury.

Moon, J. and Richardson, J. J. (1985) *Unemployment in the UK*. Aldershot: Gower.

Murray, C. (1984) *Losing Ground: American Social Policy, 1950–1980*. New York: Basic Books.

Park, A., Clery, E., Curtice, J., Phillips, M. and Utting, D. (2012) *British Social Attitudes*. London: National Centre for Social Research.

Piachaud, D. (1997) 'The Growth of Means Testing', in A. Walker and C. Walker (eds) *Britain Divided*. London: CPAG, pp. 75–83.

Pierson, P. (2001) *The New Politics of the Welfare State*. Oxford: Oxford University Press.

Rein, M. and Wadensjö, E. (1997) *Enterprise and the Welfare State*. Cheltenham: Edward Elgar.

Taylor-Gooby, P. (ed.) (2001) *European Welfare States under Pressure*. London: Sage.

Taylor-Gooby, P. (2004) 'New Risks and Social Change', in P. Taylor-Gooby (ed.) *New Risks, New Welfare?* Oxford: Oxford University Press.

Waine, B. (1995) 'A Disaster Foretold? The Case of Personal Pensions', *Social Policy and Administration*, 29(4): 317–34.

Walker, A. (1991) 'Thatcherism and the New Politics of Old Age', in J. Myles and J. Quadagno (eds) *States, Labor Markets and the Future of Old Age Policy*, Philadelphia: Temple University Press, pp. 19-36.

Walker, C. (1993) *Managing Poverty: The Limits of Social Assistance*. London: Routledge.

Walker, C. (2011) 'For Universalism and Against the Means Test', in A. Walker, A. Sinfield and C. Walker (eds) *Fighting Poverty, Inequality and Injustice*. Bristol: Policy Press, pp. 133–52.

Commentary

What were the lasting effects of Thatcher's legacy for social security?

PETER TAYLOR-GOOBY

Hill and Walker provide an incisive analysis of the social security reforms of the 1979–90 Thatcher government and comment on their longer-term impact. The main objectives of the reforms were to cut spending, weaken national insurance rights to benefits for people of working age and restructure pensions to cut state and extend private provision. A further shift, planned or not, was a change in the discourse surrounding social provision to deepen stigmatic divisions between deserving and undeserving claimants of working age. The chapter argues that it is the ideological shift that may be the most influential (and damaging) legacy of Thatcherism in social security.

The cuts were real but failed to save any cash. As unemployment increased and inequality and poverty escalated (partly as a result of Thatcherite economic, social and industrial policies, discussed elsewhere in this collection, partly due to longer-run secular trends in the global economy) benefit spending as a whole rose to wipe out any savings. The national insurance system for those of working age was damaged under Thatcher and further weakened under John Major. Earnings-related supplements were cut, entitlement straitened and insurance based and means-tested unemployment benefits aligned in the Jobseeker's Allowance. The attempt to expand private pensions to substitute for the ending of the State Earnings-Related Pension resulted in a costly and damaging failure, as private companies were found to be mis-selling pensions to those who would be better off in the state system (Goode Report 1993). The division between deserving and undeserving poor has been embedded in the UK system since Beveridge made work record the main factor in entitlement to national insurance unemployment, sickness, disability and survivors' benefits and established a less attractive means-tested system for those who were given benefits because they were simply too poor to survive otherwise. Under Thatcher the continued tightening of work tests and the attack on the poor of working age entrenched the division more firmly.

The legacy of the failure to cut spending

Social security spending had grown annually by between 5.5 and 7.2 per cent between the later 1950s and the late 1970s (Browne and Hood, 2012, figure 4.2). In the first five years of the Thatcher government annual growth fell to 5 per cent, and in the later 1980s to just 1.5 per cent. Spending then recovered somewhat, but did not return to the earlier rates until after the turn of the century. As the chapter points out, the Thatcher era saw the massive expansion of two areas of means-tested spending: housing benefit and family support, initially through Family Credit, which later formed the basis of Tax Credit in the 2000s. Both were established before 1979 but expanded massively to account for about 14 per cent of all social security spending by 1990 and more than 20 per cent by 2012 (Browne and Hood, figure 4.3 and table 2.1).Higher spending in this area, despite a Treasury commitment to cut growth, resulted from the rapid increase in poverty and in housing costs during the 1980s, continued through the 1990s but was restrained in the early 2000s by minimum wage and tax credits under New Labour.

The failure to contain social security spending points to a contradiction within market liberalism. Liberal logic assumes that, given freedom to operate, markets will set returns in relation to the value of individual labour. Living standards of those in work at the bottom of the labour market are then set by wages. Benefits for able-bodied people out of work must be substantially below the lowest wages, to maintain work incentives. Any move to set benefits higher will promote dependency. By a similar logic any benefits paid in respect of children will encourage people to have larger families than is rational. Welfare should be kept to the minimum that is politically tolerable.

The contradiction lies between the market logic and the fact that, in a period of increasing wage inequalities (exacerbated by policies to undermine employment protection and union rights) and high unemployment, market wages may fall below levels at which people could sustain anything approaching a decent life. Extra benefits are then necessary to enable low income families (whether in work or not) to raise children and afford housing, especially in areas of high housing demand. The result is an expansion of the highly targeted welfare necessary to meet these needs. The difficulties of reconciling the cost of a decent life and the wages available to those at the bottom have persisted, so that tax credit has expanded and increasingly emphasized the element (Child Tax Credit) directed towards children's needs and housing benefits payment have continued to grow. Universal Credit (to be phased in from April 2013) seeks to tighten work incentives and contain the pressure for continuing expansion of spending in a number of ways: by combining all means-tested benefits for those of working age, ensuring that work incentives are rigorously policed through a privatized Employment Service, largely paid by results, and at the same time curtailing housing benefit rights and committing to lower levels of uprating, so that the value of the benefit falls in real terms over time.

The outcome is likely to be a substantial increase in poverty, already emerging and estimated at 21 per cent among children and 12 per cent among adults, in absolute terms, by 2015 (Joyce, 2012, table 3). Whether the new programme can be sustained as living standards right at the bottom fall even further is unclear.

Pension privatization

Pensioners are by far the biggest group entitled to social security benefits and tend to turn out at elections. Consequently governments find it hard to cut pensions, although pension spending accounts for some 42 per cent of the total social security budget. Pensioners may also receive housing and community charge benefits and benefits for care and disability. The Thatcher solution was to cut state pension uprating, instituting a gradual process of cut-back, terminate the previous government's programme to expand national insurance pensions greatly and promote private pensions through subsidies.

The failure of the industry to guarantee pensions better than those the state offered, under the previous government's scheme, pointed to a basic conflict within the industry. On the one hand, pension are an attractive business with a long-term predictable contribution income and clear and calculable commitments, and with investments exempt from taxation. On the other, there are real difficulties in maintaining profits and expanding private pensions beyond middle class people with consistent work-records and substantial incomes to cover those who cannot afford to pay large contributions and who may be out of work at various stages during their life-course. Various programmes to expand the role of private pensions under the Major and Blair governments failed to resolve this issue and develop the role of private pensions.

Current policies combine four elements: first a rise in the state pension age to 66 in 2020 and to 67 by 2028, cutting particularly the commitment to lower working class people, to men and to those living in the least healthy areas of the country and of cities, who tend to die sooner; secondly, a new flat-rate state pension, available to those with 35-year work records; thirdly, a new national occupational pension scheme into which all those without alternative private pensions will be automatically enrolled (although they may then opt out); and fourthly, maintaining the existing means-tested provision to bring those without adequate support from the other schemes up to a minimal standard of living. The new system will be relatively simpler than previous systems. The government assumes it will encourage investment in private pensions, since investment in these will not simply be set against entitlement to means-tested state pensions for those with work-records. Whether the new national occupational pension has resolved the problem of ensuring sufficient income and low enough management charges to ensure a decent return for relatively low-income people is at present unclear. However, pension policy may have moved beyond the assumption of the Thatcher period that the dominant force in pensions could be private provision to accept that a substantial state scheme is needed to provide acceptable benefits for low to middle earners in an unequal labour market.

Stigmatizing the undeserving poor

Benefits stigma continues to be a major force in the politics of welfare. It sustains the distinction drawn repeatedly between strivers and shirkers in ministerial pronouncements and damages attempts to promote more humane and inclusive welfare on the left (Baumberg et al., 2012). The morality governing welfare debates becomes much more a question of ensuring that benefits are kept below wage levels to ensure fairness to lower-paid families, who are valued over the poor because they are seen to take responsibility for their own circumstances. It is less concerned with social inclusion and humane treatment of the less fortunate: a liberal individualism rather than a shared collectivism.

Issues for the left

Social security spending continues to rise and pension privatization has not happened, but people are increasingly suspicious of those on benefits. The contradiction between low wages, high rents and minimal acceptable living standards undermined the programme to cut benefits; the gap between the contributions many people can reasonably pay and the amounts needed to keep the pension industry profitable constrains attempts to privatize pensions. However, the idea that poor people do not deserve benefits unless they can prove that they are responsible market actors trumps any attempt to establish a humane, generous and inclusive welfare system in policy debate. One verdict on Thatcher's legacy might be that the policies failed but that the ideology grows ever stronger.

There are two main directions in current responses: programmes to end the stigmatization of working age claimers; and policies which tackle the problem at root in the labour market.

Remoralizing social security

Recent proposals fall into three groups. First, one logic undermines the shirker/striver division by pointing to the groups in poverty who are not responsible for their condition: low-paid workers and children. Official figures show that in 2010/11 59 per cent of household below the poverty line contained at least one member in paid work (DWP, 2012). Many of the benefit claimers in those household are not themselves earning, but the statistic dramatizes the importance of low wages in generating poverty and creating the need for an expansive welfare system in the UK.

Children are at rather higher risk of poverty than adults and are particularly hard hit by current reforms, which direct the benefit cuts away from pensioners and single people and towards low-income families and particularly the women and children in them. The main reason for this is simply that these are the groups who are most likely to be poor, already receive most in means-tested welfare and therefore are most vulnerable to cuts. The New Labour programme of expanded Child Tax Credit in the early 2000s rested on the acceptability to voters of benefit spending on children. The Coalition government has so far not repealed the Child Poverty Act of 2010 which commits it to targets it is unlikely to reach. A programme directed at child poverty may well be the most viable area for an expansion of social spending.

Second, several schemes side-step the moralism of the stigma argument and appeal to an economic logic through social investment. The provision of childcare and of family-friendly working will generate an economic return since it enables women to take part in paid work. Ben-Galim estimates the return from a national childcare scheme at £5,000 a year in saved benefits and extra taxes if the women who are released into paid work earn average wages, £1,250 if they earn the minimum wage (2012). Comparable returns might be expected from an elder care scheme, although at a lower level due to the weaker skills of many of the group who would then be in employment.

Third, a number of programmes (for example Horton and Godfrey, 2009; Bell and Gaffney, 2012) seek to reframe entitlement as a matter of contribution rather than need. Contribution indicates that the claimer has put something into society and is therefore entitled through the principle of reciprocity. The obvious problem is that such a scheme is limited and finds it hard to include those at the bottom of the labour market, with the lowest wages from which to contribute and with a high risk of unemployment. Contribution systems are likely to have an inbuilt bias against women who generally receive lower wages and whose work records are damaged by time spent in child or elder care. Most schemes tackle these issue by blanketing in time spent in care-work, with the state paying the contributions. The most ambitious scheme, by Horton and Gregory, expands this idea to value community service or training (which may lead to a future contribution) in the same way. One issue is that the more the contribution principle is extended, the greater the risk of dilution and a weaker political defence of entitlement.

The root of the problem

The problem that wages at the bottom of the labour market are simply too low to sustain a decent life style underlies many of the issues discussed above. It explains the expansion of welfare for those of working age and the difficulties in running a national insurance or contribution based pension or social security system. Minimum wage legislation in the early 2000s went some way to addressing this problem. At the levels set by the Low Pay Commission, the minimum wage does not seem to have damaged businesses or employment. However it is clear that minimum wages are not adequate to keep many families out of policy. The Living Wage is calculated by Loughborough University (outside London) and by the Greater London Authority (for London) as the minimum necessary to sustain a decent standard of living. It is currently set at about 20 per cent above the minimum wage outside London and nearly 40 per cent above it in London, to allow for higher rents and fares.

Research by the Resolution Foundation and IPPR indicates that many businesses could adjust if the Minimum Wage was raised to living wage levels, but that the higher wage bills would create problems in areas such as retail and catering (Pennycook, 2012). In these areas a move to 90 per cent of the Living Wage in the first instance is a possibility.

Conclusion

This chapter shows that the chief legacy of Thatcherism is not so much policy reforms (which were largely unsuccessful) but the embedding of a moralistic ideology which views benefit claimers of working age as work-shy scroungers. Those who wish to move towards a more generous and humane welfare state must find ways to circumvent or confront this ideology. Any shift will be a slow process. The discussion above points to various arguments that can be used to defend better benefits for children and for women, investment in childcare and a more generous contributory welfare system. Low wages lie at the heart of the problem. To be effective reforms must raise bottom end wages to a level adequate to sustain a decent family life, an approach sometimes termed 'pre-distribution'. The alternative is continued high levels of spending on unsatisfactory means-tested support to bridge the gap between low wages and the cost of a minimum decent life, with many voters unsympathetic to the needs of the poor whom they see as failures in the jobs market or workshy.

References

Baumberg, B., Bell, K. and Gaffney, D. (2012) *Benefits Stigma in Britain.* London: TurnToUs.

Bell, K. and Gaffney, D. (2012) *Making A Contribution.* London: Touchstone.

Ben-Galim, D. (2011) *Making the Case for Universal Childcare.* London: IPPR.

Browne, J. and Hood, A. (2012) *A Survey of the UK Benefits System*, IFS, BN13, http://www.ifs.org.uk/bns/bn13.pdf (accessed 23.1.2013).

DWP (2012) *Households below Average Income 1994–5 to 2010–11.* London: DWP.

Goode Report (1993) *Pension Law Reform: The Report of the Pension Law Review Committee*, 2 vols. London: HMSO.

Horton, T. and Gregory, J. (2009) *The Solidarity Society.* London: Fabian Society.

Joyce, R. (2012) *Tax and Benefit Reforms Due in 2012–13, and the Outlook for Household Incomes*, BN126. London: IFS.

Pennycook, M. (2012) *What Price a Living Wage?* London: IPPR/Resolution Foundation.

4
The legacy of Thatcherism for education policies: markets, managerialism and malice (towards teachers)

PETER DOREY

> I believe that the only way to make a major improvement in our education system is through privatisation to the point at which substantial fraction of all educational services is rendered to individuals by private enterprises. Nothing else will destroy or even greatly weaken the power of the current educational establishment – a necessary precondition for radical improvement in our education system. And nothing else will provide the public [state] schools with the competition that will force them to improve in order to hold on to their clientele.
>
> (Milton Friedman, *Washington Post*, 19 February 1995)

Secondary education and the teaching profession have experienced a process of relentless reform since the late 1980s, but they have by no means been alone. Across the public sector, there has been a permanent revolution enacted through innumerable reforms and centrally imposed 'initiatives', but these have all been based on similar assumptions and critiques, and thus entailed remarkably similar policy prescriptions. All have derived from a neo-liberal premise that publicly delivered and funded services are prone to inherent inefficiency and poor quality, due to the absence of competition and consumer choice, which in turn obviates any obligation by public sector professionals to improve either their own performance, or the level of service provided to the public. According to this perspective, initially propounded by the New Right, but subsequently embraced by New Labour, monopolies beget mediocrity.

The logical policy prescription, therefore, is either to privatize public services *in toto* or, when this is not judged feasible and practicable, to 'marketize' them by instilling the principles and practices of the private sector into the public sector. Secondary education (as well as the NHS) has provided excellent case studies of this process since the late 1980s, having been subject to the mantra of choice and competition; choice for parents and competition between schools, and attempts to link funding to success in attracting pupils, by virtue of a school's success vis-à-vis exam passes and other criteria. This component of marketization has sought to imitate the profit motive, whereby improved performance yields more 'customers' and thus increased revenues.

Yet in education (and other parts of the public sector), this neo-liberal objective has been accompanied by a parallel process of managerialism, whereby the power and autonomy of professionals and other street-level bureaucrats have been consciously eroded, and supplanted by stricter managerial control and stronger bureaucratic hierarchies, coupled with the imposition of sundry performance indicators and targets. These, in turn, have spawned a new regime of inspections and audits both of individual and institutional performance and goal attainment, invariably couched in a discourse of accountability, transparency and value-for-money.

In conjunction with this dual process of marketization and managerialism, the Thatcherite legacy in secondary education has bequeathed the ritual denigration and demonization of teachers themselves. Since the 1980s, the teaching profession has been routinely blamed for a range of social problems pertaining to illiteracy and innumeracy among young people, declining deference and anti-social behaviour. Teachers have variously been accused of failing to maintain academic standards and discipline in the classroom, due either to incompetence or 'trendy' (or 'progressive') teaching methods. These alleged failings have thus legitimized the aforementioned managerialist regime in secondary education, while simultaneously enabling politicians to invoke a populist assault on 'bad' or 'incompetent' teachers who are 'failing' pupils, their parents and employers. In this discourse, ministers depict themselves as being 'out there' on the side of parents and employers against the 'self-serving' teachers and the 'vested interests' of their trade unions.

The Thatcherite critique of education in post-war Britain

The Thatcherite critique of secondary education[1] was an integral part of its more general antipathy towards the public sector and the welfare state, and as such, enshrined similar objections and objectives, often articulated within a set of highly populist discourses. Moreover, this critique clearly enshrined both neo-liberal and neo-conservative dimensions, reflecting Gamble's summation of Thatcherism as 'free economy and strong state', whereby reducing the role of the State in the economic sphere, in order to revive freedom and liberty, was accompanied by an expanded or more interventionist role for the State in the non-economic sphere, in order to restore social discipline and traditional morality.

The neo-liberal aspect of the Thatcherite critique of education (and the public sector in general), which shared a strong similarity with the perspectives and which had been consistently articulated by the Institute of Economic Affairs (IEA) throughout the 1960s and 1970s, concerned the near monopoly of education provision which existed, largely as a consequence of comprehensive schools, and the consequent diminution of choice this entailed for parents who could not afford to send their children to a private school. According to this perspective, teachers in these schools had little incentive to improve the quality of their teaching, because local parents were a de facto captive audience. In effect, this scenario seemingly confirmed the Right's premise that limited choice and lack of competition yielded low standards.

However, alongside this perspective was a neo-conservative critique which posited that the allegedly poor standard of much secondary education was a consequence of 'progressive' or 'trendy' teaching methods. These were attributed largely to the ethos and methodologies inculcated via teacher training courses and colleges, under the auspices of the then Department of Education and Science (DES). Certainly, according to Margaret Thatcher (reflecting on her time as Education Secretary in the 1970–74 Heath government), 'the ethos of the DES was self-righteously socialist ... Equality in education was not only the overriding good,

---

[1] The focus of this chapter is exclusively on secondary education, and as such, we will not discuss reforms of higher (university) education, even though there are many similarities between the two sectors, in terms both of the type of reforms enacted since the late 1980s, and the rationales or discourses invoked to legitimize them.

irrespective of the practical effects of egalitarianism on particular schools; it was a stepping stone to achieving equality in society.' Moreover, she was highly critical of the extent to which the DES had 'become as closely connected with its clients as the DES was with the teaching unions, in particular the National Union of Teachers (NUT) . . . a large number of DES senior civil servants . . . and the NUT leaders were on the closest terms', sharing 'a common sympathy' (Thatcher, 1995: 166). Similarly vituperative views were expressed by two Conservative secretaries of state for education, Kenneth Baker (1993: 168) and John Patten (1995: 196–7).

At the same time, Thatcher believed that 'too many teachers were less competent and more ideological than their predecessors' (Thatcher, 1993: 590). Such views were shared by one of Margaret Thatcher's closest advisers in the Downing Street Policy Unit, Alfred Sherman (2005: 107, 108), who averred that in post-1945 Britain: 'The education establishment . . . had brought standards steadily down', while also alluding to the pernicious influence of 'Marxoid dons' in shaping higher education policy since the 1960s. Thatcher's successor, John Major, himself denounced 'the giant left-wing experiment in levelling down' (Major, 1992: 9), 'the failed nostrums of the 1960s and 1970s' (Major, 1993: 31), and 'the fads and fashions that short-changed an entire generation of children . . . called . . . progressive education' (Major, 1997: 20).

These two critiques were clearly reflected in the reforms of secondary education enacted during the 1980s, particularly towards the end of the decade; the neo-liberal emphasis on choice and competition, and the concomitant empowerment of parents as consumers or customers (on behalf of their children) accompanied the neo-conservative objective of exercising greater control over *what* was taught in the classroom, as well as *how* teaching was conducted. In effect, schools and teachers were to be subject simultaneously to the discipline of the market and the discipline of the State.

The Thatcher governments' reforms (1979–90)

Beyond spending curbs, the main education policy initiative of the first (1979–83) Thatcher government was the 1980 introduction of the Assisted Places Scheme, whereby financially less well-off parents could receive financial assistance, via a government fund, to enable their child(ren) to attend a fee-charging independent school. Apart from this particular

initiative, education reform was not yet a priority for the Thatcher governments, primarily because during the first half of her premiership, the
Cabinet was focused mainly on economic issues, most notably attempting
to reduce inflation, curbing public expenditure (albeit with limited success),
cutting income tax, privatizing various nationalized industries and
weakening the trade unions. Only during the course of the mid- to late
1980s did reform of education (along with the NHS) move towards the top
of the Conservatives' policy agenda, as ministers became both more
confident and more radical, and sought to extend their hitherto economic
radicalism to social policy (Thatcher, 1993: 278–9), and thereupon introduce
market principles into to the provision of education *and* health. This would
also serve to emasculate the 'over-mighty' professionals and policy communities who allegedly dominated these spheres of social policy; they
would henceforth be subject to the discipline of 'the market'.

A further reason for the increasing priority ascribed to education reform
during the latter half of the 1980s was that Thatcherite ministers became
increasingly irked at what they viewed as the excessive influence and often
'extremist' policies of local authorities during the 1980s, most notably
those under Labour control. Many on the Left sought to use local
government as a means of resisting Thatcherism, and thus of promoting
policies which were in diametric opposition. This provided the context in
which Thatcher used her 1987 conference speech to claim that many
schoolchildren were being denied a proper education, because of the
manner in which left-wing councils and LEAs were promoting their own
anti-racist, anti-sexist and anti-homophobic agenda. According to
Thatcher (1987): 'Children who need to be able to count and multiply are
learning anti-racist mathematics . . . Children who need to be taught to
respect traditional moral values are being taught that they have an
inalienable right to be gay.'

Similar condemnation had been expressed the previous year, when a
right-wing think tank, the Hillgate Group, published a pamphlet entitled
Whose Schools? A Radical Manifesto which insisted that: 'Schoolchildren
had to be rescued from indoctrination in all the fashionable causes of
the Radical Left: "anti-racism", "anti-sexism", "peace education" (which
usually means CND propaganda) and "anti-heterosexism" (meaning the
preaching of homosexuality.' The vital solution was for schools to be
'released from the control of local government', thereby 'depriving the
politicised local education authorities of their standing ability to corrupt
the minds and souls of the young' (Hillgate Group, 1986: 4, 13, 18).

In the context of these factors, the third Thatcher government embarked on a major reform of secondary education. Indeed, so profound and far-reaching was this reform, enshrined in the 1988 Education Reform Act, that it subsequently served as the lodestar for subsequent reforms of education throughout the next two decades. The Act's main provisions were:

- transferring the responsibility for the management of schools from local education authorities (LEAs) to schools' own governing bodies
- enabling schools to 'opt out' of LEA control, and instead become 'grant-maintained', whereupon they would be funded directly by central government
- establishing a 'National Curriculum' through which all pupils would study the same 'core' subjects until they chose their GCSEs at the age of 14
- creating a new form of educational establishment, namely City Technology Colleges, to increase the provision of vocational education
- facilitating 'open enrolment', so that parents could exercise greater choice in deciding which local school to send their child(ren) to
- the abolition of the Inner London Education Authority (ILEA).

These measures reflected several Conservative objectives concerning the development of secondary education in post-1945 Britain. First, by transferring the management of schools to their own governing bodies, the educational role of local government would be significantly reduced, thereby weakening the influence both of the Left in various town halls, and the 'education establishment' or policy community at local level.

Second, but following directly on from this, the 1988 Act enshrined the neo-liberal objective of shifting power away from LEAs towards parents, thus heralding a relentless process of consumerization and marketization of education (and elsewhere in the public sector, not least in the NHS). In this context, parents were to be transformed into rational consumers, by being offered greater choice in deciding which school they wished to send their children to. Put another way, this was also part of a general Thatcherite concern to downgrade and reduce the role of 'producer interests'; in this case, LEAs and teachers themselves.

Third, but again logically following on from the last objective, Thatcherism sought to promote competition between schools, as each aimed to make itself attractive to parents choosing the best school for their children. According to Thatcherism's neo-liberal and populist discourses, such competition would serve to raise academic standards, on the basis that parents would eschew the weaker schools in favour of those which could demonstrate educational excellence. This, in turn, would compel teachers to 'raise their game' far more effectively than any number of ministerial exhortations and Whitehall decrees, for unless they did so, their school would experience a diminishing pupil intake and concomitant loss of government funding, leading ultimately to redundancies and possible closure of their school altogether.

Fourth, the National Curriculum – described by two academic critics as 'a bureaucratic device for exercising control over what goes on in school' (Lawton and Chitty, 1987: 5) – aimed to ensure that all state schools delivered a common syllabus until pupils reached the age of 14. Not only would this mean that pupils studied the same 'core' subjects until their GCSEs, it also meant that meaningful comparisons could henceforth be drawn between schools. This led ineluctably to a subsequent obsession with league tables, which purported to provide parents with clear evidence of which schools were the best and most academically successful, and thus enable these 'customers' of secondary education to make rational decisions about the best school for their children. Or as Robin Squire (1995), as Minister of State for Schools, trenchantly argued:

> Providing access to performance information on a consistent basis is essential to inform choice and drive up standards. None of us should underestimate the way in which the information revolution spearheaded by performance tables has helped to focus us all on achievement and outcomes ... Performance tables are here to stay.

Indeed, league tables then became increasingly utilized (and fetishized) throughout other parts of the public sector, particularly in the NHS and, more recently, universities.

However, alongside this neo-liberal dimension, the National Curriculum also incorporated clearly discernible neo-conservative elements, most notably in the prescribed content of particular academic subjects, and the manner in which these were to be taught. This was particularly evident in the teaching of history, with the (then) Education Secretary, Kenneth Baker, insisting that 'the programmes of study should have at the core the history of Britain, the record of its past and, in particular, its political, constitutional and cultural heritage' (*The Times*, 14 January 1989).

In this context, many Conservatives – including Thatcher herself (see Judd, 1989) – not only sought to promote a particular version of history, namely one which sought to construct or convey a specific narrative of

British achievements and national identity, they also assumed or implied that subjects such as history could – and most certainly should – be taught 'objectively' through the conveyance of factual knowledge. This, of course, assumed that 'the facts speak for themselves' – a highly conservative assumption, in so far as it discourages closer consideration or critical reflection of the 'real' world or the status quo, and instead encourages acceptance of 'common-sense' views which apparently require no further explanation or justification.

Such a perspective was certainly encouraged by neo-conservatives, as evinced by the Hillgate Group's insistence that 'Our' (British) culture 'must not be sacrificed for the sake of misguided relativism'. Moreover, the Group claimed, it was vital to promote *British* history and heritage precisely in order to 'reconcile our minorities, to integrate them into our national culture and to ensure a common political loyalty' (Hillgate Group, 1987: 4). In this context, neo-conservatives have been characterized as 'cultural restorationists' (Apple, 1989; Ball, 1993: 6; Phillips, 1996) seeking to revive or return to a mythical or nostalgic past, one characterized by British 'greatness', hierarchy, social discipline and veneration of tradition.

One other crucial manifestation of the promotion of neo-conservatism and traditionalism through secondary education concerned sex education, particularly the portrayal of homosexuality. This aspect of Thatcherite neo-conservatism was not directly enshrined in the National Curriculum itself, but emanated from the 1988 Local Government Act, Section 28 of which stipulated that: 'A local authority shall not . . . promote the teaching in any maintained school of the acceptability of homosexuality as a pretended family relationship' (for a discussion of 'Section 28', see Evans, 1989/90). This particular clause clearly reflected the 1987–90 Thatcher government's determination to ensure that schoolchildren were taught that the traditional heterosexual married family was the only morally acceptable type of sexual relationship, and that other households, lifestyles or relationships – especially those comprising a same-sex couple – were morally undesirable or socially inferior.

It should be noted that while 'section 28' was largely a response to the alleged promotion of gay rights by so-called 'loony Left' Labour councils and LEAs, it also reflected a moral panic about the spread of AIDs during the latter part of the 1980s, with some neo-conservatives or proponents of traditional morality viewing this as a 'gay plague', and even God's wrath against homosexuals. The AIDS epidemic thus provided a further rationale for those Conservatives who wanted to curb the 'promotion' of homosexuality via sex education lessons in Britain's schools, and instead venerate the traditional married family or 'Victorian values' in the realm of lifestyles and morals.

A more general feature of the education reforms initiated by the Thatcher governments, and which wholly reflected their increasing disdain for many teachers in general and the teaching unions in particular was the exclusion of the teaching profession and its representative bodies from educational policy-making, and the consequent manner in which reforms were imposed by ministers, rather than being enacted through bargaining and negotiation. Viewing teachers and their unions a classic 'producer interest', and their relationship with the Department of Education and Science as that of 'producer capture' (as noted in the ministerial quotes above), the Thatcher governments assiduously sought to weaken the education policy community, thereby asserting firm governmental and ministerial authority over the professions.

Exactly the same process of marginalization was evident in the aforementioned reforms of the NHS in 1989–90, whereupon the medical profession was variously depicted as a selfish, self-serving producer interest whose influence and power needed to be subordinated both to the interests of patients and the enhanced authority of hospital managers. As such, both in education and the NHS, front-line professionals were no longer viewed as allies, but as adversaries, and policy change was increasingly based on confrontational imposition, rather than consensual incrementalism.

Consolidation under John Major's premiership

John Major replaced Margaret Thatcher as Conservative party leader and Prime Minister in November 1990, but it was not until July 1992, just a few months after Major's Conservative government had been re-elected (albeit with only a 21-seat parliamentary majority), that a White Paper on education was published, presaging the consolidation and entrenchment of the reforms enshrined in the 1988 Education Reform Act. Entitled *Choice and Diversity: A New Framework for Schools*, the White Paper provided the basis for the 1993 Education Act, formally introduced by John Patten, which:

- streamlined the 'opting-out' process to make it easier and quicker for schools to opt out of LEA control (reflecting a concern among ministers

that not nearly enough schools has so far availed themselves of this opportunity)
- established the Funding Agency for Schools, which would allocate and administer the finance disbursed to those schools which opted to become grant-maintained
- further reduced the role of LEAs in education provision, the aim being to transform them into 'enablers' and coordinators of education services, rather than direct providers
- permitted all schools to specialize in one or more subjects, alongside their teaching of the core subjects in the National Curriculum
- established 'Education Associations' which would investigate 'failing' schools, and in so doing, could decide that the school needed to be taken out of LEA control and become grant-maintained – or simply closed down altogether.

The 1993 Education Act appeared to constitute the completion of the reforms enacted by the Thatcher governments during the late 1980s. Certainly, they were imbued with exactly the same objectives and principles, namely increasing parental choice, promoting competition between schools, raising academic standards, 'liberating' schools from LEA control and interference, fostering greater diversity, facilitating accountability and further marginalizing the education policy community or 'establishment'. In essence, the 1993 Education Act aimed to widen and deepen the dual processes of marketization and managerialism in secondary education in Britain.

However, Major also shared his predecessor's concern to imbue secondary education with a stronger or more explicit neo-conservative content, an objective which was evident in his speech to the 1992 Conservative party conference, when he eulogized 'traditional' teaching methods and their emphasis on the '3 Rs' (reading, writing and arithmetic), while scorning 'trendy' teaching methods and 'political correctness' in the classroom. Major insisted that 'teachers should learn how to teach children how to read, not waste their time on the politics of gender, race and class'. These views were clearly shared by his education secretaries, with one of them, John Patten (speaking at the same conference), averring that: 'All too often, the problems in education lie . . . with 1960s theorists, with the trendy left and with the teachers' union bosses', while Kenneth Clarke (1992) complained that 'anti-academic, anti-intellectual eccentric views have permeated too many of our schools'.

One key institutional innovation enacted during John Major's premiership was the establishment, in 1992, of the Office of Standards in Education (Ofsted). As its appellation clearly implied, Ofsted's formal role was to ensure that schools and their teachers were providing a good quality of education, this defined according to a range of criteria. Although schools had always been subject to external audits of their teaching, Ofsted's inspections purported to be more rigorous and independent (of LEAs), and thus a more effective and reliable evaluation of educational standards and teaching proficiency. Its reports, and the criticisms enshrined within them, were also often deliberately high profile, and given prominent media attention, whereas the former HMI reports rarely sought or garnered such publicity.

Meanwhile, an indirect consequence of the Thatcherite reform of education seems to have been a 'spill-over' of problems beyond the classroom and school gates. For example, various authors (Farrall, 2006: 262–3; Jones, 2003: 134–5; Timmins, 2001: 424, 519, 566) have noted that an increase in staff–pupil ratios meant that teachers were increasingly struggling to maintain control over larger classes, whereupon behavioural problems and disruption by disaffected pupils also increased. This, in turn, led to a (further) loss of morale among teachers, with increasing numbers of them going on 'sick leave', quitting the profession altogether or taking early retirement.

To address such problems, and also to focus on the pupils who were most likely to secure good academic grades – a vital consideration once school league tables were published – more pupils were 'excluded' from school for disciplinary offences and disruptive behaviour. Some of these 'problem pupils' then roamed the streets or loitered in shopping arcades, possibly drifting into petty crime or other forms of anti-social behaviour, and *inter alia* adding to the workload of the local police. Moreover, for some of these excluded pupils, the ensuing lack of qualifications and/or the 'acquisition' of a criminal record then rendered them virtually unemployable, whereupon they swelled the ranks of the emerging 'underclass', perhaps becoming involved in more serious criminality in adult life.

One consequence of the constant denigration of teachers by ministers, much of the media and senior figures in Ofsted, was relentless to undermine the authority and respect they had formerly enjoyed, whereupon some pupils and parents had few qualms about ignoring, insulting, and sometimes assaulting, teachers. Of course, ministers invariably claimed that bad behaviour in the classroom was largely a consequence of poor teaching or inadequate pupil-management skills by teachers, on the grounds that 'good teachers' would be able to command the attention and respect of their pupils – irrespective of the class sizes. In this regard, ministers conveniently overlooked their own role, and also that of Ofsted, in undermining the status of teachers through constant criticism.

Enthusiastic extension under Tony Blair's premiership

Of the many areas of public policy in which New Labour generally continued a Thatcherite trajectory, and articulated a very similar discourse, education was one of the most prominent. Indeed, Warwick Mansell (2009) has claimed that: 'Often, in education, it has proved more Thatcherite than Thatcher herself.' Undoubtedly, along with the formal rejection of nationalization and public ownership, education was undoubtedly one of the policy areas where New Labour was most keen to differentiate itself from Old Labour, which it sought to do by not only enthusiastically embracing and extending public sector reform, but also invoking similar rhetorical rationales to the Thatcher-Major governments. Indeed, education (like most other parts of the public sector) was subjected to a permanent revolution from 1997 to 2010, leaving many teachers and school heads punch-drunk from new legislation, regulatory changes, structural reorganizations, top-down targets and Whitehall initiatives.

An early indication of the extent to which New Labour was readily embracing much of the Thatcherite agenda was provided in 1996, when Peter Mandelson and Roger Liddle published a 'manifesto' for the remodelled party entitled *The Blair Revolution: Can New Labour Deliver?* Although this was critical of various aspects of Thatcherism, its primary aim was to disavow Old Labour and the Left, and thereby persuade the electorate that New Labour was a wholly new party from the one which had existed in the 1970s and 1980s. This was particularly evident in Mandelson and Liddle's (1996: 91) trenchant criticisms of post-war education policy, for they alleged that:

> The educational system in Britain has always given priority to the interests of an academic elite rather than to high general standards of education . . . The teacher unions have tried to focus the public debate about education on pay and resources, rather than the curriculum and pupil attainments: on inputs rather than outputs. The educational egalitarians regard the structure of schools as far more important than the quality of what is learned.

Given such criticisms, it is perhaps not surprising that many of New Labour's early pledges concerning education shared a strong similarity with the discourses and reforms invoked by the Thatcher-Major governments. For example, Mandelson and Liddle emphasized that New Labour 'wants to allow schools the maximum freedom to develop their own distinctive ethos and identity' in terms of excellence and developing specialisms in particular subjects, such as science or music, for example. Furthermore, they emphasized that 'where there are ideological presumptions in favour of mixed ability teaching, these should be abandoned in favour of what achieves the best results for that school'. It was envisaged that this clear move away from standard comprehensive schooling (strongly associated with Old Labour and the Left) could derive from 'a successful compact with local businesses' (Mandelson and Liddle, 1996: 94; see also, Labour Party, 1995).

Certainly, New Labour readily accepted the Thatcherite view that the education system should be much more concerned with serving the requirements of employers and business, by ensuring that school leavers (and university graduates) attained the qualifications or acquired the 'transferable skills' which would render them attractive to employers. As Jones observes, 'educational priorities were presented squarely in terms of servicing market-driven growth' (Jones, 2003: 144). This was deemed more important than ever before, because in an increasingly global economy characterized by highly mobile transnational companies and flows of capital, it was imperative to attract inward investment, and a major means of achieving this was to offer a well-qualified or highly-skilled workforce. Hence New Labour's explicit strengthening of the links between education, the economy and the professed or perceived needs of big business.

However, probably the strongest similarity and continuity between New Labour's education reforms and those pursued by the 1979–97 Thatcher-Major governments concerned the increasing diversity and fragmentation of secondary schools, coupled with the discourse of choice and competition. This diversification was explicitly intended simultaneously to empower parents through providing them with a greater variety of schools to choose from – and *inter alia* show that New Labour was firmly on the side of the consumer, rather than the producers or providers, of education – while also improving academic standards by virtue of injecting even more competition into the education system. After all, as Tony Blair's first Secretary of State for Education, David Blunkett (2001: 44) declared: 'Every other sector has had to embrace diversity and respond to its customers. It is not only inevitable, but right that this too becomes a requirement of any twenty-first-century school.'

The Blair premiership thus witnessed several new types of school, such as Beacon schools, City Academies, Faith schools, Foundation/Trust schools, and Specialist schools. This burgeoning plethora of schools – what Chitty (2009: 74) deems a 'bewildering array' and Smithers (2001: 405–6) has referred to as a 'jumble of a system' – is somewhat ironic, because New Labour had previously insisted that it was standards, not structures, which were important, yet the Blair governments actually presided over a major restructuring of secondary education. Of course, the Blairite response would be that this restructuring, by facilitating much greater parental (and pupil) choice and inter-school competition, would itself serve to improve standards.

Crucially, in extending the Thatcherite agenda of choice, competition and diversity in secondary education, and encouraging a plurality of schools and specialisms, New Labour unequivocally distanced itself from those on the Left or among Old Labour who continued to defend comprehensive schools, and were anxious about the re-emergence of 'selection' on the basis of ability *á la* the old grammar schools. In this context, Blunkett (2001: 41, 44) accused the Left of 'ideological inertia ... dogma and inflexibility', and whose consequent 'attachment to a particular form of comprehensive education meant that 'it could see no value in diversity or specialisation within education'.

Consequently, alongside this continued pursuit of marketization and consumerism in education, with its discourses of choice and competition, New Labour also strengthened key aspects of managerialism or 'New Public Management' (NPM), whose key characteristics include: stronger management *of* (rather than by) professionals in the public sector; adoption of private sector techniques of management and 'incentivization'; emphasis on performance indicators, outputs and results, and associated mechanisms of audit, appraisal and evaluation; fragmentation of institutions in order to weaken monopolies and foster competition between public service providers; imposing stronger financial discipline, and linking funding to performance or attainment of specified targets (see Flynn, 2007; Hood, 1991, 1995; Pollitt, 1990, 2003). Certainly: 'A particular feature of NPM in practice has been an attack upon the traditional autonomy ... of the established professions – medicine, teaching, etc.' (Hill, 2009).

We can see, therefore, that the bulk of New Labour's education policies were clearly and firmly located within the paradigm shift wrought by Thatcherism. As Smithers (2001: 416) notes:

> What is remarkable . . . is how little it differed at root from the [education] policies of the previous Conservative administrations. Many of the education reforms which the Conservatives had introduced from 1988 onwards, and which were bitterly attacked by the Labour opposition of the time, now became the backbone of the Blair programme. The National Curriculum, tests and league tables, financial delegation to schools and a beefed-up inspection service, were all enthusiastically embraced by New Labour.

Certainly, New Labour adopted many of the neo-liberal elements of Thatcherism, in terms of promoting competition between schools, permitting the private sector an increasing role in sponsoring and managing schools and linking education more explicitly to the apparent needs of employers and the economy. However, the Blair governments seemed a little less concerned with some of the neo-conservative aspects of Thatcherite education policy.

For example, the National Curriculum was streamlined somewhat (a process actually begun during the latter stage of John Major's premiership), whereupon the Blair governments placed a much stronger emphasis on improving literacy and numeracy, particularly at primary school level (which is beyond the remit of this chapter). Moreover, the streamlining of the National Curriculum was intended to enable secondary schools to specialize in particular subjects or activities, whereupon they could place a stronger emphasis on, for example, the teaching of music. In other words, beyond English and maths, the Blair governments were a little less prescriptive about the teaching or content of particular academic subjects via the National Curriculum.

However, the Blair governments' most notable departure from Thatcherite neo-conservatism manifested itself in the realm of sex education, for while there remained a formal emphasis on the importance of family life, there was also a willingness to acknowledge the legitimacy of relationships other than those comprising a married heterosexual couple. Indeed, in 2000, the Department for Education and Employment published *Sex and Relationship Education Guidance*, which stated that:

> It is up to all schools to make sure that the needs of all students are met in their sex education programmes. Young people, whatever their developing sexuality, need to feel that sex and relationship education is relevant to them and sensitive to their needs. The Secretary of State for Education and Employment is clear that teachers should be able to deal honestly and sensitively with sexual orientation, answer appropriate questions and offer support.
>
> (Department for Education and Employment, 2000: 12–13)

In accordance with this more enlightened stance, the Blair governments also repealed 'Section 28', although owing to Conservative opposition in the House of Lords, the relevant legislation did not reach the statute book until 2003.

The Conservative-Liberal Democrat Coalition after May 2010

When David Cameron was elected Conservative leader in December 2005, he instigated a wide-ranging internal policy review as an integral part of a professed commitment to modernizing the party, and thereby render it relevant to the twenty-first century. Initially at least, it seemed as if a more conciliatory and constructive approach would be applied to the public sector, particularly health and education, for an interim report from the public sector improvement group candidly admitted that the previous Conservative administration had subjected public services to excessive 'audits' and inspections – 'this approach has run its course' – and exaggerated the extent to which they could and should mimic the private sector. It was now recognized that 'a private corporation which publicly shamed its employees in the way that government has done in recent years would not long survive', and hence the new approach was to be one of seeking a partnership with public sector professionals (Perry and Dorrell, 2006: 4).

In similar vein, David Willetts (2006), a prominent Conservative front-bencher, party intellectual and post-Thatcherite 'modernizer', declared that: 'We want to raise . . . standards by working with the professions, not beating up on them.' David Cameron (2007) himself complained that the erstwhile modernization programme had served to 'disempower the professionals whose vocation is all that makes the public services work'. Consequently, he pledged that under a Conservative government, when essential changes were introduced into the public services, they would show due 'deference to the manners and customs of the people who work in the public services and the people who use them'. What has emerged thus far with regard to education policy since the Conservatives formed a Coalition government with the Liberal Democrats in May 2010, has been a combination of carrot-and-stick towards the teaching profession (although with perhaps rather more stick as time has passed). On the one hand, there have been pledges that teachers will be accorded more respect, and granted

123

greater powers to tackle disruptive pupils, in the classroom, as well as afforded greater protection from (often malicious and false) allegations of assault or sexual abuse by disaffected pupils. The Conservatives have also mooted the notion that some public services, including schools, might be transformed into cooperative ventures which would be managed, at least in part, by their staff, thereby freeing them from state or LEA control and politico-bureaucratic interference.

Yet these pledges have been accompanied by the continued incantation of a discourse which promotes choice and competition through marketization and consumer sovereignty ('parent power'). Indeed, the 'big idea' in the sphere of education policy has been the enthusiastic advocacy of 'free' schools, whereby it is envisaged that businesses, employers, parents, philanthropists, and sundry community or voluntary groups, including religious bodies or churches, will establish and manage schools. For the Conservatives, this is wholly commensurate with their continued determination to reduce what remains of the role of local (education) authorities and thereby foster the revival of intermediary non-state institutions at local level: Edmund Burke's 'little platoons' for the early twenty-first century. These objectives also seem readily compatible with the Liberal Democrats' promotion of political decentralization and community activism.

Free schools receive their funding from the Department of Education, via the Education Funding Council, but enjoy greater autonomy (than schools governed via LEAs) over such aspects as the length of the school day, the curriculum, and how they spend their budget. In rejecting allegations that such schools constitute a form of stealth privatization of secondary education, the Department has insisted that free schools are not-for-profit organizations, and that any financial surplus which might accrue must be directly reinvested in the school. The first 'free schools', 24 in total (14 of them in London, and five in Manchester) were opened in September 2011, and a further 55 in September 2012 (although the government had originally envisaged 79).

Alongside the promotion of 'free schools', the Coalition government, via the Education Secretary, Michael Gove, sought a major expansion of academy schools, which are also independent of LEA control and funding. Instead, although the bulk of their funding emanates directly from the government, some of it will derive from sponsorship by non-state actors, most notably individual businessmen/women and private companies, who are also then permitted to share in the management of 'their' academy, including its curriculum content and academic specialism(s). These academies can either be new schools, or replace existing schools which are deemed to be 'failing'. Needless to say, proponents of such schools claim that their independence from LEAs, and the input of individual entrepreneurs or private companies, will inevitably result in higher academic standards, and *inter alia* benefit pupils from disadvantaged backgrounds who have previously been 'let down' by low expectations and/or substandard teaching in 'bog-standard' comprehensive schools. Critics, of course, view academy schools as a form of stealth privatization of education, and the increased colonization and domination of civil society and civic institutions by wealthy individuals and big business.

One other continuity evinced by the Coalition government vis-à-vis education policy was the continued denigration of the teaching profession. Regardless of the conciliatory rhetoric articulated by senior Conservatives when in Opposition, and which had emphasized the need to treat public sector professionals as partners, the reality since 2010 is that Conservative ministers – and senior figures in Ofsted – swiftly reverted to blaming teachers for sundry educational and social problems, thereby perpetuating the discourse about 'bad' teachers 'failing' the country's children. Certainly it is very rare for illiteracy, innumeracy or bad behaviour among pupils to be blamed on those parents who refuse to read to their children, or fail to teach them basic manners and any sense of right and wrong; it is always deemed to be the fault of the teachers.

The legacy of Thatcherism in education

As in many other spheres of politics and public policy, the legacy of Thatcherism vis-à-vis education in Britain only became apparent during the two decades following Margaret Thatcher's November 1990 resignation as Conservative party leader and prime minister. This is because although the Thatcher governments' most radical reforms of education were only introduced during the final two years of her premiership, their key principles and objectives, and also their discourses, constituted the basis of virtually all education reforms enacted by subsequent governments, Conservative, New Labour and Conservative-Liberal Democrat Coalition alike. These similarities and continuities, collectively constituting the Thatcherite legacy, have been evident in five particular features of education policy and reform since the 1988 Education Reform Act.

First, there has been a continuation of 'marketization'. Indeed as a consequence of the paradigm shift to neo-liberalism presaged by Thatcherism,
'the market' has become fetishized since the 1980s, so that the response to
virtually any social or economic problem is to introduce or extend the
principles, practices and processes of the private sector, while denigrating
state 'interference', bureaucracy, allegedly selfish self-serving professionals
and the trade unions. This, of course, reflect the neo-liberal mantra that
'consumer choice + institutional competition = improved standards'.

This process of marketization has also fostered the increasing involvement of the private sector in 'delivering', funding, shaping or sponsoring
educational services, a process which was greatly extended and accelerated
by the Blair governments from 1997 onwards, for as Ken Jones has noted,
'New Labour aimed not only to relate public-sector activity more closely
to the expressed needs of business, but also to involve private interests
more actively in the delivery of social services . . . including education'
(Jones, 2003: 145). In this context, it has been suggested that marketization
has entailed both the promotion of choice within the state sector, via the
creation of competition between schools, and 'by increasing the range of
realistic alternatives to the state sector . . . alternative forms of school
provision' (Dale, 1989/90: 9, 10).

One notable consequence of this relentless process of marketization has
been an accretive blurring of the boundaries between the public and private
sectors in education, reflected in, and reinforced by, the increasing
fragmentation of the education system, as a consequence of the plethora of
schools, educational services, education quangos, external 'stakeholders'
and private companies or consortiums, which have burgeoned since the
late 1980s. This is itself a manifestation of the wider shift from government
to governance in Britain since the 1980s, a phenomenon which 'places an
emphasis on vertical co-operation between institutions and tiers or levels
of government, and on horizontal co-operation between public, private and
voluntary sectors at the local level' (Goldsmith, 1997: 7; see also Pierre and
Stoker, 2000: 29; Rhodes, 1997: 53; Richards and Smith, 2002: 15, 4, 2; Stoker,
2004; Wilson, 2000: 258).

The second aspect of education policy which has been characterized by
considerable continuity since 1988 has been the extension and intensification
of managerialism and the NPM. This has been evident not only in terms of
the strong subordination of teachers to head teachers, school governors, and
stronger organizational hierarchies in general, but also via the associated
imposition of sundry performance indicators and targets.

Indeed, New Labour added a plethora of ostensibly quantifiable targets to raise standards, in tandem with (and so not instead of) competition between schools. These targets pertained to a range of criteria and desired outcomes in secondary education, such as literacy and numeracy rates among children at particular ages, for example, or the numbers of children from poor backgrounds proceeding to sixth form or university. In this regard, Fergusson suggests that New Labour's approach to 'modernizing' secondary education was 'more interventionist, and considerably more managerialist. Outcomes remain the focus, but they are now constituted as targets and benchmarks, rather than just comparisons with other institutions' (Fergusson, 2000: 208).

However, although New Labour's approach was widely criticized for its intensification of managerialism and target-setting, its strong focus on improving the educational performance and attainments of pupils from poor backgrounds did suggest a serious commitment to enhancing or strengthening equality of opportunity via the education system, even if the actual bureaucratic mechanisms for pursuing this laudable goal were often open to criticism.

Certainly, the recourse to managerialism and sundry performance indicators has spawned an 'audit regime' throughout much of the British education system (as elsewhere in the public sector), although Scotland and Wales, particularly post-devolution, have avoided or reversed some of the excesses inflicted on schools and teachers in England (see, for example, Birrell, 2009: 69–72; Cairney, 2011: chapter 8). To 'measure' performance and target attainment, along with other criteria pertaining to efficiency, value for money (VFM), and so on, school teachers (and university lecturers) have been subject to a relentless process of inspection during the last two decades, often of a highly bureaucratic character involving extensive and time-consuming form-filling and box-ticking. It has sometimes seemed as if the teachers are being tested as much as their pupils. This both reflects and exemplifies the emergence of an 'audit culture' (Power, 1997) under the auspices of a 'regulatory state' (Moran, 2003).

Indeed, one academic expert on Soviet politics and political economy has compared the contemporary public sector in Britain to aspects of the former Soviet Union, in terms of the degree and mode of bureaucratization, central planning and target-setting. Of course, the ideological origins are polar opposites (Marxism-Leninism and neo-liberalism), but the consequences in terms of the micro-management and constant monitoring of public services and their front-line staff are remarkably similar, and invariably enshrine the same internal contradictions, dysfunctionalities, bureaucratic game-playing and perverse incentives – all of which eventually contributed to the spectacular and long overdue collapse of the Soviet Union (Amann, 2003).

One other consequence of the audit regime in secondary education (and elsewhere in the public sector) is the manner with which it unwittingly promotes or provides perverse incentives to focus on particular aspects of the professional role to the exclusion of others, because it is often only those activities or outcomes which can be directly measured and quantified that are defined as important; if it cannot be, or is not going to be, measured via an audit, or is not listed as a specified performance indicator, then it is not deemed important. Professional autonomy and judgement are once again subordinated to bureaucracy and managerialism; the manner in which teaching is performed, and how pupils are taught, becomes bureaucratically determined, in order to ensure that it can be measured and monitored. The bureaucratic tail wags the professional dog.

So, for example, the imperative for schools and teachers to secure more GCSE grades, and thus improve their league table position and attract more 'customers' (pupils and parents), has led to widespread complaints – not least from the teaching profession itself – that teachers are 'teaching to the test'; teaching their pupils how to write 'model answers' in order to pass exams, and thereby improve their school's league table position, rather than actually facilitating genuine learning, understanding and critical thinking. Thus has Warwick Mansell (2007) lamented this shift to 'education by numbers' and 'the tyranny of testing'.

The third continuity which has characterized education policy and reform under successive government since the Thatcher premiership is the almost relentless denigration of teachers – what Stephen Ball (1990: 18) has termed a 'discourse of derision' – by politicians and senior figures associated with Ofsted, and strongly echoed by pro-Conservative newspapers. Teachers have repeatedly had their competence and professionalism impugned, and been deemed culpable for many of society's wider problems owing to their alleged failure to maintain academic standards or impose discipline in the classroom. The former head of Ofsted, Chris Woodhead has long been a *bête noire* of many teachers, due to his strong criticism of 'bad' teachers and teaching unions, the 'education establishment', and trenchant criticism of aspects of state education. For example, in his book *Class War*, Woodhead (2003: 114) claimed that: 'If the public has a low opinion of teachers, it is, in part at least, because too many teachers have for too long failed to teach their children . . . Across the system as a whole . . . standards are too low', although he did acknowledge that there were some excellent individual teachers, and claimed to understand their frustration at mounting bureaucracy. However, he also expressed a clear view about inspections of schools which is also often implicit in many ministerial pronouncements, namely that 'the "competence and confidence" of good teachers is enhanced by inspection. Good teachers know they have nothing to fear from Ofsted.'

Rather more recently, one of Woodhead's successors, Sir Michael Wilshaw (who became head of Ofsted in January 2012) has made various inflammatory comments which have further alienated much of the teaching profession. For example, he has claimed that: 'If anyone says to you that "staff morale is at an all-time low" [in a school] you know you are doing something right' (Quoted in *The Guardian*, 24 January 2012), while a few months later, he trenchantly dismissed teachers' claims that their job was stressful, and alleged that complaints about stress were too often advanced by teachers, particularly school heads, as an excuse for their own inadequacies or failings (BBC News, 2012).

Of course, the contempt towards teachers and educationalists displayed by successive governments and Ofsted since the late 1980s also under-pinned a fourth enduring legacy of the Thatcherite reforms of secondary education, namely the exclusion of the education profession from policy-making, along with the erstwhile role of LEAs, and thus the deliberate weakening of the education policy community. As elsewhere in the public sector since the 1980s, particularly in the NHS, front-line pro-fessionals and their representative organizations have often been viewed as a major part or cause of the problems to be solved, and hence succes-sive governments have resolutely refused to listen seriously to their criticisms and grievances. On the contrary, when front-line staff have sought to highlight the negative impact or problems engendered by relentless public sector reform and the concomitant bureaucracy thus engendered, the ministerial (and media) response has invariably been to depict education (and health service) professionals as self-serving 'producer interests' who are resistant to change for entirely selfish reasons, or who are inveterate whingers and whiners. It is also implied that public sector professionals who do not enthusiastically embrace the dual pro-cesses of marketization and modernization must want to turn the clock back to the 1970s, or are afraid of being accountable to their service users or the taxpayer.

Certainly, in education and health policy alike, Thatcher much preferred to seek advice and inspiration from New Right think tanks, such as the Adam Smith Institute, the Centre for Policy Studies and the Institute of Economic Affairs (Bochel and Bochel, 2003: 51–2; see also, Chitty, 2009: 133; Desai, 1994; Jones, 2003: 125; Riddell, 1991: 143), along with politically sympathetic individuals such as Brian Griffiths, Ferdinand Mount and Alfred Sherman, all of whom served in her Policy Unit during the 1980s. One major consequence of these developments was that the 1988 Education Reform Act was largely 'assembled *in secret* . . . There was a determined effort *not* to consult with either the DES [Department of Education and Science] or the civil servants or chief education officers or local politicians' (Maclure, 1988: 166, emphasis in original).

Later, from May 1997 onwards, Tony Blair appointed figures such as David Miliband (not yet an MP) as head of the Downing Street Policy Unit, Miliband having formerly been a researcher at the 'progressive' think tank, the Institute for Public Policy Research. Meanwhile, Andrew Adonis was appointed as Blair's special adviser on education in 1998, before himself replacing Miliband as head of the Policy Unit in 2001, and then becoming a Labour spokesman on education in the House of Lords. Blair claims that Adonis 'was not afraid to think without ideological constraint. He totally "got" New Labour' (Blair, 2010: 266). Indeed, it has been claimed that 'Adonis wielded enormous power and influence in the formulation of New Labour's education policy', and that to a very large extent, 'education policy was determined by Tony Blair and Andrew Adonis' (Chitty, 2009; 138).

The fifth legacy of Thatcherism has been the increasingly explicit linking of education to employment, and the extent to which education is viewed in economic or instrumental terms, both by governments and employers, with the latter's views now accorded much greater respect and reverence than those of teachers and educationalists themselves. For example, since the 1980s, successive secretaries of state for education and prime ministers have exhorted schools (and universities) to be more responsive to the needs of business and employers, this responsiveness to be evinced through the type of courses offered, curriculum, content and the imparting of 'transferable skills' via teaching and assessment.

Moreover, this increasingly close and explicit link between education, the economy, and the needs of employers has been strengthened further by the process of globalization, for this has enabled ministers to legitimize education reforms on the basis of ensuring that Britain has a workforce which can contribute to the requirements of the economy in an increasingly competitive international market. By the same token, ministers have variously emphasized the importance of attracting inward investment by convincing transnational companies that Britain has suitably educated and qualified workers.

Neo-liberalism and globalization have thus yoked education, employment, and the economy closely together in Britain since the 1980s, to the extent that the primary function of schools (and universities) is to provide employers with a suitably qualified or trained workforce, although ministers have variously sought to legitimize education reform in terms of providing children from poor backgrounds with a better quality 'learning experience', in order that their own employment prospects and career opportunities are enhanced. This is in spite of – or perhaps precisely because of – the allegations by some critics of contemporary education reform that socio-economic inequalities are actually becoming wider and more entrenched, and that social mobility is diminishing.

Conclusion

Education reform did not feature prominently during the early stages of the Thatcher premiership, largely because Conservative ministers focused primarily on economic and industrial issues, most notably attempts at curbing inflation and public expenditure, privatizing nationalized industries and emasculating the trade unions. By the late 1980s, however, Thatcher and her closest ministerial colleagues turned their attention to social policies, with a view to extending market principles to education and the NHS, and other public services, while also strengthening managerial authority over professionals in schools and hospitals. The discipline of the market was to be buttressed by the discipline of the NPM, so that teachers and doctors were rendered much more responsive and deferential both to their 'customers' and the new cadre of managers in the public sector, some of whom were appointed by virtue of their background and experience in the private sector. With schools (and hospitals) also opened up to private sector investment and 'partnerships', the hitherto boundaries between the public and private sectors has increasingly become blurred – which has had implications for the much vaunted goals of increasing 'accountability' and 'transparency'.

Although the initial reforms introduced by the third Thatcher government were consolidated by John Major's Conservative administration from

1990 to 1997 (it was during his premiership that Ofsted was established, and school league tables became fetishized), it was the 1997–2010 Blair governments which really ensured the lasting legacy of Thatcherism in the sphere of education policy. New Labour enthusiastically adopted or extended many of the reforms enacted by the Thatcher-Major governments, and invariably invoked the same discourses – markets, competition, choice, accountability, raising standards, confronting 'self-serving' producer interests and prioritizing the wishes of parents and employers.

Of course, this entailed a continuation of the denigration of the teaching profession which had begun (at least in earnest) back in the 1980s. New Labour, just as much as their Conservative predecessors and Ofsted, continued to blame teachers for many educational and social problems, and although, if directly challenged, they would insist that they were only criticizing a minority in the profession, the references to 'bad teachers' and 'failing schools' were so frequent that it often seemed as if teachers en masse were under political attack.

The post-May 2010 Conservative-Liberal Democrat Coalition has further entrenched the Thatcherite legacy in secondary education, with an extension of marketization, in the guise of free schools and more academies, and the associated discourse of parental choice and inter-school competition. There has also been a continued insistence on the need to raise educational standards and improve both literacy and numeracy among pupils, which, in turn, entails stricter managerialist regulation of the teaching profession and either additional, or new, targets set by central government. There have also been further attacks on the alleged failings of teachers and the teaching profession, which in turn serves to legitimize the latest tranche of education reforms, and enables the government to present itself as being 'out there' on the side of dissatisfied parents and employers.

Margaret Thatcher resigned as Conservative leader and prime minister in November 1990, just two years after her government had introduced its first major reform of secondary education. Yet subsequent governments, including – or especially – New Labour, widened and deepened the type of reforms which were first introduced by the 1987–90 Thatcher government, so that what was once viewed as radical is now widely accepted as orthodox by mainstream politicians. So deeply entrenched and hegemonic do these reforms seem to have become that most politicians now seem to accept that 'There is no alternative' to extending markets in those spheres of civil society which have not (yet) been directly privatized. In the realm of education policy (as elsewhere), the legacy of Thatcherism endures – along with the concomitant contradictions and dysfunctionalities.

References

Amann, Roy (2003) 'A Sovietological View of Modern Britain', *The Political Quarterly*, 74(4): 468–80.

Apple, Michael (1989) 'Critical Introduction: Ideology and the State in Education Policy', in Roger Dale (ed.) *The State and Education Policy*. Milton Keynes: Open University Press.

Baker, Kenneth (1993) *The Turbulent Years*. London: Faber.

Ball, Stephen (1990) *Politics and Policy Making in Education* London: Routledge.

Ball, Stephen (1993) Education, Majorism and the 'Curriculum of the Dead', *Curriculum Studies*, 1, 195–214.

BBC News (2012) 'Ofsted Chief Sir Michael Wilshaw: Teachers not Stressed', 10 May, http://www.bbc.co.uk/news/education-18025202.

Birrell, Derek (2009) *The Impact of Devolution on Social Policy*. Cambridge: The Policy Press.

Blair, Tony (2010) *A Journey*. Hutchinson.

Blunkett, David (2001) *Politics and Progress; Renewing Democracy and Civil Society*. London: Politico's.

Bochel, Hugh and Bochel, Catherine (2003) *The UK Social Policy Process*. Basingstoke: Palgrave Macmillan.

Cairney, Paul (2011) *The Scottish Political System since Devolution*. Exeter: Imprint Academic.

Cameron, David (2007) 'The Conservative Approach to Improving Public Services', http://www.conservatives.com/News/Speeches/2007/01/David_Cameron_The_Conservative_approach_to_improving_public_services.aspx. (speech on 26 January).

Chitty, Clyde (2009) *Education Policy in Britain*, 2nd edn. Basingstoke: Palgrave Macmillan.

Clarke, Kenneth (1992) 'Education's Insane Bandwagon Finally goes into the Ditch: an Ideology's Demise allows Common Sense to Return to Schools', *The Sunday Times*, 26 January.

Dale, Roger (1989/90) 'The Thatcher Project in Education: the Case of the City Technology Colleges', *Critical Social Policy*, 9(3): 4–19.

Department for Education and Employment (2000) *Sex and Relationship Education Guidance*. London: Department for Education and Employment.

Desai, Radhika (1994) 'Second-hand Dealers in Ideas: Think-tanks and Thatcherite Hegemony', *New Left Review*, 203, 27–64.

Evans, David T. (1989/90) 'Section 28: Law, Myth and Paradox', *Critical Social Policy*, 9(3): 73–95.

Farrall, Stephen (2006) '"Rolling Back the State": Mrs. Thatcher's Criminological Legacy', *International Journal of the Sociology of Law*, 34: 256–77.

Fergusson, Ross (2000) 'Modernizing Managerialism in Education', in John Clarke, Sharon Gewirtz and Eugene McLaughlin (eds) *New Managerialism, New Welfare?* London: Sage.

Flynn, Norman (2007) *Public Sector Management*, 5th edn. London: Sage.

Gamble, Andrew (1988) *The Free Economy and The Strong State: The Politics of Thatcherism*. Basingstoke: Palgrave Macmillan.

Goldsmith, Michael (1997) 'Changing Patterns of Local Government', *ECPR News*, 9(1).

Gove, Michael (2009) 'A comprehensive programme for state education', http://www.conservatives.com/News/Speeches/2009/11/Michael_Gove_A_comprehensive_programme_for_state_education.aspx, speech on 6 November 2009.

Hill, Michael (2009) *The Public Policy Process*, 5th edn. Harlow: Pearson Longman.

Hillgate Group, The (1986) *Whose Schools? A Radical Manifesto*. The Hillgate Group.

Hillgate Group, The (1987) *The Reform of British Education: From Principles to Practice*, Claridge Press.

Hood, Christopher (1991) 'A Public Management for all Seasons', Public Administration, 69(1): 3–19.

Hood, Christopher (1995) 'Contemporary Public Management: A New Global Paradigm?', *Public Policy and Administration*, 10(2): 104–17.

Jones, Ken (2003) *Education in Britain: 1944 to the Present*. Cambridge: Polity.

Judd, Judith (1989) 'Thatcher Changes Course of History', *Observer*, 20 August.

Labour Party, The (1995), *Diversity and Excellence: A New Partnership for Schools*.

Lawton, Denis and Chitty, Clyde ((1987) 'Towards a National Curriculum', *Forum*, 30(1): 4–6.

Maclure, Stuart (1988) *Education Re-formed: A Guide to the Education Reform Act 1988*, Hodder & Stoughton.

Mandelson, Peter and Liddle, Roger (1996) *The Blair Revolution: Can New Labour Deliver?* London: Faber.

Major, John (1992) *The Next Phase of Conservatism: The Privatisation of Choice*, Conservative Political Centre.

Major, John (1993) *Conservatism in the 1990s: Our Common Purpose*, Carlton Club/Conservative Political Centre.

Major, John (1997) *Our Nation's Future*. Conservative Political Centre.

Mansell, Warwick (2007) *Education by Numbers: The Tyranny of Testing*. London: Politico's.

Mansell, Warwick (2009) 'New Labour has learnt well from Thatcher', *Times Education Supplement*, 17 April.

Moran, Michael (2003) *The British Regulatory State: High Modernism and Hyper-Innovation*. Oxford: Oxford University Press.

Patten, John (1995) *Things to Come*. London: Sinclair-Stevenson.

Perry, Baroness and Dorrell, Stephen (2006) *The Well-Being of the Nation: Interim Report of the Public Service Improvement Policy Group*. The Conservative Party.

Phillips, Robert (1996) 'History Teaching, Cultural Restorationism and National Identity in England and Wales', *Curriculum Studies*, 4(3): 385–99.

Pierre, Jon and Stoker, Gerry (2000) 'Towards Multi-Level Governance', in Patrick Dunleavy, Andrew Gamble, Ian Holliday and Gillian Peele (eds) *Developments in Politics 6*. Basingstoke: Macmillan.

Pollitt, Christopher (1990) *Managerialism and the Public Services*. Oxford: Blackwell.

Pollitt, Christopher (2003) *The Essential Public Manager*. Maidenhead: Open University Press.

Power, Michael (1997) *The Audit Society: Rituals of Verification*. Oxford: Oxford University Press.

Rhodes, R.A.W. (1997) *Understanding Governance: Policy Networks, Governance, Reflexivity and Accountability*. Buckingham: Open University Press.

Richards, David and Smith, Martin J. (2002) *Governance and Public Policy in the UK*. Oxford: Oxford University Press.

Riddell, Peter (1991) *The Thatcher Era and Its Legacy*. Oxford: Blackwell.

Sherman, Alfred (2005) *Paradoxes of Power: Reflections on the Thatcher Interlude*, ed. Mark Garnett. Exeter: Imprint Academic.

Smithers, Alan (2001) 'Education Policy', in Anthony Seldon (ed.) *The Blair Effect*. London: Little, Brown and Co.

Squire, Robin (1995) 'Speech to the Secondary Heads' Association', *Department for Education and Employment News*, 234/95, 18 October.

Stoker, Gerry (2004) *Transforming Local Governance: From Thatcherism to New Labour*, Basingstoke: Palgrave Macmillan.

Thatcher, Margaret (1987) 'Speech to Conservative Party Conference', 9 October, http://www.margaretthatcher.org/document/106941.

Thatcher, Margaret (1993) *The Downing Street Years* London: HarperCollins.

Thatcher, Margaret (1995) *The Path to Power*. London: HarperCollins.

Timmins, Nicholas (2001) *The Five Giants*. London: HarperCollins.

Willetts, David (2006) Quoted in *The Guardian*, 'Tories Admit Past Mistakes over Public Service Workers', 6 September.

Wilson, David (2000) 'New Labour, New Local Governance?' in Robert Pyper and Lynton Robins (ed.) *United Kingdom Governance*. Basingstoke: Macmillan.

Woodhead, Chris (2003) *Class War: The State of British Education*. London: Time Warner.

Commentary

English passions: Thatcherism and schooling

KEN JONES

Peter Dorey is right to identify marketization and managerialism as central features of Thatcherism in school education. Bequeathed to subsequent generations by the 1988 Education Reform Act, these are policy legacies that that have been invested in, and developed, by all governments since. He is right, also, to trace alongside these neo-liberal emphases, a set of neo-conservative preoccupations with authority and cohesion that under-pinned aspects of policy, and policy rhetoric, in the 1980s, and continue to do so in the post-2010 period of coalition government.

Europe

In these senses, we can think of Thatcherism as a matrix for an evolving policy ensemble that we could call English neo-liberalism. We would then need to establish what this 'Englishness' consists of. Many researchers have noted the growth, since the 1980s, of a global policy orthodoxy in education, developed through the OECD, the EU, the World Bank, and shaped in broad terms by neo-liberal principles (Ball, 2008; Lingard, Laval and Weber, 2002; Rizvi and Lingard, 2000). In Jenny Ozga's summary, there was in post-1993 Europe:

> A shift toward decentralisation, devolution and deregulation as key principles of restructuring. In education – to a greater or lesser degree depending on context – these changes enhanced institutional autonomy and school-based management and were accompanied by enhanced parental choice of school, and by greater competition between schools ... These policy developments reflected the dominance of neo-liberal principles in the design of reform and restructuring programmes, so that decentralisation and devolution were pursued with the aim of enabling the market to operate effectively.
>
> (Ozga 2009: 150–1)

It is thus possible to speak of principles of deregulation, loosely under-stood as school autonomy and marketization – as, in short, 'global'. From this point of view, England might be seen as one local instance of a general tendency, and the significance of any peculiarly national characteristics thereby diminished.

The same point might be made about the cultural politics of European education. There is much to suggest that there is nothing specifically English about cultural conservatism. The 2004 ban on the wearing of the 'veil' in French schools has been replicated in Belgium and parts of Germany. Angela Merkel's pronouncement that German multiculturalism had failed (Weaver, 2010), the Berlusconi government's attempt to teach migrants separately from classes of native Italian speakers (Jones, 2009), and the French National Assembly's 2005 requirement that lycées should teach the 'positive values of colonialism' all speak of nationalisms that in some ways are even more sharply formulated than those of English education. In the same frame, we could put the tendency of European parties of the Right to define themselves against the spirit of '1968', and the disorder it brought to education (Jones et al., 2008). Luc Ferry, the academic who became minister of education in the Raffarin government of 2002–4, made his philosophical name with a critique of 'la pensée 68'. Mariastella Gelmini, Berlusconi's education minister, regarded the 40 years since 1968 as a reprehensible period that needed 'dismantling' (Barzano and Grimaldi, 2013). Thus, when Michael Gove, Secretary of State for Education, claimed that it was in the 1960s that 'the role and authority of the teacher and traditional subject knowledge had been undermined' he was not lacking for company (Gove, 2013).

However, for Ozga, and for others, the recognition of a general tendency is accompanied by an insistence that England has a special place within it. 'The reliance on market mechanisms was especially strong in England', writes Ozga, supporting Seddon's view (1996) that the relationship between 'markets and the English' had become a binding one. The same can be said of managerialism, which Dorey defines in terms of 'stronger bureaucratic hierarchies, coupled with the imposition of sundry perfor-mance indicators and targets [and] a new regime of inspections and audits'. Here again, England is exceptional. Grek et al., reviewing forms of edu-cational regulation across Northern Europe, describe England as 'the most advanced regulatory state' (2009: 121); Ozga suggests that though the shift towards such forms of regulation is common across the EU, England represents an 'extreme version' of it (2009: 151).

Likewise, in relation to cultural conservatism, England is unusual in the consistency, across more than three decades, with which governments have sought to distance themselves from a period when teachers and policy-makers attempted in the name of access, modernization, and equal opportunity, to change inherited patterns of learning, teaching, assessment, and selection (Jones, 2003). Although they have differed over questions of multiculturalism, both Labour and Conservatives have implemented a curriculum organized around various motifs popularized by the Right – phonics, basic skills, ability grouping, and frequent testing.

To explain why England's status in these policy areas is 'advanced' and 'extreme', we need some understanding of English neo-liberalism's path dependency. Thatcher, as Dorey shows, was convinced that the Department of Education and Science was a socialist apparatus, committed to equality. She was not alone in this belief. A similar notion, that the school system had been captured by producer interests, operating in tandem with a liberal establishment to depress standards and 'put the inherited values of their society up for sale' (Norman, 1977), animated the pamphlet-writers and think tanks that proliferated in the 1970s and 1980s: the Black Papers, the National Council for Educational Standards, the Hillgate Group, the Adam Smith Institute and so on (Jones, 1989). These organizations were the drivers of a Conservative policy that rose into political ascendant. They supplied it with a discourse, identified points of attack and sketched new policy frameworks. The effect of their work was to make Conservatism militant.

Conservatism presented education as being in a state of emergency, a state that required strong intervention by government to restore the teaching of 'moral values' and 'basic educational skills' and to destroy the influences that led to schools being centres of 'political indoctrination' and 'sexual propaganda' (Conservative Party, 1987). Given this analysis, policy change proceeded via confrontation. Institutions, organizations and practices which were thought responsible for the subversion of schooling were made the objects of media scandal, or closed down, like the Inner London Education Authority, or subjected to stronger discipline. The high point of this approach was reached in the 1980s, but governments, especially Conservative governments, have remained permanently on the alert since then to suppress signs of a re-emergence of past deviations. Michael Gove was especially watchful of this danger, writing for the *Daily Mail* an article headlined, 'I refuse to surrender to the Marxist teachers hell-bent on destroying our schools: Education Secretary berates "the new enemies of promise" for opposing his plans' (Gove, 2013). From a position such as Gove's, it becomes necessary to push policies as far as they will go, or else the enemies of promise will triumph.

A tendency on the part of education-focused politicians towards sharp political contestation, against opponents whom it is important to defeat rather than accommodate, has thus been one of the legacies of Thatcherism. Conversely, the world of education has never accepted market managerialism, still less cultural conservatism, as basic orientating principles. The effect on English policy-making has been to deconsensualize it, a feature that seems to me one of Thatcherism's strongest legacies; questions not just of resources, but of forms of organization and curricular principles, are permanently at stake. English neo-liberalism is shaped by its encounter with that which it tries to suppress.

Britain

In the British context, Thatcherism and its legacies appear very strongly as peculiarities of the English. Since the devolution of educational authority to Edinburgh, Cardiff, and Belfast, beginning in 1999, the differences in orientation have become plainer. In none of the Celtic countries have global policy orthodoxies been without influence. The involvement of private companies in education provision, decentralization and performance management have been features of post-devolution Scotland (Grek et al., 2009; Poole and Mooney, 2006); Northern Ireland has adopted much of the policy repertoire of decentralization, school autonomy and school improvement (McGuinness, 2012); Wales, especially since the results of the Programme for International Student Assessment (PISA) in 2009, which revealed it as the worst-performing of UK countries, has moved towards a system of annual grading of schools with closure as a penalty for low performance (Hughes, 2010).

Researchers are unequivocal in their judgement, however, that despite these influences, policy, discourse and practice in the three countries are markedly different from England. Neo-liberalism may be a global force, but countries encounter it on different terms. Gareth Elwyn Jones (2006) claimed that post-devolution policy in Wales was inflected by historically rooted social democratic emphases on equality, and by acceptance that government should work with, rather than against, the 'policy community' of education. Arnot and Ozga (2010), analysing the politics of the SNP government, make a similar point. They identify a policy narrative that has as an 'overarching theme':

> the pursuit of economic prosperity, or more recently, survival, in order to achieve a 'wealthier and fairer, healthier, safer and stronger, smarter and greener Scotland' that can be easily understood and referenced across the different public and social policy fields. Importantly, it links wealth and fairness; economic growth is defined as a public good.
>
> (Arnot and Ozga, 2010: 338)

These emphases are not only discursive: educational organization is not marketized, managerialism tends to be related to consensual goals, and national culture is configured in curricular terms of inclusivity and diversity.

These national differences were in some senses the products of national histories. In other ways, they were the unintended results of a Thatcherite period of militancy. The impulses towards confrontation that made Thatcher's government able to shape the field of English education around its project, had the opposite effect in other countries. The introduction of a national curriculum in Wales, for instance, served to codify cultural and historical differences with England – a codification that was bound to be in tension with English cultural conservatism. More immediately, when Scottish teachers, in the mid-1980s, went on strike over pay, their cause was seen as a national one. 'Could it be', asked an official of the EIS, the teachers' trade union, 'that George Younger is no longer Secretary of State for Scotland, but the minister applying English education policies to the Scottish education system?' (Ross, 1986: 85). Nationalism linked to united teacher action was a potent strategy. Teachers retained their negotiating rights, and union influence remained strong. Subsequent aspects of the Conservative programme were muted in Scotland: no national curriculum was introduced; attempts were defeated to introduce the universal testing of primary school students in ways that would allow the construction of league tables of school success and failure. If anything, the Conservative effort to export the English model to a semi-autonomous country, where levels of support for the Right were very low, only increased the demands for a break with London. Thatcherism, through the medium of education policy, contributed to a weakening of the union.

An unsteady tribunal

Foucault's 1979 suggestion that neo-liberalism creates 'a kind of permanent economic tribunal' from whose perspective every area of social practice is monitored, judged and shaped, was prophetic – and certainly more insightful than that of his English Conservative contemporaries. It is doubtful whether the collection of literary intellectuals, philosophers, Hayekians and anti-communists who constituted the vanguard of the Right imagined the iron cage of marketized managerialism that would be constructed on the basis of their passions. Yet contemporary English neo-liberalism is still marked by their way of doing educational politics. Dogmatic and agonistic, fighting on both cultural and institutional fronts, aiming to rewrite the national curriculum and to privatize the management of as many schools as possible, the policy of the Cameron government is nothing if not the heir of Thatcherism. This adds to rather than mitigates the unsteadiness of its policies. Neo-liberalism has unmade conditions that enabled a certain kind of collective security, and required individuals, possessing very different levels of economic and cultural resources, to find new means of coping with matters of employment, social care, housing – and education. In response to this situation, the devolved polities of Britain have attempted to devise a politics that presents collective ways of responding to them. Neo-liberalism in England has no such interest. There lies its distinctive feature – and, probably, its weakness.

References

Arnot, M. and Ozga, J. (2010) 'Education and Nationalism: the Discourse of Education Policy in Scotland', *Discourse: Studies in the Cultural Politics of Education*, 31(3): 335–50.

Conservative Party (1987) 'The Next Moves Forward: the Manifesto of the Conservative Party': http://www.conservative-party.net/manifestos/1987/1987-conservative-manifesto.shtml

Barzanò, G. and Grimaldi, Emiliano (2013) 'Discourses of Merit. The Hot Potato of Teacher Evaluation in Italy', *Journal of Education Policy* (published online).

Gove, M. (2013) 'I refuse to Surrender to the Marxist Teachers Hellbent on Destroying our Schools' (23 March): http://www.dailymail.co.uk/debate/article-2298146/I-refuse-surrender-Marxist-teachers-hell-bent-destroying-schools-Education-Secretary-berates-new-enemies-promise-opposing-plans.html#ixzz2QG0uDtzp

Grek, S., Lawn, M., Lingard, B., and Varjo, J. (2009) 'North by Northwest: Quality Assurance and Evaluation Processes in European Education', *Journal of Education Policy*, 24(2): 121–33.

Hughes, S. (2010) *Has Devolution Delivered for Students?* Research Service, National Assembly for Wales: http://www.assemblywales.org/ki-018.pdf

Jones, G.E. (2006) 'Education and Nationhood in Wales: An Historiographical Analysis', *Journal of Educational Administration and History*, 38(3): 263–77.

Jones, K. (1989) *Right Turn: The Conservative Revolution in Education*. London: Radius.

Jones, K. (2003) *Education in Britain: from 1944 to the Present*. Cambridge: Polity Press.

Laval, C. and Weber, L. (2002) *Le nouvel ordre éducatif mondial.OMC, Banque mondiale, OCDE, Commission Européene*. Paris: Syllepse.

McGuinness, S. (2012) 'Education Policy in Northern Ireland: a Review', *Italian Journal of Sociology of Education*, 4(1): 205–37.

Norman, E.R. (1977) "The Threat to Religion', in C.B. Cox and R. Boyson (eds) Black Paper. London: Temple Smith.

Ozga, J. (2009) 'Governing Education Through Data in England: From Regulation to Self-evaluation', *Journal of Education Policy*, 24(2): 149–61.

Poole, L. and Mooney, G. (2006) 'Privatizing Education in Scotland? New Labour, Modernization and 'Public' Services', *Critical Social Policy*, 26(3): 562–86.

Rizvi, F. and Lingard, B. (2000) 'Globalization and Education: Complexities and Contingencies', *Educational Theory*, 50(4): 419–26.

Ross, D. (1986) *An Unlikely Anger: Scottish Teachers in Action*. Edinburgh: Mainstream.

Seddon, T. (1996) 'Markets and the English: Reconceptualising Educational Restructuring as Institutional Design', *British Journal of Sociology of Education*, 8(2): 165–85.

Weaver, M. (2010) 'Angela Merkel: German Multiculturalism has "Utterly Failed"'. *The Guardian* (17 October).

5
The housing legacy of Thatcherism

ALAN MURIE

Housing policy was a key element in the Conservatives' electoral success in 1979 and the mobilization of a cross-class electoral base. The right for council tenants to buy the dwelling that they lived in, which formed an emblematic policy that helped to define Thatcherism, was introduced immediately following election, rewarding a key section of the electorate and changed patterns of property ownership. The right to buy (RTB) delivered a multiple contribution to the Thatcherite project by selling public sector assets, generating capital receipts, reducing public expenditure and expanding home ownership. Early action to deregulate private renting and cut housing capital expenditure further contributed to a shift from a managed- to a market-based approach to housing. This emerged step by step with subsequent changes in housing finance and subsidy, further deregulation of private renting and the promotion of housing associations.

The policy detail associated with the RTB emerged from an era of state-subsidized home ownership. It formed part of a strengthened pattern of rights for council tenants and adopted the welfare paternalist language of exclusive rights, bureaucratic determination of entitlements and explicit grants (discounts) that protected purchasers from market costs. Later deregulations and privatizations were more compatible with freeing the market and liberal economics but the package as a whole represented continuity with earlier practices and grew out of long-standing debates within the Conservative party. There were precursors and prototypes for individual policies (selling council houses, modifying subsidies, deregulating housing finance, and private renting) but what emerged was innovative and distinctive. The quantitative shift in sales of dwellings and cuts in council building and housing public expenditure was unprecedented. Terminating local discretion over council house sales and sustained and concerted action across housing policy was designed to dismantle local

143

authorities' role, undermine mutualism and leave market processes to determine what happened in housing.

Housing was prominent in governments' agendas between 1979 and 1997 and merits discussion in any consideration of the legacy of Thatcherism. Housing policy evolved over 18 years but nothing introduced after 1979 reversed the approach established at the outset. Although this identifies the whole period with Thatcherite policy approaches three phases of policy are evident. The first embedded the most distinctively Thatcherite housing agenda of privatization, demunicipalization and deregulation affecting home ownership and private renting. Before the flagship RTB policy was incorporated in legislation, a general consent, issued immediately following election in 1979, enabled council dwellings to be sold on the same terms, and increased discretionary sales. Policies on council rents, management and maintenance reduced the attractiveness of council housing and strengthened the appeal of the flagship policy while changes in planning and council house building were designed to facilitate private development.

These policies continued to deliver until 1997 and beyond. But, once the new approach was embedded, a second policy phase introduced complex reforms of housing subsidy and housing benefit and deregulated housing finance and private renting. A third phase, after 1986, responded to the failure of previous changes to trigger sufficient private investment in new building or private renting and housing associations' repositioning themselves as vehicles to channel private finance into rented housing. Government relocated housing associations from the public to the private sector and paved the way for further demunicipalization through housing stock transfers from councils to housing associations. This introduced private finance into a newly defined social rented sector. Housing associations, as not-for-profit bodies, could borrow private finance because of access to government grants and regulation by a government agency – the Housing Corporation.

Context

Housing policy between 1979 and 1997, and since, has been influenced by critiques from different traditions within the Conservative party and elsewhere. The encouragement of home ownership appealed to a neo-conservative view of the family and family home and severing dependency

144

on the state. The Conservative promise of a property owning democracy had not initially been predicated on housing but expanding home ownership offered an opportunity to realize that goal. At the same time all political parties were responding to the distinctive managed, regulated housing legacy from 60 years of UK housing. The maturation of the housing market put the post-war consensus of support for both home ownership and council housing under strain. The absence of political support for private landlordism was long-established and periodically reinforced by evidence of low standards and exploitation. Private renting was the tenure of last resort and both home ownership and council housing, as aspirational tenures, expanded at its expense. However, as private renting declined, there was less scope for home ownership to expand through transfers from it. The ambition to expand home owner-ship increasingly called into question the share and growth of council housing and supplemented critiques of municipal socialism, the waiting list society and inefficient subsidy systems. By 1976 a Labour govern-ment was referring to home ownership as the natural tenure and the Conservative party, which competed with Labour to champion council house building in the 1950s, increasingly adopted a residual approach. When some local housing authorities increased council house sales in the 1960s Conservatives regarded this as a vote winner capable of breaking Labour's appeal to council tenants (Forrest and Murie, 1990; Murie, 1975).

State intervention over sixty years had left what was, by international standards, an unusual legacy. Public sector housing had expanded rapidly after the introduction of Exchequer subsidies in 1919 and especially after 1945. By 1979 some one in three dwellings were owned by local authorities and new towns (not-for-profit housing associations and cooperatives were minor partners). Council housing comprised older, debt-free, stock that cross-subsidized high-debt stock. Its market value was well in excess of outstanding debt. The stock represented a long-term manageable collective asset enabling housing to be provided at rents below market levels. The cash expenditure needed to bridge the gap between costs of provision and rent charged was much lower than would be needed to bridge the gap to market rents. Political debate ignored the underlying strength of council housing finances and its established position as a high quality alternative to market provision. Instead, it tended to focus on the inefficiency or unfairness of subsidizing the rents of higher income tenants, to rail against object subsidies and bureaucratically determined rents as distorting the market and to extol the merits of choice in a deregulated market. The collective public housing legacy was a dwelling stock attracting high demand and high satisfaction. The ageing of the sector and the development of medium- and high-rise flats damaged its reputation but it was far from being the last resort. There was competition to access most council housing and the purchasers of council homes before, as well as after 1979, included households that could have afforded to buy elsewhere but had remained tenants because they valued their home and neighbourhood more than being a homeowner. Privatization would prove popular because what the state had built was popular.

Housing policy in the 1970s also involved managing the private sector. Established private tenants generally benefited from security of tenure and regulated rents and, since 1972, rent allowances had been available for all private tenants. Building societies, which dominated lending for house purchase, were mutual organizations subject to distinctive legal and regulatory measures. The growth of home ownership was encouraged through tax reliefs and local authorities were encouraged to adopt a comprehensive housing policy: using powers to buy land, build for rent or sale, acquire existing dwellings for different purposes including clearance or improvement, lend for house purchase, lend to housing associations, provide grants for dwelling repairs, improvements, conversions or adaptations and respond to homelessness, and housing need. Between the wars, and after 1952, ministers enabled councils to decide whether to sell council houses, and many had done so.

By the 1970s the private rented sector was too small to meet the needs of the lowest income groups – which increasingly relied on public housing. At the same time long waiting times for council housing made home ownership attractive for new households able to access mortgages. The outcome was not a polarized tenure structure. The poorest households were present in all tenures and often stayed put even if their incomes rose. In 1980 some 18 per cent of households in the highest three income deciles and 34 per cent of households in the middle four income deciles were council tenants (Murie, 2006). Households in the lowest income deciles were most concentrated in private renting and the pattern of social segregation in terms of class and race related to tenure but also to the history, reputation and attractiveness of parts of tenures.

In 1979 this managed housing system involved a variety of forms of state intervention, regulation, collective provision and mutual organization. Although its role in housing the poorest households had increased, the state did not provide a safety net exclusively for the poorest but offered various services for different groups and provided rented housing that was generally better than in the private sector. The managers of both state and regulated private sectors were significant urban gatekeepers criticized for their cultural and professional practices, paternalism and discrimination, but the system provided much more than an ambulance service within a free market system. Esping-Andersen's (1990) depiction of the UK as close to such a minimalist liberal welfare state model was based on analysis that made little reference to housing. Rather than being the wobbly pillar of the welfare state, housing, in some places in Britain, was the robust, redistributive pinnacle of the local welfare state, operating alongside a wobbly national welfare system and successfully competing with the private sector.

Thatcherite policy

Not everything in housing changed under the governments of Margaret Thatcher and John Major (see e.g. Malpass, 1990; Malpass and Murie, 1999; Mullins and Murie, 2006). Conservatives regarded housing policies and particularly the RTB as having significantly contributed to electoral success in 1979 and as a continuing electoral asset. Housing cutbacks accounted for 75 per cent or more of all public spending reductions in 1980 and mandatory legislation gave almost all public sector tenants the right to purchase their homes with more generous discounts than under previous discretionary policies (Jones and Murie, 2006). Although charitable housing associations successfully lobbied to escape the RTB, the Housing Corporation used this legislation to approve the sale of co-ownership housing and effectively wiped this sector out. Home ownership was further encouraged through tax reliefs (peaking in value in 1990), building for sale, shared ownership, rent to mortgage, homesteading and improvement for sale schemes. The RTB delivered the largest capital receipts of any privatization programme (almost £27 billion between 1979 and 1996) and facilitated wider taxation and public expenditure plans. It was enhanced by legislation in 1984 and in 1986 and enabled some 2 million households to buy. Legislation in 1980 also changed subsidies and enabled government to raise council rents and restrict expenditure on management, repairs and maintenance. Over time, local authorities ceased to build, buy land or provide mortgage loans and retreated from comprehensive, locally responsive housing strategies. In part, this reflected the nationalization of housing policy. Central government operated tighter controls over what councils could and had to do. Increased rents in council, housing association and private sectors, along with changes in employment and incomes, generated more claims for rent rebates and allowances. The Social Security and Housing Benefits Act (1982) unified existing schemes for assistance with housing costs and contributed to shifting from general 'bricks and mortar' assistance towards benefits based on individual tests of needs and incomes.

New shorthold and assured tenancies introduced in 1980 were designed to revive private renting by reducing tenants' rights and enabling landlords to set rents and regain possession more easily. The Building Societies Act (1986) enabled building societies to compete with banks in the personal finance sector and to offer unsecured loans and a full home-buying service, including estate agency, conveyancing and insurance. Financial deregulation changed practices in housing finance and increased lending to private landlords and housing associations. Although lending for private renting was slow to respond, the capacity to borrow on wholesale markets ended the need for mortgage rationing. Banks and building societies increased their mortgage lending but increased capacity and competition to lend added to inflationary pressures.

The distinctive approach to housing policy established in the first two Thatcher administrations was not reversed by subsequent governments but some responses diluted and then diverted policy. The housing association movement had successfully orchestrated opposition to the inclusion of charitable housing associations under the RTB in 1980 and again in 1982. This subverted government intention and left most housing associations able to develop strategies without their stock being eroded through sales. Some individual housing associations, seeing their ambitions in relation to new development thwarted by major reductions in housing capital expenditure, independently explored ways of using private finance, along with their reserves, to pursue their objectives. These associations, faced with government policy that constrained their continued growth, reacted by taking initiatives to break the mould and successfully negotiated private sector loans. Following this, they persuaded a reluctant Department for the Environment to endorse private financing and the Treasury was persuaded to agree that private borrowing would not count as public expenditure. Malpass (2000) discusses this as the incorporation of 'independent' housing associations as agents of government. Whether or not this overarching discourse is accepted, associations were not passive. They helped to shape subsequent arrangements acceptable to government – with new housing association investment funded partly by private lenders. Housing association lettings after 1989 were assured tenancies (escaping the constraints of fair rents and, for non-charitable associations, the right to buy). Housing associations' capacity increased and with private renting they formed an 'independent' rented sector – contrasting with the public sector (Malpass, 2000; 174; Murie, 2008a). At least initially, and until buy-to-let landlords increased, housing associations became the standard bearers for alternatives to state provision. Privately financed housing associations required less subsidy than local authorities and their private loans were outside public expenditure – they could build more dwellings than local housing authorities for a given level of public expenditure. Every pound of public expenditure levered in additional private finance in a way that could not apply to local authorities. But the resulting rents and, consequently, continuing housing benefit costs were higher.

The Housing Act (1988) introduced new private tenancies, changed the financial regime and tenancy arrangements for housing associations and introduced Tenants' Choice. This reflected government's new aspiration to enable supposedly dissatisfied council tenants to choose their landlord. However, doubts about the suitability and integrity of disposals to private landlords led ministers to determine that disposals must be to regulated landlords. The emerging programme to transfer council stock was not part of the original Thatcherite policy. It empowered regulated housing associations as the best vehicle for new affordable rented housing and for giving council tenants a choice between their existing landlord and an alternative. Tenants' Choice transmogrified into a local authority initiated policy to transfer stock, facilitate private investment in rented housing, generate receipts and pay off debt. Almost no transfers were initiated by tenants and almost all were to housing associations. The result was consistent with government's dislike of municipal housing, and this de-municipalization continued through the remaining period of Conservative government and was adopted energetically by its Labour successor. Government set out the criteria under which it would consent to stock transfers with the Housing Corporation, Scottish Homes and Housing for Wales responsible for approving, scrutinizing, regulating and monitoring prospective and new landlords. Transfers usually triggered rapid rent increases – often alongside investment and improved management and repairs. This generated increased housing benefit expenditure and ministers had accepted that restructuring the ownership of housing involved discounting asset sales and increased social security support. The process of transfer was planned and programmed to take account of financial consequences. Both of these elements could be contrasted with concerns to move to market pricing and to reduce public expenditure.

Deregulation failed to generate significant new construction but higher rents and housing benefits added to the poverty trap for lower income tenants. The formula was not working from a housing market, economic or public expenditure point of view. Although housing benefit was adjusted downwards by referring to regional average rents rather than meeting 100 per cent of rents charged in all cases, the government concluded (DoE, 1995) that social rented housing was the most cost-effective way to provide long-term housing for low income households. Subsidizing social landlords to charge below-market rents was cheaper than paying housing benefit on market rents: it also reduced dependency on benefits, improved work incentives and increased the prospect of breaking out of benefit (1995: 26). While levels of house building remained low changes in housing benefit and private tenants' rights increased housing insecurity.

The legacy of Thatcherite policy

Assessing the legacy from policy is not straightforward and is not the same as an evaluation focused on the expressed aims of policy and whether they were achieved. Some immediate outputs from policy changes are temporary or superficial but the concept of legacy focuses on sustained effects that enable or limit what happens in the longer term. Consequently, this chapter refers to lasting outcomes that reshaped the market, the governance of housing and households' opportunities and attitudes. The discussion refers to outcomes that can be directly linked to policy changes (for example, changes in ownership of housing) and more complex outcomes involving other factors in addition to policy change.

Ownership

Between 1979 and 1997 the housing stock increased (by almost 3 million dwellings), home ownership expanded (by 14 percentage points), and the local authority sector declined from housing almost one in three households, to housing fewer than one in five (Tables 5.1 and 5.2). Council house sales, stock transfer and low levels of new construction and acquisition combined to reduce council housing for the first time since 1919.

Table 5.1 Dwellings by tenure UK, 1976–97

	All dwellings (000s)	Owner occupied %	Local authority %	Housing association %	Private rented %
1976	20,608	53.8	31.6	14.8	
1981	21,586	56.4	30.4	2.2	11.0
1986	22,600	61.5	26.1	2.5	9.9
1991	23,550	66.6	21.8	3.1	8.5
1997	24,721	67.8	17.9	4.6	9.6

Source: DCLG

Table 5.2 Households* by tenure England, 1981–2008

	All households (000s)	Owner occupied %	Social rented %	*Housing Association (dwellings) %	*Local authority (dwellings) %	Private rented %
1981	17,225	57.2	31.7	2.3	26.8	11.1
1991	19,309	67.6	23.0	3.1	19.8	9.4
1997	19,877	68.6	21.0	4.8	16.5	10.5
2008	21,407	68.3	17.7	9.2	8.3	13.9

Source: DCLG Table 801

* Household data refers to a combined social rented tenure because households do not accurately distinguish between local authority and housing association tenure. This split is consequently based on data for dwellings.

Between December 1988 and March 1997, 54 local authorities in England transferred their housing stock of around 250,000 dwellings. These transfers together with private financing, facilitated housing associations' growth. In spite of reductions in tenants' rights, rising rents and the business expansion scheme (BES), the private rented sector declined until 1989 and only increased slightly by 1997. This increase was affected by rising demand from a greatly expanded population of full-time students, changes in the scale and nature of immigration and lenders' increased funding of buy-to-let mortgages (Kemp, 2009). In 1988, 59 per cent of lettings in the private rented sector had been regulated. By 1997/98 this figure was 9 per cent. Assured tenancies over this period rose from 4 per cent to 66 per cent.

Most of the growth of home ownership was attributable to some 2 million RTB purchases by 1997. Purchasers were typically more affluent, middle-aged tenants living in attractive properties and likely to have remained as tenants had they not exercised the RTB. Most bought with no intention of moving or making a speculative gain and purchased with a bank or building society mortgage that was low relative to property value (because of discounts). A new cohort of borrowers emerged with a transfer of debt from public to private sectors. The best properties in the best locations sold most and this pattern along with the lack of new council building reconcentrated council housing in less attractive urban estates, flats and non-traditional dwellings. RTB sales benefited the existing generation, which had graduated to valuable locations and properties at the expense of households awaiting the opportunity to succeed them as tenants. Because the receipts from sales were used to reduce local authorities' debt and then to replace the general need for additional local government borrowing, they were rarely used for housing related activities. Until Labour's Decent Homes policy after 1997, receipts grew without being used to address the backlog in repairs or increasing homelessness.

If we move beyond the generation directly affected by policy, the complexity of the legacy increases. Some growth in home ownership proved temporary as some sold council houses were resold to private renting (with fewer to social renting). The proportions involved vary between places: in parts of London around 25 per cent had become privately rented by 2002 (Jones and Murie, 2006) and on large council estates in Birmingham up to 40 per cent of growth in private ownership was private renting (Murie, 2008b). One perspective is that the RTB temporarily inflated the level of home ownership: substantial subsidies (discounted prices) inflated effective demand for house purchase. In subsequent transactions, at market prices, putative owner-occupiers have no equivalent subsidy and buy-to-let purchasers could prove willing and able to pay more. What purported to be a populist response to the demand for home ownership became a two-stage transfer. Initial privatization was a state subsidized transfer from collective to individual ownership, not exposed to market processes. In the subsequent commodification stage transfers to a deregulated private rented sector neither matched household aspirations nor politicians' commitments to home ownership and responsible renting. Deregulation eventually enabled increasing incomes to be capitalized in property and increased multiple dwelling ownership. At the other extreme, the opportunities available to lower income households were reduced by continuing housing shortage, the smaller size of the social rented sector and house price inflation.

The assumption that the RTB would leave an uncomplicated legacy of expanded home ownership needs modification in view of subsequent transfers to rental tenures. The dismantling of council housing and co-ownership also stretched the home ownership sector and altered its price profile, its geography and its stratification (see Dorling, Chapter 8 in this collection, on other matters relating to geographical shifts during this period). Sales affected the neighbourhood attributes associated with parts of the home ownership sector – ownership in mixed and minority tenure environments is marketed and valued differently from elsewhere. The method of expansion of home ownership added to its differentiation and increased the attention given to which parts of the home ownership sector conferred status, creditworthiness or realizable wealth.

The RTB and promotion of home ownership reduced collective investment designed to provide for households in housing need and placed the emphasis on individuals making provision for themselves as they would with other commodities. In this sense it dismantled the shared 'insurance' against housing shortage and exclusion, changed the pattern of household opportunity and increased risk. The financial strength and asset base that was the collective legacy from previous public investment in housing and could potentially support an attractive alternative to private sector provision was dismantled. It terminated further progression towards a low-debt, mature sector able to provide high quality housing at affordable rents without subsidy. This reduced the possibility of developing a sustainable alternative to high-cost private provision and profoundly weakened the council sector's capacity to respond to homelessness, meet housing need and redistribute opportunity. The remnant council sector was less attractive and varied than previously.

Thatcherite policies changed the size of the public sector and further narrowed its social base. Residualization of council housing was identifiable before 1979. The decline in private renting reduced its capacity to house the poorest households and both the pool of demand for council housing and the characteristics of new council tenants changed. This happened irrespective of local allocation policies. Greater targeting of council housing, especially owing to the decline of private renting strengthened the fit between council housing and income, employment status and occupation. However, as long as the sector housed 30 per cent or more of all households it would provide more than residual welfare housing. It is the combination of shrinking and targeting that dismantled this earlier vision. The relabelling of public housing as social housing partly reflected a narrower social role but the policies adopted further concentrated poverty, with vulnerable, transient and 'troublesome' households in areas with problems. This legacy would only prove temporary if there was a prospect of rebuilding the share and reach of public sector housing. But this was almost impossible to imagine in view of the discourses around council housing and public expenditure and the erosion of the asset base that could have cross-subsidized growth and been a potential platform for expansion. Even if the political debate had not been reset by Thatcherite policies there was no going back. Once transferred out former council houses were too expensive to buy back. The financing of later expansion through acquisition or new construction would require new subsidy up front or require housing benefit to assist with the higher rents needed to cover costs. And where social rented housing was a better way of providing affordable housing than higher rent private provision, housing associations' new position outside the public expenditure collar and with maturing stocks made them the preferred vehicle for expansion.

Housing shortages

One tenet of Thatcherite housing policy was that public sector investment crowded out the private sector. Rolling back the state would leave space for private developers and investors to roll in. New building by local authorities and new towns duly fell – to the lowest peacetime level since 1920 – and was negligible by 1997/98. New building, however, was insufficient to meet the needs generated by demographic change (see David, Chapter 6, in this collection). It fluctuated at lower levels than previously and fluctuated more than when local authorities were active builders and provided stimulus in an economic downturn. The use of planning powers to make private developers contribute to affordable housing provision (after 1992) did not produce enough affordable housing where it was needed and was least effective in periods of downturn.

Table 5.3 Housing performance 1980–97

Housing completions UK	1980	1997
Public sector	88,590	1,543
Housing associations	21,422	28,249
Private sector	131,974	160,910
All dwellings	241,986	190,702

Source: Based on Mullins and Murie (1996)

Government responded by periodically increasing public expenditure through housing associations but their increased activity (Table 5.3) was insufficient to bridge the gap. Continuing housing shortage exacerbated problems of homelessness, affordability, overcrowding, sharing and lack of mobility and choice. All of these historically familiar problems increased in, or after, the 1980s. They impacted unevenly socially and geographically and were greater in areas of shortage and high demand. The market responded not by increasing construction but by subdividing properties, increasing overcrowding and sharing, bringing substandard dwellings into use and increasing rents (and housing benefit costs).

Housing costs and social security transfers

An important legacy of Thatcherite policy was a step change in housing indebtedness, changing the household budgets and risks faced by a generation of existing households. While rents are paid continuously throughout occupation, homeowners purchase outright or face front-loaded mortgage costs. Unless the property is remortgaged housing costs eventually fall back to the levels needed for maintenance. RTB purchasers changed their lifetime pattern of housing costs. RTB discounts (averaging over 40 per cent of market value) reduced front-loaded costs. Although mortgage payments were sometimes lower than rents most purchasers had higher real costs that declined over time. Transfers from public ownership increased private sector debt: more households had mortgages and were exposed to fluctuating interest rates. At some stages – notably in the early 1990s – very high interest rates coincided with low or declining house prices. The processes and consequences arising from loss of income, employment or relationship breakdown for new homeowners were different from those had they had remained tenants. They faced additional risks and opportunities associated with movements of interest rates and house prices. The advantages gained from changed tenure status depended on what, when and where people bought. Housing shortages and, following financial deregulation, the greater capacity and willingness of banks and building societies to lend, increased house prices and costs for new entrants to the housing market. In an environment of rising income inequality the practice of basing lending on multiples of income (with higher multiples and a willingness to lend more than 100 per cent of house value) added to inflation and drew the market away from what was affordable by lower- and middle-income groups. The sustainability of home ownership down the income scale weakened and generated greater need for assistance with housing costs. Changes in incomes, employment and job security put home ownership beyond the reach of some while others could buy more than one property.

Tenants experienced real increases in rents because of council and housing association rent policies and because deregulated private rents rose rapidly in the environment of housing shortage. This increase in housing costs affected the residual income available for other expenditure. It is not surprising that measures of poverty excluding housing costs saw a significant increase and the longer-term legacy of housing policies was to increase the numbers of households with insufficient income available to meet non-housing expenditures.

The development of housing benefit after 1982 only partly protected tenants against rising rents and rent caps became more significant in the 1990s. Government housing policies (along with economic recession and widening social inequality) shifted costs to the social security budget. The housing benefit bill increased with private sector rent allowances over-taking rent rebates in the public sector. The apparent legacy of reduced housing public expenditure had only been achieved because social security expenditure had increased to take the strain. The combined costs of rent rebates and rent allowances in Great Britain increased from £3.4 billion in 1986/87 to over £11.4 billion in 1996/97. In that period rent rebates rose from £2.4 billion to £5.6 billion and rent allowances from £996 million to £5.8 billion. Income support for homeowners also grew in this period: from £351 million to £867 million. Changes in rents and subsidy meant that council housing in aggregate moved into surplus (Table 5.4) and generally low-income tenants were subsidizing the rents of lower income neighbours.

Table 5.4 Assistance with housing costs 1980–97

	1980/81	*1997/98*
Mortgage interest tax relief (£m) UK	2,188	2,700
Average tax relief (£) UK	335	250
Net subsidies for LA housing GB (£m)	2,130	(674)
Housing benefit UK		
Rent rebates: number	1,330	2,762
Rent rebates average payment per person (£ per annum)	240	1,893
Rent allowances: number	240	1,829
Rent allowances average payment per person (£ per annum)	199	2,818

Source: Based on Mullins and Murie (1996)

Organizational control and capacity

The policies outlined above profoundly altered housing practices. Many households experienced changes in ownership and management, who they sought help and advice from, where they obtained finance from and who they made payments to. Relationships with familiar councils and building societies gave way to new relationships sometimes with unfamiliar organizations with different names and accountabilities. This amounted to a changed system of urban governance especially related to financial institutions, local government, private landlords and housing associations.

The approach to housing involved further centralization of policy. Local authorities withdrew from mortgage lending, their new house building shrank and other elements in a comprehensive housing service diminished in importance. The RTB and stock transfer shifted responsibility for housing finance, management and maintenance from local authorities to the private and third sectors. This, in turn, changed employment and accountability and how and where residents sought support and addressed complaints. Housing had been a key area for most local authorities and engaged local councillors: where the service was reduced in scale, wholly transferred or transformed to a purely strategic role local government's role diminished. The private sector and housing associations increased in importance and a new generation of housing associations were the direct products of local authority stock transfers. Without local authority housing management acting as the neighbourhood manager (or policeman?) disordered estates could be more difficult to manage and different mechanisms were needed to deal with some neighbour disputes, changes in occupation and neighbourhood management. Initiatives designed to improve estates were overwhelmed by increasing concentration of problems and a reduced capacity to address them (see Murie, 1997a) and increased inequality exacerbated problems and their concentration (see Farrall 2006: 267–9 and Farrall and Jennings, Chapter 7 in this collection). The issues arising from poorly managed, private tenancies affected homeowners and tenants in neighbouring properties and became more common sources of tension. The management of cities and neighbourhoods became more fragmented.

Housing associations and the Housing Corporation were not initially (or ever) the favourites of Conservative governments. They were regarded as part of the managed system that required reform and were subjected to attacks and expenditure cuts from the outset (Murie, 2008a). In view of this, their expansion and the increased importance of their regulators was remarkable. Housing associations successfully colonized the privatization agenda by accessing private finance and offering an alternative to municipal ownership through new building and stock transfer that was acceptable to different sections of government support. They enabled government to honour commitments to regulate and guarantee responsible renting better than if transfers had been to deregulated private landlords. A government espousing deregulation introduced a new regulatory regime to manage this significant privatization: the legacy of privatization and deregulation was a more complex set of rules, rights and regulation. Housing associations increased their share of the market and by 2008 owned more dwellings than local authorities in England.

The Thatcherite agenda was the catalyst for a sustained period of housing association growth and reorganization. Changing practice, finance and regulation triggered mergers and group structures. Housing associations became the largest voluntary organizations in the UK with their regulator among the largest quangos. The merged, developing housing associations and groups became larger than local authority landlords had been. While they were responsive to government and regulators they had considerable autonomy and chose where to put their energies and resources. Their independence was important for private funders as well as for their own boards and members. Their governance and not-for-profit status, distinguished them from private landlords and they were closer to the collective model previously associated with council housing. In both cases, large stocks of dwellings with historic debt provided a maturing asset that was (in the long term) cheaper for government than dependence on private renting. In this perspective an important part of the Thatcherite legacy is a new organizational and financial arrangement to deliver a similar alternative to the private market as that previously available as council housing – but with less conventionally democratic regulation and accountability. As long as housing association rents were below market levels their call on housing benefit was less than private renting. But the business plans of housing associations were best served by higher rents and rents that rose faster than inflation. The temptation to push rents up also offered the prospect of more houses built for a given level of initial government grant to associations. Although there were adverse consequences for tenants not entitled to 100 per cent benefit (and by strengthening the poverty trap), the argument to accept rising rents because so many tenants were entitled to all of their rent being met by housing benefit tended to hold sway. Government, housing associations and lenders colluded in a process that generated affordable housing with an unsustainable reliance on social security expenditure. In the longer term and after 2010, the consequences for housing benefit expenditure rendered this model unsustainable.

The example of housing associations demonstrates that the legacy of Thatcherism was shaped by influences beyond government. The scope and impact of new policies was affected by changes that had been working through the housing system for some time. Increasing income inequality (see Walker, Chapter 9 in this collection), changes in employment and immigration and the growth of the student population also affected outcomes. Not all tenants chose to exercise the RTB and not all housing associations embraced private finance and chased development funds. Although resistance to Thatcherite housing policy was weak or short-lived, local authorities, housing associations and private sector bodies reacted in different ways. Some councils and tenants enthusiastically embraced stock transfer while others rejected it. The legacy reflects a variety of practice in implementation and realization on the ground.

The deregulation of building societies and financial institutions speeded the process of merger and enlargement and initiated active demutualization. Restructuring of the housing finance industry followed, leaving a small number of very large institutions dominating the market, borrowing from other institutions on the wholesale lending market to meet mortgages. A number of building societies merged and most of the largest demutualized and converted into banks. Local and medium-sized organizations providing financial services declined. Many familiar high street names departed and with them the relationships that had existed with small savers. The old practices, where local managers were important gatekeepers, potential borrowers needed records of saving and a deposit to negotiate a loan, and lenders were often cautious about both valuations and loan to value ratios, gave way to a more centralized system run by head offices and with competition to respond to demand and make more generous offers with loans meeting or exceeding values. These changes increased access to mortgages, enabled fuller funding of RTB purchases with larger immediate capital receipts for the Exchequer than if local authorities had funded sales and facilitated a growth in buy-to-let mortgages. In the longer term, increased competition to lend, and wholesale borrowing rather than drawing on small savers as in the past, fuelled house price inflation and fed affordability problems. This and the willingness to use wholesale borrowing to purchase securitized loans without sufficient care were key elements in the credit crunch after 2007 and the consequent prolonged low levels of house building and lending for home ownership.

Insecurity and inequality

The RTB and reduced new construction affected future housing costs and access. With reduced levels of new housebuilding the supply of housing and flow of new lettings in the social rented sector would eventually decline as vacancies that would have emerged in the social rented sector instead occurred in the private sector. The changing size, type and location of the social rented stock, higher rents and increased turnover demonstrate the direct impact of Thatcherite policy on the nature and role of the sector.

Households accepted as homeless by local authorities more than doubled in Great Britain between 1979 and the early 1990s and the proportion of new council tenants who had previously been homeless increased. In England 16 per cent of new secure council tenancies were let to homeless households in 1980/81, 46 per cent in 1991/92 and 25 per cent in 1997/98. The comparable figures for these years for London were 27 per cent, 76 per cent and 51 per cent. There were more homeless households housed in temporary accommodation. In 1980, 1,330 households in England were housed in bed and breakfast hotels and a total of 4,710 in some form of temporary accommodation. In 1997 these figures were 4,520 and 54,930. Increased inequality was at its most pronounced in affecting people with the least capacity to gain access to housing. The Housing Act (1996), reduced the chances of homeless persons obtaining long-term housing from local authorities and housing associations but could not obscure the growth of insecurity and homelessness (see Carlen, 1996).

Increased inequality affected access to different tenures and qualities of housing but shortages and greater dependence on market processes introduced different risks for people within the private sector. The certainties and securities supposed to follow home ownership proved unreliable for some and the practice of lenders as well as government in supporting homeowners with difficulties had major loopholes. The periodically high levels of arrears and repossessions affecting homeowners provide evidence of increased risks and insecurities. As home ownership expanded so its diversity increased. The legacy was not a single tenure providing the same opportunities and rights. Rather than creating a nation of homeowners joined by common interests and benefits from property ownership the outcome was highly differentiated and stratified. Increased home ownership provided an investment, a source and store of wealth and a potential for intergenerational transfers but the realizable wealth differed enormously between regions and parts of markets and according to when and where people bought.

The practice of lenders and willingness to provide loans equal to, or in excess of, value increased access to home ownership but added to house price inflation and affordability problems and left more households exposed to mortgage arrears and repossessions during crises. These problems were increasingly evident alongside a new phenomenon of unsecured debts and significant negative equity in the economic and house price downturns during the early 1990s (and after 2008). Those who bought at the wrong time and with the largest loan to value ratios faced negative equity affecting their mobility as well as wealth and indebtedness. The greatest absolute gains went to households with higher lifetime earnings.

Even where tenants in the new deregulated private sector were able to maintain their rent payments and were 'good' tenants, their landlord could easily terminate the tenancy. At the same time the sale of council housing had not removed the problems associated with that tenure: it either made very little difference to the functioning of neighbourhoods or introduced greater challenges to management and maintenance of property. There is little evidence that increased tenure mix led to greater income and social mix than had existed previously but the capacity for neighbourhood management through a 'monopoly' landlord was reduced. The inequality between neighbourhoods appears to have increased as market processes replaced 'paternalistic', or 'inefficient' public management. The popular and media images of 'estates' ignored their mixed tenure nature. Privatization rarely changed neighbourhood reputations and inequality may have consolidated them.

Conclusions

Eighteen years of Conservative government had an important effect upon housing in Britain. The reorientation of expenditure and investment activity, the ideological opposition to municipal activity, and privatization marked a clear break with the past. However, the mechanisms used and the resulting legacy are much less coherent than the rhetoric implied. The legacy attributable to the Thatcher and Major governments does not reflect some master plan and the expectations of government were not always detailed or explicit. Government did not privatize housing as it did railways, gas or electricity and the desire to bring the disciplines of the market to bear on housing was compromised by the electoral appeal of the RTB and the neo-conservative preoccupation with home ownership. The RTB identified individual households as the only potential purchasers, provided a huge state subsidy incentive to buy and was far from being a market transaction. Where sitting tenants chose not to buy, there was no offer to sell to other investors. At the same time the deregulation of private renting and development of housing associations came to depend on public expenditure. In order to reduce direct state provision, the state increasingly sponsored and supported independent and private provision. It encouraged the 'market' by subsidy and special treatment as well as deregulation. The housing policy agenda did not sever dependency on the state but in the long term increased it. As the election of 1997 demonstrated, expanded home ownership also failed to provide a new electoral base for Thatcherite Conservatism.

Deregulation of housing finance increased capacity to lend and borrow and contributed to inflation in housing costs. It also impacted on the wider economy and the costs and availability of funds for other activities. The deregulated system was less tied to home ownership and generated more loans for buy-to-let properties and the expansion of private renting at the expense of more popular tenures. Both council housing and home ownership declined and the aspirations of new households to become homeowners were increasingly frustrated. Private renting, where it housed benefit-dependent households, formed part of this market along with officially defined social landlords. This new social rented sector operated with different categories of landlord, higher rents and private finance but depended on state assistance with housing costs. The view that the benefit system could take the strain arising from the reorganization of housing left a growing housing benefit bill that would eventually need review. In this sense, the legacy was an unhealthy and unstable financial base for the future of housing. Later debates around housing benefit and wider social security reform indicate the failure to provide a sustainable legacy and to address the complex issues around housing and social security rights.

These considerations mean that the legacy of Thatcherite policy is less about reduced public spending or increased home ownership than about higher housing costs, dependency on means-tested benefits, housing inequality and insecurity. The opportunity for one generation was to consolidate advantages already secured through council housing; but the legacy for the next generation was greater risk, uncertainty and inequality in housing. The shift from a managed to a market system left individuals more exposed to the effects of market fluctuations, housing shortages, low housing standards and homelessness. Periods of economic downturn (notably the recession following 2007) demonstrated the fragility of the new formula, its overdependence on planning gain and inability to sustain house building. New housing construction consistently lagged behind demographic and normative calculations of what was needed and the market generated increased sharing and overcrowding, substandard housing, increased segregation and neighbourhood differences.

The expressed intention of Thatcherite policy had been to deliver a populist agenda around expanding home ownership as the normal tenure associated with citizenship and personal wealth. But some of the mechanisms used to achieve this were not repeatable and its expansion stretched the sector beyond what was sustainable and fractured it. While satisfaction and status associated with some (expensive and exclusive) parts of home ownership were very high, in other parts they were much the same as for social renting (Murie, 1997b). Deregulation of housing finance, in the context of wider income inequality, created a more differentiated home ownership sector and added to house price inflation and affordability problems. It also facilitated the growth of buy-to-let mortgages by a new generation of private landlords. The expansion of private renting following deregulation was partly the second stage of transfer from state ownership but also involved direct and successful competition with people trying to become homeowners. Home ownership became less accessible for some households at a time when good quality, well managed, affordable renting was also declining.

The growth of home ownership at the expense of council housing transferred debt from public to private sectors. It is plausible to speculate that this affected wider attitudes to debt, risk, savings and work as well as towards inequality and collective provision. The RTB directly shifted assets from the public sector and served to symbolize the assertion that a new political economy could make a difference to individual households and could do so quickly. Some households felt wealthier individually or felt they had new opportunities and this may have offset economic and policy changes that, collectively, made them poorer.

Dismantling council housing reduced the financial and organizational capacity of local authorities in housing. Local government retained enabling and strategic roles but its position in housing production and in housing and neighbourhood management was weakened. The view that the private sector had been crowded out of housing development by local authority activity and would expand as council building declined, proved erroneous. The private sector's failure to fill the gap left by reduced council development strengthened the case for increased housing association contributions. Housing associations also compared favourably with private landlords in terms of long-term costs to the public purse and other factors. They duly replaced local authorities as the major source of new rented housing: the banks and building societies that lent to them and the agencies that regulated and channelled public funds to them became more important in housing production and management and in wider neighbourhood management and governance. But this whole edifice relied on state support through housing benefit.

Dismantling council housing further damaged its status and reputation and weakened its political support. Public and media perceptions of what council housing was were redefined to relate to the remnant sector rather than the whole sector as it was built. The remnant of council housing, after more affluent tenants had bought, housed a greater concentration of lower-income and benefit-dependent households. This enabled a less complex, opportunistic debate about worklessness, security of tenure and housing rights than when more tenants were affluent and 'deserving'. Council housing was more easily stereotyped as a source of dependency and council tenants demonized as undeserving. Nevertheless, there is reason to hesitate before accepting this as the enduring legacy. The insecurity and poor quality of housing associated with parts of deregulated private renting highlights strengths in council housing and competition to access social rented housing was sustained by the inadequacies of some private rented alternatives. The unexpected legacies of Thatcherite policy included confirmation of the superiority of regulated, non-profit collective forms of housing in providing good accommodation for lower-income and vulnerable households and greater confidence in mutuals than in privately owned banks. Just as the strengths of mutuals and council housing had not prevented attacks upon them, these legacies will not prevent future attacks. However, if social landlords (and mutuals in the financial sector) operate better services than significant parts of the competing private sector and retain an organizational capacity valued by individual households, governments and others wanting to sustain housing supply and quality they are likely to remain significant players.

The new deregulated, market-based system that replaced the old paternalistic, subsidized, bureaucratic and inefficient managed system inflated housing costs, increased housing inequality and insecurity, failed to deliver housing supply and required increasing public subsidy. In the longer term it proved susceptible to boom and bust, contributed to crises in banking and the wider economy; and the failure to maintain mortgage lending undermined the promise of wider home ownership. The policy and institutional legacy bequeathed to subsequent administrations was deeply flawed and problematic.

References

Carlen, P. (1996) *Jigsaw: A Political Criminology of Homelessness*. Buckingham: Open University Press.

Department of the Environment (1995) *Our Future Homes*. White Paper.

Esping-Andersen, G. (1990) *The Three Worlds of Welfare Capitalism*. Cambridge: Polity Press.

Farrall, S. (2006) 'Rolling Back the State': Mrs Thatcher's Criminological Legacy, *International Journal of the Sociology of Law*, 34(4): 256–77.

Forrest, R. and Murie, A. (1990) *Selling the Welfare State*, 2nd edn. London: Routledge.

Jones, C. (2003) *Exploitation of the Right to Buy Scheme by Companies*. London: Office of the Deputy Prime Minister.

Jones, C. and Murie, A. (2006) *The Right to Buy: Analysis and Evaluation of a Housing Policy* . Oxford: Blackwell.

Kemp, P. (2009) 'The Transformation of Private Renting', in P. Malpass and R. Rowlands (eds) *Housing Markets and Policy*. London: Routledge, pp. 122–42.

Milner Holland Report (1965) *Report of the Committee on Housing in Greater London*. London: HMSO.

Malpass, P. (1990) *Reshaping Housing Policy: Subsidies, Rents and Residualisation*. London: Routledge.

Malpass, P. (2000), *Housing Associations and Housing Policy: A Historical Perspective*. Basingstoke: Macmillan.

Malpass, P. and Murie, A. (1999) *Housing Policy and Practice*, 5th edn. Basingstoke: Macmillan.

Mullins, D. and Murie, A. (2006) *Housing Policy in the UK*. Basingstoke: Palgrave.

Murie, A. (1975) *The Sale of Council Houses: A Study in Social Policy*, Occasional Paper, 35. Birmingham: CURS, University of Birmingham.

Murie, A. (1997a) 'Linking Housing Changes to Crime', *Social Policy and Administration*, 31(5): 22–36.

Murie, A. (1997b) 'The Housing Divide', in R. Jones et al. (eds) *British Social Attitudes: The 14th Report*. Farnham: Ashgate, pp. 137–50.

Murie A. (2008a) *Moving Homes: The Housing Corporation 1964–2008*. London: Politico's.

Murie A. (2008b) 'Social Housing Privatisation in England', in K. Scanlon and C. Whitehead (eds) *Social Housing in Europe II*. London: London School of Economics, pp. 241–60.

Meanwhile, attempts were made to stimulate the supply of rented housing by alternative providers: housing associations and private landlords. First, the Housing Act 1988 deregulated all new private lettings and reduced security of tenure for tenants. And in order to stimulate investment in the newly deregulated private rental market, the Finance Act 1988 temporarily extended the Business Expansion Scheme (BES) to include new property companies letting accommodation on assured tenancies at market rents. The BES – which had originally been set up by the Conservatives to foster an 'enterprise culture' – provided very generous tax breaks for individuals buying shares in new small companies.

This temporary extension to the BES prompted a short-lived surge of investment in new residential property companies. Since it was essentially a tax-driven phenomenon, it is not surprising that few of these new companies lasted for much longer than the minimum four-year holding period for the shares. Nor did the scheme kick start investment in private rental housing more generally. The decline of private renting did finally come to an end but there was only modest growth in the number of households living in this tenure.[1] While the changes introduced by the 1980 Housing Act helped facilitate this development, the early 1990s slump in house prices was probably of greater significance (Crook and Kemp, 2011).

Second, the Housing Act 1988 also deregulated rents on new housing association lettings. In addition, the government reduced capital grant levels, and made associations rely on private finance instead of public sector loans, for new construction. This new financial regime opened the capital markets to housing associations, but also exposed them to greater financial risk (Hills, 1991) or what the housing White Paper referred to as 'the disciplines of the market' (DoE, 1987). In effect, these changes converted housing associations from quasi-public to quasi-market agencies.

Taken together, the changes introduced in the wake of the 1987 housing White Paper represented the most fundamental reform of housing policy since the Second World War (Kemp, 1989). Moreover, they were part of a wider set of 'quasi-market' reforms introduced at the same time by the Thatcher government, not just in housing, but also in education and health (Le Grand, 1990).

---

[1] The recent sharp growth in private renting did not take off until the turn of the century (Crook and Kemp, 2011).

Conclusions

The sale of council houses to sitting tenants is indelibly associated with Thatcherism, but as Murie points out, such sales had been taking place on and off for many years. It was the statutory right to buy and the large discounts that were novel.[2] The RTB was not just about selling council houses. In fact, it made a three-fold contribution to the Thatcherite project: it simultaneously increased homeownership, reduced the number of council dwellings and (via the receipts it generated) helped to lower public spending (Kemp, 1992).

Highly popular with council tenants and voters, the RTB seemed to epitomize what Thatcherism was about to many supporters: it offered council tenants an opportunity for self-improvement and wealth accumulation; freedom from an overbearing nanny state; and the prospect of a home that they could proudly call their own and which, in due course, they could pass on to their children. Indeed, for Thatcherism, home ownership was a self-evident and unalloyed good and an almost virtuous state, in a sharp contrast to the perceived serfdom of council tenancies.

Although it has received much less public attention, the strategy of demunicipalizing rental housing was more radical and more difficult to engineer. And even if the main policy instrument – large-scale voluntary stock transfers to new housing associations – was developed by local rather than central government, it was constructed in an environment of constraints and incentives created by the Thatcher governments. Moreover, it was dependent upon the emergence of a new common sense about the perceived inefficiency and paternalism of council housing.

This delegitimization strategy was an essential precursor to the emergence of large-scale, voluntary stock transfers of former council housing. To date, over half of all local authorities have sold their housing stock (Pawson and Mullins, 2010). The success of this new narrative, and the transfer of large swathes of council housing to new quasi-market landlords, ranks alongside the right to buy as Thatcherism's most lasting achievements in housing policy.

---

[2] However, it is worth recalling Heath's 1974 general election manifesto had promised to introduce a right to buy if the Conservatives were returned to office.

References

Booth, P. and Crook, T. (eds) (1986) *Low Cost Home Ownership*. Aldershot: Gower.

Crook, T. and Kemp, P.A. (2011) *Transforming Landlords: Housing, Markets and Public Policy*. Oxford: Wiley-Blackwell.

Department of the Environment (1977) *Housing Policy Review*. London: HMSO.

Department of the Environment (1987) *Housing: the Government's Proposals*. London: HMSO.

Forrest, R. and Murie, A. (1988) *Selling the Welfare State*. London: Routledge.

Hall, S. (1985) 'Authoritarian Popularism: A Reply to Jessop et al.', *New Left Review* 1(151), May–June. http://newleftreview.org/ (accessed 1 April 2013).

Hills, J. (1991) *Unravelling Housing Finance*. Oxford: Clarendon Press.

Hills, J. and Mullings, B. (1990) 'Housing: A Decent Home for all at a Price within their Means', in J. Hills (ed.) *The State of Welfare*. Oxford: Clarendon Press.

Kemp, P.A. (1989) 'The Demunicipalisation of Rented Housing', in M. Brenton and C. Ungerson (eds) *Social Policy Review 1988–9*. Harlow: Longman.

Kemp, P.A. (1992) 'Housing', in D. Marsh and R.A.W. Rhodes (eds) *Implementing Thatcherite Policies*. Buckingham: Open University Press.

Le Grand, J. (1990) 'The State of Welfare', in J. Hills (ed.) *The State of Welfare*. Oxford: Clarendon Press.

Pawson, H. and Mullins, D. (2010) *After Council Housing*. Basingstoke: Palgrave Macmillan.

Pollitt, C. (1993) *Managerialism and the Public Services*. Oxford: Blackwell.

Whitehead, C. (1983) Housing under the Conservatives, *Public Money* (June): 15–16.

6
What were the lasting effects of Thatcher's legacy for families in the UK?

MIRIAM E. DAVID

> I was asked whether I was trying to restore Victorian values. I said straight out that I was. And I am.
>
> (Margaret Thatcher, speech to the British Jewish Community, 1983)

> We must strengthen the family. Unless we do so, we will be faced with heart-rending social problems which no government could possibility cure or perhaps even cope with.
>
> (Margaret Thatcher, quoted in Wicks, 2012)

Introduction

In this chapter I will discuss the Thatcherite legacy for families and family policies from a gender and feminist perspective. This discussion will necessarily also consider the changing demographic, socio-economic and political contexts, and the role that Thatcherite policies had in the wider global contexts. I will also consider the changing roles of women with respect to employment, education and training, as part of the changing landscape of family and social policies. There is, of course, a distinction to be drawn between 'the family' as part of the ideological apparatus of the Tory party and family policies which may or may not align. Indeed, I will argue that, despite much of the Thatcher rhetoric about a return to 'Victorian virtues' or 'traditional family values' to underpin education and social or family policies, there was an inexorable trend towards women's participation in employment, whatever their family structures and circumstances (married or lone or single-parent). There is, therefore, a paradox at the heart of both Thatcherite policies and their legacy for families.

At the same time, wider changes in the economy, towards a 'knowledge economy', also contributed to lasting changes in the contribution of women, and education, to the global economic system. In other words, Thatcher herself argued in the 1950s for a liberal-feminist position, which she came to 'represent' or 'symbolize' beyond her administrative terms (1979–90) (see Arnot, David and Weiner, 1997). Yet in many respects, whilst the 'traditional' 'nuclear family' was one of the cornerstones of both the welfare state and Conservative ideology (Moroney, 1976; Mount, 1982), the changes in the economy presided over by Thatcher did much to undermine the institution of the family so constructed. Drawing on the work of Nancy Fraser (1997), I will consider the wider long-term impacts, rather than effects, of Thatcherite policies and reprise some of my earlier considerations in David (2003).

Both the Conservative and New Labour governments of the 1990s and first decade of the twenty-first century increased 'individualization' as part of these wider and global socio-economic shifts. This has essentially entailed new public policy trajectories away from a sharp distinction between the public and private, where the latter has been seen largely as the 'family' linked to an increasingly privatized or marketized economy. Interestingly, these shifts have entailed the incorporation of 'personalization' practices within family, education, including higher education, employment and social policies (David and Clegg, 2008). This has also meant that the ideas underpinning the so-called 'second-wave' feminist project of 'the personal is political' have been incorporated into the understandings of personalization without acknowledgement or recognition.

There have, then, been complex changes within family and social policies linked to care and work in wider socio-economic and political processes: moves away from a sharp distinction between public and private. This has meant that there have continued to be huge inequalities between families, especially those with dependent children, despite the fact that women have participated in education and employment on unprecedented levels since the 1980s. Thus there has been a paradox at the heart of the Thatcherite legacy for family policies: moves towards sexual or gender equity in employment, education and public life but the burden of care remaining largely on women in families, especially those poor and disadvantaged families largely headed by mothers. This has remained both a moral and economic project, with lasting implications.

I take a critical perspective on the changing political and socio-economic contexts at the time, and the contested effects of Thatcherism during her three administrations. I will develop an appraisal of the longer term effects, and impacts, on families into the second decade of the twenty-first century, and the continued rise of 'neo-conservatism' or 'neo-liberalism' as part of the current Coalition government's policy developments on care, family, education, employment and training, and women. I do so using feminist standpoint theory (Harding, 1996) and thus from my own positioning as a feminist academic sociologist of social and educational policy and activist thinking and writing about women, families and Thatcherism (David, 2003). As others have argued in this book, the issues of effects and impacts, whilst different, are both contested notions. There have continued to be huge and growing inequalities between families, especially those with dependent children, despite the fact, as noted above, that women's public participation in employment and education has grown inexorably.

The paradox at the heart of the Thatcherite legacy for family policies is that effective moves towards sexual or gender equity in employment, education and public life leave the burden of care largely on women in families, thus maintaining and enhancing social and economic inequalities or conditions of poverty versus privilege. Indeed, it has been argued that shifting the boundaries between the private family and public policies, through increasing forms of employment for women in families has doubled the burden of family responsibilities. And in times of austerity and recession, women as wives and/or mothers of dependent children are the first to feel 'the pinch' or the burden of such economic responsibilities. David Willetts, Conservative Minister for Higher Education, in the current Coalition government, has written a polemic about the impacts of changing public policies on families across generations entitled *The Pinch: How the Baby Boomers Took their Children's Future – and Why they Should give it Back* (2010). He lays the blame squarely on public policies for social welfare and feminists especially, arguing that 'feminism trumped egalitarianism' (2010: 208). In this he represents an unreconstructed Thatcherite both in terms of family values and family policies.

As Hay and Farrall argue in their introduction, there is also the thorny question of 'time' in relation to effects and/or impact (immediate or longer term) and the concept of periodization (or what I called 'waves' (David, 2003), linked but not synonymous with 'waves' of feminism which may also be linked with age generations or cohorts). The term 'wave' with respect to forms of feminism both nationally and internationally entered the political and social lexicon in the late twentieth century (Banks, 1986; David, 2013; Hewitt, 2010). This was to contrast generations of feminist political activity, and seeing 'first-wave' feminists as those involved in political campaigns for women's suffrage in all countries (see, for instance, Banks, 1986). In the UK suffragettes and suffragists were seen as politically active at the turn of the twentieth century and into the 1930s when there was a sense that they had successfully achieved their aims.

'Second-wave feminism' arose after the Second World War in many European and North American countries as many of these generations began to question the limited effects of women's suffrage on wider social and familial changes. As beneficiaries of the expansion of educational opportunities into the 1960s and 1970s such women began to argue for more extensive public and social policies including for women and children and linked to education. Arising from the student movements of the 1960s and 1970s, linked to civil and human rights, the women's movement also became involved in developing the evidence within academia to account for women's continuing subordination through family and education (David, 2003, 2013). A huge panoply of ideas and theories began to develop in the global academy around these issues, linked as they continued to be with activism and political campaigning. 'Second-wave' feminism became a strong and analytical perspective within and across the arts, humanities and social sciences in academia (David, 2003; Hewitt, 2010; Weiler and David, 2008). The term 'third-wave feminists' and beyond, has been applied to subsequent generations of feminist academics whereby they have developed a strong theoretical and analytical perspective, including considerations of post-structuralism and the 'post-socialist condition' (Butler, 1990; David, 2013; Fraser, 1997).

More recent generations of women as feminists in the global academy have indeed developed more theoretically informed and gender-sensitive analyses of the relations between families and the wider socio-economic and political systems (Morley, 2003; Ringrose, 2012). They have also explored the longer-term effects of socio-economic developments upon increasing inequalities and the growth of increasing individualization. This theoretical sociological approach draws upon the work of Beck and Giddens (1995), linked as it is with wider analyses of socio-economic change (Clegg and David, 2006; David and Clegg, 2008). However, it has also been imaginatively developed with respect to gender and from a feminist perspective, with increasingly subtle analyses of developments for young women and girls, the so-called 'sexualization' thesis (Epstein,

Kehily and Renold, 2012; Ringrose, 2012; Ringrose and Renold, 2012). Let me start, however, with an overview of the importance of the family in Thatcherite thinking and a 'snapshot' of the position of families and their constitution during the period from the late 1970s.

Thatcherism and the family

Margaret Thatcher was elected to office as leader of the Conservatives in 1975 after the Heath government fell (in 1974), and in 1979, when the Callaghan government failed to secure a majority, she came to power as prime minister. The characteristics of Thatcherism with respect to the 'family' were at this early stage deeply contradictory, and there was no attempt necessarily to rescind earlier (Labour) legislation which had promoted equal opportunities for women, but there was an immediate ideological commitment to family values and being 'morally right' (Levitas, 1986; Lewis, 1983). The ideology of the family was also expressed in those early days of Thatcherism as being about a commitment to 'Victorian values' or virtues and drew on the work of American conservative historians such as Gertrude Himmelfarb (1976). It was taken up in the UK by Sir Keith Joseph, a Conservative MP who supported Thatcher in her bid to become leader of the Conservatives. He was later seen as 'the father of Thatcherism' through the setting up of a Conservative think tank – the Centre for Policy Studies (CPS) – which tried to develop an ideology of the family in keeping with traditional Victorian values and virtues.

The notion of 'the family' as a social institution has underpinned most societies and social policies but this is not an uncontested notion. The notion of the family lay at the heart of the welfare state as it developed in post-war Britain, although it was being critiqued from social and feminist perspectives (Moroney, 1976; Wilson, 1977). However, from the foundations of the welfare state until Thatcher became prime minister, there was a bipartisan political consensus about the partnership between the state, or government, and families for meeting social needs and providing social care (see David, 1986, 1998; Mishra, 1984).

What, if anything was different about Thatcher's position with regards to this institution? For Thatcher, the traditional heterosexual married couple as a nuclear family was the cornerstone for meeting basic needs and social cohesion (David, 1990; Mount, 1982; Pascall, 1997: 292–3). This idea was developed in government, not only through the CPS but also by appointing the Conservative writer, Sir Ferdinand Mount to advise the Family Policy Group, a secret Cabinet cabal, in 1982–83. This group was nicknamed 'the Family Patrol Group' by the late Labour MP, Malcolm Wicks, who had been the Director of the Family Policy Studies Centre (from 1983 to 1992), in direct opposition to Conservative values and policies (David, 1986: 154).

It was Mount's book, *The Subversive Family: An Alternative History of Love and Marriage* (1982) which set out most clearly both a Conservative ideology and an approach to family policies. It was both an attack on feminist approaches to the family and on those who argue for state intervention to sustain family life. His thesis was that the family is a 'natural' unit that has survived the vicissitudes of hundreds of years, and is best left unfettered by government regulations. Nevertheless, he articulated a clear view of the right and 'proper' family form – a heterosexual union, formed by marriage and nourished by children and grandchildren. He assumed that it is only this family that should be allowed free rein.

> The defenders of the family . . . assert always the privacy and independence of the family, its biological individuality and its rights to live according to its natural instincts. It is for this reason that, even in societies where male supremacy is officially total, the family asserts its own *maternal* values.
>
> (my emphasis; quoted in David, 1986: 154)

The family was to be responsible for looking after itself and its own without interference from the state, a return to the situation that prevailed in the nineteenth-century Victorian era. It was seen by many key Thatcherite thinkers as standing as the bulwark against the encroachment of the 'nanny state' (Pascall, 1997: 293).

As I have shown elsewhere (David, 1990: 133), the first Thatcher administration cut back public expenditure in such a way as to resuscitate the 'traditional' family, penalizing lone families (see also Walker, Chapter 9 in this collection). However, such efforts were counter-productive (David, 1990), and coupled with wider shifts (see below) only served to encourage more women, especially lone mothers, into the labour market. Policies in social services (including the freezing of child benefit, and culminating in the introduction of the Jobseeker's Allowance, paid for those under 25 at a lower rate) ultimately only served to impoverish families, especially those headed by a lone mother, and increase young people's dependency on them during this period (Abbott and Wallace, 1989: 85). Other legislation during this time imposed new burdens on families, by, for example, making parents responsible for their children's criminal behaviour; Lister, 1994: 361); and by encouraging families to take on the burden of caring for older relatives, in effect, foisted most of this work on women in the families concerned.

Trends in family formation and labour market participation

In line with many other European and North American countries, the UK saw decreases in rates of marriage with attendant increases in rates of cohabitation as a growing new family form. The proportion of women aged 18–49 who were married fell from 74 per cent in 1979 to just over 60 per cent by 1990 (Lister, 1994). Cohabitation for women in the same age group rose from 11 per cent in 1979 to 22 per cent in 1990, with a commensurate rise in the number of births outside of marriage. For example, the proportion of births to single women, as a proportion of all births, rose from 5 per cent in 1945 to 27 per cent in 1987 (Lister, 1996: 53). Similarly, with the changes in the divorce law, divorce rates increased dramatically, trebling in a 20-year period (1970–90) (Lister, 1996: 127) and the number of children living in reconstituted or lone-parent families inevitably increased during this same period.

In 1979 12 per cent of families were headed by a lone parent, but by 1990 this had risen to 20 per cent, with the biggest increase being amongst single, never-married, mothers (Lister, 1994: 352–3). Haskey (1998) has shown the cumulative percentages of marriages which ended in divorce between 1951 and 1989, including considering a hypothetical marriage cohort (1998: 42). He also demonstrated the growing percentages of all families with dependent children headed by lone mothers and by lone fathers between 1971 and 1995 (ibid.: 43).

What was abundantly clear was not only that the vast majority of such families were headed by lone mothers, but that there was a dramatic shift from widowed lone mothers (3 per cent in 1971 to 1 per cent in 1991) to single lone mothers or divorced lone mothers (5 per cent each in 1991), with separated lone mothers accounting for 3 per cent in 1991. Altogether the proportion of lone-parent families with dependent children doubled from 8 per cent in 1971 to about 20 per cent in 1991, with the proportion of lone fathers remaining relatively constant at about 2 per cent). Thus the period also witnessed the rise of lone-mother families, or what the USA called female-headed households (David, 1983, 1986).

Alongside these trends 'at home' or in changing the family form, there were similarly dramatic changes in the labour market. For example, in 1979 64 per cent of females aged 16–59 were economically active, but by 1994 this had risen to 72 per cent (and set against a period of rampant unemployment it must be remembered). The greatest take-up of work appeared to be amongst the younger generations; of those aged 18–24 in 1979 52 per cent were economically active, whilst by 1994 this stood at 73 per cent. Those with young children also saw increases in economic activity, rising from 31 per cent to 52 per cent over this same period (albeit, working mainly part time; Pascall, 1997). Yet the trends reversed for some groups, with the percentage of lone parents in work declining from 47 per cent in 1979 to 42 per cent in 1992 (Lister, 1994: 353). When we look at men, we see a decline in employment during this period; in 1979 92 per cent of men of working age were economically active, declining to 86 per cent in 1994 (Pascall, 1997).

The impacts of these changes were to challenge both the 'traditional' family as a lived experience for many people, and to start to erode the extent to which it could be employed (as part of the welfare state) as the vehicle for providing social support. But these were not the only challenges the family faced. The increase in owner-occupation (fostered via the Housing Acts of the 1980s – see Murie, Chapter 5 in this collection) required a secure income just at a time when many men were losing work or moving to 'flexible' (i.e. temporary) working arrangements. Thus changes in the economic and housing sectors had knock-on effects for families (Abbott and Wallace, 1989: 85). Thatcher's stance towards various institutions in the labour market (such as trade unions and wage councils) also produced effects for women's labour market participation (and hence changed the internal dynamics of families) in that low paid and part-time work became more plentiful for families struggling on husbands' low wages and women as wives and mothers were forced into these jobs, because even a low wage was better than no wage. Cuts in the budgets of education departments meant that families needed to pay for extra activities associated with supposedly free compulsory education – books, music lessons, and educational trips. Changes in taxation policies have also not helped the family; reducing income tax threshold, raising VAT and National Insurance contributions have all left lower paid families worse off (see Walker, Chapter 9 in this collection). As such, wider social trends, common-sense responses to changing labour markets and some of her own government's policies have meant that families were weakened (in some cases indirectly, via policies pursued in another policy arena), not strengthened during Thatcher's period in office.

The paradox of gender equality and women's family responsibilities

There is a deep paradox (Morley, 2011) at the heart of these challenging considerations which remains contested: this relates to the changing position of women within families, employment and public politics/ policies, and the role of women within these changes. There is now no question that women's positioning within families and employment has changed markedly over the last 30–50 years, in not only the UK, but internationally, but that change is part of wider socio-economic and political changes, so that women of all social classes and ethnicities remain relatively unequal. Thatcherism's lasting effect and/or impact has *not* been about 'Victorian values' so much as about social class inequalities and *individualism/individualization or personalization*. Women's education and working/employment patterns, including caring for dependent children, have changed greatly and women are no longer confined to the household and housework but patriarchal patterns remain and are paradoxically both occluded and more overt.

These kinds of socio-cultural as well as socio-economic changes lie at the heart of the Thatcherite project, leading to paradoxical processes, both within families and public policies. Several official policy reports have made a claim for gender equity, for example, amongst students accessing higher education (HEPI, 2009; Morley, 2011). However, this report only considers the bare numbers, and does not investigate the cultural and socio-economic contexts in which the changes are taking place. In other words, the 'feminization thesis' is a gloss on the wider changes taking place, in which women remain relatively subordinate. For example, it ignores the impact of caring on women's identities (Leathwood and Read, 2009; Morley, 2011). On the other hand, much public policy debate remains blind to the evidence about the shifting gender balance in either education or employment and the relatively modest moves towards gender equity (David, 2009; Hey and Morley, 2011). In other words, as there have been moves towards a knowledge-based economy globally as well as nationally, women have been afforded opportunities to participate in education and employment, and not just remain within the 'family'. However, these socio-economic changes have not substantially transformed gender relations either in employment, education (including higher education) or the 'family'.

Reflections on Thatcherism 1979–90

When Thatcher came to power as prime minister in 1979 I was an academic in social policy at the University of Bristol, a feminist activist and member of an emerging collaborative group of feminist academics in the social sciences. We had begun the process of developing women's studies and materials around family and social policies for intra- and extra-mural courses when Thatcher was elected leader of Conservatives in 1975 in rather challenging circumstances (David, 2003: 61). Indeed, our innovative work was on the theme of sexual divisions in the changing socio-economic and policy contexts of post-war Britain, and we tried to develop materials for courses and research around a definition of 'the family' that hinged on the question of women's 'work' inside and outside the family in terms of employment and caring work for children and husbands: what was conventionally known as housework (Land, 1976; Wilson, 1977). Given that these questions, which later became known as gender equality, had only just begun to emerge on academic agendas' source materials were hard to come by (see for example, Bristol Women's Studies Group, 1979; David, 2013). Nevertheless, we struggled to locate and theorize these questions and develop feminist knowledge through feminist and collaborative peda-gogies. Although we were academics, we also saw our project as one of campaigning for political and policy change, in the direction of greater social and economic equality as well as what was then known as sexual equality.

There was, then, an interweaving of the women's movement and campaigning for social and political changes, and the emerging so-called 'second-wave feminism' from late 1960s and into 1970s about women and the 'family'. At the first major national women's liberation conference, held at Ruskin College, Oxford, in 1970, because of the preponderance of women involved who had recently been university students, and linked as they were with social, civil and human rights campaigns, a series of campaign goals were articulated as 'demands' upon the state, or government. The original four demands were all around the question of transforming women's position in relation to work, either in the family as forms of domestic labour and care or in the labour market. Thus one was for equal pay; a second was for forms of subsidized childcare (and what were then called 24-hour day nurseries); equal educational and employment opportunities; and abortion and contraception. In other words, these were all aimed at freeing women from the burdens of family care and work.[1]

The late 1960s and early 1970s were deeply contradictory and contested social times with the rise of 'equality movements' in a post-war period of political consensus and yet the relatively lukewarm commitments to social policy changes. Under Harold Wilson's Labour government, the Equal Pay Act (EPA) of 1970 was passed, to be fully implemented by 1975. This was the result of social and political campaigning amongst women for employment changes. During the early 1970s, the Labour government, although committed to social democracy was deeply unpopular, and a Conservative government elected, during which time Thatcher was appointed Secretary of State for Education. Her policies and actions during this period of the Heath's Conservative government were quite contradictory in that she implemented cuts in the schools budgets – such as limiting of social welfare through the provision of milk for schoolchildren – to enable them to be able to work. On the other hand, she did not rescind policies of comprehensive education, and more importantly, she developed policies for young children such as nursery education, outside the social care budget. She also was innovative in commencing the expansion of higher education by allowing for mature women students. Equally importantly the EPA 1970 was not rescinded, and when Labour came to power again in 1974 they moved to develop a linked policy of the Sex Discrimination Act (SDA) 1975. This Bill had been in the process of development when Labour was voted out of office, and the Conservatives had not promulgated this particular commitment to equal employment and educational opportunities (David, 2003).

Under the 1974 Labour government the SDA and EPA were to be implemented from 1975, and they contained a monitoring body to check on the progress and implementation of equal opportunities, namely the Equal Opportunities Commission (EOC). This body was modelled on the

---

[1] In the 1980s three more demands were added: namely freedom of expression of sexuality and orientation; tackling violence against women; and legal and financial independence.

USA and had party political consensus. Thus the first deputy chairman of the EOC was Elspeth Howe, the wife of the shadow Conservative Chancellor of the Exchequer Geoffrey Howe. From 1975 to 1979 the EOC was quite proactive in pursuing policies for equal opportunities in terms of sexual discrimination, and ensuring not only individual discrimination but also monitoring class actions. A particularly famous action related to girls' and boys' equal access to grammar school education. Through the EOC's Tameside inquiry in 1976 it was shown that local education authorities (LEAs), and Tameside, in particular, assumed that boys did better than girls at age 11 and should be entitled to more grammar school places. Indeed, the LEA had more boys' grammar school provision than for girls. However, girls' educational achievements were shown to be better than boys at age 11, and so more were discriminated against in access to selective secondary education.

Given this, the commitment to equal opportunities legislation appears to have been insufficient to effect changes for women in relation to men and families; the Thatcherite legacy remains a relatively lukewarm commitment to equal opportunities in public life. It remains the case that whilst there are more women now participating in public office or employ-ment, they still remain relatively subordinate to men, even in political positions (see Childs, 2008; Childs and Webb, 2010).

During Thatcher's periods of office as Secretary of State for Education (1970–73) and as Prime Minister (1979–90) there were a number of policy changes with respect to equal opportunities for women with caring responsibilities. As already noted, as Secretary of State for Education, Thatcher was responsible for improvements in the public provision of nursery education and the subsequent opening up of opportunities for combined childcare and education, during the early period of her time as Prime Minister (New and David, 1985). Whilst these provisions of forms of public care and education enabled some mothers of pre-school children to think about forms of paid employment, the public ideological commitment remained to early childcare and pre-school within families, by mothers.

Moreover, and far more significant for the implementation of equal opportunities were the fiscal and economic policies set in train by the government which shored up inequalities between families of different socio-economic backgrounds and also on the grounds of parenthood. Motherhood continued to be not only a strong concept for the caring work in families, whilst fatherhood had little material significance within families but more as 'the breadwinner' (Land, 1976). Cutbacks to social welfare benefits fell more heavily on mothers of dependent children, especially from poor families. Moves to support fathers on the birth of a child, or when they had young and dependent children, were frustrated by the lack of Conservative commitment. During this period of office the European Union (EU) was moving towards granting paternity and parental leaves for sick children but the British commitment to taking these policies forward and implementing the EU directive was opposed by the then relevant minister, Michael Portillo, in 1994, illustrating the weak commitment to equal opportunities. One of the key changes, as a more welcome development rather than legacy, is that there is less hostility to men being involved with childbirth and childcare than 30 years ago.

Throughout Thatcher's terms of office, there was an array of ideological and substantive conflicts especially over what was later, in 1998, called the 'fragmenting family'. Drawing on a review essay about women, family and 'work' that I wrote for a collection of critical essays about a decade of Thatcherism (David, 1990: 117) three different approaches were identified.

The 1979–83 Thatcher administration tried to reduce 'the nanny state' by cutbacks in public expenditure on social services aimed at supporting the traditional nuclear family (and penalizing lone-mother families). However, as noted above, the initial effects were the reverse – increasing forms of part-time employment. The 1983–87 Thatcher administration attempted to change the governmental infrastructure for the delivery of social services (via the Fowler Review, 1984) and to reduce social services support for families (by shifting the responsibility from statutory to voluntary organizations). This became known (in 1986) as 'care in the community'. Edwina Currie (then a junior health minister) tried to ensure 'self-help' schemes for families as part of the project of helping the community to care, adding to the already burgeoning voluntary 'helper' projects. The 1987–90 administration sought to develop more explicit alternative social policies to those of the social democratic era. These, too, were particularly significant for women's lives inside and outside the family, although all were expressed in gender-neutral terms. The two most significant – The Education Reform Act 1988 and the Children Act 1989 – mark the apotheosis of Thatcher's social policies, in that the Education Reform Act demonstrated how far the Thatcher government had moved away from any commitment to equal opportunities whereby parents were given a major involvement in running schools, thereby accentuating the differential resources available to schools (see Dorey, Chapter 4 in this collection). Furthermore, the Children Act 1989 did not try to reduce social or economic inequalities between parents.

What became the Children Act 1989 was only about children in non-traditional families and it contained no provisions for universal early childhood education (despite the commitment to nursery education, a decade earlier, which Thatcher had shown when she was Secretary of State for Education). The immediate twin-effects of the implementation of free market policies for social welfare were the 'privacy of the (genderless) family, coping on its own . . . private businesses for schemes of childcare for under fives . . .' (David, 1990: 136). In addition, the form of the changes made has been to increase sexual and social inequalities both in families and the labour market, at that point, reversing trends of the previous three decades. It would be difficult to gainsay these effects as lasting effects of the Thatcherite legacy, and well into the twenty-first century.

It is clear, therefore, that the Thatcher administrations had a tremendous impact on women's lives both inside and outside the family. However, that impact was not quite as Thatcherite rhetoric might have led us to believe. It is the case that opportunities for women, including many who are mothers of dependent children, to participate in the largely male form of the labour market have increased. That, however, did not free them from their primary responsibilities for dealing with the care of their dependent children. The Thatcherite welfare state reversed the commitment to equality of opportunity to a commitment to privacy and freedom from state control. Moreover, the diversity between families masks the real effects of such policies. Childcare is still the task that confronts the majority of mothers, who are challenged by the lack of social and economic support afforded them, either from their partners in the privacy of the family or from the state, to give them choices over the mix of care and paid employment.

Post-Thatcherism and its immediate effects: the rise of neo-liberalism and the Major administrations

When Thatcher resigned in November 1990, there began to emerge a series of theoretical and methodological perspectives to consider the long-term effects on various political administrations. From my own feminist perspective there arose an array of both changing feminist and socialist critiques and, at the same time, moves to examine changing socio-economic and political contexts. For example, Fraser's *Post-Socialist Condition* (1997) was taken up with vigour by many analysts of the growth of economic liberalism and is becoming what has now been seen as a major economic system – neo-liberalism. The attempt was to consider the rupture of traditions and additions of proliferation of post-theories, that is, post-structuralism; post-modernism and growth in political sphere of 'personal responsibility'.

This was seen as the slow shifting trajectories from the personal is political and the social or cultural or biographic turn to the newly coined term 'personalization'. In David (2003) an analysis and 'periodization' of economic and social change from the vantage point of the early twenty-first century was presented, arguing that the Major administrations were in effect a continuation of Thatcherism but in rapidly changing economic times and financial crises. There were more moves towards the free market through, for example, the introduction of vouchers for public services. This was a signal of further privatization and the rise of neo-liberalism (David, 2003: 133). The growth of Conservative policies had particularly significant effects on women and the family (David, 2003: 142).

For example the American Neo-Conservative pundit Charles Murray was invited to comment upon changing British family life under Thatcher by yet another (but linked to the Conservative CPS) think tank – the Institute of Economic Affairs (IEA). His original article entitled *The Emerging British Underclass* was published in the UK, in *The Sunday Times* (1989) and it was subsequently reprinted as an IEA pamphlet in 1990. What Murray argued was that the effects of free market policies were to produce not just inequalities between families in social class terms but an *underclass* of dependent men and women who were either the women raising children on their own or men who were feckless and not in gainful employment. This essay caused an enormous controversy amongst social scientists and commentators. In 1994, Murray was invited to comment again. Given the furore, four of us were invited to make further commentaries: two of us as social policy analysts (Pete Alcock, and myself), with two political commentaries (by Melanie Philips and Sue Slipman) (Murray, 1994).

I argued that Murray's argument was fundamentally flawed (1994: 53–8) as he had distinguished only two groups of working-class women or mothers with dependent children – the so-called New Victorians and the 'New Rabble'. His argument added up to being about how the underclass is made up only of (young) women with illegitimate children living in poverty. Such was the success of his appeal to Conservative family values that the pamphlet was expanded and republished in 1996, edited by the now Labour peer, Ruth Lister (Lister, 1996). There was also a particular focus on the changing trends in divorce and illegitimacy and especially the increasing numbers of women rearing children alone. However, it was clear and obvious that these women did not have suitable suitors (those available were not attractive as potential partners). This kind of argument about the 'underclass' with the moral undertones of disapprobation about their fecklessness continued in yet another publication from the IEA (Conway, 1998), which was a largely positive commentary on the virtues of the free market in social welfare (apart from my critique – David, 1998).

This kind of perspective on the marketization of social welfare has become so completely accepted that it is no longer a cause for concern, and at the same time, feminism has become completely occluded. The process of shifting discourses was also exemplified by yet another IEA pamphlet (David, 1998). However, given the more sober and analytical approach with articles by John Haskey, then Director of the Social Statistics Unit in the Office of National Statistics (ONS), and Kathleen Kiernan then Reader in Social Policy at the London School of Economics, this collection was not as sensationalist as previous ones had been. However, Patricia Morgan (1998) provided a rather dramatic piece with evidence of diverse family types, including lone mothers, and the figures on divorce. Throughout the 1990s there was an escalation of debate about the changing figures on divorce and lone motherhood, laced with commentary about the moral degradation of such families.

Over a decade later, and well into the second decade of the twenty-first century, there is now a much more clearly analytical approach to the changes for women around motherhood. For example, the Economic and Social Research Council has funded a number of social research projects that do not moralize about the changing demographic evidence (which has certainly been a dramatic legacy of the Thatcherite era) but take a more sociological and analytical perspective. One major effect of the Thatcherite period is the changing demography of families, and the increasing trends towards fragmentation, social diversity and multiculturalism. However, these trends do not necessarily cause concern, unless they increase inequalities such that families cannot participate on an equal basis in economic activities, or that the burden of care remains largely with mothers, with little access to economic support or resources.

In another sober analysis of the key changes in women's lives in the postwar period, linked to both social and educational changes, Arnot et al. (1997) argue that, despite Thatcherism and attempts to maintain social inequalities, there was a secular trend towards gender equality in education and forms of employment. We focused on the gender gap in girls'

educational achievements at school from the 1980s, looking at first the
closing and then reversal of the traditional gender gap. We argued that:

> in the UK schooling appears to have broken with the traditions of the gender
> order. It is this decisive break with the social and educational past that lies
> behind the closing of the gender gap.

(Arnot et al., 1997: 156)

Using our own positioning as academic feminists in education and social
sciences, we also showed the contradictions around Thatcher herself in her
values and ideologies and educational policies of individualism. Drawing
on her autobiography we argued that she found herself in a contradictory
position, found it very hard to impose Victorian family values (1997: 42–7)
and indeed singularly failed (1997: 47). She appeared to accomplish the
very opposite and to enhance the advancement of women's educational
and public achievements such that 'ordinary' girls began to desert the
traditionally female educational avenues directed towards family life.

Post-Thatcherism and its long-term effects: neo-liberalism and New Labour: Blair administrations 1997–2007

After two post-Thatcher administrations led by John Major, there is a
question about the Thatcherite legacy of social and sexual or gender
inequalities under the Labour administrations of 1997–2010. Was this one
of continuation or transformation and what were the shifts and changes
across the subsequent three New Labour administrations (viz. 1997; 2001
and 2005)? Initially, it could be argued that the New Labour project (David,
2003: 167) shifted the ideologies towards *understanding the political as
personal.* For example, Levitas (1998) provided a very careful analysis of
discourses underpinning New Labour from the moral underclass debate
(MUD) to the social inclusion discourse (SID) and even more radically to
the redistribution of economics debate (RED). However, she identified all
as present to varying degrees under the incoming Labour administration.
The initial position taken by the administration was largely to continue
with MUD modified slightly by SID, but with little attempt to shift towards
RED. Indeed, although there was a dramatic shift in the composition of
New Labour's women MPs, nicknamed 'Blair's babes' (Childs, 2008) and
with Harriet Harman appointed as Secretary of State for Social Services,
no minister for women was initially appointed and Harman had to hold

the portfolio jointly and without any additional pay for the responsibilities. Whilst there was some surface evidence of shifting moves towards gender equity in political life, this was more a question of continuity with weak forms of equal opportunities, than a radical break with the past, and set alongside the requirement to maintain cuts in child benefit, the Labour administration seemed to have continued with the Thatcher legacy in terms of family or women's responsibilities for their dependent children.

However, there was a significant shift in terms of developing an explicit commitment initially with respect to women's equality with the creation of a Women's Equality Unit in the government's Cabinet Office (David, 2003). The differences in the personal lives of the Thatchers with those of the Blairs (David, 2003: 173) seemed to augur well for advancing gender equalities in public life, in particular, the fact that Cherie Blair was a professional working wife and working mother. There was no talk of conflicts of interest or women's relative inequality but these trends were not to last, and the legacy of continuing inequalities alongside women's inequalities continued unabated. Moreover, although Lord Giddens became a key policy adviser to Blair, and attempted to develop a new policy path (Giddens, 1998), this never had quite the dramatic influence that was claimed for it (David, 2003: 172).

Policy transformations during the Blair, and subsequent Brown, Labour administrations have to be seen partly as an incorporation of Thatcherite policies of marketization and what has become known as neo-liberalism through policies such as Private Finance Initiatives (PFI) and Public-Private Partnerships (PPP) for developing social welfare as well as Giddens' attempt to carve a third way between past social democracy and Thatcherism. These policy developments have also to be seen alongside wider socio-economic changes, and demographic changes both nationally and internationally. In particular, from the point of view of family and gender policies, the development of what became known as the global knowledge economy and the processes of globalization had major implications for transforming inequalities.

Economic developments through increasing technologies, such as information and communication led to a dramatic growth in the knowledge industries and the knowledge society. Here education, and higher education especially, became a much more significant part of the British and global economy, such that the term 'knowledge economy' became de rigeur. The term 'academic capitalism' was coined in the USA by Slaughter and Leslie (1997) and developed as a key concept for understanding the role of higher education in international economic development, and the USA itself (Slaughter and Rhoades, 2004). Thus the expansion of what became known as mass higher education was a part and parcel of these developments. Included here especially were mass changes in women's enrolment in higher education over a 25-year period to the beginning of the twenty-first century (David 2003: 167–73).

These changes in the form of the economic system both nationally and globally towards education as a key component not only had implications for social but also for gender inequalities. Whilst there were some remarkable shifts for women's participation in higher education, this did not mean that women's equality was achieved, despite the rhetoric advanced by organizations such as the Higher Education Policy Institute (HEPI, 2009). Indeed, the 'feminization thesis' of higher education became a major debating point of the end of the first decade of the twenty-first century (Leathwood and Read, 2008; Morley, 2011). The more general question of feminization of employment, and not only professional employment, has also been raised. Alan Milburn, a former Labour minister chaired a government inquiry into social mobility which produced findings showing the continuing exclusion of women from senior professional positions (David, 2009; Milburn, 2009). Thus there are paradoxes in the debates about the positioning of women in relation to forms of employment. And at the other end of the social scale, the question of disadvantaged and working-class women in access to employment also remains somewhat occluded. For example, New Labour's policy of supporting young, largely poor, people leaving school who became known as Not in Employment, Education or Training (NEETs), also ignored the question of gender. However, young pregnant women remained the target of policy disapprobation, continuing the Thatcherite moral reprehension, although not fully counted as NEETs (Alldred and David, 2007).

These changes in policies towards education and employment were part of a broader shift in how individuals were treated as part of the changing nature of the now waning welfare state, given the various moves to limit local and community control and government. The notion of individual responsibilities rather than a more general idea of family or social relationships underpinning social responsibilities were increasingly developed as part of the trajectory from Thatcherite economic liberalism. During the Blair period of office they became increasingly known as personalization and individualization, whereby individuals were expected to take their own responsibilities, without the traditional sharing with aspects of the welfare state. These were seen as part of the processes of shifts towards a knowledge economy with its attendant exacerbation of social, economic and gender inequalities. This is, therefore, a paradoxical aspect of the Thatcherite legacy with not only the effects of moves towards neo-liberalism and market forces and/or privatization and voluntarism but also personalization.

An example of this development can be found in a critique of the changes with respect to women and higher education. An international debate about second-wave feminism and the changes seen in educational research over a 30-year period, especially the moves between the personal and the political was convened with the American educational historian and feminist scholar Weiler (see Weiler and David, 2008) to assess the comparative effects across metropolitan countries. The ways in which individualization and personalization work through work, employment and higher education were reviewed (David and Clegg, 2008), demon-strating how personalization through personal portfolios, study skills, and so on, had become a central facet of the knowledge economy or academic capitalism. The implications of these shifts and changes are that personal responsibility and personalization have become the key features of the moves to neo-liberalism, and its increasingly complex new forms with education and training alongside employment in the ascendancy, and the decline of the role of the welfare state and social or public policies. A new moral order of private and personal social, economic and familial responsibilities is on the ascendance again.

Conclusions: the Thatcherite legacy for the second decade of the twenty-first century?

There has clearly been a huge array of policy changes and developments, given the globally changing political and economic environment towards personal responsibilities and what is now frequently referred to as personalization or individualization. There is also now a critique that lends itself to reconfiguring the concept around notions of sexualization, and the additional commodification of sexual activities and prowess, even amongst young and teenage schoolchildren (Ringrose, 2012). However, despite all these activities, there is a key and central trajectory towards personalization policies, altering the public–private balances and forms of social and economic responsibility. Whilst the lasting effects of

Thatcherism on social and economic policies around women and family are contradictory and paradoxical they remain vitally important: they ensure lasting inequalities on social class grounds and limited 'social mobility', but the major shift and change is that women are no longer confined to the family in terms of domestic labour and housework in the ways they once were at the height of social democracy. Nevertheless, this has not meant a massive increase in public participation in education, care or employment. Indeed, whilst Murray's association with the IEA is no longer publicly prominent, the ideological positions that they espouse remain clearly in the ascendance in Conservative party thinking and have remained at the heart of the Coalition government's policy mantras on women, family, care, education and employment. The moral focus on personal responsibility, along with patriarchal power lies at the heart of these developments, and along with it a deeply misogynistic set of ideologies. In this respect, David Willetts has become a key ideologue for traditional Conservative family values and their implementation in respect of higher education. As noted above, his book, *The Pinch* (2010) sets out a Conservative critique of public welfare, social and economic policies and argues for a new agenda for the future, ensuring that class inequalities remain, whilst the so-called stark differences between the generations are rectified. He concludes that:

> You might say that no one can do anything about the brute luck of the year in which they were born, and there is nothing much government or anyone can do about fairness between the generations – apart, perhaps, for those transfers from parents and grandparents to which this book might have given a nudge. Some critics wished the book had offered a ten-point plan, but there are other places for that debate. I am trying here to get people to think about the whole issue of the obligations between the generations.
>
> (Willetts, 2010: 269)

On the other hand, there is now far more evidence about the diverse cultural patterning in education, care, training and/or employment. One key methodological advance in this scholarship has been around how to account for the diverse ways in which policies impact upon social and cultural inequalities. There have, therefore, been developments in theories around what is now known as intersectionality (Brah and Phoenix, 2004) – about the links and connections between gender, ethnicity, race or diversity and social class. The fact that Thatcher was a woman is deeply significant to women's occlusion and erasure and yet, at the same time, middle-class women's successful involvement in education, including universities. Inequalities have changed and yet remain constant, so that individual middle-class women may achieve but elitism remains endemic and pervasive in social and economic and political policies (see Willetts (2010) for a Conservative elaboration of this point). The debates have shifted from concerns with sexual equality to the weaker form of equal opportunities and renamed gender equity. Moreover, there remains official contestation over whether the pursuit of any form of equality or equal opportunities can be sustained in an era of austerity. This is, indeed, redolent of the Thatcher years: a long-lasting legacy of moral puritanism tinged with social elitism in respect of education, employment or training. This is indeed a neat conjuncture of social policies and continuing inequalities in a changed socio-economic climate and era of austerity.

References

Abbott, P. and Wallace, C. (1997) *An Introduction to Sociology: Feminist Perspectives.* London: Routledge.

Alldred, P. and David, M.E. (2007) *Get Real About Sex: The Politics and Practice of Sex Education.* Maidenhead: Open University Press.

Arnot, M., David, M. and Weiner, G. (1997) *Closing the Gender Gap: Post-war Education and Social Change.* Cambridge Polity Press.

Banks, Olive (1986) *Becoming a Feminist: The Social Origins of 'First Wave' Feminism* Athens, GA: The University of Georgia Press.

Barrett, M. (1980) *Women's Oppression Today: Problems in Marxist-Feminist Analysis.* London: Verso.

Beck, U., Giddens, A. and Lash, S. (1995) *Reflexive Modernization.* Cambridge: Polity Press.

Brah, A. and Phoenix, A. (2004) 'Ain't I a Woman? Revisiting Intersectionality', *Journal of International Women's Studies*, 5(3): 75 ff.

Butler, J. (1990) *Gender Trouble: Feminism and the Subversion of Identity.* London: Routledge.

Childs, S. (2008) *Women and British Party Politics.* London: Routledge.

Childs, S. and Webb, P. (2011) *Sex, Gender and the Conservative Party.* London: Palgrave Macmillan.

Conway, D. (ed.) (1998) *Free-Market Feminism.* London: IEA Health and Welfare Unit; Choice in Welfare No. 43.

Clegg, S. and David, M. (2006) 'Passion, Pedagogies and the Project of the Personal in Higher Education', *21st Century Society*, 1(2): 149–65.

David, M. (1983) 'The New Right, Sex, Education and social policy: towards a new moral economy in Britain and the USA', in J. Lewis (ed.) *Women's Welfare, Women's Rights.* London: Croom Helm.

David, M. (1986) 'Moral and Maternal: The Family in the Right', in R. Levitas (ed.) *The Ideology of the New Right*. Cambridge: Polity Press.

David, M. (1990) 'Looking after the Cubs: Women and "Work" in the Decade of Thatcherism', in I. Taylor (ed.) *The Social Effects of Free Market Policies*. London: Harvester-Wheatsheaf.

David, M. (1998) 'Free Market Feminism: a Rejoinder', in D. Conway (ed.) *Free-Market Feminism*. London: IEA Health and Welfare Unit; Choice in Welfare No. 43.

David, M. (ed.) (1998) *The Fragmenting Family: Does It Matter?* London: IEA Health and Welfare Unit, Choice in Welfare No. 44.

David, M. (1998) 'Education, Education, Education', in H. Jones and S. MacGregor (eds) *Social Issues and Party Politics*. London: Routledge.

David, M. (2003) *Personal and Political: Feminisms, Sociology and Family Lives*. Stoke-on-Trent: Trentham Books.

David, M. (2013, forthcoming) *Feminism, Gender and Universities: Passion, Pedagogies and Politics*. London: Routledge and the Society for Research in Higher Education.

David, M. and Land H. (1983) 'Sex and Social Policy' in H. Glennerster (ed.) *The Future of the Welfare State: Remaking Social Policy*. London: Heinemann.

David, M. and Clegg, S. (2008) 'Power, Pedagogy and Personalisation in Global Higher Education: the Occlusion of Second Wave Feminism? *Discourse, The Cultural Politics of Education*, 29(4): 483–98 (special issue ed. Kathleen Weiler and Miriam David, The personal and political: Second Wave Feminism and educational research).

Epstein, D, Kehily M.J., and Renold, E. (2012) 'Culture, Policy and the Un/marked Child: Fragments of the Sexualization Debates', *Gender and Education*, 24(3): 249–55.

Fraser, N. (1997) *Justice Interruptus: Critical Reflections on the 'Postsocialist' Condition*. London: Routledge.

Giddens, A. (1998) *The Third Way*. Cambridge: Polity Press.

Glennerster, H. (ed.) (1983) *The Future of the Welfare State: Remaking Social Policy*. Brighton: Harvester-Wheatsheaf.

Harding, S. (1986) *The Science Question in Feminism*. Ithaca, New York and London: Cornell University Press.

Haskey, J. (1998) 'Families: Their Historical Context, and Recent Trends in the Factors Influencing their Formation and Dissolution', in M. David (ed.) *The Fragmenting Family: Does It Matter?* London: IEA Health and Welfare Unit; Choice in Welfare No. 44.

Hey, V. and Morley, L. (2011) Imagining the University of the future: Eyes Wide Open? *Contemporary Social Science*, 6(2): 165–75.

Hewitt, M. (ed.) (2008) *No Permanent Waves Recasting Histories of US Feminism*. Rutgers: The State University.

Higher Education Policy Institute (2009) *Male and Female Participation and Progression in Higher Education: A Report*. Oxford: HEPI.

Himmelfarb, G. (1968) *Victorian Minds*. New York: Knopf.

Land, H. (1976) 'Women: Supporters or Supported?' in D.L. Barker and S. Allen, *Sexual Divisions and Society: Process and Change*. London: Tavistock.

Leathwood, C. and Read, B. (2009) *Gender and the Changing Face of Higher Education: A Feminized Future?* London: SRHE and the Open University Press.

Levitas R. (ed.) (1986) *The Ideology of the New Right*. Cambridge: Polity Press.

Levitas, Ruth (1998) *The Inclusive Society? Social Exclusion and New Labour*. London: Macmillan.

Lewis, J. (ed.) (1983) *Women's Welfare, Women's Rights*. London: Croom Helm.

Lister, R. (ed.) (1996) *Charles Murray and IEA Pamphlets on the Underclass Debate*. London: IEA Health and Welfare Unit in association with *The Sunday Times*.

Milburn, A. (2009) (Chair of the Panel) *Unleashing Aspiration: The Final Report of the Panel on Fair Access to the Professions*. London: the Cabinet Office.

Mishra R. (1976) *The Welfare State in Crisis*. Brighton: Harvester-Wheatsheaf.

Morley, L. (2003) *Quality and Power in Higher Education*. Maidenhead: SRHE and the Open University Press.

Morley, L. (2011) 'Misogyny Posing as Measurement: Disrupting the Feminisation Crisis Discourse', *Contemporary Social Science*, 6(2): 223–37.

Moroney, R. (1978) *The Family and the State*. London: Longman.

Mount, F. (1982) *The Subversive Family: An Alternative History of Love and Marriage*. London: Jonathan Cape.

Murray, C. (ed.) (1994) *Underclass: The Crisis Deepens*. London: IEA Health and Welfare Unit; Choice in Welfare series No. 20.

Pascal, G. (1997) *Social Policy: A New Feminist Analysis*. London: Routledge.

Taylor I. (ed.) (1990) *The Social Effects of Free Market Policies* Brighton: Harvester-Wheatsheaf.

Ringrose, J. (2012) *Postfeminist Education? Girls and the Sexual Politics of Schooling* London: Routledge.

Ringrose, J. and Renold, E. (2012) 'Slut-shaming, Girl Power and "Sexualisation": Thinking Through the Politics of the International SlutWalks with Teen Girls', *Gender and Education*, 24(3): 333–45.

Slaughter, S. and Leslie, L. (1997) *Academic Capitalism: Politics, Policies and the Entrepreneurial University*. Baltimore: John Hopkins University Press.

Slaughter, S. and Rhoades, G. (2004) *Academic Capitalism and the New Economy. Markets, State and Higher Education*. Baltimore: John Hopkins University Press.

Weiler, K. and David, M. (eds) (2008) 'The Personal and Political: Second Wave Feminism and Educational Research', *Discourse, The Cultural Politics of Education*, 29(4): 483–98 (special issue).

Wicks, M. (1978) *Old and Cold: Hypothermia and Social Policy*. London: Heinemann.

Wicks, M. (2012) 'A late Labour MP and former Minister for Science under a Labour Administration (2007-9) was Dedicated to Relieving Poverty and Insecurity'. Obituary in *The Guardian*, 1 October, p. 24.

Willetts, D. (2010) *The Pinch: How the Baby Boomers Took their Children's Future – and Why they Should Give it Back*. London: Atlantic Books.

Wilson, Elizabeth (1977) *Women and the Welfare State*. London: Tavistock.

Commentary

Women, the family and contemporary Conservative party politics: from Thatcher to Cameron

SARAH CHILDS and PAUL WEBB[1]

The noted tension between the family and women within conservative thought and practice – key to Miriam David's chapter – remains absolutely central to contemporary Conservative politics. Liberal feminism has undoubtedly triumphed, with its values permeating British society, and women have unquestionably made significant advances in the public sphere over the last few decades, most notably in education and employment, even if gender (and other) differences mediate women's experiences therein.[2] Yet women's fulsome participation in the public sphere is widely acknowledged to be constrained by their gendered experiences in the private sphere. As a consequence, many women find it difficult to achieve the status of the competitive and seemingly unencumbered individual demanded by, and rewarded in, the public sphere, and valorized by neo-liberals. For many women this is about the gendered expectations and practices of motherhood. But even those who are not mothers are frequently treated as if they are, or one day will be (which is why there may be reluctance to employ women of childbearing age).[3] In any case, the non-mother who should theoretically be able to compete on an equal basis with

---

[1] This commentary draws heavily on Childs and Webb (2012).
[2] This is not to deny continuing horizontal and vertical segregation in paid employment; the pay gap between women and men; women's greater tendency to work part time; sex and pregnancy discrimination; and post-childbirth underemployment.
[3] http://www.dailymail.co.uk/news/article-513264/Sir-Alan-Sugar-Why-I-think-twice-employing-woman.html

men – presuming the absence of sex discrimination – may very well find herself responsible for elder, and other dependant, care, especially in her own middle and older age.

A belated acknowledgement that British society no longer reflects a mythical 1950s female domesticity, together with a realization that the Conservative party needed, for reasons of electoral competitiveness, to 'catch up' with these societal changes, underpinned an explicit feminization of the Tory party post-2005. Feminization would address both the under-representation of Conservative women in UK politics and update the party's policy position vis-à-vis women's issues. In respect of the latter, conservatives in general and the Conservative party in particular confront women's roles and experiences, constrained by their own ideological underpinnings. In 2010 the party proffered a manifesto in parts clearly informed by liberal feminism, and David Cameron the party leader, and later Prime Minister of the Coalition Conservative-Liberal Democrat government, declared that a Conservative government in 2010 would be the 'most family friendly' in Europe.[4]

The latter claim begs questions for contemporary Conservatives of what the family is, and what it should be (the distinction between descriptive accounts of existing family forms and normative accounts of the ideal family type) and the extent to which its current leaning owes anything to the earlier Thatcherite stance on families. Given the recent statutory provision for gay marriage, as well as wider rhetorical support for the institution overall, one might contend that marriage – now inclusive of both gay and straight couples – is the Conservative standard that delineates the family. This updated definition sits easily amongst the party elite, and indeed, wider society more generally, especially younger people,[5] but many Conservative MPs and party members,[6] regard marriage by its very definition as a union between a man and a woman. Cameron is adamant, though, that he is pro-gay marriage *because* he is a conservative not despite his conservatism.[7] He maintains too that to be 'for' marriage is not to be

---

[4] http://news.bbc.co.uk/2/hi/uk_news/politics/7298364.stm; http://www.huffingtonpost.co.uk/2012/07/10/david-cameron-family-friendly-country-pledge-rejected_n_1661928.html; http://www.guardian.co.uk/commentisfree/2011/sep/11/observer-editorial-family-friendly-policies

[5] http://yougov.co.uk/news/2013/02/04/how-gay-marriage-row-threatens-tories/

[6] http://www.telegraph.co.uk/news/politics/david-cameron/9845610/Grassroots-Tories-betrayed-by-David-Cameron-over-same-sex-marriage.html

[7] Cameron made this clear at the 2011 Conservative Party conference.

'against' the unmarried. What remains unanswered, however, is whether and how the government will privilege the married over the non-married substantively as well as symbolically. Electoral and Coalition politics, as well as wider economic context will no doubt constrain the government here. It also remains to be seen whether Cameron's restated commitment to introduce marriage tax relief prior to the 2015 election will be sufficient to placate those who regard gay marriage as an attack on, and not a bolstering of, marriage and the family. At the same time, if the Coalition goes down this road of privileging marriage it may well be regarded as re-contaminating the Conservative party by those voters who regard marriage as either a 'lifestyle choice' independent of any moral value, or something that one aspires to but may not necessarily achieve.[8]

While some elite Conservatives have sought to broaden the definition of the family in a more inclusive fashion, and in the face of not insignificant traditionalist consternation, conservative framing of some families as 'broken' in recent years has dominated political debate. Indeed, it is one of the reasons for the party emphasizing marriage in its policy reviews and later government priorities. In this there are clear continuities with the rhetoric and ideological analysis of the Thatcher era. Depicting family breakdown as a key characteristic of a wider 'broken' British society is closely associated with the Centre for Social Justice (CSJ). A highly influential think tank during the party's policy review process prior to 2010, its analysis has been brought directly into government via Iain Duncan Smith, the current Secretary of State for Work and Pensions, and previous party leader and ex-Director of the CSJ. In various publications, the CSJ highlights and seeks to redress the problem of 'fractured families'. Single-headed, either because they were from the outset 'fatherless', or because of cohabitation, separation or divorce, such families are depicted as dysfunctional due to factors including mental health issues, and drug and alcohol dependency. These families are also associated with crime, unemployment and poverty, and are said to be caused, in no small part, by welfare state benefits which support if not promote the practice of single parenthood, for example, by what the Party terms the 'couples' penalty'.[9] Though present across classes, there is especial concern that fractured

---

[8] Campbell and Childs (2010) talk of marriage tax relief as the 'golden hello' to the younger and blonder second wife; one which penalizes the abandoned first wife.
[9] http://www.centreforsocialjustice.org.uk/UserStorage/pdf/Pdf%20Exec%20summaries/BBExecFamilyBreakdown.pdf

families are most prevalent amongst the poorest in society, and that there is significant inter-generational reproduction, with single mothers begetting single mothers.

The extent to which such framings resonate with the wider public mood will likely influence the terms of inter-party competition over the family in the run up to the 2015 general election. At present this is playing out most explicitly in the context of debates about welfare reform, and the deserving and undeserving poor, updated through the modish language of 'shirkers v. strivers'.[10] Here there are some signs of opposition from the Labour party as well as disquiet on behalf of the Conservatives' Coalition partner. Yet it is not yet definite how Labour or the Liberal Democrats will ultimately position themselves. Labour in early 2013 chose to vote against the government's Benefits Up-rating Bill, which capped increases at 1 per cent – a stand that positioned them against public opinion and, in the words of the *Observer* political commentator Andrew Rawnsley, on the side of 'skiving fat slobs'.[11] There is indeed extensive media copy and apparent public support – especially in the Conservative-supporting *Daily Mail* newspaper – for accounts that attack 'third generation' non-working households; and mother-headed households with multiple children dependent upon state benefits. At present, counter-narratives remain marginal, lacking significant public currency.

Alongside and arguably in tension with explicit rhetorical claims and policy interventions focused on the family, constituted as a single undifferentiated unit, is the Conservative party's acceptance of women's greater participation in the public sphere. And when Conservatives recognize the disadvantages that some women face therein, as they increasingly do, at least at the elite level, Conservatives are challenged to reconsider their accepted understandings of gender and gender relations. On paper at least, conservative conceptions of the family sit uneasily with much feminist analysis. Reforms identified by many feminists as necessary to bring about gender role transformation, especially the sharing of domestic responsibilities, and for society to accommodate all human beings' care needs, appear to be oftentimes beyond their terms of reference (Campbell, 1985): conservatives speak of individuals and not structures; discrimination and

---

[10] http://www.guardian.co.uk/politics/2013/jan/07/nick-clegg-protests-shirkers
[11] http://services.parliament.uk/bills/2012-13/welfarebenefitsuprating.html; http://www.guardian.co.uk/politics/blog/2013/jan/08/mps-vote-benefits-cap-live-blog; http://www.guardian.co.uk/commentisfree/2013/jan/05/labour-party-bill

not oppression; and critique a positive role for the state. In the contemporary party the concept of choice is deployed to reconcile the potentially opposing goals of women's equal opportunities in the public sphere and conservative gender roles in the private sphere. In other words, families, as private institutions, should decide how to reconcile work and family life. In so doing the Conservative party formally side-steps normative questions about what women (and by implication men) *should* do. Government's role is to enable choice, not to overtly favour one particular option. There is within this stance little appreciation of the possibility of power inequalities within families; that women and men may have competing and, or conflicting interests; that women may be less free to make a real choice given wider economic, social, political and cultural structures and norms; and that government policies may implicitly (so by default if not by design) support traditional gendered outcomes.

That said, the 2010 Conservative party general election manifesto was much more competitive on what has been called the 'women's terrain', with considerable attention given to women's work/life balance. Specific policy pledges would:

1   force equal pay audits on any company found to be discriminating on the basis of gender
2   extend the right to request flexible working to every parent with a child under eighteen . . . [and ultimately] extend the right . . . to all
3   oblige JobCentre Plus offices to ask employers if their vacancies could be advertised on a part-time or flexible basis
4   introduce a new system of flexible parental leave which lets parents share maternity leave between them.

All of these pledges are congruent with liberal feminist values. They might also be said to stretch the limits of liberal arguments about state intervention, and to stretch conservative reluctance to admit that gender differences result not from individual actions but are more systemic. However, we must look beyond a party or a government's policies that explicitly focus on women (Celis and Childs, 2012). Apparently non-gendered policies can have significantly gender-differentiated effects. The government's response to criticisms of austerity politics that have negatively and disproportionately affected women is that such outcomes are an unintended consequence rather than a conscious ideological goal. Critics point out, however, that even if that is the case, what remains lacking is the integration of feminist analyses in government policy-making: a failure to see 'gender'. It is clear too that there are some in the Conservative parliamentary party who take an explicitly anti-feminist and socially conservative line on a whole series of policies, not least those linked to work/life balance, such as greater maternity, paternity and parental leave, and who contest the 'business' case for flexible working (Childs and Webb, 2012). There has also been in this Parliament a more explicit socially conservative (Americanized) position articulated by individual MPs on abortion.

The extent to which Conservative party actors are at ease with liberal feminist values and associated policies varies. In a recent survey of party members three main ideological tendencies were identified: *Thatcherites* are the most hostile to gender equality. *Traditional Tories*, whilst less 'feminist' than *Liberal Conservatives* at the general level, are on a range of specific policy areas related to women's issues, more progressive. (Traditional Tories are the most numerous, working class and the most female.) Conservative women party members are, moreover, more pre-disposed to feminism than the men – on issues such as equal oppor-tunities, women's suitability for politics, and the impact of women's paid work on family life. More specifically still, there are sex differences in party members' attitudes towards childcare. The issue of equal pay polarizes womens' and mens' views yet further. And on economic policy women are more 'dry' (see also Campbell and Childs, 2013). With regard to both policies there is, therefore, the distinct possibility of significant intra-party sex divisions.

In seeking to attract women voters the Conservative party is influenced by electoral considerations as well as by ideological ones. Historically, the women's vote was firmly in the party's reach, and the grey women's vote has remained critical to Conservative party support (Campbell, 2006). Yet the apparent emergence of a modern gender gap amongst younger women (the gender generation gap) at the time of the new Labour governments, made Cameron keen to win over middle-income working women. In 2010 he looked to have achieved this (Campbell and Childs, 2010). Mid-way through the Parliament he appeared to be struggling to hold on to these women (Campbell, 2012). Like the other parties, the Conservatives need to recognize that in making representative claims for women, significant differences exist between women, not least in respect of class, race, sexuality, disability and age. Given this heterogeneity, women are likely to have different and sometimes conflicting interests (Celis and Childs, 2013). To illustrate: access to affordable childcare for working women may be in tension with enhanced pay and conditions for women working in the sector, if the latter makes childcare more expensive; and whilst 40-something women may desire greater benefits and services in respect of childcare, older women might want the government to prioritize social care, given what is known about women's greater longevity and poverty in old age.

The contemporary Conservative party has evidently undergone a process of feminization in the last decade. They have more women MPs than ever before and they are addressing women's concerns to a much greater extent, and in a more feminist fashion. At the elite level the Tories' claim to be the party of the family is not felt to be incompatible with liberal feminist views of gender roles and relations and an inclusive definition of marriage. (Their position on the latter should not be dismissed as mere symbolism; gay people in the UK are in the process of acquiring new formal rights which should deliver substantive effects.) Government should enable families to make their own decisions about how best to reconcile participation in both the public and private spheres. Many feminists will no doubt take issue with this; question whether women have real choice; and highlight the implicit preferences underpinning policy and rhetoric, in other words, query the symbolic and substantive impact of Conservative party and Coalition policies for women.

Midway through the Parliament, Cameron's family friendly status would be met with disbelief by critics.[12] Austerity policies aimed at reducing the deficit[13] have negatively impacted the financial health of all but the very richest families, hence all the talk of the 'squeezed middle',[14] and public attention to the rise of food banks.[15] Substantial reductions to welfare budgets have given rise to attendant cuts to services.[16] Social

[12] http://www.guardian.co.uk/politics/2012/sep/19/government-with-ominous-intent
[13] Variously Labour politicians, leftist commentators, and civil society groups representing women, children and the poor.
[14] http://www.telegraph.co.uk/comment/personal-view/8845151/The-squeezed-middle-why-Ed-Milibands-phrase-defines-the-new-political-battleground.html; http://www.guardian.co.uk/politics/2011/feb/28/ed-miliband-cost-living-crisis-squeezed-middle
[15] One illustration of the impact of recession on poorer families http://www.guardian.co.uk/commentisfree/2012/dec/19/2012-year-of-the-food-bank
[16] http://www.guardian.co.uk/politics/2010/jul/04/women-budget-cuts-yvette-cooper; http://www.telegraph.co.uk/women/womens-politics/9726738/Autumn-Statement-2012-Theresa-May-We-dont-look-after-women-anymore.html; http://www.wbg.org.uk/RRB_Reports.htm; Ruth Lister, talk at the University of Birmingham, 2012, http://www.birmingham.ac.uk/Documents/college-social-sciences/government-society/polsis/research/all-in-it-together.pdf

care,[17] admittedly a long-standing issue, is frequently said to be in crisis.[18] And taking one especially gendered provision – domestic violence services – local authorities' capacity to meet need has been significantly limited by funding cuts.[19] Benefit levels have been reduced too,[20] alongside the introduction of greater means testing, notably to child benefit.[21] The commitment to introduce a marriage tax allowance, portrayed as *the* pro-family policy in the run-up to the election has still to be implemented,[22] amidst the antipathy of Liberal Democrats,[23] and at least some Tory MPs' reluctance to distinguish between children with married and non-married parents. Even the self-acclaimed childcare reforms, which aims to reduce the costs and improve quality via, for example, increasing 'child–carer' ratios, faces considerable derision.[24] And whilst legislation to legalize gay marriage was successfully passed in the Commons in 2013, as noted above, more Conservative MPs voted against rather than in support of the Bill, albeit on a free vote.[25]

Sex, gender and the family remain, as they did when Thatcher was party leader, unsettled issues within the contemporary Conservative party: at the elite level policies have been advocated that sit quite comfortably with liberal feminist goals even as individuals directly around Cameron have flown 'kites' for policies that directly challenge them. This disjuncture is real: the party cannot, one at the same time, advocate more flexible working and yet see such regulations as 'red tape' getting in the way of business;

[17] http://www.dilnotcommission.dh.gov.uk/

[18] http://www.ageuk.org.uk/home-and-care/care-in-crisis-campaign/; http://www.mencap.org.uk/news/article/social-care-crisis-exposed

[19] Professor Sylvia Walby, talk at the University of Birmingham, 2012. http://www.birmingham.ac.uk/Documents/college-social-sciences/government-society/polsis/research/all-in-it-together.pdf

[20] www.parliament.uk/briefing-papers/LLN-2013-004.pdf

[21] http://www.dailymail.co.uk/news/article-2257728/Child-benefit-chaos-engulfs-Tory-MPs-Downing-St-orders-politicians-check-family-status-tax-inspectors.html; http://www.guardian.co.uk/money/2013/jan/03/child-benefit-changes-what-they-mean

[22] http://conservativehome.blogs.com/thetorydiary/2013/02/cameron-says-he-feels-very-strongly-about-married-tax-allowance-but-delays-its-introduction-for-four.html

[23] http://www.telegraph.co.uk/news/politics/9787866/Nick-Clegg-tax-breaks-for-married-couples-would-sting-the-unmarried.html

[24] http://www.guardian.co.uk/commentisfree/2013/jan/29/hofit-six-toddlers-in-bugy-truss-childcare; http://www.guardian.co.uk/money/2013/jan/29/childcare-reform-proposals-fierce-criticism

[25] http://www.guardian.co.uk/society/2013/feb/06/gay-marriage-male-tory-mps; https://twitter.com/philipjcowley/status/299054633853263873

one cannot champion women in the workplace and yet fail to enable the provision of affordable childcare upon which such participation is premised; and if the Coalition has too frequently failed to address the gendered effects of its wider policies then removing statutory provision for gender equality audits can but signal a trumping of business/economic interests over women's gender equality interests. To try to determine which of the ideological inheritances dominates in this period of Conservative government, albeit a Coalition one, is premature. The 'battle' over gender politics both within the party (at the different levels) and between the party and its leftist and feminist critics, continues.

References

Campbell, B. (1987) *The Iron Ladies, Why do Women Vote Tory?* London: Virago.

Campbell, R. (2012) 'What Do We *Really* Know about Women Voters? Gender, Elections and Public Opinion', *Political Quarterly*, 83(4).

Campbell, R. (2006) *Gender and the Vote in Britain*. Colchester, Essex: ECPR Press.

Campbell, R. and Childs, S. (2010) '"Wags", "Wives" and "Mothers" . . . But what about Women Politicians?', *Parliamentary Affairs*, 63(4).

Campbell, R. and Childs, S. (2013) '"To the Left, To the Right": Representing Conservative Women's Interests', unpublished paper first presented at the 2012 ECPR Joint Session of Workshops, University of Antwerp.

Celis, K. and Childs, S. (2013) '"Good" Substantive Representation: A Feminist Economy of Claims', paper prepared for ECPG Biannual Conference, Barcelona.

Childs S. and Webb P. (2012) *Sex, Gender and the Conservative Party: From Iron Lady to Kitten Heels*. Basingstoke: Palgrave.

7
Thatcherism and crime: the beast that never roared?

STEPHEN FARRALL and WILL JENNINGS

Introduction

In this chapter we will review the impacts which Thatcherite social and economic policies had on the UK's experience of crime. Our chapter proceeds by first discussing criminological thinking on recent political shifts and their relationship with crime/the criminal justice system (hereafter CJS). We then consider what one *might* have expected from a 'fully-realized' Thatcherite agenda for the CJS. In line with others we find little by way of radical Thatcherite impact in the CJS during the period from 1979 until 1993. Nevertheless, we will still suggest that there *has* indeed been a Thatcherite legacy for the CJS (and crime more generally), but this largely operated in indirect and often unanticipated ways. We shall conclude with some thoughts on the extent to which criminologists have ignored the earlier work on the 'contradictory' (Levitas, 1986: 11) nature of the New Right and how ignoring the neo-conservative strand of thinking has affected criminologists' understanding of crime and its relationship to politics.

Thatcherism, neo-conservatism, neo-liberalism

Criminologists, along with many other branches of the social sciences, have become increasingly exercised and excited by the concepts relating to neo-liberalism. As Philip Cerney (2004, cited in Larner et al., 2007) has noted, this term has started to replace terms such as 'Thatcherism' or 'Reaganomics', or even 'neo-conservatism'. This trend can be seen in two very good contributions to the debates about crime and politics in the UK. For example, Reiner (2007) refers extensively to neo-liberalism, does not mention neo-conservatism at all and refers to the New Right only in passing. Similarly, Bell (2011) chooses to focus on neo-liberalism, and mentions neo-conservatism only in passing. What is strange is that if one looks back only a matter of 25 years or so, both neo-conservatism and neo-liberalism were seen as being more-or-less equally weighted themes of a wider New Right project (Gamble, 1998; Hayes, 1994 or Hay, 1996; Levitas, 1986). Trends relating to the use of such terms are plotted in Figures 7.1 and 7.2.

Figure 7.1 shows a growing use of the term 'Thatcherism' with a high point in 1989 (31 articles published that year). After this, use of the term wanes. This contrasts with interest in neo-liberalism. Here one sees a growing use of the term – from the early 1990s until 2009 (110 publications that year).[1]

Few – at least within criminology – seem to have either spotted this trend or appeared concerned by it if they had. However, O'Malley (1999) reminds us that some of the recent trends in penality owe rather more to neo-conservativism than they do neo-liberalism (O'Malley, 1999: 187). Herein, and as part of our wider exploration of the legacy of Thatcherite social and economic policies for crime in the UK, we wish to explore the ways in which neo-liberal and neo-conservative strands of thought and policy enactments have influenced crime and responses to crime in the UK since the early 1980s.

Let us commence, then, with a recapping of the two strands of New Right thinking, starting with neo-liberalism.[2] Hay (1996) notes that neo-liberals were concerned to reassert the free market, increase individual liberty and freedom, reduce inflation, and saw limiting government spending, reducing the size of the state and bringing down levels of taxation as the vehicles for achieving these goals. For Gamble (1989: 5) the libertarian New Right believed that: state intervention did not work; alternatives to the market were flawed; government failure was more common than market failure; and citizens' rights were violated by state

---

[1] A similar graph for neo-conservatism (not shown) is rather more patchy, with no clear trend and a very low N of publications in any one year – 9 in 2008 being the highest.

[2] For good summaries of the histories of neo-liberalism and neo-conservatism, see the texts quoted in the passages above; most start with some discussion of where these ideas came from and a brief chronology of key events.

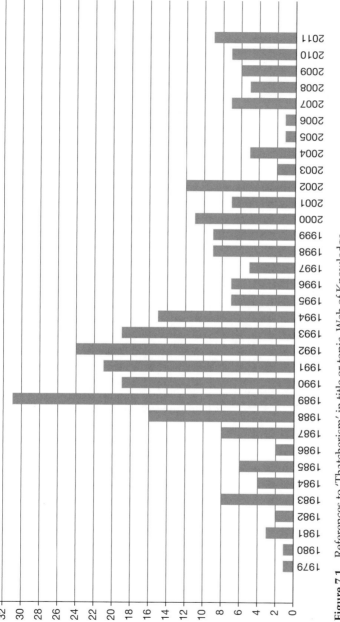

Figure 7.1 References to 'Thatcherism' in title or topic, Web of Knowledge

210

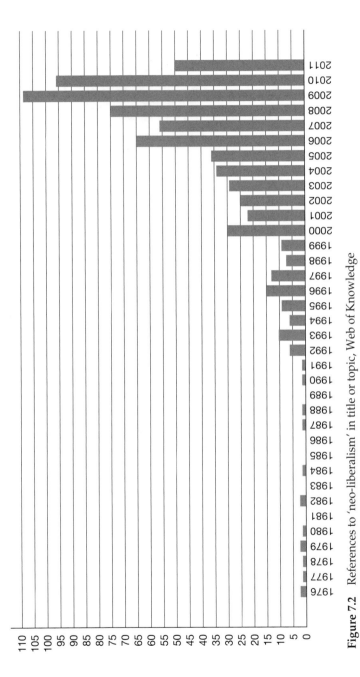

Figure 7.2 References to 'neo-liberalism' in title or topic, Web of Knowledge

intervention. The Thatcher administrations aimed their policies at reducing the role of the state (Gamble, 1989: 7) via the privatization of key services hitherto provided by government. Gamble recounts the principal objectives of privatization: greater freedom of choice; greater efficiency; the reduction of the Public Sector Borrowing Requirement; reduction in the costs of public sector pay; the removal of key decisions from the political arena altogether; increased share ownership amongst the citizenry; the promotion of liberalization and competition; an increase in active citizenry and a reduction of state dependency (1989: 11). To this Leys (2001: 3) adds the desire to make the state serve business interests, and to reduce the government's exposure to political pressure from the electorate. As Levitas notes (1986: 7) such concerns were rather limited to economic matters. Neo-conservatism, on the other hand, had a slightly different set of 'instincts'. These included: (re)imposing traditional values (such as respect of property/authority, decency and discipline); the active role of the state to police and enforce moral behaviours; the reduction of the welfare state to tackle the 'dependency culture'; the upholding of the importance of the nuclear family; and the restoration of social hierarchy (Hay, 1996; but see also Hayes, 1994 and essays by both Gamble and Edgar in Levitas, 1986). Marwick (2003: 241) adds that Thatcherism also expressed overt hostility toward the 'permissiveness' associated with the 1960s.

It is clear then, that even a cursory glance at the political science literature on phenomena such as Thatcherism or the New Right acknowledges that these creatures are made up of different strands of thinking and desires for the economy and society (indeed, Levitas argues that the contradictory nature of the New Right is a strength, 1986: 11). Yet few criminologists have either: (a) fully recognized this distinction, or (b) thought about how these strands of New Right thinking may relate to one another, or even, that their relationship to each another might have evolved over time. What does viewing the Thatcherite legacy through the lenses of neo-conservatism and neo-liberalism do to our understanding of the Thatcherite legacy for the CJS? This is a question we return to later. Let us now turn to a consideration of how we might have expected Thatcher to have shaped the CJS.

What might a 'Thatcherized' CJS have looked like?

As noted above, few (Newburn, 2007) have found very much evidence of a radical Thatcherite influence on the CJS. What might one have expected had the Conservative governments of 1979 to 1990 attended to the issue of crime with the same vigour that they attended to, for example, housing or the economy? Hypothesizing what might have happened is never an easy task, however, and in order to imagine what a 'Thatcherized CJS' might have looked like we have relied upon the rhetoric of Thatcher during her time as leader of the Conservative party. In her final election broadcast on the eve of the 1979 election, Thatcher referred to 'feeling safe in the streets' (Riddell, 1985: 193). Prior to that, she had claimed that the country wanted 'less tax and more law and order' (Savage, 1990: 89). In March 1988 Thatcher expressed her opinion that social workers were also to blame for rises in crime as they 'created a fog of excuses in which the muggers and burglars operate' (Riddell, 1989: 171). She also stated that she would 'never . . . economise on law and order' (Savage, 1990: 91). She was also in favour of capital punishment (Thatcher, 1993: 307). Such sentiments can be interpreted as a desire for a CJS which did not embrace penal welfarism, favoured crime control models of policing, and which tended towards harsher penalties.

Although 'law and order' was brought to the fore by the Conservatives in the 1979 election campaign (Downes and Morgan, 1997: 93) there was very little policy change. In fact, there was a notable absence of legislation on crime in the first two post-1979 sessions of Parliament (Windlesham, 1993: 153). Whitelaw referred to the idea of a 'short, sharp, shock' for young offenders, but did not pursue the idea (Windlesham, 1993: 159). The Police and Criminal Evidence Act 1984, which grew out of a Royal Commission started in 1978, gave new rights to those suspected of having committed an offence (Windlesham, 2001: 135), although the Act had initially caused consternation amongst civil liberties groups and the opposition (Windlesham, 1993: 185–92). Hurd's memoirs suggest that, as Home Secretary, he was isolated from the Cabinet and left, in effect, to deal with law and order in a reactive rather than a proactive fashion (Hurd, 2003: 349–72). Whilst the Criminal Justice Act 1988 empowered the Attorney-General to appeal against 'overly-lenient' sentences, despite this, the prison population in this period actually fell (Windlesham, 1993: 241) – a consequence of earlier restrictions placed on the sentencing of young people following the 1982 and 1988 Criminal Justice Acts (themselves based on ideas put forward in 1974; Faulkner 2001: 110). As this suggests, criminal justice under Thatcher was characterized more by continuity of consensus politics than it was by Thatcherite radicalism.

With the arrival of Major as Prime Minister, there were a number of important changes in key ministries, with Baker becoming Home Secretary.

Like Hurd before him, Baker was a liberal on many matters. The Criminal Justice Act 1991 strengthened non-custodial sentences, providing guidelines for sentencing, making custodial sentences only available if no other sentence could be justified and reducing maximum sentences for theft and non-domestic burglary (Faulkner, 2001: 115). Again, there was little sign of a hard-line 'Thatcherite' approach; rather, 'the wets' pursued liberal crime policies and gave enlightened thinking on such matters the space to flourish within the Home Office.

It was only from 1992 that crime became much more prominent on the policy agenda. After expulsion from the ERM and the signing of the Maastricht Treaty, Major needed to unite his party, and 'law and order' was an obvious target (Faulkner, 2001: 122). However, this focus was not merely a diversionary tactic; crime *had* risen unexpectedly in 1989–92. Data from the British Crime Survey suggested that crime was under-reported and relatively few criminal acts resulted in court convictions. This was particularly troublesome for the Conservatives, who, having increased expenditure on the CJS for 14 consecutive years, had little to show for their efforts (see; Baker, 1993: 450–1; Balen, 1994: 233; Thatcher, 1993: 626). In early 1993, the first criticisms of the Criminal Justice Act 1991 were voiced by members of the judiciary and the media. Accordingly, the Criminal Justice Bill 1993 was amended to abolish unit fines and also remove sentencing guidelines (Faulkner, 2001: 125). Faulkner – amongst others – interpreted this as signalling that the government no longer wanted to limit the use of imprisonment (Faulkner, 2001: 125–6). Howard – very much Thatcher's man (Thatcher, 1993: 852) – took over at the Home Office in May 1993. During his first speech as Home Secretary at the Party conference (in 1993 and during which he claimed that 'prison works'), Howard outlined several new 'tough' measures, many of which became part of the Criminal Justice and Public Order Act 1994. The Act resulted in the erosion of the right to silence, the introduction of secure training for persistent juvenile offenders, the criminalization of squatters and demonstrators, changes in laws of evidence (making conviction easier), increased penalties and periods of custody for young offenders, and restrictions on the use of bail (Faulkner, 2001: 126). Yet, it was his speech to the 1995 conference that would become a landmark in penal history (Windlesham, 2001: 4). Howard successfully captured the prevailing mood, following the abduction and murder of James Bulger in February 1993 (Hay, 1995), that 'something must be done about crime', with his desire to move to a system of mandatory minimum sentences and a return to economic utilitarian arguments on deterrence. From this point onwards, there was a dramatic increase in incarceration rates (Windlesham, 2001: 8–25). Although judges, lords and two former Home Secretaries (Hurd and Baker) criticized the proposals, the tone was set for the future of the criminal justice agenda, as the parties increasingly sought to outdo one another in their toughness in response to crime (Windlesham, 2001: 24). Finally, in 1997, the Crime (Sentences) Act was passed, although it did not come into effect until early 1999 (under Labour). This Act introduced various mandatory sentences and reversed earlier efforts to reduce imprisonment (Faulkner, 2001: 126). So the obvious efforts to 'get tough' occurred *after* Thatcher's period in office.

A Thatcherite legacy?

The foregoing review may well lead the reader to wonder how it is that we have the temerity to persist with our claim of being able to identify a Thatcherite legacy for the CJS. We do so by pointing to four key social and economic arenas in which Thatcherite influence can be (and has been) convincingly documented (Thompson, Murie, Hill and Walker, and Dorling, in this collection). These four are: changes in economic policies and outcomes; changes in the housing market (led by a raft of housing acts); changes in the provision of social security, and, finally, changes in education policies (especially after 1988). We take each in turn, and each in the order in which they were focused upon by the Thatcher administrations (Hay and Farrall, 2011).

Economic change

During the 1970s, the gradual discrediting of the trade-off between unemployment and inflation that had been identified by the Phillips curve,[3] in particular with the experience of stagflation in a number of advanced economies including Britain, led successive British governments to retreat from Keynesian fiscal policies and embrace, to varying degrees, monetarist

---

[3] The Phillips Curve (now no longer used) describes the inverse relationship between unemployment and inflation (such that when unemployment is high inflation is low, and vice versa). The validity of the Phillips Curve diminished after the 1970s, when several prominent economies experienced both high levels of unemployment and high levels of inflation.

policies. As control of the money supply and the prevention of inflation were prioritized above full employment, levels of unemployment rose during the 1980s (Figure 7.3). The terms of the 1976 IMF loan to Britain's Labour government had required cuts to public expenditure and helped advance monetarist thinking (Burk and Cairncross, 1992). This was part of a wider debate about the 'overloaded state' as UK policy-makers struggled to cope with the growing range of issues that confronted them – further adding to scepticism about Keynesian demand management and the merits of 'big government'. The tenor of the economic policies pursued by the Thatcher and Major governments itself changed considerably over time; interest in monetarism emerged in the mid-1970s, peaking between 1981 and 1984. Monetarism was slowly abandoned after 1983, followed by a focus on privatization and financial deregulation (1983–86), which contributed to the so-called 'Lawson boom' of 1986–88. Following this, inflation rose, sterling joined the Exchange Rate Mechanism (ERM) and successive budgets reduced personal taxation (with privatization of public-

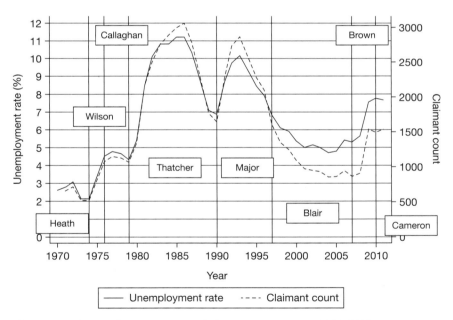

Figure 7.3   Unemployment rate and claimant count rate, 1970–2011

Source: Office for National Statistics, *Labour Market Statistics* (2012)

215

owned ventures used to pay for this between 1986 and 1990). Economic restructuring in the form of further deindustrialization (which had started in the late-1960s; Tomlinson, 1990) was associated with rising unemployment, which some have argued led to increasing social and political polarization (Walker and Walker, 1997). Liberalization of financial markets and the tax regime from the 1980s onwards contributed to rising economic inequality (Figure 7.4) as the Thatcher government abolished higher rates of taxation, reduced corporation tax, and increased indirect taxation, such as VAT, which had a greater marginal effect on the less well-off. Although the exact nature of the policies pursued varied over time, our chief concern is with the impact that these policies had on unemployment and economic inequality (which, by and large, was to increase each of these over time). As shown in Figure 7.3, unemployment grew rapidly during the early 1980s. Some regions were hit harder than others.

The 'Lawson boom' did result in a short-lived reduction in the unemployment but this rose again during the recession in the early 1990s. Economic inequality is plotted in Figure 7.4, showing inequality steadily rising from the mid-1970s before plateauing during the early 1990s and then rising again after 2000 (with the horizontal lines indicating periods of economic change under the Heath, Wilson, Callaghan, Thatcher, Major, Blair, Brown and Cameron governments). If one considers standard, international measures of the distribution of wealth in a nation, such as the Gini coefficient, one sees growing inequalities in the UK from the late 1970s (Stymne and Jackson, 2000). These inequalities increased dramatically from the early to mid-1980s at a time when others countries saw declines in the Gini coefficient (see Dorling, Chapter 8 in this collection). Atkinson (2000: 364–5) notes that between the end of the Second World War and the late 1970s the trend in the distribution of wealth in the UK was strongly egalitarian. However, after the end of the 1970s, this picture changed dramatically. Between 1979 and 1985 widening inequality was due to many families losing their incomes as unemployment rose (Atkinson, 2000: 365). From 1985 to 1990, however, the inequalities were due largely to government policies (Atkinson, 2000: 365). Timmins (2001: 375) is not alone in noting the marked widening in the gap between rich and poor during the Thatcher years, reporting that as early as the late 1980s the first signs that the UK was becoming a more unequal society were emerging (2001: 449). Walker (1990) reports that the number of people reliant on income support increased by 45 per cent during the period from around 3 million in 1979 to 4.35 million 1989. If one includes the claimants' dependants, as many as

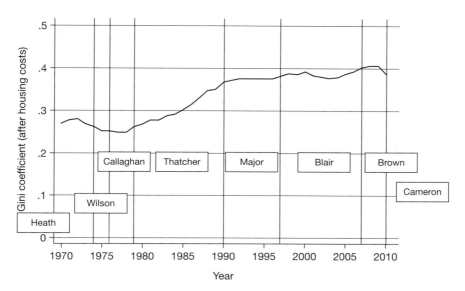

Figure 7.4   Income inequality (Gini coefficient), 1970–2010

Source: Institute for Fiscal Studies (2012)

7 million people were reliant upon income support during the 1980s. Further evidence in the mid-1990s suggested that the poor in the UK were getting poorer (Timmins, 2001: 507). With long-term unemployment endemic in some parts of the UK, many residents found themselves reliant on benefits for extended periods of time, which made working cash-in-hand or claiming and working more socially acceptable (Timmins, 2001: 526).

There is growing evidence that indicators of the economic cycle or economic outcomes such as the rate of unemployment (Cantor and Land, 1985; Hale and Sabbagh, 1991; Pyle and Deadman, 1994) or levels of income inequality (Chiricos, 1987; Land et al., 1990) are associated with higher rates of offending. Such a link between the economic cycle and crime runs in parallel with the identification of partisan business cycles (Hibbs, 1977), in the link between electoral politics and the economic cycle, manifested in systematic differences between macro-economic outcomes (specifically the inflation/unemployment trade-off identified by the Phillips curve) under left and right political parties. The combined insight from such accounts is that macro-economic policies and outcomes are not wholly exogenous to either politics or to crime rates. Using time series analyses for the period between 1961 and 2006 (Jennings et al., 2012) we find that changes in the unemployment rate are associated with changes in the rate of recorded property crime in England and Wales. Interestingly, there is also evidence that the crime-unemployment link strengthened during this period, suggesting that the economic changes brought about by the Thatcher administrations contributed to a shift in the crime-economy nexus. In sum, then, the consequences of Thatcher's economic radicalism were a profound increase in levels of unemployment, economic inequality and social polarization that were reflected in a steep increase in rates of crime, and reinforcement of the unemployment-crime link.

Changes in the housing market

The election of the Thatcher government brought a dramatic paradigm shift in housing policy, with a concerned and radical attempt to extend home ownership (Murie, Chapter 5 in this collection). The Housing Act 1980 was key to this process, and resulted in a rise in home ownership from 55 per cent in 1979 to 64 per cent in 1987. Following an initial burst of sales, from 1982, the number of council house sales began to fall (Kemp, 1992: 68), prompting further discounts in 1984 and 1986. Thatcher's third term focused on the privatization of rented housing. The Housing Act 1988 was aimed at transferring council houses to housing associations or allowing private landlords to bid for the running of council properties. At around this time, the impact of changes elsewhere to the running of the welfare state started to impact on housing in the UK. The Social Security Act 1988 increased homelessness amongst those aged 16–18 (Atkinson and Durden, 1994: 196), thereby increasing demand for basic, affordable accommodation at a time when the housing system was ill-placed to cope with extra demands. By 1990, the discounts being offered to tenants in council housing had reached 53 per cent. This accelerated the ongoing residualization of both council tenants and the council housing stock (Murie, Chapter 5 in this collection). The result was the ghettoization of large sections of the inner city in 'new enclosures with high turnover, transient populations, drawn from the most vulnerable sections of community in a context of high unemployment and widening social inequality' (Murie, 1997: 28). The process of residualization was also fostered by the Housing Act 1985, which placed a duty on local councils to house homeless people (Atkinson and Durden, 1994: 192). This created a situation in which better-off families either bought houses in 'good' council estates and left after a short while to move 'up' the ladder or left without buying, leaving the less well-off living alongside those who the councils had a statutory obligation to house and who often had considerable social and economic needs. Radicalism in the housing arena had significant consequences and spill-over effects. The right to buy one's own council house, coupled with the Housing Act's requirement (1985) that local councils house homeless people and the impacts of the Social Security Act 1988 (which were aimed at reducing the costs of social security in general), created a situation in which dis-advantaged members of society were corralled together in areas that became known as 'sink estates' and in which low-level anti-social behavi-our and crime became commonplace. This was to become an important element of the context in which crime and criminal justice policy would eventually be radicalized.

Changes in social security provision

There was considerable continuity in policy in this area that the election of Thatcher in 1979 did little to alter (Farrall and Hay, 2010) – at least initially. This was at least, in part, because the incoming Thatcher government lacked a clear sense of what to do about social security (McGlone, 1990: 160). Yet they were very clearly committed to the idea that benefits had become too generous (Pierson, 1996: 215). As in many other policy domains, there was a clear Thatcherite instinct, but it was not yet clear precisely how this was to inform a more radical reform agenda. Reflecting this instinctive commitment to reduce benefits, the Conservatives altered the 'up-rating rule', linking benefits to rises in prices, not earnings (Walker, 1990: 34), slowly impoverishing those receiving such benefits (Howard, 1997: 93), contributing further to widening inequalities and, as our model-ling above suggests, ultimately, to crime. In 1983, the Department of Health and Social Security (DHSS) produced new regulations that introduced banded limits on payments relating to board and lodging (McGlone, 1990: 162). This, in effect, resulted in a freeze on all board and lodgings pay-ments, followed by a cut and a restriction placed on the payment of benefits for unemployed people under 25 years. They would now need to move every two to eight weeks to remain eligible for payments – thereby increasing the number of young homeless people (McGlone, 1990: 162), who, in turn, were trapped in situations in which they were more likely to become involved in crime (Carlen, 1996). Further developments saw housing benefit cut (Hill, 1994: 247) and earnings-related short-term benefits abolished (Hill, 1999: 166). In April 1984, Norman Fowler announced a comprehensive review of social security spending (McGlone, 1990: 163), which argued that the benefit system needed reform, resulting in the Social Security Act 1986. From around 1987, we see the start of the second (more radical) stage of changes (McGlone, 1990: 160). Unlike the first, in which there was an attempt to enforce a new philosophy via the old structures, this saw a conscious effort to break with past policies (Pierson, 1996: 203–6: Walker, 1990: 34). Commentators typically see 1988–90 as representing the high point of radical legislation, some even claiming that it rivals the legislation of 1944–48 in terms of its radicalism (Glennerster, 1994: 322). In 1986, 16- and 17-year-old claimants lost the right to income support under the Youth Training Scheme, whilst those for 18–24-year-olds were reduced (Hill, 1994: 248). The Social Security Act 1986 saw the ending of free school meals and cuts in housing benefit, producing a 10 per cent reduction in claimants between February and May 1988 (McGlone, 1990: 168). Changes to the rules also meant that fewer people were eligible for unemployment benefit (Howard, 1997: 87).

Following the departure of Thatcher from office, a number of Thatcherite ministers took hold of key departments, most notably Peter Lilley as Minister for Social Security and Michael Portillo at the Treasury. Following these appointments, the pace of change in social security policy quickened considerably (Howard, 1997: 84). The 1993 Party conference saw Portillo announce a two-year review of social policy and public spending. Oddly for a 'spending minister', Lilley supported this, claiming that he wanted to rethink the role of social security (Glennerster, 1994: 319). Unemployment Benefit was re-titled Jobseeker's Allowance in 1995, emphasizing a shift in thinking on entitlements and responsibilities (Hill, 1999: 170). Those aged under 25 received a lower rate (Howard, 1997: 87). The Jobseeker's Allowance was means tested after the first six months, with entitlement reduced after that point (Hill, 1999: 171; Howard, 1997: 87–8). The changes in the social security system – ostensibly aimed at alleviating poverty and financial hardship – in fact stemmed from the need to halt the rise in expenditure that followed the increase in unemployment in the early 1980s. Some have argued that it was the 'reduced redistributive ambitions of the Government' which were to blame for changes in Gini coefficient after the mid-1980s (Atkinson, 2000: 370) – prior to this point the changes in Gini were due to unemployment. As we have shown elsewhere (Jennings et al., 2012), the effects of benefits expenditure was to act as a break on the rate of property crime.

Changes in education policies

Whilst the Education Act 1980, along with all education acts (up to 1988) is seen as incrementalist, big changes took place in the education sector from the mid to late 1980s (see Dorey, Chapter 4 in this collection). In 1986, there was a marked shift in thinking, as New Right approaches came to dominate the government's approach to education and schooling (Tomlinson, 1989: 183). The Education Reform Act 1988 was radically to change secondary education in the UK. As a result, staff–student ratios rose throughout the 1980s and 1990s, arguably leading to greater disruption in classes, more exclusions and greater levels of staff absenteeism. In Major's first Cabinet in 1990, Clarke became Education Minister. Within six months, he had published two White Papers that were to change the face of higher and further education in the UK, just as the 1988 Act had reformed secondary education (Scott, 1994: 338). Changes in personnel at the National Curriculum Council and the Schools Examinations and Assessments Council also resulted in a greater Thatcherite control of education policy than the Thatcherites had enjoyed whilst she was in power (Scott, 1994: 339).

The Education Act 1992 continued the work of streamlining the opting-out process, further limiting the role of LEAs (Dorey, 1999: 149). The Education Act 1993 further enabled and encouraged the opting out of LEA control by schools (Scott, 1994: 341). In this respect, education policy under Major represented a continuation of the momentum generated at the end of Thatcher's administration. In 1992, the first league tables of school exams were published (Timmins, 2001: 519). These had the unfortunate side effect of encouraging schools to exclude unruly children (school exclusions rose throughout the 1990s, reaching a peak of 12,668 in 1996–97; DFeS, 2001). Dumped on the streets, excluded children only served to cause further problems for local residents and the police (Berridge et al., 2001). As such, school exclusions helped to create anti-social behaviour and the need for the Crime and Disorder Act 1998. Bynner and Parsons (2003: 287) show that those in school between 1975 and 1986 had twice the rate of temporary suspensions (15 per cent for males and 6 per cent for females) as the generation of children before them (7 and 3 per cent, respectively). The radicalism of the reform of the education system served to make the management of schools harder by raising staff–student ratios and it had a series of spill-over effects for communities and policing in terms of the numbers of young people excluded from schools. As with changes in the economy, housing provision and social security provision, the side effects included (but were not limited to) widening inequality, unemployment, 'sofa-surfing', the creation of 'sink estates' and an increase in excluded pupils. All of these were to have significant ramifications for both crime and the criminal justice system.

What happened to crime?

Crime, of course, had been rising steadily during the 1960s, albeit it from a very low base, having not exceeded 1 million recorded crimes per annum until the 1960s. Total recorded crime increased from 2.5 million in 1979 and 4.5 million in 1990 (an increase of 179 per cent). Not all offences saw the same rates of increase (Figure 7.5). Burglary and theft saw dramatic increases, whilst violent and sexual offences rose more slowly, but continued to increase into the early 2000s. Whatever the nuances, there is no denying the overall rise in crime throughout the 1980s and into the first half of the 1990s. Crime was generally rising before 1979, but the rate of increase picked up after early 1980s and further accelerated in early 1990s. The steepest rises in the rate of burglary and theft occurred during the 1980s and early 1990s, coinciding with sharp increases in the level of unemployment and inequality.

Such dramatic changes in crime rates did not go unnoticed by the public; and the expressed level of public fear of crime (as measured in the British Crime Survey) is illustrated in Figure 7.6. Again we see steady increases throughout the 1980s until its crescendo in 1994, before declining thereafter. The rising crime rate was not recognized by the public as a serious problem earlier, in, say, the mid-1980s (which saw the riots in various English cities) as such events were cast at the time very much as problems resulting from the state of the economy, which was identified as the 'real problem' in need of attention. So although crime was rising during the period, the economy still overshadowed it as the 'most important problem' facing the country in regular surveys of public opinion (Farrall and Jennings, 2012).

This increase in crime appeared to have a number of consequences for public attitudes. First there was an increase in the proportion of people wanting increased spending on the police and prisons, combined with a decrease in public preferences for spending on social security (see Figure 7.7).[4] It also appeared to 'harden' attitudes towards offenders, as

[4] Since 1983, the British Social Attitudes Survey has asked a regular question about the spending priorities of the public: 'About items of government spending. Which of these would be your highest priority for extra spending?'

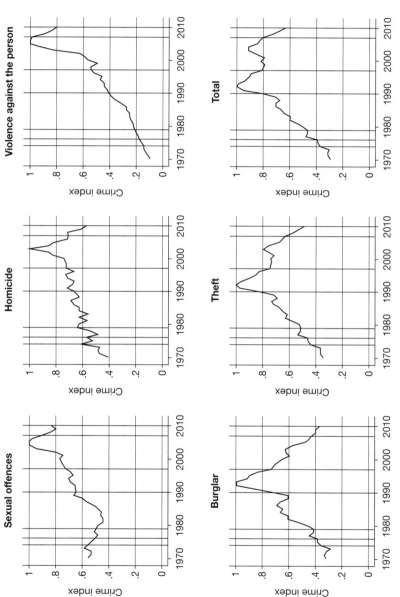

Figure 7.5 Property crime per capita (Home Office recorded statistics)

Source: Home Office (various). The introduction of revised counting rules in 1998 presents a challenge for longitudinal analysis of crime rates in England and Wales. The figures presented here are transformed using a multiplier for post-1998 values to adjust for inflation in the number of recorded crimes due to this change. The value of the multiplier is equal to the ratio between the number of crimes recorded according to the old rules and the new counting rules in 1999.

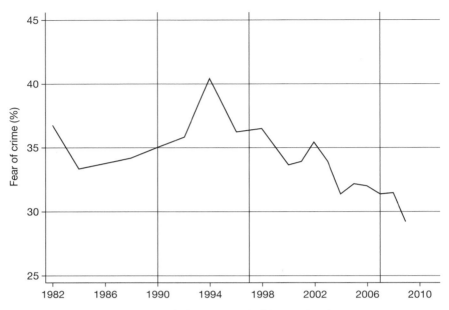

Figure 7.6   Percentage worried about crime (BCS 1982–2009)

measured by the proportion of people prepared to see the harsher treatment of suspects.

To what extent did crime occupy the attention of British government during this period? The proportion of the policy agenda presented at the start of each session of Parliament in the Queen's Speech referring to criminal justice is plotted in Figure 7.8 for the period between 1970 and 2010. Over this period, there was a low level of government attention to criminal justice between the 1970s and early 1990s, with between 1 and 8 per cent of the content of the policy agenda dedicated to the issue of law and order. There was a short-lived upturn in attention (to 10 per cent) in 1979 (the first programme of the Thatcher government). However, the most sizeable escalation in concern occurred in the Major government's programme of October 1996 in which there was a jump to 15 per cent of the total of the Queen's Speech. After a brief lull in attention during the period between 1997 and 2000, the amount of policy content in the speech dedicated to crime rose to almost a fifth. Through plotting a LOWESS[5] line

[5] Locally Weighted Scatterplot Smoothing.

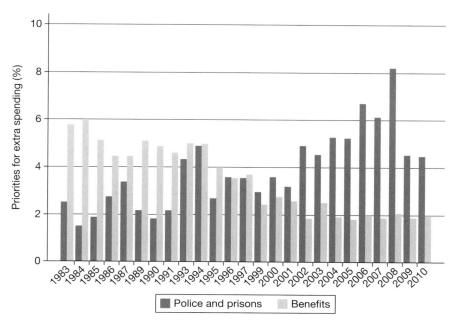

Figure 7.7   Priorities for extra spending, British Social Attitudes Survey 1983–2010

of best fit through the data points, it becomes evident that while there was an upward trend during the 1970s and 1980s, there was a more pronounced escalation of political attention to crime after 1990, which only started to subside in 2005. The period between 1995 and 2005 therefore observed a greater proportion of the annual government agenda dedicated to the issue of crime than at any other point since the 1970s (and indeed since the start of the post-war period).

Statistical modelling (Farrall and Jennings, 2012) shows that changes in the national rate of crime were associated with changes in the attention of British government to the issue of crime, while public concern about the issue also influenced the policy agenda. From the mid-1990s, just as the fear of crime had reached a peak and as crime started to challenge the economy as the issue that public considered to be the 'most important problem' facing the country, government – hardly unsurprisingly – became more active in attending to the issue in their annual programme of executive and legislative proposals. In summary, there are dynamic and lagged effects at work; over time the population responds to rising crime levels (with

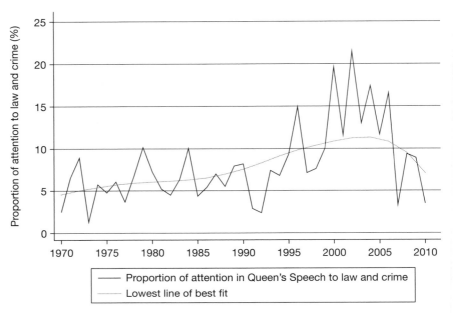

Figure 7.8 Proportion of attention to law and crime in Queen's Speech (with LOWESS line of best fit)

heightened anxiety), which, in turn, leads to government's attention on crime. In this case, the attention afforded to crime was lagged so much that crime was actually on the decrease just as government ratcheted up its own attention on crime. But this is not the whole story, for Jennings et al. (2012) also find that the rate of incarceration (i.e. the ratio of convictions to the size of the prison population): (a) rose sharply during the early 1990s, and (b) is negatively correlated with crime – so 'getting tough' with offenders did appear to reduce the property crime rate.

Conclusion: thinking again about the neo-conservative and neo-liberal influences

Let us think again about the two strands of New Right thinking which characterized the governments of both Thatcher and Major. As documented above (see also Hay and Farrall, 2011: 446, table 1) the social and economic changes pursued by the Thatcher government were initially characterized by a concern with economic matters (and so, by and large, were neo-liberal rather than neo-conservative). As time progressed, and as the Conservative ministers started to get to grips with the civil service machinery, so they started to target rather more neo-conservative issues (such as tackling welfare dependency, via the Fowler Review, see above, which did not start to change benefits until April 1987). However, as crime rose and as public sentiment about crime also shifted, the issue started to rise up the agenda and so the government in the early 1990s started to recognize that it needed to 'do something' about crime – a problem, in large part, the result of economic change. As such, developments post-1993 tended to reflect a neo-conservative approach to crime (as opposed to a neo-liberal one), viz. Howard talking 'tough' on crime; immediate rises in the prison population (which grew by 2.5 per cent p.a. from 1945 to 1995, but by 3.8 per cent p.a. 1995–2009; MoJ, 2009: 4), and a rise in average sentence lengths (Newburn, 2007: 442–4; Riddell, 1989: 170). This 'toughening' of sentencing options led to an increase in the daily prison population (the MoJ's own research points to tougher sentences and stricter enforcement, MoJ, 2009: 2–3, following mandatory minimum sentences – aimed at burglars and drug traffickers – as a cause). There were also increases in exclusion from schools (documented above).

Like O'Malley before us (1999), we find it hard to attribute this entire 'toughening' to neo-liberalism. Rather, our explanatory model points to the influences of both neo-conservatism and neo-liberalism, although each played a role in a slightly different way. The coexistence of structural social and economic forces that have long-term effects on the rate of crime with policy-making and public agendas that have far shorter time horizons point to one of the limitations of existing understanding of the relationship between crime and the criminal justice agenda. It suggests that whilst structural change in both society and the economy is an underlying determinant of crime, the political and public agendas reflect shorter-term considerations that tend to create demand for immediate policy solutions. This is consistent with the theory of punctuated equilibrium in public policy (Baumgartner and Jones, 1993), where long-run stability in policy-making is subject to occasional seismic shifts when existing institutions and issue definitions break down and pressure for change exceeds a threshold. The 1990s was one such period, as long-term trends in crime rates, combined with increasing public concern about the importance of the issue of crime (as well as increased inter-party competition over their law and order credentials), contributed to demand for policy solutions and tougher measures on criminal justice. This set of observations about the post-war British experience underpins our feedback model of the relationship between crime, politics, social change and the economy (Figure 7.9). It suggests that long-term social and economic changes (notably in the British case, deindustrialization), inform change in the preferences and priorities of political parties and the wider public, each of whom further stimulate interest in this issue. This, in turn, contributes to politicization of the issue of crime, through competition between parties, as well as creating pressure for government action and new policy solutions. Changes in government can also lead to changes in social and economic policies, with the election of the Thatcher government in 1979 leading to changes in the distribution of wealth, routine activities and social and economic structures in Britain.

Given that the levels of crime are, in part, the consequence of wider social, economic and political structures, the feedback model suggests that, consistent with a wide field of empirical inquiry, changes in social and economic structures contribute to changes in levels, forms and experiences of crime and victimization. In response, such socio-economic forces can lead, over extended periods of time, to calls for new ways of tackling and dealing with crime and its perceived causes. In this respect, changes in social and economic policies (even those not directly related to crime) may result in underlying changes in behaviour which create further pressure for governmental action. There is a complex feedback process where the consequences of public policies in one domain can have subsequent effects on society and policy in another (Figure 7.9). Such policy feedback processes can occur in isolation from social change – such as between the

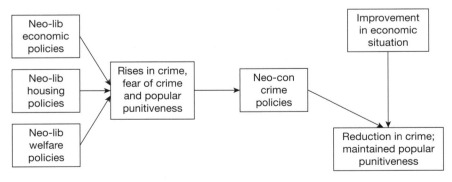

Figure 7.9   A model of neo-liberal and neo-conservative policies and crime

political and public agenda, and, say, between media, public and legislative attention.

For the issue of crime, however, social and economic conditions also prescribe the limits of the sorts of policy responses available. This feedback model, grounded in theories of agenda-setting and policy change, provides a means for explaining the rise in crime and of the criminal justice agenda under the 1979–97 Conservative governments.

It informs representation of the complex interaction between society, the economy, policy and politics along the following lines: taking office in 1979, the Conservatives responded to growing pressures for economic and social reforms that had emerged in Britain during the 1970s through adoption of neo-liberal macro-economic policies as well as embarking on widespread privatization of council housing. However, some aspects of their policies only served to prolong the economic hardship and augment earlier processes of deindustrialization. Later, neo-liberal and neo-conservative social policies cascaded through other branches of state activity between 1981 and 1989 (Hay and Farrall, 2011) falling most heavily on social security, education and local government. This programme of government policies resulted in a shift in the underlying social and economic conditions of Britain, in particular in terms of unemployment and inequality. However, these policies also had impacts on actual crime levels, contributing to production of a further policy problem (rising crime) which was manifested in surveys of the public's fear of crime and its identification of crime as an important issue facing the country.

Although the economy–crime link strengthened during the 1980s, there was initially limited government action on this growing social problem. Eventually, increased political attention was given to the issue of crime, such as in the Queen's Speech (described above). Crime, moreover, became politicized as parties sought to establish reputations for competence in handling of the issue, with inner-city disorder, prison riots and high-profile criminal cases adding to further politicization. In Britain then, the economic policies emerging from the economic crises of the 1970s (at time t_1) had effects on society and the economy, which in turn affected crime rates (at t_2), and which meant that crime later became a focus of further political and government attention (downstream at t_3). The Thatcherite agenda was therefore inadvertently self-fulfilling as neo-liberal policies in one domain (macro-economics) produced social problems that required neo-conservative solutions in another (criminal justice, Farrall and Hay, 2010; Hay and Farrall, 2011).

On the basis of the evidence presented here, it is possible to argue that classic neo-liberal accounts of the origins of crime and of social and economic policies in Britain are wrong. Changes in national crime rates (and in particular property crimes, representing a large proportion of the overall level of crime) can be linked to economic causes. The monetarist policies of Milton Friedman and others, which became increasingly influential over both Conservative and Labour governments during the 1970s and 1980s, and which were associated with high levels of unemployment and increasing income inequality to provide a buffer against inflation, can be indirectly linked with subsequent upturns in the rate of property crime (Pyle and Deadman, 1994) and later rightward shifts of criminal justice and policing policies. Economic restructuring, in particular deindustrialization (which whilst not initiated by the Thatcher governments, certainly accelerated under them), also contributed to social unrest. This illustrates the self-fulfilling character of modern neo-liberal and neo-conservative economic and social policies, as one of the inadvertent features of the rise of monetarist thinking during the 1970s and 1980s was the subsequent rightward shift in the position of the major British political parties on the issue of law and order, offering policy solutions that were 'tough on crime'. It suggests that the policies of economic management of the Conservative governments did little to alleviate – and arguably exacerbated – some of the existing social and economic conditions that gave rise to future calls for conservative (i.e. more punitive) criminal policies under both the Major and Blair governments. Whilst the election of the first Thatcher government in 1979 was a response to the social and economic problems of the 1970s, some of its policy outcomes, in particular further job losses, increasing deindustrialization and rising inequality, consolidated already existing problems which later led to increases in crime rates and fuelled the subsequent rise of law and order on the political agenda in the 1990s. These processes occurred over the period of three decades, starting well before the election of the Conservative government in 1979 and continuing long after the resignation of Thatcher in November 1990. Thatcherite legacies in law and order were sustained in the long term more through their continuing influence over macro-economic policies than through the myth of its 'hard right' approach to criminal justice.

References

Atkinson, A. B. (2000) 'Distribution of Income and Wealth', in A.E. Halsey and J. Webb (eds) *Twentieth-Century British Social Trends*. London: Macmillan.

Atkinson, R. and Durden, P. (1990) 'Housing Policy in the Thatcher Years', in S. Savage, and L. Robins (eds) *Public Policy Under Thatcher* London: Macmillan.

Atkinson, R. and Durden, P. (1994) 'Housing Policy since 1979', in S. Savage, R. Atkinson, R. and L. Robins (eds) *Public Policy in Britain*. Basingstoke: Macmillan.

Baker, K. (1993) *The Turbulent Years*. London: Faber & Faber.

Balen, M. (1994) *Kenneth Clarke*. London: Fourth Estate.

Baumgartner, F. and Jones, B. (1991) 'Agenda Dynamics and Policy Subsystems', *The Journal of Politics*, 53(4): 1044–74.

Becker, G. (1968) 'Crime and Punishment', *Journal of Political Economy*, 76: 169–217.

Bell, E. (2011) *Criminal Justice and Neoliberalism*. London: Routledge.

Berridge, D., Brodie, I., Pitts, J., Porteous, D. and Tarling, R. (2001) 'The Independent Effects Of Permanent Exclusion from School on the Offending Careers of Young People'. Home Office RDS Occ. Paper No. 71.

Burk, K. and Cairncross, A. (1992) *'Goodbye, Great Britain': the 1976 IMF Crisis*. New Haven, CT and London: Yale University Press.

Bynner, J. and Parsons, S. (2003) 'Social Participation, Values and Crime', in E. Ferri, J. Bynner and M. Wadsworth (eds) *Changing Britain, Changing Lives*. London: Institute of Education.

Cantor, D. and Land, K. (1985). 'Unemployment and Crime Rates in the post-World War II United States', *American Sociological Review*, 50: 317–32.

Cerney, P. (2004) 'Mapping Varieties of Neoliberalism', paper at the International Studies Association, Montreal, Canada, March 2004 (cited in W. Larner et al., 'Co-constituting After Neoliberalism', in K. England and K. Ward (eds) (2007) *Neoliberalization* Oxford: Blackwell).

Chiricos, T. (1987) 'Rates of Crime and Unemployment' *Social Problems*, 34(2): 187–212.

Dorey, P. (1999) 'The 3 Rs – Reform, Reproach and Rancour', in P. Dorey (ed.) *The Major Premiership*. Basingstoke: Macmillan.

DFeS (2001) *Permanent Exclusions from Maintained Schools in England*, Issue 10/01 (November).

Downes, D. and Morgan, R. (1997) 'Dumping the "Hostages to Fortune"'? in M. Maguire, R. Morgan and R. Reiner (eds) *The Oxford Handbook of Criminology*, 2nd edn. Oxford: Oxford University Press.

Farrall, S. and Hay, C. (2010) 'Not So Tough on Crime?' *British Journal of Criminology*, 50: 550–69.

Farrall, S. and Jennings, W. (2012) 'Policy Feedback and the Criminal Justice Agenda: an analysis of the economy, crime rates, politics and public opinion in post-war Britain', *Journal of Contemporary British History*, 26(4): 467–88.

Faulkner, D (2001) *Crime, State and Citizen*. Winchester: Waterside Press.

Gamble, A. (1989) 'Privitization, Thatcherism, and the British State', in A. Gamble and C. Wells (eds) *Thatcher's Law*. Cardiff: GPC Books.

Gamble, A. (1998) *The Free Economy and the Strong State*, Macmillan, Basingstoke.

Glennerster, H. (1994) 'Health and Social Policy', in D. Kavanagh and A. Seldon (eds) *The Major Effect*. London: Macmillan.

Gunn, S. and Bell, R. (2003) *Middle Classes*. London: Phoenix.

Hale, C. and Sabbagh, D. (1991) 'Testing the Relationship between Unemployment and Crime', *Journal of Research in Crime and Delinquency* 28(4): 400–18.

Hayes M. (1994) *The New Right in Britain*. Pluto Press, London.

Hay, C. (1996) *Restating Social and Political Change*. Buckingham: Open University Press.

Hay, C. and Farrall, S. (2011) 'Establishing the Ontological Status of Thatcherism by Gauging its "Periodisability"', *British Journal of Politics and International Relations*, 13(4): 439–58.

Hibbs, D. (1977). 'Political Parties and Macroeconomic Policy', *American Political Science Review*, 71: 1467–87.

Hill, M. (1994) 'Social Security Policy under the Conservatives', in S. Savage, R. Atkinson, and L. Robins (eds) *Public Policy in Britain*. Basingstoke: Macmillan.

Institute for Fiscal Studies. (2012) *Living Standards, Poverty and Inequality in the UK: 2012*. London: Institute for Fiscal Studies.

Hill, M. (1999) 'Rolling Back the (Welfare) State', in P. Dorey (ed.) *The Major Premiership*. Basingstoke: Macmillan.

Hough, M. and Mayhew, P. (1983) *The British Crime Survey: First Report. Home Office Research Study 76*. London: HMSO.

Howard, M. (1997) 'Cutting Social Security', in A. Walker and C. Walker (eds) *Britain Divided*. London: CPAG.

Hurd, D. (2003) *Memoirs*. London: Abacus.

Jennings, W., Farrall, S. and Bevan, S. (2012) 'The Economy, Crime and Time: an Analysis of Recorded Property Crime in Britain, 1961–2006', *International Journal of Law, Crime and Justice*, 40(3): 192–210.

Kemp, P. (1992) 'Housing', in R.A.W. Rhodes and D. Marsh (eds) *Implementing Thatcherite Policies*. Buckingham: Open University Press.

Land, K., McCall, P. and Cohen, L. (1990). 'Structural Covariates of Homicide Rates', *American Journal of Sociology*, 95(4): 922–63.

Levitas, R. (1986) 'Introduction', in R. Levitas (ed.) *The Ideology of the New Right*. Oxford: Polity Press.

Leys, C. (2001) *Market-Driven Politics*. London: Verso.

Marwick, A. (2003) *British Society Since 1945*. London: Penguin Books.

McGlone, F. (1990) 'Away from the Dependency Culture?' in S. Savage and L. Robins (eds) *Public Policy Under Thatcher*. London: Macmillan.

MoJ (2009) *Story of the Prison Population 1995–2009 England and Wales*. Ministry of Justice, Statistics Bulletin (July).

Murie, A. (1997) 'Linking Housing Changes to Crime', *Social Policy and Administration*, 31(5): 22–36.

Newburn, Tim (2007) 'Tough on Crime: Penal Policy in England and Wales', *Crime and Justice*, 425–70.

Office for National Statistics (2012) *Labour Market Statistics*. London: ONS.

O'Malley, P. (1999) 'Volatile and Contradictory Punishment', *Theoretical Criminology*, 3(2): 175–96.

Pierson, C. (1996) 'Social Policy under Thatcher and Major', in S. Ludlam and M. Martin (eds) *Contemporary British Conservatism*. Basingstoke: Macmillan.

Pyle, D. and Deadman, D. (1994) 'Crime and the Business Cycle in Post-War Britain', *British Journal of Criminology*, 34(3): 339–57.

Reiner, R. (2007) *Law and Order*. Cambridge: Polity Press.

Riddell, P. (1985) *The Thatcher Government*, 2nd edn. Oxford: Basil Blackwell.

Riddell, P. (1989) *The Thatcher Decade*. Oxford: Basil Blackwell.

Savage, S. (1990) 'A War on Crime?', in S. Savage and L. Robins (eds) *Public Policy Under Thatcher*. London: Macmillan.

Scott, P. (1994) 'Education Policy', in D. Kavanagh and A. Seldon (eds) *The Major Effect*. London: Macmillan.

Stymne, S. and Jackson, T. (2000) 'Intergenerational Equity and Sustainable Welfare', *Ecological Economics*, 33(2): 219–36.

Thatcher, M. (1993) *The Downing Street Years*. London: HarperCollins.

Timmins, N. (2001) *The Five Giants*. London: HarperCollins.

Tomlinson, G. (1989) 'The Schools', in D. Kavanagh and A. Seldon (eds) *The Major Effect*. London: Macmillan.

Walker, A. (1990) 'The Strategy of Inequality', in I. Taylor (ed.) *The Social Effects of Free Market Policies*. Brighton: Harvester.

Walker, Alan and Walker, Carol (eds) (1997) *Britain Divided*. London: CPAG.

Windlesham, Lord (1993) *Responses to Crime* (vol. 2). Oxford: Oxford University Press.

Windlesham, Lord (2001) *Responses to Crime* (vol. 4). Oxford: Oxford University Press.

Commentary

Thatcherism and crime:
the beast that never roared?

DAVID DOWNES

Overall, this is a highly stimulating chapter, which makes out a virtually unanswerable case for Thatcherite policies on crime postdating her lengthy period of office. Moreover, the stress on revising standard depictions of Thatcherism as basically neo-liberal, and neglecting the resurgence of neo-conservatism in the 1990s, is well conveyed. The combined effect of neo-liberal economic policies generating steep rises in unemployment, inequality and poverty, and neo-conservative policies to deal with the consequent rising crime rates and the erosion of social cohesion proved a lethal mix.

However, it remains the case that the most potent development was the shift to neo-liberalism in economic policy, which *required* a subsequent resort to neo-conservatism to deal, as the authors convincingly argue, with the unwanted effects of their policies. However, there is a certain tautology here, as the definition of neo-conservatism seems largely to consist of the resort to tougher criminal justice policies that it is designed to explain. The focus of most criminologists on the neo-liberal shift is therefore not so chronic a perspective. For example, their argument can be seen as supplementing that by David Garland on 'late modernity', which he sees as a process of social and cultural change resulting from profound structural changes – deindustrialization, deregulation, consumerism and growing inequality combined with changes in family and household structure and social ecology that made for rising crime. It was the 'reactionary reading of late modernity' by Thatcher and Reagan which both fuelled and narrowed blame for steeply rising crime to the individuals committing it. Such is the basis for the emergence of what Garland termed the 'culture of control',[1] which could be characterized

---

[1] David Garland (2001) *The Culture of Control.* Oxford: Oxford University Press.

as a profound shift from welfare to penal capital. That this sequence is far from inevitable is a conclusion to be drawn from much comparative criminology (see, for example, Cavadino and Dignan, 2007; Lacey, 2010; and Nelken, 2012).

Farrall and Jennings are indubitably right to discern the lack of synchronization between Thatcherite social populism and its conversion into punitive penal policies in Britain as a problem that demands far more attention than it has so far received. With Reagan there is no such problem: US imprisonment rates started to soar during his presidency. But the reverse happened under Thatcher, indeed a brief decarceration 1989–92 even returned prison population levels to those of a decade earlier. That could not be explained by neo-liberalism, but by liberal morality in a more traditional sense, the kind emanating from Bentham and Mill, and influencing key Home Office policy-makers, encouraged by practitioner success in deflecting young offenders from custody, to pursue a 'quiet revolution' in non-custodial sentencing.

Other points which might be given more emphasis by Farrall and Jennings are:

1   Labour's disarray throughout most of the 1980s meant that the Tories' inability to tackle rising crime did not pose an electoral problem for the government. The Tory lead on 'law and order' was an undisturbed comfort zone until the very end of the decade, when the crime rate rose far more steeply.

2   More importantly, far from hounding the Tory government for being 'soft' on crime, Labour policy was quite the reverse: to criticize them for not pursuing non-custodial penalties radically enough. If Labour had berated the government at this stage for being insufficiently 'tough on crime', it is hardly conceivable that the Conservatives would have countenanced so liberal and reductionist a penal policy.

3   Labour's criticisms of the government for economic and social policies fuelling the crime rate were brushed aside as excuses for those responsible. The Conservative success in 'responsibilization' at times rang perilously thin, as in Norman Tebbitt's explanation for crime as flowing from 'human evil'. More plausibly, Margaret Thatcher consistently cited the 1960s as a period of full employment and rising crime, and the 1930s as one of high unemployment and (quite falsely) stable crime rates, as disproof of any attempt to link rising crime to her social and economic policies. Criminals were to be seen as wholly

responsible for their offences, and any other explanation amounted to excusing law-violation.[2]

4   The domination of the neo-liberal agenda in economic policy was more rapid than that of neo-conservatism in social policy, which was still opposed in key respects by the 'One Nation' strand of Conservative policy-making, notably in criminal justice, where successive Home Secretaries, especially William Whitelaw and Douglas Hurd, contrived a balance between liberal measures and tougher penalties. And Margaret Thatcher did leave her ministers alone to 'get on with it'. This was crucial, as an unusually dedicated number of higher echelon Home Office administrators – notably Brian Cubbon and David Faulkner – were able to assemble the case for, and persuade ministers of, the urgency of reducing the prison population, by wide-ranging reforms to sentencing and non-custodial alternatives. Hence, while the rhetoric of the government on law and order remained abrasive, actual policy-making began to move in the direction of a more sparing use of imprisonment and more constructive community penalties as the 1980s wore on.

5   Thus, until Michael Howard and Tony Blair entered the 'arms race' on crime control, criminal justice policies were more a matter for the judgement of individual Home Secretaries than Party ideology. As Douglas Hurd wrote:[3] 'Indeed, to an extent which surprised me, the Prime Minister left me alone to cope with problems of law and order . . . In general, I realized that she favoured a tough line and strong penalties. But whereas on broadcasting she chaired the relevant committee of ministers and constantly intervened on all matters of policy, on this wider and more important sector she held back. She also supported me on some decisions, particularly on prisons, which she must have found unpalatable.' Such restraint was all the more remarkable given her intense antipathy to law-breaking. Following the

---

[2] Early in their first Parliament, November 1997, New Labour came to embrace much the same position, embodied in the title – *No More Excuses* – of a White Paper on youth justice. This was the cornerstone of the Crime and Disorder Act 1998 which *inter alia* created Anti-social Behaviour Orders. See Downes and Morgan (1997) for an analysis of the 'dumping' of this and other 'Old Labour' hostages to fortune; Denis Jones (2001) for a severe critique of the Audit Commission reports which provided its empirical base; and Owen Jones (2012) *Chavs: The Demonization of the Working Class*, for an unusually detailed analysis of the 'chav' phenomenon as the latest phase in the stigmatization of wayward and largely jobless youth.
[3] Douglas Hurd (2003: 341).

riots in Brixton and Toxteth – '"Oh, those poor shopkeepers!" she cried on seeing the first pictures of riot and looting in Toxteth. A lot of Margaret Thatcher's character is expressed in that single phrase.'[4]

6   A leitmotif connecting different policy fields was the attack on the power of local authorities to set their own agenda. Thus, in housing, the Right to Buy and, more crucially, the prohibition on local councils using the funds thus created to build again, quickly led to both beggary and homelessness. In education, bypassing local education authorities in ordering curriculum changes and league tables fed into higher rates of exclusion. All of this was basically driven by the assault on left-wing authorities' scope for pursuing even mildly social-democratic policies. The central state accrued even more power as a result. The strong, central 'watchman' state is fundamental to neo-liberalism and practically the first act of the incoming Thatcher administration in 1979 was to implement the generous recommendations of the Edmund-Davis committee, set up by the previous Labour government, on police pay.

7   The role of Tony Blair as Shadow Home Secretary in activating the belated Thatcherite U-turn is seen in the timing of his 'Tough on crime, tough on the causes of crime' speech, coming three months after the James Bulger case and four months before Michael Howard's 'Prison works' speech in October 1993. Following their fourth successive electoral defeat in early 1992, Labour were now ditching key elements of their previous policies on law and order to rebrand themselves as *the* party on that front. Though the Tories had long held a comfortable lead on that issue – for example, in September 1987 they polled[5] 50 per cent support by contrast with Labour's 14 per cent – the gap had been greatly narrowed, even under 'Old' Labour's more liberal policies, to 40 per cent and 26 per cent on 30 March 1992. By September 1993, following Blair's 'Tough on crime' speech, though before Michael Howard's 'Prison works' re-positioning of the government on that front, the difference had virtually disappeared, with the Tories on 23 per cent and 'New Labour' on 21 per cent. Blair's strategy proved

[4] Hugo Young (1989: 239).

[5] To the question including 'law and order': 'I am going to read out a list of problems facing Britain today. I would like you to tell me whether you think the Conservative party, the Labour party or the Liberal Democrats has the best policies on each problem.' MORI: see note below.

so popular, politically and eventually in electoral terms, that by May 1994 Labour moved ahead of the Tories on law and order by a margin of 31 per cent to 26 per cent, a lead they were to hold almost unbrokenly until 2003.[6]

A major irony of these developments is that the belated activation of Thatcherite policies on crime, law and order was in part due to the conversion of New Labour under Blair's leadership to quasi-Thatcherite policies. Indeed, the polling trend suggests that the steep rise in the crime rate between 1988 and 1992, arguably the result of the Conservatives' neo-liberal economic policies of the 1980s, was in its turn eroding confidence in the Conservative government. There was no need for Tony Blair to abandon what was coming to be derided as the 'Old' Labour approach to crime control. But the fact that he did so, along with his successor as Shadow Home Secretary, Jack Straw, made a 'tough' Conservative response inevitable. The ensuing rivalry as to which party could be 'toughest' led to a doubling of the prison population within just over a decade, as well as the much-criticized creation of Anti-Social Behaviour Orders, the extension of mandatory sentencing powers, and the expansion of partially indeterminate sentences, an 'arms race' best captured in Jonathan Simon's concept of 'governing through crime'. A second irony was that despite a continuing drop in the overall crime rate, the popularity of New Labour governments on that issue fell to the point, in 2003, when the Conservatives reclaimed their traditional lead as the party 'with the best policies on law and order',[7] all of which suggests that New Labour's, and Blair's, ever more tortuous attempts to outdo the Tories on 'law and order' had begun to lose credibility. As Farrall and Jennings conclude, the Thatcherite legacy in criminal justice is proving a disturbingly durable fixture.

References

Downes, D.M. and Morgan, R. (1997) 'Dumping the 'Hostages to Fortune'?' in M. Maguire, R. Morgan and R. Reiner (eds) *Oxford Handbook of Criminology*, 2nd edn. Oxford: Oxford University Press.

[6] Bobby Duffy et al. (2010) *Closing the Gaps: Crime and Public Perceptions*. Ipsos MORI, 24 March. See also www.ipsos-mori.com/researchpublications/researcharchive/poll.aspx?oItemID
[7] Ipsos MORI.

Garland, D. (2000) *The Culture of Control*. Oxford: Oxford University Press.

Hurd, D. (2003) *Memoirs*. London: Little, Brown.

Jones, D. (2001) '"Misjudged Youth": A Critique of the Audit Commission's Reports on Youth Justice', *British Journal of Criminology*, 41: 362–80.

Jones, O. (2012) *Chavs: The Demonization of the Working Class*, updated edn. London: Verso.

Lacey, N. (2008) *The Prisoners' Dilemma: Political Economy and Punishment in Contemporary Democracies.* Cambridge: Cambridge University Press.

Nelken, D. (ed.) (2012) *Comparative Criminal Justice and Globalization.* Farnham: Ashgate.

Simon, J. (2007) *Governing Through Crime: How the War on Crime Transformed American Democracy and Created a Culture of Fear*. New York: Oxford University Press.

Young, H. (1989) *One Of Us: A Biography of Margaret Thatcher*. London: Macmillan.

8
Mapping the Thatcherite legacy: the human geography of social inequality in Britain since the 1970s

DANNY DORLING

Introduction

British academics of my generation, and some a great deal younger, are often fascinated by Thatcherism and its legacy. When reviewing Peter Dorey's book, *British Conservatism: The Politics and Philosophy of Inequality*, Emily Robinson (2011) explained that the book helped answer Kevin Hickson's plea for more work to be done on the Conservatives' attitudes to inequality:

> As both Hickson and Dorey point out, Conservative positions on inequality have often been mistaken for an offshoot of pragmatism: given that inequality exists, an acceptance of it can easily be seen as simply realistic. However, as both go on to demonstrate, the defence – and even promotion – of inequality are core tenets of Conservative thinking. In fact, as Dorey's title suggests, this could be seen as the defining feature of British Conservatism, uniting the party across the lines of moderation and radicalism, paternalism and laissez-faire.
>
> (Robinson, 2011: 307)

The promotion of inequality, mostly as an indirect result of policy but also as a direct result of the belief that 'tall poppies' should not be cut down, was one of the main Thatcherite legacies (see Walker, Chapter 9 in this collection). Not just the inequality that grew under Thatcher's actual years in office, but the beginnings of the promotion of the idea that growing inequalities were a 'good thing' and should be encouraged (see Figure 8.1). Following 1997, as the legacy continued, if a little muted, this led to New

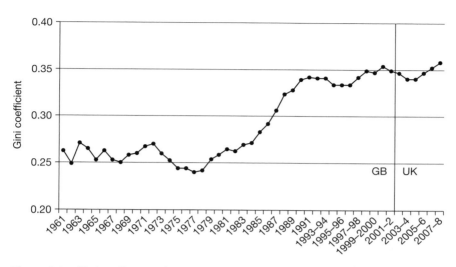

Figure 8.1 Gini coefficient of equivalized inequality in income after tax and before housing costs, 1961 to 2007–8

Source: Institute for Fiscal Studies
Note: Data are for Great Britain before 2002–3 and for UK subsequently.

Labour politicians suggesting that it was equality of opportunity that mattered most, not equality of outcomes. Equality of outcomes could diverge, or so these former (New) sons and daughters of toil (Labour) suggested, with life-chances becoming progressively more unequal, just as long as the more immeasurable 'opportunities' or 'capabilities' people had to prosper were apparently being made available and presented upon a slightly more level playing field.

Figure 8.1, and many other similar diagrams, suggest to me that the rising, and then high, period of inequality synonymous with Thatcherism began shortly after 1977 and has continued largely unabated to the present day (on periodization see Hay and Farrall, 2011). Following the coalition victory of 2010 the Thatcherite legacy of promoting inequality was renewed with extra vigour. The Health and Social Care Act 2012 was passed allowing up to half of NHS hospital beds to be privatized, for other parts of the legislation researchers later found that 'it is not possible to do in the real world that which the bill purports to achieve' (Jones, 2012). The state checks on the market mechanisms that the Bill proposed would not work because of random variation in short-term health outcomes. What was being offered to people after more than three decades of Thatcherism was an increased 'opportunity' to be lucky, win the lottery, or an inheritance, and secure access to healthcare on the basis of their economic circumstances. In education reintroductions of old-fashioned school examinations were announced to increase the opportunity children had to fail to gain any qualification from school. At the same time, social housing rules were changed to make it harder for young people in expensive cities to find shelter. In health, education and housing outcomes were becoming more unequal, but in each area it could be said that opportunities to succeed or fail were widening. To the generation that grew up under Thatcher's initial terms of office (the ones when she was prime minister), it felt a little as though we had been here before, but this was not automatically the case. Figure 8.2 shows one view from those times.

Figure 8.2 shows an old computer graphic of unemployment rates as they stood two years after Thatcher was swept to power in 1979. The altitude of areas on the map, which itself is an equal population cartogram, is drawn in proportion to the proportion of jobless people. As area on the map is drawn in proportion to people the volume being shown is the volume of unemployed jobseekers in 1981. Note how high unemployment was in Scotland and in the far north, how a low-lying ring of relative prosperity encircled London, but how also, in general, areas around the coast often faired badly.

The recession of the early 1980s was like a social storm which swept south from the north of the UK and which, in particular, reduced men's chances of gaining employment and of living into old age. It blew southwards, round the coasts, into inner London and the cores of some other southern cities but it was a social wind which went strangely still over the more rural parts of the Home Counties – places that never felt the economic cold. The 1980s recession had begun earlier, in the late 1970s along the Clyde and a little later on the Tyne and Mersey, but Thatcherism allowed its progress to be both encouraged and exacerbated (see figure 8.1 in Dorling, 2012, and figure 14b in Dorling, 1996).

Where there were small signs of economic weakness, in any community at any particular time, the doctrine of Thatcherism, of not 'supporting the weak', prised open the cracks to grow. Elsewhere in Europe industries were not repeatedly decimated so often. In Britain where there was a little discord in communities, for instance between police and other groups, these tensions were stoked to grow to hatred during the Thatcher years. Miners, football supporters, urban adolescents: all would fight pitched

The Distribution of Unemployment in Britain 1981

Rate shown as surface height, volume in proportion to the number of unemployed upon the population cartogram. Resolution 300 by 450, based on ward figures.

Figure 8.2 1980s style computer mapping of 1980s unemployment

Source: Dorling, 2012, figure 7.13

243

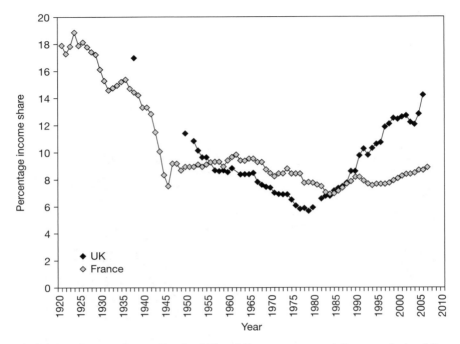

Figure 8.3 Income Inequality the UK and France compared. Income share of the best-off 1%, France and UK

Note: For the UK, until 1974, the estimates relate to income net of certain deductions; from 1975, estimates relate to total income. Until 1989 estimates relate to tax units but, from 1990, estimates relate to adults. Data for the UK is patchy prior to 1951.
Source: The World Top Incomes Database

battles at some point as the authorities were egged on by the doctrine of economic efficiency.

Where error or injury had been done to communities during the initial early 1980s recession, subsequent neglect led to doubt over the future viability of poorer neighbourhoods and ensured despair among many inhabitants as levels of depression rose quickly. A kind of Victorian darkness settled in many inner-city and industrial neighbourhoods, and a new kind of sadness, but only in some places, only in some parts of Britain. Elsewhere in affluent Britain, in the places which profited, the living was more often easy and becoming easier. And, elsewhere in Europe, as Figure 8.3 shows, people shared what they had more fairly. There were fewer winners and fewer losers. The inequality trends in Britain were not repeated nearby, especially not just across the channel in France. Looking exactly when the trend in Figure 8.3 in the UK changed – 1977/78, France has a flatter trend line.

If you were a young man brought up in relative affluence *outside* the urban cores of the North, Wales, Scotland or Northern Ireland, you might think that the 1980s had been a period of great economic success. The 1980s and 1990s were not bad places to be for those in London and the South-East, or the 'Home Counties' and some of the commuter towns in them. For the residents of many of the smaller southern towns, increases in apparent social harmony, the reinforcement of what they saw as 'home truths', of their faiths and of hope in a Greater Britain in the future were common. Other places saw crime and murder rates more than double (see Farrall and Jennings, Chapter 7 in this collection; Dorling, 2005), unemployment soar (see Thompson, Chapter 2 in this collection), drug use become endemic, and the new misery set in, but that was not among 'our people' as Margaret Thatcher used to describe those she saw as worthy of any respect.

Mrs Thatcher

> May I just thank you very much. And I would just like to remember some words of Saint Francis of Assisi . . .
>
> Where there is discord, may we bring harmony.
>
> Where there is error may we bring truth.
>
> Where there is doubt, may we bring faith.
>
> And where there is despair, hope.
>
> (Margaret Thatcher, on taking office, 4 May 1979)

It is important not to conflate Thatcher with Thatcherism. For example, the name 'Charles Darwin' will now forever on be synonymous with Darwinism, a name which is now mostly an empty vessel to fill with what we now think about his ideas (Powell, 2012). So, too, Mrs Thatcher's corporeal existence is now subsumed within others' ideas of what it is she stood for. But it is worth looking back a little more closely at her. After misquoting St Francis, she then talked in some detail of her father. Margaret rarely mentioned having had a mother. She was an admirer of

245

Ronald Reagan (see Figure 8.4). It can also be useful to look back on the precursors to the rise of Thatcherism by using points in the life of the lead actor in the drama herself.

Margaret Hilda Roberts was born in 1925 during the end of an era of aristocratic inequality. When Margaret Hilda was a child she saw that adults would doff their hats in her Lincolnshire market town as their betters passed by (Waugh, 1945). Young Margaret first attended grammar school, and was then separated from most local children, just as unemployment reached new heights in 1936. After the age of 11 she would not have mixed at school with the majority of the children of her town but mostly with the daughters of the more affluent residents, which included her parents who owned two shops. Because she did not quite get the grades, it was only after one student dropped out, in 1943, that she arrived at Oxford to begin

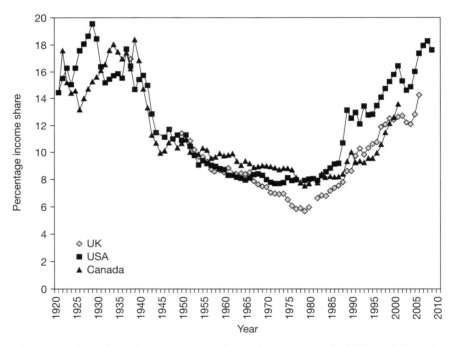

Figure 8.4 Trends in Britain were similar to those seen in the USA and Canada. Income share of the best-off 1%, USA and Canada

Note: For both Canada and the USA the estimates exclude incomes from capital gains.
Source: The World Top Incomes Database

a degree in chemistry, which she completed in 1947 (Margaret Thatcher Foundation, 2012). She became a mother in 1953 and an MP in 1959. Early on she was most noticed for getting in a little trouble after voting for the restoration of birching in 1961 and for helping to ensure her party was not fashionable during the swinging Sixties (Campbell, 2007). The 'young female Member for Finchley had joined with five other Tories on the Standing Committee in support of an amendment to restore flogging moved by the 74-year-old Member for Ayr, Sir Thomas Moore. (The other five were all much older than Mrs Thatcher, three of them military or naval men)' (2007: 134).

At age 36, in 1961, Mrs Thatcher was far from being an ordinary woman. She preferred the company and attitudes of older men from another era – she married one of those – but the reason for reeling out all these dates and reminding you that she was in favour of flogging, and hanging too, and racist anti-immigration policies (2007: 437) is not to show that she was about as politically incorrect as it is was possible to be, even by the standards of those times, but to illustrate just how quickly the world around her was changing. The figures quoted below are for the UK, but consider also Figure 8.4 from 1925 to 1961 and what was occurring at the same time in the USA where Friedrich Hayek, one of Thatcherism's architects (and one of her favourite authors), lived from 1950 to 1962 and complained about the social progress he saw.

In 1925 the richest 1 per cent of people in the UK took home 22 per cent of all income; by 1936, as Margaret Hilda first walked to her grammar school, that grossly unfair share had fallen to 18 per cent; by 1941 as she took (and initially failed) her exams to allow her to later enter her Oxford college, the income share of the richest 1 per cent fell to 'just' 13 per cent; by the time she left Oxford, in 1947, that share was 11 per cent; when she first became MP (in 1953) the income share of the richest 1 per cent had fallen just below 10 per cent and, by the time she was voting with the old naval men to bring back flogging, in 1961, the richest 1 per cent were taking home less than 9 per cent of all income, nearer to 8 per cent the year after. These are very low rates of inequality for the UK, but are rates that have been enjoyed by the citizens of Japan and Germany since 1945 (Figure 8.5).

Almost every year of Margaret Roberts's formative years, privilege and power was rapidly ebbing away from the rich in Britain. Later more equitable Germany and Japan would begin to economically supersede Britain (Thatcherites never understood the key reasons were those two

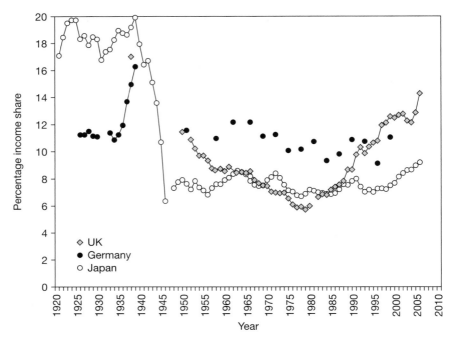

Figure 8.5 Comparitive levels of inequality in Germany and Japan. Income share of the best-off 1% Germany and Japan

Note: In Japan the estimates exclude incomes from capital gains. In Germany the estimates are excluding capital gains apart from 1925–1938 and are only for the Federal Republic from 1960 to 1991.
Source: The World Top Incomes Database

countries' greater levels of post-war economic equality). To a young woman so rapidly social climbing, so quickly removing herself from those below her, it must has felt as if the country she was so very patriotically proud of was on a road to some kind of serfdom. The faster she rose up the ranks and climbed up the greasy pole of school and entrance exam success, with her financially appropriate marriage to Denis Thatcher, that much wealthier, older, divorcee; the faster she secured political success. However, throughout the 1960s and early 1970s the monies she and those around her were gaining – by getting ahead of others, by rent-seeking and profiteering – was rapidly ebbing way. And the Germans and Japanese were moving ahead. No wonder she and 'her people' were angry.

In 1975, when Margaret became leader of her party, the annual incomes of the richest 1 per cent in the UK had fallen to just 6 per cent of national income for the first time in British history. The very rich, on average in that year 'only' received six times the arithmetic mean income of the country. Imagine a well-paid top London banker 'only' receiving six times what a factory worker got. You might think that was six times too much, but that was almost the lowest the UK richest 1 per cent ever reached. They reached their precise historic minima in 1978, the year before she became prime minster, the first year after which income inequality again began to

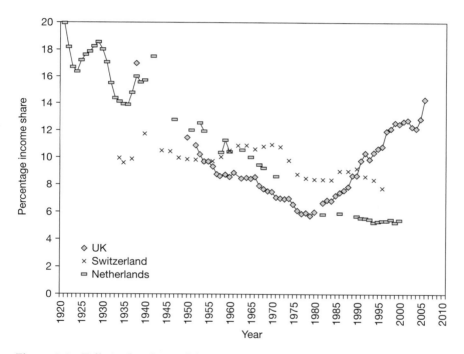

Figure 8.6   Falls in the share of the top 1% in the Netherlands and Switzerland since 1940. Income share of the best-off 1%, Netherlands and Switzerland

Note: In the Netherlands, up to 1946, the series is based on tabulated income tax data; between 1950 and 1975, estimates are based on tabulated data produced by the Central Bureau of Statistics; from 1977 they are estimated based on micro-data from the Income Panel Survey (IPO) and using tax and other administrative data. Swiss estimates do not include capital gains.

Source: The World Top Incomes Database

relentlessly rise. And there was no need for that inequality to rise. Figure 8.6 shows what else could have been possible.

The rising tide of inequality

Approaching the issues along these lines allows one to appreciate just how closely the declining fortunes of the richest 1 per cent in the UK correlated with Thatcher's political education and then turned as she took office. Her ascendancy was the precise point at which these inequalities began again to increase. Of course it was not just her. She was mostly a symbol for the men behind her, those who backed her and thrust her forward, and of the ideas of men like Hayek, von Mises (1975), and others so shattered by the events of the Second World War that they though that almost any government, planning or sharing was evil.

Thatcherism is not about a woman but about a trend that the politics associated with this surname gave rise to. It was a trend she was part of, a trend which began before she was born and which carried on long after she had left office. It is a historically interesting question to ask just how much this politician, brought up in a remote market town, trained in chemistry (not PPE) and married into the class she would later benefit most, understood of what was happening to British society before she gained power or even became Education Secretary, but she rallied against the status quo and was the Thatcherites' symbol of a powerful force for change.

Figure 8.7 shows just how important Thatcherism was for fundamentally changing UK society and, key here, that society's human geography. It is a more detailed version of one of the lines in Figure 8.3, but showing more than just the best-off 1 per cent. The top graph is dominated by the black line, which is the average income of the very richest of all, of the best-off 0.01 per cent of all people in the UK. Around 1912, the richest, on average, each received over 400 times mean average incomes (much more again than the median average). Today the very richest see their share heading back up towards 150 times the mean. We might even be tempted to a little speculation as to whether Thatcherism might be ending now (see the blip at the end of Figure 8.7), but it is too early to tell. The economic crises of 2008–12 could be its death throes. To paraphrase what the Chinese premier Zhou Enlai said in commenting on changes in France in 1968, or in the UK 2008, 'It is too early to say.' What we can be sure of is the temporal coincidence between the all-time low in the incomes of the very richest,

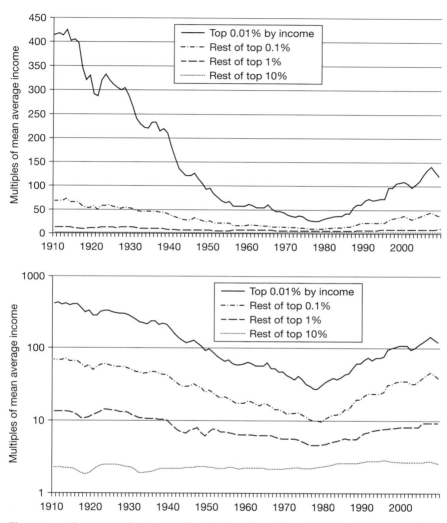

Figure 8.7 Incomes of the best-off in the UK 1910–2009 (top half). Incomes of the best-off in the UK 1910–2009 (compared to average, on linear & log scales) (bottom half)

Source: The World Top Incomes Database, missing data interpolated, original source: Atkinson, 2007, http://g-mond.parisschoolofeconomics.eu/topincomes/as accessed 11th June 2012; for details to the interpolation see Dorling, D. 2013, figure 2

and Mrs Thatcher's elevation to power just after 1978. In terms of defining a pivot point, few graphs showing social changes are as clear as Figure 8.7.

Figure 8.7 shows the most basic set of consistent measures we have of economic inequalities in Britain that span almost a century in time. Missing values have been interpolated here (for details of that process and similar trends in other social measures see Dorling, 2013). They are interpolated to present a picture that is simpler than it would otherwise look. However, the overall trend is clear: inequalities were huge, fell consistently for 70 years and then rose consistently for 30 years. The pivot point was 1978. The later parting of the ways between 'the 9 per cent' and 'the 1 per cent' after 1990 is the other major feature of note and the very recent falls in the remuneration of the very best-off of all will require careful and close attention in the immediate years to come. Thatcherism could be ending now, even with arch-Thatcherites in power.

It is this graphic (Figure 8.7) which best explains the importance of Thatcherism. In other countries the same graph shows a different trend which behaves in very different ways. In many countries inequalities carry on falling throughout the 1980s and 1990s, just as earlier in this chapter the case of the Netherlands and Switzerland was described (see Figure 8.6). There is almost nothing at all 'international' in the temporal trends revealed in Figure 8.7. In fact, nowhere else in Europe is the same as the UK when it comes to inequality profiles and projections. Only the USA and, to a lesser extent, Canada have similar trajectories, and in both of those cases equalization was not progressing throughout the 1920s and 1930s, as was the case in the UK, but only began with the advent of the Second World War. Because the graphs in Figure 8.7 show how many times average incomes members of the richest tenth, 1 per cent, 0.1 per cent and 0.01 per cent of society receive in income a year, greater changes in the futures of just one group can be overshadowed by larger changes for others. For 'the 1 per cent' their multiple of average income is identical to their share of national income. If the top 1 per cent received ten times average incomes then they receive 10 per cent of all income. Groups above the top 1 per cent can enjoy incredible incomes because there are fewer of them. The top 1 per cent can never enjoy much more than 25 per cent of all income as, above that, those at the very bottom begin to starve.

As Thatcher came to power the UK share of the top 1 per cent rose to 6 per cent in 1979, 7 per cent by 1984, 8 per cent by 1988, 9 per cent by 1990, and then there followed a very brief dip (when John Major became prime minister), then a rise following Major's 1992 election victory to 10 per cent by 1993, rising quickly to nearer 11 per cent by 1995, 12 per cent by 1997, rising a little slower in the first years of the New Labour government, but still to almost reach 13 per cent by 2001. Thatcherism continued after New Labour came to power, that was part of what made it 'New'. Liberal Leader Nick Clegg would complain of this in the 2010 election campaign, but he did little while in office as Deputy Prime Minister to tackle income inequality. In office Nick Clegg was just as Thatcherite as New Labour had been.

It is true that there was a brief dip in the upwards inequality trend during Gordon Brown's 'progressive brief pause' (2001–2 – blink and you missed it), before the share of the top 1 per cent began quickly rising again to 13 per cent by 2004, 14 per cent by 2005, jumping to nearer 15 per cent by 2006, 15.4 per cent by 2007 and then a third dip, to just under 14 per cent by 2009. The third dip was associated with the immediate impact of economic crash, with factors such as initially falling income from interest on stocks and shares, but we know that fall was quickly reversed, with inequality rising again in 2010 and 2011 from other reports of the income of top financiers bouncing back (the bulk of the top 1 per cent work in banking and similar services). However, by 2012 there were again signs of restraint at the top. We are currently in a period of oscillation, possibly a third tipping point after those in 1912 and 1978. Those two tipping points could only be clearly seen long after most of the events if their respective years had been forgotten. If 2008 turns out to have been the tipping point, the end of Thatcherism, which precise prime minister or political party was in power that year will no longer be seen to have been of much importance.

A geographical perspective

What is so geographical about any of this? Why go into so much detail about what appear to be historical social and economic changes in a chapter about geography? Initially, these trends appear to be purely about falling and then rising economic inequalities, but 'the 1 per cent' were and are not evenly spread across the country. Only slightly more evenly spread are the 'next best-off 9 per cent' beneath them. Those well above the bulk of the top 1 per cent are far more geographically concentrated, almost solely in and near London, which is where almost all of the 0.1 per cent and 0.01 per cent reside (see Hennig and Dorling, 2012 on the geography of 0.01 per cent). It is possible to chart how the 1 per cent became a little more evenly spread geographically as their share of income falls and how they rapidly geographically segregated into exclusive enclaves and southern towns, villages and cities as they became richer again. However, it is with political patterns and voting that the geography becomes clearer quickest, so let us turn to that and to some more social graphics from the 1980s on geographical swings in voting to try to illustrate the effect that Thatcher's rise to power had.

The polarization of voting

A simple geographical measure of polarization is the segregation index (Simpson, 2004). When applied to Conservative voters by parliamentary constituency this index is the measure of the minimum number of Conservative voters who would have to move constituency were all constituencies to return an identical share of Conservative votes. (That political party is used here because it is the most consistently defined over this period as well as being Thatcher's party). Table 8.1 illustrates that people voted Conservative in remarkably similar numbers in most constituencies between 1931 and early 1974. Elections were decided much more by the national swing than by issues of tactical voting and political geography. During those years one would have only had to move as few as 4 per cent of Conservative voters, and never more than 8 per cent, to have exactly the same number/proportion voting in each area. Six years after economic inequalities began to fall (in 1912), the 1918 'Khaki' election saw the greatest political polarization, exacerbated by the political machinations of the time and Liberals not standing against Tories in many seats. As a result, as Table 8.1 shows, polarization as indicated by voter segregation shot up to almost 20 per cent, dropping only to 14 per cent in 1922, but then fell gently downwards to almost 6 per cent by 1959 before rising up to 8 per cent by the February election of 1974 and then suddenly jumping to almost 11 per cent in the October election of that year.

If you want a moment when everything changed, when Thatcherism was conceived, it was during the spring and summer months of 1974 (see also Hay, 1996; Heffernan, 2000; and Jessop et al., 1990 on similar attempts to identify a 'starting point'). The economic tipping point might have been 1978, but the political tilt occurred earlier. It was then that people in the South-east of England swung rightwards, voting polarized sharply and, a year later, Margaret's party would elect her as leader. Political polarization

Table 8.1 Segregation of Conservative voters 1885 to 2010 – all general elections

Election	Concentration	Election	Concentration
1885	7.11%	1951	6.77%
1886	5.53%	1955	6.93%
1892	5.81%	1959	6.24%
1895	4.70%	1964	6.51%
1900	4.39%	1966	7.69%
1906	6.67%	1970	8.04%
1910 Jan	7.91%	1974 Feb	8.01%
1910 Dec	6.24%	1974 Oct	10.72%
1918	19.30%	1979	9.17%
1922	14.44%	1983	10.59%
1923	11.57%	1987	11.84%
1924	10.62%	1992	11.88%
1929	9.24%	1997	13.94%
1931	9.23%	2001	15.05%
1935	9.65%	2005	15.69%
1945	7.21%	2010	16.40%
1950	6.74%		

Source: Dorling 2010. See also: http://www.sasi.group.shef.ac.uk/injustice/files/Figure13.xls
and Norman Tebbit's objection to the measure only being shown for Conservatives (letter
New Statesman, 5 July 2010: http://www.readperiodicals.com/201007/2073707111.html)

dropped a fraction during the 1979 election itself but then rose relentlessly, subsequently to reach the post-First World War maxima in 2010. Table 8.1 above of voting polarization turns out to be a good indicator of when social divisions in general were also widening and falling.

The proportions in the table above might appear modest but you really need to see what was involved in these rises in polarization, or recognize why even the slight rise from 9.2 per cent in 1979 to 10.6 per cent in 1983 and 11.8 per cent by 1987 was shocking. Figure 8.8 shows how a political vacuum opened up in the centre of politics in Britain as voters in constituencies swung away from the political centre during these years. Labour areas became more Labour, Tory more Tory, and hence the numbers of voters rose who would have had to be moved across a political boundary to ever achieve a more even geographical distribution rose election after election.

To understand Figure 8.8 you need to know that each triangle contains the space of all possible election results in any one election. Within each triangle every constituency is placed as a dot. The precise location of the dot depends on the share of the vote between the three main parties. If most

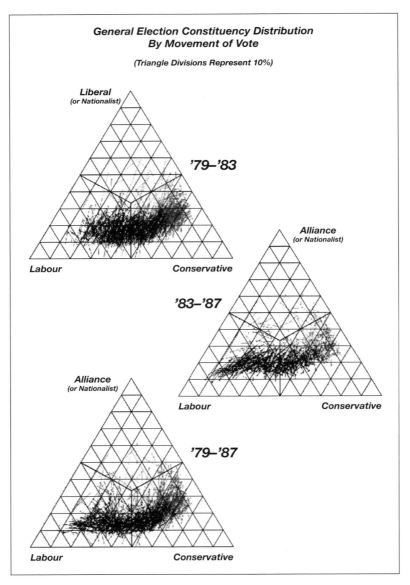

Figure 8.8 Westminster Constituency swings on the Electoral Triangle 1979–87.

Source: Dorling 2012, figure 1.8

Note: Each constituency is represented by an arrow showing how voting there changed.

of the vote is to Labour then the dot is drawn towards the bottom left of the triangle. If most of the vote is to the Conservatives then it is drawn towards the bottom right, and if most of the vote is to the various groupings of Liberal parties (SDP/Liberal/Alliance) then it is drawn further up. The vote share decides the precise position. Between any pair of elections the dot for a constituency changes position as the vote share changes within the constituency. The change on the diagram between the two dots can be shown by an arrow. The arrowhead is draw at the later election point to show the overall direction of change over time. Groups of politically similar constituencies can be seen to be 'flocking' as they swing in similar directions, or 'scattering' when there is less of a pattern to the flow of votes in voting space.

Over the 1979–87 period as a whole, Labour areas became more Labour, arrows to the left swung to the left, Conservative areas become more Conservative and, in many, the main opposition became the Liberals, SDP and later the Liberal Democrats (known at the time as 'The Alliance'). The hole that appeared in the middle of British politics, in the middle of the triangles in Figures 8.8 and 8.9 was a political vacuum, a fall in moderation and that itself was one initial result of Thatcherism. Later on the hole filled up again as Labour moved to the right to fill it.

Trends in local election results show even more clearly the schisms that opened up under Thatcher's period of immediate tenure. In Figure 8.9 a dot is drawn to show the vote share in every county division in England, the areas used to elect county councillors in the years 1981, 1985 and 1989. The net of an electoral tetrahedron is also shown for Scotland to illustrate how polarization within a four-party system can be visualized and how there too evidence of a political vacuum opening up could be seen by the end of this period of initial change, by 1988.

In 1981 in England the distribution of county councillors was quite even across voting space. A great many seats are shown as dots in a histogram beneath the electoral triangle as in these no Liberal Party (or Alliance) candidates stood. The size of the dots is proportional to the electorate. There is a hint of white space in the centre of the triangle as there are slightly fewer seats in which all three main parties gain a near identical share of the vote than might be expected if there were no geographical issue to voting.

By 1985 the white space in the centre has opened up a little more. County council seats were beginning to move away from the political centre of the image, at least those that were ever anywhere near that centre. The *entire* distribution in fact shifted a little to the edges (see original source for more

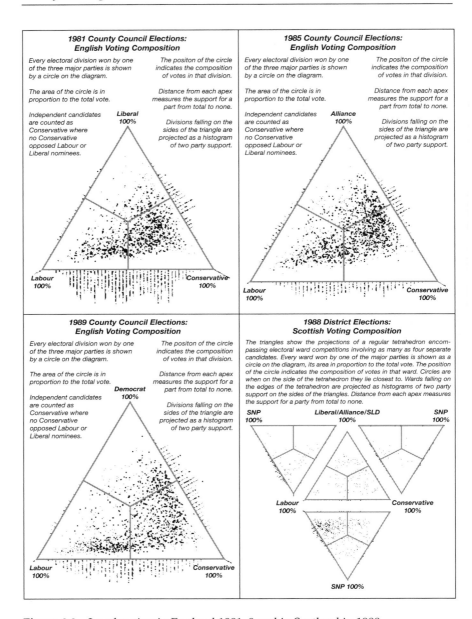

Figure 8.9 Local voting in England 1981–9 and in Scotland in 1988

Source: Dorling, 2012; figures 7.4, 7.5, 7.6 and 9.16 (of the electoral tetrahedron)

diagrams showing this, albeit in tedious detail, but using early three-dimensional surface visualization techniques). After 1985, as all the three main parties tried to ensure that their voters had a chance to vote for them, everywhere, there were fewer seats placed around the edges of the triangle and also fewer where there is a single unopposed candidate (illustrated by the strings of seats drawn at the corners of the triangle).

What began as a shift between 1981 and 1985 became a rout between 1985 and 1989. The political centre can be seen in Figure 8.9 to almost completely hollow out in just those four years. In hindsight, it is less surprising that one response to the growing vacuum was the splitting of the SDP from Labour and then its alliance with the Liberals. By 1989 county divisions, county council seats, are either Liberal/Alliance–Tory contests or Tory–Labour battles, and this was only if there was much of a fight to be had at all. More areas became safe local or even very safe national seats. The country had polarized politically, faster in the late 1980s than the early 1980s and ever since then this polarization has continued. It continued to such an extent and degree that the Conservative party failed to gain a majority at the 2010 national general election because so many of the extra votes they won were piled up in areas they had already secured by 2005 (Dorling, 2010).

The final quarter of the diagram in Figure 8.9 shows how, in Scotland and by 1988, the hole in the middle of politics was also very clear to see north of the border, the dots representing local councillors forming a ring around places that no longer existed, such as places where roughly a quarter of voters each voted Tory, Liberal, Labour and SNP. In hindsight these diagrams show *when* the schism was formed. They were first drawn between 1989 and 1991 using data from just a few years before. Back then it was far from clear just how important and semi-permanent what had just occurred would be. The political ground shifted in the 1980s and it is still moving in the same directions it first shuddered out towards then. Looking at these diagrams is a little like looking at an electoral autopsy. They show when the break first occurred.

I include all these diagrams (and Table 8.1) because if you lived through those years as a youngster it is easy to think that your times were special and something very unusual was occurring. However, viewed both in hindsight and in context, something very odd, even unprecedented, in terms of voting was occurring. Whole places were moving towards political poles and away from the centre ground. Viewed conventionally and geographically this is now known as the north/south divide widening; a divide widening in voting as well as wealth, health, educational changes and employment fortunes. Viewed in detail in political space it is clear that the drifts were near universal, they were found both within the north and south as well as between them.

The new geographies of England

Thatcherism did not suddenly create a new political map. Long before Mrs Thatcher's three governments were put in power England dominated Britain, Northern Ireland was marginalized and London reigned supreme. And this is all despite many decades of population decline within the capital. However, in the early 1970s there were a few years when the population centre of the country moved north (see Dorling and Atkins, 1995: 34, figure 16). By the 1980s that had ended. Figure 8.10 provides a single image to illustrate how dominant London was five years before the 'Big Bang' of financial deregulation in 1986.

After Mrs Thatcher left office the legacy of her tenure continued. Figure 8.11 shows how, during those following ten years of the 1990s, there was actual population decline in the North-west of England and around the rivers Clyde, Tyne and Tees. In contrast, the South-east, and especially London, boomed. There was, in effect 'managed decline' outside the core zone. This managed decline began with Michael Heseltine but continued under first John Major, and then Tony Blair, both contemporaries of Thatcher.

There was no slow-down under Tony Blair's tenure in the economic and social polarization of the country. Table 8.2 shows how mortality rates continued to polarize – if anything a little faster under Blair than Thatcher – between areas of the country. It was migration which drove these changes. Those who could, moved. They moved towards more prosperous areas. Years later this internal migration became apparent when measured in terms of the numbers of people dying per year in each place at each age.

New Labour as 'Thatcherism continued'

Thatcherism changed how we thought, what we aspired to. It dumbed down collective social aspiration while building up individual senses of entitlement. Towards the end of New Labour's period of office even

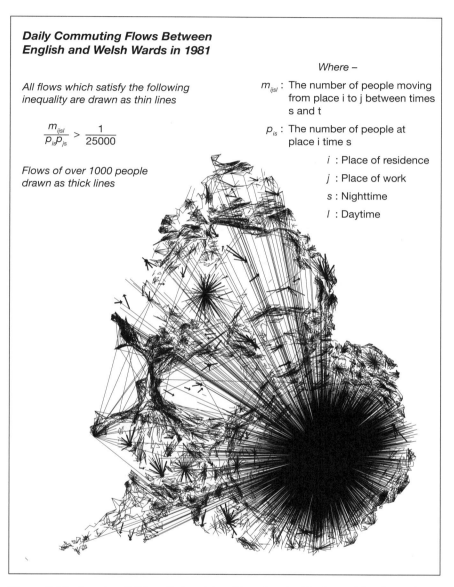

Daily Commuting Flows Between English and Welsh Wards in 1981

All flows which satisfy the following inequality are drawn as thin lines

$$\frac{m_{ijsl}}{p_{is}p_{js}} > \frac{1}{25000}$$

Flows of over 1000 people drawn as thick lines

Where –

m_{ijsl} : The number of people moving from place i to j between times s and t

p_{is} : The number of people at place i time s

    i : Place of residence

    j : Place of work

    s : Nighttime

    l : Daytime

Figure 8.10 London 1981 – all absorbing (the other 'spider' was Manchester)

Source: Dorling, 2012, figure 6.14

261

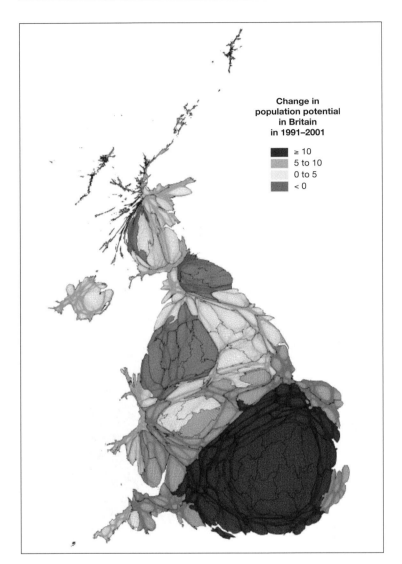

Figure 8.11 During the 1990s Thatcherism continued on the ground, if not name. London and the Home Counties grew while Merseyside, Tyneside and Clydeside continued to decline.

Source: UK population Censuses 1991 and 2001, population potential calculated for this book by local authority (see figure 9.3); 1991 statistics subtracted from 2001 and population – weighted mean shown.

262

Table 8.2 Geographical inequalities in health in Britain 1921–2007

SMR 0-64	1921–30	1931–39	1950–53	1959–63	1969–73	1981–89	1990–98	1999–2007
Tenth of standardised mortality ratio								
1 (worst)	138	136	131	136	131	137	149	149
2	122	120	118	123	116	120	123	123
3	113	112	112	117	112	114	114	115
4	108	106	107	111	108	108	108	109
5	104	103	103	105	103	102	99	101
6	97	97	99	97	97	96	94	95
7	90	89	93	91	92	92	91	90
8	83	85	89	88	89	89	86	83
9	78	81	86	83	87	84	78	77
10	72	73	82	77	83	79	73	70
Ratio of worst to best	1.91	1.85	1.60	1.76	1.58	1.74	2.04	2.12
Rll	2.50	2.35	1.96	2.25	1.92	2.17	2.64	2.79

* Data series is not continuous, with no data for the 1940s and gaps in mid-1950s, mid-1960s, and from early 1970s to early 1980s; nor are time periods always of wqual duration. For 1980, we used the harmonic mean of decile SMRs for the two periods of which it was composed (1981–85 and 1986–89).

Note: Confidence interval in original paper

The Guardian, then its staunchest backer, was listing the basic achievements of that government as if they were greater achievements, as if repairing and rebuilding schools was some kind of rocket science:

> Invited to embrace five more years of a Labour government, and of Gordon Brown as Prime Minister, it is hard to feel enthusiasm. Labour's kneejerk critics can sometimes sound like the People's Front of Judea asking what the Romans have ever done for us. The salvation of the health service, major renovation of schools, the minimum wage, civil partnerships and the extension of protection for minority groups are heroic, not small, achievements.
>
> (*The Guardian*, 30 April 2010)

However, the key and reiterated undertaking by the 'New' Labour administration that governed Britain in the early years of the twenty-first century was not honoured. This undertaking had been announced by Prime Minister Tony Blair in the annual Beveridge lecture of 1999: being poor, he said, 'should not be a life sentence': it was a '20 year mission – but I believe it can be done' (BBC News, 1999). This pledge was reaffirmed by his successor Gordon Brown at the Labour Party conference of 2008:

> Brown acknowledged that economic times were 'tough' but said the government was 'in it for the long haul' in the complete elimination of child poverty by 2020. He also promised to continue record investment in Sure Start and introduce free nursery education for two-year-olds in up to 60 areas. 'For me, the fairer future starts with putting children first – with the biggest investment in children this country has ever seen. It means delivering the best possible starts in life with services tailored to the needs of every single precious child.'
>
> (Ahmed, 1999)

However, by the time that the 'New' Labour government had departed the political stage, it was possible to make a more sober appraisal of the 'Blair Years' (1997–2007) in relation, at least, to the state of the nation's children. The proportion of children living in a family that could not afford to take a holiday away from home had risen; so too had the number of children whose parents could not afford to let them have friends round for tea. Likewise, the number of children who were too poor to pursue a hobby and the number of children living in single-parent families without access to a car had risen. It all became much worse after 2010 with the economic crisis, partly because New Labour's record was more like a continuation of Thatcherism rather than something new. In 1991 in his Beveridge lecture, Tony Blair had said: 'In Beveridge's time the welfare state was associated with progress and advancement. Today it is often associated with dependency, fraud, abuse, laziness. I want to make it once again a force for progress' (BBC, 1999). However, in practice, 'New' Labour pursued that self-same populist and punitive approach, happy to label benefit claimants as feckless and to regard taxation as the Victorians had done – as charity, something one did for the poor.

This is not to deny that the New Labour government did achieve a great deal for children. It greatly reduced the numbers living in the worst poverty. It improved both education chances and narrowed education divides and it governed over a period when young peoples' chances of gaining a job improved greatly, especially in the poorest areas, and national youth suicide rates fell quickly (in contrast to rises in young adult suicide rates during the previous Conservative administration). However, when it came to assessing their legacy as regards inequality overall, and inequality between the access to income and wealth enjoyed by different groups of children in the UK, their record was poor. The geography of Thatcherism became further entrenched.

Following on as the next wave of Thatcherism, New Labour also paved the way, in so many ways, for some of the worst policy decision of the next

(Coalition) government. They introduced student fees, which the next government would increase to £9,000 a year – the most expensive in Europe. They began the privatization of the National Health Service which the next government would then expand upon. And they allowed life chances between groups of young adults to diverge rapidly, which is why young parents today are bringing their children up in such widely different circumstances, often without knowing much of each others' lives – less than their parents' knew.

A heroic Labour government from 1997 to 2010 would have achieved so much more. It would have been heroic to have reduced income and wealth inequalities (and, by doing so, bring down rates of poverty towards normal western European levels). It would have been heroic to have refused to take part in America's wars (as Labour refused when in power from 1964 to 1970). It would have been heroic to have reigned in the bankers before the crash. That kind of a government would have been comparable with other contemporary governments in other countries, with progressive politics in Britain's past, and with the 1997 dream that 'things can only get better', New Labour fell far short. Here is what Julian Baggini had to say on Labour's record in office in that same issue of *The Guardian* as quoted from above:

> I think this has been an under-appreciated government. The last 13 years have been immeasurably better than the previous 18, and the return to Conservatism, in its current shape at least, appals me. But the game is up, both for a system which protects two parties which most people do not support, and a government that just cannot now hope to be re-elected with a majority.
>
> (Baggini, 2010)

What do we find when, instead of announcing 'immeasurably better' we actually measure? Here are some attempts (with the help of many others) to measure this apparently immeasurable betterment. What is interesting is to note that when this is done we again do not appear to see too great a change from the Thatcherism to New Labour via John Major.

Among British adults during the 1997–2005 Blair years, the proportion unable to make regular savings rose from 25 per cent to 27 per cent; the number unable to afford an annual holiday away from home rose from 18 per cent to 24 per cent; and the national proportion who could not afford to insure the contents of their home climbed a percentage point, from 8 per cent to 9 per cent. However, these national proportions conceal the way in which the rising exclusion had hit particular groups especially hard, not least a group that the Blair government had said it would help above all others: children living in poverty. The sources for all these facts are in Dorling (2011: 117–43). Brown's very short term as prime minister was a little less damning statistically, but too short and turbulent a time to yet easily dovetail with the record to date.

Another failure of New Labour was its record on *real* rates of youth unemployment. They remained high throughout 1997–2010 so that just before the London riots of 2011 unemployment rates amongst young black men rose again to above 50 per cent. Rates for young black women had reached that level in 2009 (Figure 8.12). I say again, as this last occurred when Mrs Thatcher was in power.

The comparison of poverty surveys taken towards the start and end of Tony Blair's time in office found that, of all children, the proportion living in a family that could not afford to take a holiday away from home (or just

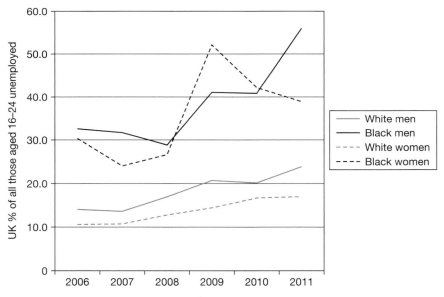

Figure 8.12 Unemployment rate of men and women, black and white, aged 16–24, 2006–11, Q4, United Kingdom

Source: Drawn from data at: hhtp://www.guardian.co.uk/news/datablog/2012/mar/09/black-unemployed-young-men. Sourced in turn from Labour Force Survey 2012.

to visit relatives) rose between 1999 and 2005, from 25 per cent to 32 per cent. This occurred even as the real incomes of most of the poorest rose; they just rose more for the affluent, making holidays more expensive for all and subtly changing what it meant to go on holiday. Similarly, as the rich became richer and housing became more expensive and more unequally distributed, the number of school-age children who had to share their bedroom with an adult or sibling over the age of 10 and of the opposite sex rose from 8 per cent to 15 per cent nationally.

Encouraging buy-to-let landlords in a new wave of privatization did not help reduce overcrowding. It was in London that such overcrowding became most acute and where sharing rooms rose most quickly. Keeping up appearances for the poor in London was much harder than in Britain as a whole, not simply because London had less space, but because within London other children were so often very wealthy. Greatly reducing the numbers of children living in households below 60 per cent of median incomes still leaves many children in those households and in some cases it became harder to achieve the child poverty goal in 2005 as compared to 1999 as overall inequalities increased as mean incomes rose faster than mediums. Even among children at the same school, the incomes of their parents had diverged and, consequently, standards of living and expectations of the norm did too.

Nationally, the proportion of children who said their parent(s) could not afford to let them have friends round for tea doubled, from 4 per cent to 8 per cent. The proportion who could not afford to pursue a hobby or other leisure activity also rose, from 5 per cent to 7 per cent, and the proportion who could not afford to go on a school trip at least once a term doubled, from 3 per cent to 6 per cent. For children aged below the age of 5, the proportion whose parents could not afford to take them to playgroup each week also doubled under the Blair government, from 3 per cent to 6 per cent.

Concealing poverty becomes ever more difficult in an age of high and increasingly unequal consumer consumption and it becomes easier for us to imagine why someone might be tempted to go further into debt in order to pay for a playgroup rather than spend another day at home with a toddler or to pay for a school trip rather than asking their child to pretend to be ill that day. Debt rose greatly amongst families with children under New Labour (or the continuation of Thatcherism as argued here). The worse-off resorted to the increasing number of dodgy lending and saving schemes set up by loan sharks or Christmas clubs such as 'Farepak' which went bust. One Farepak victim made it clear what growing inequality meant:

> I have got four children, all at various ages. Like I say, you can't tell the little two, Father Christmas can call next door, but he can't call here you know. And with my husband being on sick as well, having to pay the mortgage and feed four kids and whatever, and £37 a week is not a lot.
>
> (Spalek and King, 2007)

The second most expensive of all consumption items are housing costs – rents or mortgages – and these have also diverged as income inequalities have increased. Having to move to a poorer area, or being unable to move out of one, is the geographical reality of social exclusion. People get further into debt trying to avoid this. The most expensive consumer item is a car. The combination of the expense and necessity of car ownership is the reason why not having a car is, for many, a contemporary mark of social failure. It is also closely connected to why so many car firms were badly hit so early on in the crash of 2008, as they were selling debt as much as selling cars.

By 2008/9, two out of three children in Britain living in a household without a car were living with only one parent. The chattels and behaviour that signal what it means to be poor change over time and in accordance with what most others have. By 2009, for a family not having a car outside London, like not being able to go on the cheapest of summer holidays, spelled stigma.

This was the outcome of having a government that was seriously relaxed about the rich becoming richer – 'as long as they paid their taxes'. (But New Labour cut Her Majesty's Revenue staff, thereby reducing tax inspectors' abilities to chase the rich for their payments.) The gaps between all families grew: celebrity, entrepreneur, affluent, hard-working, a bit slovenly, and down-in-the-mouth. Council housing became social housing with the word 'social' denoting implications of charity rather than rights.

Taxation became viewed by some in New Labour as a form of charity; something one 'did' for the poor. Jobseeker's Allowance of £9 a day was fine (as long as 'one' never imagined having to live off it oneself). But charity, or child tax credits, or Sure Start centres are simply not enough if the income gaps between people are allowed to turn into chasms. Whether our gaps can be considered cracks or chasms can be established by looking at other similarly affluent societies.

International comparisons of the quintile range of income inequality are some of the most telling comparisons that can be made between countries.

By 2005, after eight years of New Labour government, the richest fifth received 7.2 times more income on average than the poorest fifth each year – up from 6.9 times in 1997. According to the United Nations Development Programme's Annual Report (the most widely used source), this ratio was 6.1 to 1 in Ireland; 5.6 to 1 in France; 4.0 to 1 in Sweden; and 3.4 to 1 in Japan. By contrast, in the USA that same ratio of inequality was 8.5 to 1. Between 1997 and 2005 the UK moved 0.3 points towards US levels of inequality, or almost one-quarter of the way along the path to becoming as socially unequal as people are in the USA.

The great and the good of New Labour mostly cared. But caring was not enough given thinking that had been rewired by too many years of living under growing inequality, of living under Thatcherism. The people who make up what is left of the party that governed until 6 May 2010 mostly know that it made huge mistakes, that what it did was not enough compared with what most other politicians in most other affluent countries in the world achieve today; not enough compared with what the 1906 or 1910 or 1945 or 1964, or even the 1974 governments achieved, all with less time and far less money.

Conclusion

Thatcherism has shaped the contemporary human geography of the UK as surely as glaciation shaped its physical geography. Thatcherism cut through what was there before, brought great industrial cities to near ruin and elevated many small southern rural towns that had only recently been places of monotony or poverty to rise to become sought after (if often soulless) dormitory villages for London. Just how appropriate the term Thatcherism will be we will not be sure of until we know that the epoch is truly over. We already know it has not occurred elsewhere in the world in the form in which it rose in the UK. Perhaps it was part of the death-throes of Empire? We now know that in many other affluent countries some equalities grew during the 1980s. The concept of Thatcherism, however, is likely to be a both an idea and a label that sticks, not least because 1978/79 now appears to have been such a seminal turning point in many key historical series. Above I have concentrated on economic inequalities and how they rose from that point on (Hills et al., 2010), but inequalities in health turned then too (Table 8.2), as did inequalities in wealth (Townsend, 1993), which also rose just a few years later (wealth lags). Even inequalities in the murder rate rose as Thatcherism grew in ascendance (Dorling et al., 2008).

No one in the USA would call what happened there 'Thatcherite', and likewise the acolytes of Thatcherism were not simply aping Mr Reagan and the men who did that president's thinking for him. It was political glaciation in the USA too, but of a different kind. It is worth reiterating that the UK Thatcherism may well, in part, have been a long-delayed reaction to loss of empire. Reaganomics, in hindsight, was about still building an empire, still fighting the Cold War. Thatcherism was turning back the progressive tide and promoting, again, inequality. And then, in 2010 came the Coalition. Initially the poor became much poorer while most of the rich became richer. At the very top the incomes of FTSE executives continued to rise so fast that the declining value of the pound could not dent their abilities to holiday as before. But that was 'initially'. There were signs during 2012 that disgust with the rich might be growing and, in effect, disgust with the intellectual project of Thatcherism was growing. However, there were also signs of continued fear of the poor and even more reluctance to support welfare payments among the population as a whole as when Mrs Thatcher herself was making cuts. And the basic lie of Thatcherism continued: that everyone could become rich if only they tried hard enough. That if you had not become rich it was simply because you either had not tried hard enough or that you did not have the 'potential' to be a tall poppy in you. When that view is seen as an ideology and not as 'common sense', Thatcherism will have ended.

References

Ahmed, M. (2008) 'Gordon Brown vows to Enshrine Child Poverty Pledge in Law', http://www.communitycare.co.uk/Articles/2008/09/24/109514/gordon-brown-labour-will-legislate-to-end-child-poverty-by-2020.htm (accessed 29 July 2011).

Atkinson, A.B. (2007). 'The Distribution of Top Incomes in the United Kingdom 1908–2000', in A.B. Atkinson and T. Piketty (eds) *Top Incomes over the Twentieth Century. A Contrast Between Continental European and English-Speaking Countries*. Oxford University Press, chapter 4. Series updated by the same author.

Baggini, J. (2010) Quoted in part in *The Guardian* (1 May), p. 37 and in full at www.guardian.co.uk/commentisfree/2010/apr/30/lib-dems-tories-election

BBC (1999) http://news.bbc.co.uk/1/hi/uk_politics/298934.stm (accessed 30 July 2011).

Campbell, J. (2008) *Margaret Thatcher; Volume One: The Grocer's Daughter,* 3rd edn. London: Vintage (first published in 2000 by Jonathan Cape), p. 134.

Davies, C. and Davies, L. (2012) 'Tory chief whip faces mounting calls to quit as police stand by expletive claim', *The Guardian* (21 September), http://www.guardian.co.uk/politics/2012/sep/21/tory-chief-whip-andrew-mitchell-police

Dorey, P. (2010) *British Conservatism: The Politics and Philosophy of Inequality.* London and New York: I.B. Tauris.

Dorling, D. (1996) *Area cartograms: Their Use and Creation Concepts and Techniques in Modern Geography series no. 59.* University of East Anglia: Environmental Publications http://www.dannydorling.org/?page_id=1448

Dorling, D. (2010) 'Our Divided Nation', *New Statesman* (14 June). http://www.newstatesman.com/uk-politics/2010/06/election-seats-support-tory.

Dorling, D. (2011) *Injustice: Why Social Inequality Persists.* Cambridge: Policy Press

Dorling, D. (2012) *The Visualization of Spatial Social Structure.* Chichester: Wiley.

Dorling, D. (2013) 'Fairness and the Changing Fortunes of People in Britain', The Beveridge Memorial Lecture, 2012, presented to The Royal Statistical Society on Wednesday, 27 June 2012, *Journal of the Royal Statistical Society A,* 176(1): 97–128.

Dorling, D. and Atkins, D.J. (1995) *Population Density, Change and Concentration in Great Britain 1971, 1981 and 1991, Studies on Medical and Population Subjects No. 58,* London: HMSO, http://www.dannydorling.org/?page_id=1449

Dorling, D. Gordon, D., Hillyard, P., Pantazis, C., Pemberton, S. and Tombs, S. (2008) *Criminal Obsessions: Why Harm Matters more than crime London,* 2nd edn. London: Centre for Crime and Justice Studies.

Guardian, The (2010) 'Editorial' (30 April): www.guardian.co.uk/commentisfree/2010/apr/30/the-liberalmoment-has-come (accessed 29 July 2011).

Hay, C. (1996) *Re-Stating Social and Political Change.* Maidenhead: Open University Press.

Hay, C. and Farrall, S. (2011) 'Establishing the Ontological Status of Thatcherism by Gauging Its "Periodisability": Towards a "Cascade Theory" of Public Policy Radicalism', *The British Journal of Politics & International Relations,* 13(4): 439–58.

Heffernan, R. (2000) *New Labour and Thatcherism.* Basingstoke: Macmillan.

Hennig, B.D. and Dorling, D. (2012) 'The Geography of the Super-rich, Political Insight', *Political Insight,* 3(3): 42.

Hills, J., Brewer, M., Jenkins, S., Lister, R., Lupton, R., Machin, S., Mills, C., Modood, T. Rees, T. and Riddell, S. (2010) *An Anatomy of Economic Inequality in the UK.* London: Government Equalities Office/Centre for Analysis of Social Exclusion.

Jessop, B., Bonnett, K. and Bromley, S. (1990), 'Farewell to Thatcherism?', *New Left Review,* 179: 81–102.

Jones, R. (2012). 'End of Life and Financial Risk in GP Commissioning.'. *British Journal of Healthcare Management,* 18(7): 374–81.

Margaret Thatcher Foundation (2012) *Biography* (accessed November 2012): http://www.margaretthatcher.org/essential/biography.asp

Powell, R. (2012) 'Echoes of the New Geography? History and Philosophy of Geography', *Progress in Human Geography,* 36(4): 518–26.

Robinson, E. (2011) 'Book review' of Peter Dorey, *British Conservatism: The Politics and Philosophy of Inequality, Twentieth Century British History*, 23(2): 307–8.

Simpson, L. (2004) 'Statistics of Racial Segregation: Measures, Evidence and Policy', *Urban Studies*, 41(3): 661–81.

Spalek, B. and King, S. (2007) 'Farepak Victims Speak Out: an Exploration of the Harms Caused by the Collapse of Farepak'. See www.crimeandjustice.org.uk/opus419/Farepak_Web_Final.pdf. For the full report, see www.crimeandjustice.org.uk/farepakvictims.html. In April 2010, 'Customers who Paid for Hampers from Farepak are Expected to Receive Less than £50 each, even as Accountants and Lawyers Handling the Liquidation Rack up Millions in Fees', *The Times* (27 April 2010); and http://business.timesonline.co.uk/tol/business/industry_sectors/consumer_goods/article7108918.ece

Thatcher, M. (1979) 'Margaret Thatcher Arrives at 10 Downing Street for the first time', 4 May: http://www.youtube.com/watch?v=A23PQCndPYU

Townsend, P. (1993) 'Underclass and Overclass: the Widening Gulf between Social Classes in Britain in the 1980s', in G. Payne and M. Cross (eds) *Sociology in action: Applications and opportunities for the 1990s*. London: Macmillan.

von Mises, L. (1975, 1990, 2012) 'Economic Calculation in the Socialist Commonwealth', in Friedrich A. Hayek (ed.) *Collective Economic Planning*. Clifton, NJ: Kelley Publishing, pp. 87–130, and Auburn, AL: Ludwig von Mises Institute, 1990, available 2012 at: http://mises.org/document/448/Economic-Calculation-in-the-Socialist-Commonwealth

Waugh, E. (1945) *Brideshead Revisited, The Sacred and Profane Memories of Captain Charles Ryder*. London: Chapman & Hall.

Commentary

Mrs Thatcher's iniquitous geographies: why spatial dynamics matter

CHRIS PHILO

Mapping socio-spatial inequalities: critique and defence

> mapping even more evidence of man's [*sic*] patent inhumanity to man is counter-revolutionary in the sense that it allows the bleeding-heart liberal to pretend he is contributing to a solution when he in fact is not. . . . Nor does [our task] lie in what can only be termed moral masturbation of the sort which accompanies the masochistic assemblage of some huge dossier on the daily injustices to the population of the ghetto, over which we beat our breasts, commiserate with each other, before retiring to our fireside comforts. . . . Nor is it a solution to indulge in that emotional tourism which attracts us to work with the poor 'for a while' in the hope that we can really help them improve their lot.
>
> (Harvey, 1972: 10)

With these words – announcing the possibilities for a Marxist approach to human geography – David Harvey scathingly denounced as 'counter-revolutionary' three possible avenues open to critical social scientists addressing a social world fractured by simultaneously social *and* spatial inequalities (the latter expressed in the creation of 'ghettos' of diverse type and scale). One target was academics electing to get 'close' to the grounded experiences of those peoples and places suffering from such inequities, regarded by Harvey as 'emotional tourists' offering nothing tangible back from their endeavours. Another was academics generating comprehensive dossiers of information demonstrating how socio-spatial inequalities impact negatively upon the peoples of those 'ghettos' on the distaff side of development, progress and modernization. A third, closely related to Harvey's second, was academics wishing to map humanity's *in*humanity, and who saw their role as a painstaking mapping of socio-spatial inequality at a variety of scales from the local to the global. For these academics, certain tools from the spatial-scientific turn of the preceding decade or so could be legitimately deployed in reconstructing regional and urban patterns of wealth and poverty, alongside various other geographically variable dimensions of material and social deprivation.

Such work had started to surface in the early 1970s, but in 1972 Harvey was writing on the cusp of a burgeoning genre of inquiries sometimes termed 'welfare geography'. This latter genre – inspired in the UK by pioneering texts such as Coates and Rawstron (1971; also Coates et al., 1977) and then elaborated in diverse directions by the compelling contributions of David M. Smith (e.g., 1973, 1977, 1979, 1994) – was indeed all about the careful but imaginative tracking, tracing and translating (into [carto]-graphical form) of the iniquitous geographies displayed by contemporary society (in the UK and further afield). Harvey may have seen some merits in these endeavours, yet most likely would still have viewed them as deficient in their failure to locate such inequities in a securely Marxist conceptual frame.

Danny Dorling's oeuvre fits squarely within just such a (carto)graphic forensics of socio-spatial inequality, and he is thereby the UK's leading heir to the legacy of Smith's welfare geography. Proceeding from an extraordinary understanding of how quantitative data 'works' and an unparalleled capacity for unearthing data that genuinely measures what needs to be measured, not just what can easily be measured, Dorling has been producing outstanding (carto)graphical representations of socio-spatial inequalities of almost every shade and texture imaginable. These representations – often based not upon the land areas of jurisdictional spatial units but rather on their human population levels – undoubtedly serve as much more than just representational tools: they *do* have their own compelling aesthetic, but they are also devices for 'thinking with', provocations to reflection, amazement and even (as in his chapter) anger. It is perhaps not too fanciful to see Dorling's work as itself the logical outgrowth of his facility for exploring socio-spatial inequality being confronted by the apparent deepening of such inequality after the late 1970s – once the UK, USA and (if less aggressively) other parts of the world had embarked upon the dismal trajectories unfurled under the headings of Thatcherism and Reaganism (albeit these two 'isms' must not be simplistically conflated). I do have more to say about Dorling and Mrs Thatcher, but first let me underline the *potential* critique that Harvey's quote, nonetheless, signals for an approach such as Dorling's: as just another 'technical' exercise in charting what we know already, ultimately amounting to (clever) descrip-tion unsupported by (theoretically rigorous) explanation and disconnected from (realistic and realizable) recommendations for achieving progres-sive social change. There are important threads of critique here that cannot be entirely discounted, but my principal response would be forcefully to refute such a dismissal of Dorling's work, and instead to insist on its absolute centrality to – and its unavoidable ongoing salience for – any broader alignment of critical social scientists concerned to expose what otherwise can be so readily concealed (and where what is exposed is actually what a great many of us otherwise assuredly would *not* know).

It is arguably vital that there are academics in every generation able to put their conceptual and technical skills to the service of laying bare socio-spatial inequalities, precisely because every society in every generation is continually making anew the inequalities that it inherits. Possibly it will dampen them down, too often it will exacerbate them, and other times it will rework them so that new configurations of peoples and places come to occupy the 'lowest' rungs of the socio-spatial hierarchy while others, more fortunately, climb a few notches upwards. The map of socio-spatial inequalities may contain stubborn land masses of poverty, deprivation and malaise, ones recurring across successive maps, but the exact contours will be continually shifting and, additionally, the 'heights' of these contours and the 'steepness' of the gradients (or, in current policy parlance, the 'cliffs') between them will be continually altering. I deliberately use these kinds of topographical images because many of Dorling's maps furnish an acute sense of a three-dimensional landscape, pockmarked with peaks and troughs of wealth and poverty, which powerfully disclose the fundamentally unequal geographies of such phenomena (and their many correlates). I also stress the point about change, about one generation's maps of inequalities not being the same as the next generation's, because at the heart of Dorling's message is the thunderbolt revelation that socio-spatial inequalities in the UK *have* varied in distribution and magnitude over the years, apparently becoming *less* marked for many decades but then rapidly becoming *more* marked (right up to the present moment) following Mrs Thatcher's rise to power. Crucially too, the impression is that such a temporal shift in socio-spatial patterns has not been straightforwardly mirrored elsewhere in the world, excepting in the USA and, to an extent, Canada, which decisively opens up the delicious possibility of counterfactual argumentation. Just maybe it did not have to be like that; just maybe an alternative political-discursive imagination could have taken the UK elsewhere, towards a more socio-spatially just future; and just maybe that could still happen. Such a speculation sits well with Doreen Massey's spatial-juxtapositional vision of the future's inherent 'openness', thereby cracking apart overly defeatist, structurally determinist accounts of power, politics and inequality (Massey, 2004). Wrapping back to my basic claims, however, I would assert that, had Dorling (and his predecessors) followed Harvey's 1972 injunction by abandoning the forensic documenting of socio-spatial inequality, then temporal and spatial comparisons would have been impossible and the challenging realizations of the present chapter (and related publications) would not now be available to us.

Mrs Thatcher's geographies: denial and invention

No country can deny its geography ever.[1]

(Mrs Thatcher, 3 November 1984)

Speaking at a 'Q&A' session in New Delhi following her statement about the assassination of Mrs Ghandhi, Mrs Thatcher referenced the importance of 'geography' – an observation that she repeated on at least two other occasions (only one of which was scripted in advance).[2] True, she primarily meant 'geography' in the sense of where countries are located upon the earth's surface, particularly with reference to immediate neighbours in their own world region, but it is intriguing to note that, in general, Mrs Thatcher was not averse to speaking of 'geography'. There are many instances from her archive when she cites the importance of 'history and geography' as important subjects within a decent school education, always bracketed together but mentioned *after* the physical sciences, and the archive is also a window on statements where she explicitly confided her concern for wider 'environmental' agendas. Surprisingly perhaps, in a Q&A session at

[1] Thatcher Archive, Margaret Thatcher Foundation (henceforth TA), consulted at http://www.margaretthatcher.org./document/105783 (accessed 20/03/2013).

[2] 'no country can deny its geography as well as its history' (Q&A session following speech in Kuala Lumpar, Malaysia, 6 April 1985): TA, http://www.margaretthatcher.org./document/106010 (accessed 20/03/2013); 'We cannot deny our geography as part of Europe anymore that you can deny yours as part of the Pacific' (Speech at State Government Dinner in Sydney, Australia, 4 August 1988): TA, http://www.margaretthatcher.org./document/107312 (accessed 20/03/2013).

a 1990 Young Conservative Conference, the first question was about environmental issues, and she replied by discussing facets of the physical environment that concerned her (and where her governments were taking policy leads). She distinguished between: the 'global environment', stressing the need to protect the atmosphere from the dumping of 'waste gases'; the 'regional environment', stressing the need to protect rivers and seas from polluting emissions, as well as from the effects of 'acid rain'; and the 'immediate local environment', where the question became more one of how to keep towns and cities free from 'litter and graffiti, as well as maintaining the countryside as the home of 'scenes of great beauty' for us all to visit.[3] Significantly, she also appended a comment about the environment as *not* solely a matter of physical geography, to which I will return shortly.

In another geographical register, Mrs Thatcher has occasionally remembered her upbringing in Grantham, 'a small market town in the county of Lincolnshire in the East Midlands of England. Neither rich nor poor, neither remote nor metropolitan, it is an ordinary place' (Moore, 2011, no pagination). Asked by an Australian school pupil about her 'favourite place in England', Thatcher replied: 'I think one always feels a special bond towards the place where you were born, which in my case was Grantham, Lincolnshire.'[4] In his chapter, Dorling hints that these geographical origins are not irrelevant to understanding Mrs Thatcher, suggesting that her journey from Grantham, to the University of Oxford and then the hallways of national government in London, holds clues about her aspirational vision of social advancement. Conveniently, Grantham itself sits just south of the UK line that Dorling and co-workers have calculated as separating a advantaged 'South' from a disadvantaged 'North'.[5] Mrs Thatcher's own trajectory 'up' the UK's socio-spatial hierarchy from Grantham was mirrored in her political beliefs in how *anyone*, from *any place*, could make good largely through their *own* efforts, and that it was simply a matter of self-conviction, hard work and an enterprising spirit (and a notion of such 'enterprising spirit' also recurs throughout her archive). At the same time, she arguably retained a certain 'outsider' status in her own mind, a

---

[3] 10 February, 1990: TA, http://www.margaretthatcher.org/document/108011 (accessed 21/03/2013).

[4] Radio Interview on Australian *Schools of the Air*, Alice Springs, Northern Territory, Australia, 2 August 1988: TA, http://www.margaretthatcher.org./document/107307 (accessed 20/03/2013).

[5] See http://sasi.group.shef.ac.uk/maps/nsdivide/ns_line_detail.html.

Grantham grocer's daughter combating the political consensus associated with a certain London–Oxbridge axis of 'how to do things', and an abiding feature of her own politics was the will to be a consensus-breaker, to proceed in a thoroughly non-consensual fashion when shattering the likes of the Fordist (Big Capital/Big Labour) 'economic consensus' (Moore, 2011, no pagination). Dorling's telling additional point, though, is that, just as Margaret Roberts made it to Oxford, London and, eventually, No. 10, having arrived in the 'top' echelons of UK society, so she encountered a progressively flattening pattern of socio-spatial inequality: the 'top' peoples and places were ceasing to be so overwhelmingly 'top', and hence, in Mrs Thatcher's eyes, the incentives for people to demonstrate the acute social enterprise to reach the 'top' were dangerously diminishing. Perhaps it is over-stating the case, but Dorling's chapter does propose that Mrs Thatcher's own geography, and indeed her own feelings about that geography, were arguably far from incidental ingredients in her drive to engineer a more unequal society.

It might therefore be said that Mrs Thatcher's orientation was in some measure a *denial* of geography, notwithstanding her plea quoted above to avoid 'denying geography'. She did not want hailing from Grantham to be an obstacle to achieving the highest office, honours and rewards, but at the same time she did not want to level out spatial differences – whether richer or poorer, more central or more remote – because, in her core political philosophy, it was precisely the social *distances* between places that gave the motivational impulse needed by places (and peoples) to improve their socio-spatial standing. It was the curse of 'socialism, state intervention, debauched currency, weakened incentives and overly powerful trades unions' (Moore, 2011, no pagination) to work towards the evening out of such distances, to level the socio-spatial playing field, and thereby to remove the elemental drives to achievement. To an extent, Mrs Thatcher may have genuinely believed in 'trickle-down economics', but her crucial ambition was the creation of a 'capital-earning democracy'[6] which was completely unabashed in its pursuit of wealth generation, less so that crumbs might drop from the tables of the rich to nourish the poor, more so that the (most industrious, 'morally' responsible) members of the latter would be incentivized to try ascending the table as well. Ultimately, of course, she could not countenance too many succeeding in this respect, since that would precisely smooth out

---

[6] Speech to Centre for Policy Studies, London, 28 April 1988: TA, http://www.margaret thatcher.org/document/107228 (accessed 21/03/2013).

the socio-spatial disjunctures; and in practice, she presided over many policies which decisively widened such disjunctures. While Dorling cannot anatomize all of the various policies involved here, he convincingly measures and maps the effects of those policies, in so doing echoing various geographers at the time who detected the marked increase in socio-spatial inequalities at a regional scale (e.g., Martin, 1987, 1988).

Infamously, Mrs Thatcher declared that 'there is no such thing as society', arguably of a piece with her denial of geography, in that she wished to downplay the significance of any broader relationalities between people and places – between social groupings/classes and the localities of their work and residence – which it might be thought the responsibility of the state to 'manage'. That said, it is worth quoting more of the passage in question (from a *Woman's Own* interview in 1987):

> There is no such thing as society. There is living tapestry of men and women and people and the beauty of that tapestry and the quality of our lives will depend upon how much each of us is prepared to take responsibility for ourselves and each of us prepared to turn round and help by our own efforts those who are unfortunate.[7]

Even more arresting perhaps than the denial of 'society', then, is the following, surprisingly lyrical remark about the 'tapestry' of immediate encounters, exchanges and obligations enacted in everyday social life.[8] A connection can possibly be spied with a claim that Mrs Thatcher added about 'environment' when taking questions at the above-mentioned 1990 Young Conservative Conference:

> Environment is not only about the physical environment. It is about the standards and values, the courtesy, the conduct by which we live. That matters very much indeed and courtesy is by definition: thinking of others. It is taking pride in the school of which you are part, pride in the reputation of your company, pride in your area and setting the standards.[9]

[7] 23 September, 1987: TA, http://www.margaretthatcher.org/document/106689 (accessed 21/03/2013). Previously in the same interview, she had said: 'Who is society? There is no such thing! There are individual men and women and there are families and no government can do anything except through people and people look to themselves first. It is our duty to look after ourselves and then also to help look after our neighbour and life is a reciprocal business and people have got the entitlements too much in mind without the obligations.'

[8] In passing, it might be remarked that Mrs Thatcher's words here are not *so* different from ones sometimes uttered by current geographers and others, myself included (Laurier and Philo, 2006), who see progressive potential in the 'convivialities' of everyday life. That she could say such things is perhaps a valuable cautionary tale!

[9] See footnote 3.

Combining these elements with what we know more broadly of Mrs Thatcher's political philosophy, we arrive at a sense of a living 'tapestry' which constitutes not so much 'society' but a diversity of social 'environments', pluralized as various settings such as schools, companies and local areas. It is, hence, from within the environing 'standards', 'values', 'courtesies', 'pride' and 'conduct' of these settings that individuals (notably young people) should learn (and be imbued with) the kind of enterprising spirit mentioned earlier. In effect, then, Mrs Thatcher denied 'society' in order to (re)invent local social environments, themselves anchored in small-scale institutions, but also in the micro-dynamics of 'proper' family life, overseen by patriarchs but run by deeply pragmatic mothers like her. These organic, not externally planned or managed, family-environment assemblages were to deliver the sorts of ambitious, enterprising, capital-generating souls required as the workhorses of Thatcherite social change. In other words, Mrs Thatcher denied 'society', and hence attention to the UK's overall social geography, while inventing an alternative geographical sense of relatively discrete, self-regulating social environments (deeply 'conservative', 'moral' and family-centred). Within such a vision there was, to repeat, scant imperative to act in a trans-systemic manner to even out differences between places, to foster equal geographies. Indeed, again to emphasize the root thrust of my argument, the possibility that occupants of differently faring social environments might, as it were, compare themselves with one another as spur for some to do better, to work harder and to avoid relying on state hand-outs (or regional policies!), was arguably integral to the pervasive logic at work here.

And maybe this all sounds a little familiar? Maybe current UK Prime Minister David Cameron's stillborn notions of a 'Big Society', hinging on hopes about community-centred voluntarisms, drink from much the same trough as Mrs Thatcher's 'No Society'? They certainly veer sharply away from any meaningful attempt to redress the obscenely wide socio-spatial inequalities unleashed in the UK, entirely non-accidentally, on Mrs Thatcher's watch. One now feels incredulous at the contrasts between, on the one hand, the 'austerity' budgets of 2010–13 pressing down on the pockets and well-being of the UK's poorer citizens, and, on the other, the likes of Barclays Bank's attempts to hide the news (on budget day 20 March 2013) that nine of their senior staff were to receive circa £40 million in bonuses. One of the prime beneficiaries, Rich Ricci, the bank's investment banking boss, had apparently been at the Cheltenham Festival, a major UK horse-racing event, earlier that week, entering a horse in one race under the name of Fatcatinthehat, an intensely provocative thing to do under the circumstances (Aidan Radnedge, *Metro*, 2013). It is against this background, perhaps, that Dorling's ongoing work matters so much in chronicling the socio-spatial inequalities made by Thatcher, fanned by Blair and now, it seems, if not enflamed then entirely unchallenged under Cameron.

References

Coates, B.E. and Rawstron, E.M. (1971) *Regional Variations in Britain: Studies in Economic and Social Geography.* London: B.T. Batsford Ltd.

Coates, B.E., Johnston, R.J. and Knox, P.L. (1977) *Geography and Inequality.* Oxford: Oxford University Press.

Harvey, D. (1972) 'Revolutionary and Counter-revolutionary Theory in Geography and the Problem of Ghetto Formation', *Antipode*, 4(2): 1–13.

Laurier, E. and Philo, C. (2006) 'Cold Shoulders and Napkins Handed: Gestures of Responsibility', *Transactions of the Institute of British Geographers*, 31: 193–207.

Martin, R. (1987) 'Mrs Thatcher's Britain: A Tale of Two Nations', *Environment and Planning A*, 19: 571–74.

Martin, R. (1988) 'The Political Economy of Britain's North–South Divide', *Transactions of the Institute of British Geographers*, 13: 389–418.

Massey, D. (2004) *For Space.* London: Sage.

Moore, C. (2011) 'The Invincible Mrs Thatcher', online article from Mrs Thatcher's biographer prompted by new biopic with Meryl Streep, consulted at http://www.vanityfair.com/politics/features/2011/12/margaret-thatcher-20112 (accessed 19/03/2013).

Radnedge, Aidan (2013) 'The £40 Million Budget Day Giveaway . . . to Nine Bank Bosses', *Metro*, Wednesday, 20 March, pp. 1, 6.

Smith, D.M. (1973) *The Geography of Social Well-Being in the United States: An Introduction to Territorial Social Indicators.* New York: McGraw-Hill.

Smith, D.M. (1977) *Human Geography: A Welfare Approach.* London: Edward Arnold.

Smith, D.M. (1979) *Where the Grass is Greener: Living in an Unequal World.* London: Penguin.

Smith, D.M. (1994) *Geography and Social Justice.* Oxford: Blackwell.

9

Don't cut down the tall poppies': Thatcherism and the strategy of inequality

CAROL WALKER

In her first statement from the steps of 10 Downing Street immediately after being elected Prime Minister, Margaret Thatcher quoted St Francis of Assisi. The promise of unity implied in the words: 'Where there is discord, may we bring harmony' and 'where there is despair, may we bring hope' was in fact to be in sharp contrast to the overt neo-liberal ideology which she brought to government. This strong ideological perspective, with its goals of reducing the role of the state, promoting individual responsibility and increasing the freedom of the market, led to a steep rise in poverty and inequality. Other aspects of Thatcherism, such as family policy (see David, Chapter 6 in this collection), had a stronger neo-conservative emphasis although there are clearly elements of her ideological perspective in the social control of claimants. As will be shown, the strategy of inequality was driven chiefly by neo-liberalism. The Thatcher administrations set in train a growing divide between rich and poor, those in work and those out of work, between the north and the south, between men and women and between different black and minority ethnic groups. These social divisions impacted not only on citizens' economic well-being but also on their physical and mental health, their educational chances, employment and housing prospects (Walker and Walker 1987, 1997). As this chapter will show, at the end of her premiership, Britain was a much more socially and economically divided country than when she took office. It has remained so ever since.

The chapter looks at the rationale behind the economic and social policies that would lead to the impoverishment of large numbers of people in Britain and to a growing divide between the rich and the poor. It looks at the 'strategy of inequality' pursued by the Thatcher governments, which broke the post-war consensus on the structural causes of poverty and replaced it with individual explanations, which blamed the poor for their poverty and demonized 'dependency'. The chapter examines the rise in the numbers in poverty, the growth of inequality and the role of welfare benefits (see Hill and Walker, Chapter 3 this collection and Figure 7.4 in Farrall and Jennings, Chapter 7 this collection), taxation, earnings and cuts in the social wage in contributing to these major social divisions. In exploring the Thatcherite legacy, it is argued that, although the trend of rising poverty and inequality began to turn round under her successor, John Major's Conservative administrations (1990–97), and the strong commitment to poverty reduction of the subsequent New Labour administrations, key elements of the neo-liberal ideology which underpinned her 'strategy of inequality' survived and fundamentally changed the debate on taxation, welfare benefits and the poor. Her legacy can also be seen in the policies of the 2010 Conservative/Liberal Democrat Coalition government, which looks set to preside again over both a growth in poverty and a growing gap between the rich and the poor.

Ending the post-war consensus

In a speech in New York as leader of the Opposition, Thatcher made clear her view on what she regarded as the perverse consequences of the pursuit of equality:

> We find that the persistent expansion of the role of the state, beyond the capacity of the economy to support it, and the relentless pursuit of equality has [sic] caused, and is [sic] causing, damage to our economy in a variety of ways. It's not the sole cause of what some have termed the 'British sickness' but it is a major one. Now what are the lessons then that we've learned from the last thirty years? First, that the pursuit of equality itself is a mirage. What's more desirable and more practicable than the pursuit of equality is the pursuit of equality of opportunity. And opportunity means nothing unless it includes the right to be unequal and the freedom to be different. One of the reasons that we value individuals is not because they're all the same, but because they're all different. I believe you have a saying . . . 'Don't cut down the tall poppies. Let them rather grow tall.' I would say, 'Let our children grow tall and some taller than others if they have the ability in them to do so.'
> (Speech to the Institute of SocioEconomic Studies, 15 September 1975)

283

Thatcher's premiership ended the broad post-war consensus that one function of government was to combat poverty and to reduce, rather than increase, social and economic inequalities; weak as that might sometimes have been in the implementation, inequalities in wealth narrowed over the post-war period (see Dorling, Chapter 8 in this collection). Her abandonment of any anti-poverty strategy was consistent with the neo-liberal agenda, which determined both her economic strategy to give free rein to the market and to reduce direct taxation, and her social agenda, which was to roll back the welfare state. State intervention to tackle poverty was viewed as economically harmful because it required unacceptable levels of public spending and excessive taxation, which would stifle incentive. It was seen as socially harmful because it would have a demoralizing impact on those to whom it was directed.

With regards the welfare state, her economic and social priorities reinforced each other. The welfare state was regarded as an overbearing instrument, which had created dependency and reduced self-reliance and initiative. By continually focusing on this perceived negative threat, to the almost total neglect of the importance of the welfare state in supporting the vulnerable in times of need, the Thatcher governments created the climate in which cutting spending in this area was not only seen as economically vital but also socially necessary. Thus, in her first budget, when the need for public expenditure cuts was announced, it was made clear that no area, including social security, which had hitherto been largely protected, was to be spared. In addition to the cuts, the welfare state was subjected to successive rounds of restructuring, marketization and privatization, which gradually gained momentum through her period in office, and the impact of which also came to fruition fully only after she had been ousted. It was the poorest and the most vulnerable who were to experience the greatest losses in their financial security and their standard of living as the welfare state underwent the most radical change since the Second World War.

> 1979 represented a watershed in British social policy: the replacement of a weak and highly circumscribed consensus on the case for combating poverty . . . with a proactive 'strategy' of inequality.
>
> (Walker, 1997: 3)

Three key assumptions underpinned the Thatcher approach to social policy. First was the assertion that the welfare state creates dependency. Unlike Titmuss (1987) who used the term to justify state intervention during difficult periods in people's lives, the Thatcher governments presented dependency as being both a personal failing and morally debilitating. This emphasis became a feature of the debate on social security and those dependent upon it, and provided an important justification for cuts in this area of spending. Second was the belief that any form of welfare provision – from the family, self-help, charities, but especially that of the market – was superior to welfare from the state. This led to the transfer of many services from the public to the private sector, which resulted, for example, in a radical transfer in the provision of residential care for older and disabled people away from local authorities. Third was the primacy given to the enterprise culture and the resultant need to increase financial incentives for those at the top of the income distribution, by allowing salaries to rise and by reducing the level of taxation; the fruits of this increase in entrepreneurial activity would then, it was argued, 'trickle down' to those below.

The attack on poverty and the poor

During the Thatcher years right-wing pressure groups such as the Institute for Economic Affairs (IEA) were brought in from the cold and became major influences on, and cheerleaders for, cutbacks in the welfare state in general and the 'generosity' of the social security system in particular. Charles Murray's (1984) critical treatise blaming poverty on an underclass of lone mothers and those involved in criminal activity, with an overt racial dimension, also received widespread coverage in the UK and was cited by government ministers. The Thatcher governments were not the first to blame poverty on at least some groups of the poor but they raised the level of sustained criticism and opprobrium to a new level, from which few escaped.

First, the government questioned the very existence of poverty in Britain. The Thatcher administrations were unmoved as the evidence began to pile up about the level of the hardship caused by their economic and social policies. For example, Norman Lamont, as Chancellor of the Exchequer, notoriously said in Parliament that the huge rise in unemployment over which they had presided (after an initial election campaign based on posters with the banner headline 'Labour isn't working', above a picture of a lengthy dole queue) was 'a price well worth paying' (1991). Lord Young, the Secretary of State for Industry and reputed to be Thatcher's 'favourite minister', was similarly complacent:

General standards of living rose steadily and substantially through most of the Victorian era . . . So in looking at the generation of Victorian entrepreneurs and the result of their achievements, we need not feel guilty that their success was at the expense of the poor.

(1985: 2 cited in Walker, 1997: 6)

If there was any response it was to further justify the strategy of targeting the poor and the vulnerable through a highly negative campaign questioning their level of need and/or their level of deservingness.

The word 'poverty' disappeared from the language of all official documents to be replaced with euphemisms such as 'those in real need' and 'those in genuine need' (Walker, 1993). In his short-lived career as Secretary of State for Social Security, John Moore, in a speech entitled 'The End of the Line for Poverty' (1989), claimed that absolute poverty had been abolished and that relative poverty was a misnomer for inequality. He also said critics of government policy would find 'poverty in paradise'.

Second, and in legacy terms perhaps the most influential, was a shift from structural to individual explanations of poverty. At its most extreme, poverty was 'redefined as "dependency" which was seen as a behavioural problem caused by the welfare state itself' (Moore, 1987; Oppenheim, 1997: 18). The 1980s became the decade of the 'dependency culture'. Proponents of this thesis, led by Thatcher, secretaries of state for social security and other government ministers, maintained that people were encouraged to remain dependent on the state by the very policies which had been put in place to assist them (Moore, 1987). This approach was later to underpin the analysis of poverty propounded by the Centre for Social Justice founded by Iain Duncan Smith who later became the first Secretary of State for Work and Pensions in the 2010 Coalition government and who framed the government's radical welfare benefit reforms on this premise.

Members of the government, including Thatcher herself, launched a sustained attack on one particular group of the poor, namely social security claimants: first on the familiar front of fraud and abuse and, second, on the 'problem' of 'welfare dependency'. With regard to the first, the tackling of fraud and abuse was one of three objectives on social security identified in her government's first Queen's Speech in 1979. The 1980s was marked by a succession of measures designed to increase control within the system. These included setting up regional fraud units and, in 1982, the 'Oxfraud incident' during which hundreds of homeless people were arrested after reporting to a fake social security office (Franey, 1983).

To justify its 'dependency culture' thesis, government ministers, including Thatcher, attacked one group of social security claimants after another. Interestingly, those classed as sick and disabled largely escaped. This might have been because, in order to reduce the unemployment count, many people were recorded as sick instead, which had long-term implications for their re-employment chances and the benefits bill. Subsequently, both the New Labour and Coalition governments introduced stringent policies to radically reduce their number.

The first group to be subject to the government's opprobrium were the most obvious – the unemployed. A series of stringent measures were introduced in order to ensure that they were 'genuinely' unemployed; their benefits were cut and penalties for leaving work 'without good cause' or for being sacked were increased. Second, the government narrative in relation to older people no longer concerned the persistence of poverty among this group but the emergence of a new group: the 'WOOPIES' – well-off older people. Originally identified by the marketing industry, this idea was seized upon by government to illustrate the growing number of affluent pensioners, the existence of whom provided justification for transferring resources from the national insurance retirement pension to means-tested social assistance. In fact, as discussed later, pensioner poverty persisted during the Thatcher era. Although the proportion of pensioners in the poorest income decile fell by a half to one in eight between 1979 and 1987, this happened not because older people suddenly became better off but because younger people were even worse off and therefore displaced them into the decile above (Walker, 1993). Pensioners were 'disproportionately in the bottom half, particularly the second fifth, of the income distribution (Hills, 1998: 24) and at the end of Thatcher's period of office there were still over one million pensioner families receiving means-tested social assistance and a further 1.5 million living on incomes below social assistance levels (Giles and Webb, 1993). Third, in response to the growing poverty of young people and school leavers, the government placed the blame not on their policy to abolish social security benefit as of right to 16–18-year-olds, which alone led to an increase in homelessness, or on the record levels of youth unemployment, but on the failure of their families to support them. Focus on lone parents did not come until the end of the 1980s when, following a speech by Margaret Thatcher to the National Children's Home (1990), legislation was introduced to create the ill-fated Child Support Agency (CSA) (Cm 1264, 1990). Widely trailed as a way of ensuring that absent parents did not abdicate financial responsibility for their children, in its execution the CSA focused only on lone parents *on benefit* in an attempt to reduce the benefits bill. Many working parents who wanted the CSA to act on their behalf were to be disappointed by the lack of support they were offered.

All these initiatives had the same intention and result. By making subtle, and sometimes less than subtle, attacks on people living on state benefits, the Conservative government sought to undermine the credibility of those receiving benefits, which they and the media often referred to as 'hand-outs'. Do they really deserve help? Are they 'genuinely' poor? Also 'the poor' were defined only as those on benefit, ignoring entirely the growing numbers of working poor. In such a climate it is easier for government to withdraw from anti-poverty policies and even to pursue policies, notably cutting benefits, excluding people from benefits and increasing condi-tionality, which would lead to greater poverty for many.

The rise in poverty and inequality

During her 11 years as Prime Minister the incomes and the wealth of the richest grew exponentially. In contrast, the incomes of the poor in work were kept low by rising unemployment and below-inflation rises in the public sector, and the incomes of those out of work were cut in the most significant set of social security changes since the introduction of national provision in 1948.

As part of its strategy to make poverty 'disappear' from the social and political debate, important changes were made in the collection and publication of both low-income and unemployment statistics. Around thirty changes were made to the unemployment count, virtually all of which had the effect of reducing the total. Previously the 'poverty' figures had been based on the government's 'Low Income Families Statistics' (LIF), which set out the number of people and households living on a range of incomes relative to the prevailing social assistance rates (supplementary benefit (SB) and later income support (IS)) (DHSS, 1988). However, the government rejected the relative definition of poverty on which these were based and which had been widely accepted for over two decades since publication of *The Poor and the Poorest* (Abel-Smith and Townsend, 1965) by all political parties and in the academic literature. In the Thatcher government's first review of social security (Cmnd 9517, 1985: 12) both the relative definition and the use of supplementary benefit as a poverty line were challenged:

> Various attempts have been made to measure poverty using a relative standard. . . . There are, however, obvious drawbacks to this approach. If the level of supplementary benefit rises relative to other forms of income, more families will be counted as being in poverty even if the real incomes of all families in the population are rising. For these and other reasons there is now no universally agreed standard of poverty.

Thus in 1985 the Households Below Average Income (HBAI) series of data replaced the Low Income Families Statistics. This would have meant that it was impossible to follow the poverty trend during the Thatcher era except that the House of Commons Select Committee on Social Services (1988) were so concerned at the loss of this data that they commissioned the Institute for Fiscal Studies (IFS) to produce figures calculated on the old basis (Johnson and Webb, 1990; Social Services Committee, 1988) in order to provide some continuity. The government also collected the HBAI data biannually rather than annually, and the data often appeared up to two years after collection.

Poverty

The trend in poverty under the Thatcher governments can be measured by three poverty measures: the HBAI, which still provides the basis for measuring poverty today; the extended LIF statistics collected by the IFS and the expenditure-based approach first pioneered by the Breadline Britain Surveys (Mack and Lansley, 1985) undertaken in the early 1980s and later in the Poverty and Social Exclusion Surveys (Pantazis et al., 2006).

According to all three measures the rise in poverty under Thatcher was dramatic. In the 1960s around 10 per cent of the population had incomes below half the contemporary average; this fell to 6 per cent before housing costs (BHC) in 1977 but in 1991/92 it peaked at 21 per cent. The number of people living in households below half median income after housing costs (AHC) rose from 5.0 million to 13.9 million between 1979 and 1991/92; calculated BHC it rose from 4.4 million to 11.7 million. The rise in the number of children living in poor households (using HBAI data) was also dramatic, rising from 1 in 10 of all children to 1 in 3. Similarly, the number of people on incomes at or below SB/IS level rose from 7.7 million to 11.3 million. Thus the growth in the numbers in poverty using the new HBAI measure showed an even greater increase than under the original LIF criteria.

As a result of its strategy to concentrate on providing a minimum for those in poverty rather than tackling the wider question of social injustice, the government favoured means-tested, or as they were renamed 'targeted' and 'income-related' benefits, over universal provision (Oppenheim, 1997). The number of families receiving supplementary benefit and its successor, income support, in the UK rose from 2.9 million in 1979 to 4.1 million in 1989; the number of individuals rose from 4.6 million to 7.0 million, after peaking in 1987 at 8.1 million (Giles and Webb, 1993). The whole of the rise was among those below pension age. Three groups accounted for the rise. First, lone parents whose numbers in the general population rose from 0.8 to 1.1 million (see David, Chapter 6 in this collection), but the proportion who were dependent on SB/IS almost doubled from 38 per cent to 66 per cent. Second, the number of unemployed people on means-tested benefit rose from 1.4 to 1.8 million over the same period, though it had peaked at 3.3 million in the latter half of the 1980s when unemployment was at its highest (see Thompson, Chapter 2 in this collection). The 1980s also saw a growth in the number of long-term unemployed on means-tested benefits as a result of prevailing labour market conditions, the reduction in the length of time contributory unemployment benefit was paid and stricter penalties on those who left work 'with no good cause'. Third, there was a doubling in the numbers of people claiming as long-term sick or disabled. Much of this growth can be attributed to the high levels of unemployment during the 1980s. Lone parents and disabled people find it harder to get work in such a climate. Part of the growth in the number registered as sick or as disabled was the result of many unemployed people being recategorized as a way of reducing the unemployment count (Atkinson, 1989); a trend which subsequent Labour and Coalition governments have sought vigorously to reverse.

The expenditure-based approach to measuring poverty in the Breadline Britain Surveys (Mack and Lansley, 1985), which built on Townsend's ground-breaking approach (Townsend, 1979), provide a different measure of poverty based not on income but on 'an enforced lack of socially perceived necessities'. The levels of poverty revealed according to this measure were remarkably similar to those produced by the LIF and the HBAI series: in 1990 around 20 per cent of all households (11 million households) were living in poverty compared to around 14 per cent (7.5 million) in 1985.

During Thatcher's period of office, lone parents and their children and pensioners featured most significantly at the bottom of the income distribution. Couples without dependent children were most likely to be at the top. Nearly half the richest fifth were single, full-time workers or couples both working full time. The self-employed were polarized between the top and the bottom. Two-thirds of the poorest fifth had no earnings, but the remaining third were the working poor, who incidentally were also victims of cuts in in-work benefits such as family income supplement (later reincarnated as family credit and working tax credits) and housing and council tax benefits. Indeed, under Thatcher the number of working poor (those in full-time and part-time work and the self-employed) increased from 1.71 to 4.36 million (Pile and O'Donnell, 1997). The massive sale of council houses under Thatcher (see Murie, Chapter 5 in this collection) contributed to a shift in the position of those in social housing in the income distribution as the better off bought their homes: less than half of such tenants were in the poorest two-fifths of the income distribution in 1979; this rose to three-quarters in the early 1990s. These tenants were particularly hard hit by the successive rounds of cuts in housing benefit. Finally, people from ethnic minorities were twice as prevalent in the bottom fifth of the income distribution as they were in the population (11 per cent versus 6 per cent). This disguised substantial differences between groups: for example, in the early 1990s as many as two-thirds of the Pakistani and Bangladeshi populations were among the poorest fifth (Hills, 1998: 25).

As well as the number of people in poverty increasing during Thatcher's term of office, their level of poverty deepened (Giles and Webb, 1993: 41):

> those in the poorest decile in 1989 [were] likely *on average* [their emphasis] to be poorer than their 1979 counterparts . . . the bottom decile now contains types of individuals who are absolutely poorer than the types that used to be in the bottom decile. These people are generally characterised by unemployment, low-paid self-employment and/or high housing costs.

Furthermore, the chances of the poorest moving up the income ladder were very slim and decreased with the length of time spent at the bottom of the income distribution (Oppenheim, 1997). Rather they was merely churning at the bottom as some groups (such as the growing numbers of unemployed) displaced others (such as those over pension age) not because anyone got any better off but because others got worse off.

Income inequality

> Everyone in the nation has benefited from increased prosperity – everyone.
> (Margaret Thatcher MP, House of Commons, *Hansard*,
> 17 May 1988, col. 796, cited in Oppenheim, 1997: 22)

The very significant increase in the numbers of people and households living in poverty under the Thatcher administrations provide one part of the explanation for the unprecedented rise in inequality, which also occurred during this period. It also disproves the New Right's assertion that wealth created at the top would 'trickle down' to the bottom (Murray, 1996).

Income inequality in the UK grew rapidly between 1977 and 1990 to the highest level recorded since the war (Hills, 1995; updated Hills, 1998). This increase was greater than any other country in the OECD except New Zealand, where it grew for a shorter period (Atkinson, 1996, cited in Oppenheim, 1997) and the gap between rich and poor was wider than in any other country except the USA (Hills, 1998: 17). Part of this growing gap can be attributed to the growing dependence on means-tested benefits (see Hill and Walker, Chapter 3 in this collection). Another explanation lies in what was happening to wages and salaries and to taxation.

In the 1960s and 1970s all income groups saw their real net incomes rise, with the poorest 10 per cent seeing the greatest percentage increase (Hills, 1998, figure 2). However, under Thatcher the poorest 20–30 per cent received no benefit from economic growth. Between 1979 and 1991/92 the incomes of the poorest fifth BHC and the poorest three-tenths AHC barely rose at all (Hills, 1998: 13). The incomes of the poorest tenth BHC were the same in 1991/92 as when Thatcher had taken office in 1979; AHC they were 17 per cent lower. By contrast, those in the top 20 per cent of the income distribution did very much better, enjoying an increase both before and after housing costs. The top 10 per cent were almost 60 per cent better off BHC and over 60 per cent better off AHC.

The contrast between rich and poor is even more stark when looking at the relative share of income received by each tenth of the population. Between 1979 and 1990/91 the bottom 60 per cent saw a fall in their share of total income but the poorest tenth saw the greatest fall from 4.3 per cent to 2.9 per cent BHC and from 4.0 per cent to 2.1 per cent AHC. Those in the 7th, 8th and 9th deciles saw small changes (sometimes up and sometimes down depending on whether calculated BHC or AHC). Only the richest tenth saw their share rise, and rise dramatically: from 20.6 per cent to 26 per cent BHC and from 21 per cent to 27 per cent AHC (Hills, 1998, table 1).

Taxation

One of the lasting impacts of the Thatcher administrations was to, apparently irrevocably, embed the principle of low direct taxation into the national debate and so cut off a key means of revenue raising from future governments (Walker, 1990: 32). With the exception of the introduction of the 50p tax band introduced in April 2010 for incomes above £150,000 (subsequently reduced to 45p by the Coalition government) and, to some extent the scrapping of the 10p tax band in 2008, all movements in income tax rates since 1980, in contrast to previous decades, have been downwards. The constraints this places on governments' ability to raise revenue has a serious knock-on effect on their ability to spend, it has also led to more regressive ways of raising revenue through increases in indirect taxes and national insurance.

The reduction of direct taxation was one of the first objectives of the Thatcher administration. Her rationale was simple: high tax rates are a deterrent to hard work and, in the case of very high rates for the top paid, might deter talented people from working in the UK.

> If you look across the continent in France, you will find that they've been able to pay their managers less but get a much higher net taxed income. And the result has been that if, in fact, British companies put some of their top managers into Europe or elsewhere on French salaries at French levels of tax, they couldn't get them back because we couldn't in fact pay them a big enough gross salary to give them the net income.
>
> (Thatcher, 1975)

In the first budget under Thatcher's premiership, the higher rate of income tax was cut from 82 per cent to 60 per cent, where it was held until 1988 when it was reduced to 40 per cent (where it still stands). The Labour government belatedly introduced a 50 per cent rate on incomes over £150,000 in 2010; this was reduced to 45 per cent by the Coalition government from April 2013. The basic rate of tax was reduced from 33 per cent to 25 per cent between 1979 and 1990. Subsequently, the basic rate was further reduced under the Conservative administrations of John Major and the New Labour administrations of Tony Blair to its current level of 20 per cent.

The role of a progressive tax system, where each pays according to his or her ability to pay, is to redistribute income from the richer to the poorer. However, during and since Thatcher, the UK tax system has become more regressive. The average tax take for a married man on five times average earnings fell from 43.9 per cent to 34.3 per cent between 1979 and 1995 while for the poorest on half average income it actually increased from 10.1 per cent to 11.1 per cent (Pile and O'Donnell, 1997). Cutting tax rates is much more advantageous to the higher paid than the low paid. For example, the 1 per cent cut in the basic rate of tax in 1996 was worth 20 times as much in cash terms to those on twice average earnings as to those on half average earnings and, of course, was of no benefit to the very low paid with incomes below the personal tax allowance threshold (Pile and O'Donnell, 1997: 39).

This cut in the tax bill of the rich and the general antipathy towards raising income tax was in sharp contrast to the alacrity with which the Thatcher governments increased employees' national insurance (NI) contributions and indirect taxes. Thus, while income tax rates were reduced employee NI contributions increased from 6.5 per cent in 1979 to 10 per cent in 1994 (by 2012 they were 12 per cent). NI contributions are much more regressive than income tax as there is an upper limit above which no contributions are paid; as the very rich do not pay contributions on the whole of their income, the overall percentage they pay in NI contributions is lower than for those earning below the upper earnings limit.

Indirect taxes are similarly regressive on the poor. In 1981 the rate of VAT was virtually doubled from 8 per cent to 15 per cent (it currently stands at 20 per cent) and its tax base was extended. Most significantly, VAT was imposed on domestic fuel, an additional tax burden that particularly hit poor families who spend a higher proportion of their disposable income on fuel than higher income groups. Governments have justified the growing significance of indirect taxes in the overall tax take by arguing that, as they are taxes on spending not earnings, people have some control over how much they pay. However, this choice is not there for the poor, the majority of whose income is spent on essential goods and services. By 1995, VAT accounted for nearly 20 per cent of the income of the poorest tenth compared to 8 per cent of the income of the top tenth. This compares to 15 per cent and 7 per cent respectively a decade earlier (Giles and Johnson, 1994 cited in Pile and O'Donnell, 1997). When Thatcher came to power indirect taxes accounted for 43 per cent of tax revenue versus 57 per cent from direct taxes; in the last year of the Major Conservative government it had reversed to 54 per cent and 46 per cent, respectively.

As the data on income inequality above illustrates, this significant reduction in income tax rates for the rich in contrast to the increasing tax burden on those lower down the income distribution, far from bringing down top salaries, was accompanied by huge salary (and 'package') increases for the best paid and the burgeoning of 'telephone number' salaries at the top end during the 1980s, and indeed ever since.

The falling value of the social wage

The Thatcher goal of cutting social spending reflected her neo-liberal philosophy. First, she believed that the welfare state created dependency and reduced the individual's responsibility for their own welfare. Second, as mentioned earlier, she argued that the high cost of the welfare state necessitated unacceptably high levels of taxation which reduced people's incentive to work harder. In the adoption of monetarist economics, the first priority was to reduce public spending and no area of policy was to be given any special protection. Hers was the first, but certainly not the last, post-war government to argue that even the poor should take their fair share of the cuts. 'Social security cannot be regarded as exempt from re-examination and entitled always to take absolute priority over spending on defence, the police, hospitals or schools – or over the need for proper control of public spending as a whole' (*Hansard*, vol. 981, col. 1463, 26 March 1980).

The impact of the first significant round of social security cuts to be implemented since the Second World War is discussed by Hill and Walker (Chapter 3 in this collection). However, the poor are also more affected by cuts elsewhere in the welfare state, such as in health, education and housing. As Hills (1998: 44) points out: 'In proportion to income, these benefits in kind are much more important to those with low than with high incomes. Allowing for this is very important . . . working out the combined distributional effect of welfare services and taxation.' In an analysis of the impact of the social wage conducted for the Joseph Rowntree Foundation Inquiry into Income and Wealth, Sefton (1997) found that in 1993, the value of benefits in kind received by the poorest fifth of the population was about 70 per cent greater than for the richest fifth, though there is some variation between services. Sefton's study compared changes in income and in the social wage between 1979 and 1993 and found that when the value of the public services from which they benefit (health, education, housing subsidies and personal social services) are factored in, the gap between the top and the bottom income groups was very similar. Thus, while the social wage is more significant for the poor than for the better off (and therefore they are much more affected by cuts in welfare services) it did nothing to reduce the inequality between those at the top and those at the bottom of the income distribution during this period.

Thatcher's legacy

The election of Margaret Thatcher in 1979 marked a sea change in the development of the welfare state. It ended the post-war consensus in which the state had a clear role in protecting the vulnerable and offering them security when they were unable to support themselves. As the fall-out from her government's monetarist economic policies created growing numbers of unemployed (see Thompson, Chapter 2 in this collection), increasing numbers of lone parents and those with long-term illness and disabilities outside the labour market, and of the working poor, and the burden of her tax changes benefited the rich at the expense of those on average and low incomes, so her social policies created an environment which challenged the deservingness of those unable to support themselves and reduced investment in key public services, such as housing, education and health, which are of greatest value to the poor. Subsequent Conservative and New Labour governments did reverse and slow down the trends of growing poverty and inequality but many of the sentiments behind the Thatcher philosophy on the role of the state and its impact on the citizen have remained a potent influence on the shape of many aspects of social policy in the twenty years after she left office.

The rising trends in both poverty and inequality reversed first under the Conservative governments of John Major and then under the New Labour administrations between 1997 and 2010 (Clark and Goodman, 2001; Evans and Williams, 2009). Unlike Thatcher, Major initiated some changes to tackle poverty, not least by first lifting the freeze on child benefit and then increasing it above inflation. New Labour had a very proactive anti-poverty agenda. They introduced the minimum wage, invested significant public resources into supporting poorer families, both for those in work through the new tax credits system and for those out of work through more generous means-tested benefits, especially for children and older people. They also introduced the Sure Start scheme to provide practical support for disadvantaged poorer families before their children started school.

In contrast to the highly unequal income growth between rich and poor during the Thatcher years when the incomes of the poorest fifth grew hardly at all, during the Major years income growth was lower across the whole population but what income gains there were appeared at the lower end of the income distribution (Clark and Goodman, 2001). Under New Labour income growth continued for all groups, though much more slowly after 2002 and it again began to benefit those in the middle and upper bands of income distribution though the gap in growth between the top and bottom was less than during the Thatcher years and overall income inequality increased only slightly (Hills et al., 2009).

Poverty also began to fall after Thatcher left office. Nevertheless, the level of poverty has consistently been more than double the 3 million poor individuals living on incomes below 50 per cent of median income in 1979 (when Thatcher took office), thus demonstrating that it is much easier to drive people into poverty than to lift them out of it. New Labour policies led to significant reductions in both child and pensioner poverty until 2004/5 when they began to rise again. There was also a marked decline in persistent poverty and deprivation among families. However, despite the progress made and the considerable investment made in anti-poverty measures, most notably the means-tested tax credits system (see Hill and Walker, Chapter 3 in this collection), the New Labour administrations did not meet the targets for halving child poverty by 2010 and abolishing it by 2020, set by Tony Blair shortly after taking office. In 2010/11 2.3 million children were still living in poverty in the UK. However, this was over 1 million fewer than in 1998, the year after Labour took office and the lowest level since they began to rise in the 1980s under Thatcher.

The Child Poverty Act was passed in January 2010 just months before Labour lost the 2010 election. This set into law ambitious targets for future governments to eliminate child poverty by 2020 and established an accountability framework to monitor progress. A National Equality Panel (NEP) was set up to report on economic inequality in the UK; their report (NEP, 2010) was published shortly before the 2010 election. One of the report's main conclusions was that the major growth in inequality of the 1980s (the Thatcher years) had not been reversed. Both of these initiatives came too late, after 13 years, for the Labour government to respond to the issues raised, handing their opponents a comprehensive analysis of inequality in the UK with which to criticize New Labour's record.

One clear example of Thatcher's legacy related to the way she funda-mentally changed the political discourse and the public debate on tax. Although, in international terms, the UK is not a high tax country, the pressure on income tax is always downwards. The threat (or promise) of increases to the basic rate of tax are taken seriously by all political parties and have been eliminated from serious political discourse since John Smith's ill-fated shadow budget of 1992, which proposed tax rises. The Liberal Democrats abandoned their proposal to increase income tax by 1p in the pound in order to invest in education over a decade ago. Successive governments have continued to eschew the promotion of a fairer system of income tax in favour of a strategy of raising NI contributions, VAT and raising and introducing new indirect taxes, including on insurance, travel, fuel and alcohol. Labour belatedly increased the higher rate of income tax to 50p on incomes over £150,000 and introduced (and later very controversially scrapped) a 10p rate for low paid workers but also further reduced the basic rate of income tax to 20p and reduced the rate at which the higher rate was to be paid. Personal allowances ceased to be increased with inflation and therefore many more people were gradually brought into tax and into the higher rate of tax, even while they were eligible, in some cases, for tax credits. A significant rise in the personal allowance under the Coalition government is one of the main victories claimed by the Liberal Democrat partners, though this is of no benefit to the lowest paid workers with incomes below the personal allowance threshold and, as discussed earlier, is of even greater benefit to the higher paid.

The refusal of the political parties to even engage with the possibility of increasing taxes in order to boost government revenue has been a glaring omission from the debate on how to tackle the budget deficit, which has been the main focus of the Coalition government. As a result, public expenditure has taken the full brunt of the Coalition's strategy to tackle the deficit. Of the OECD countries, only Ireland and Iceland are planning deeper cuts in spending as a proportion of GDP and the British government's planned cuts in spending will be the biggest since the Second World War (Crawford et al., 2011). Not only will the £17 billion cut in the welfare benefits bill (with the threat of another £10 billion to come) hit the poorest, including the working poor, but cuts in other areas of welfare service spending, which are greater than any experienced by any welfare state ever, will, for reasons discussed above, again fall most heavily on the poorest.

Thatcher's second clear legacy is in the widespread acceptance of means-tested benefits by all subsequent governments (see Hill and Walker, Chapter 3 in this collection), the anti-poor rhetoric within which policy is made and the continued espousal of behavioural explanations of poverty. Alongside their anti-poverty measures, including more generous welfare benefits and widening the net of eligibility, New Labour's welfare reforms were highly focused on increasing conditionality and tightening eligibility criteria to try to get people off benefit and into work. Although presented more sympathetically than the more punitive regime of the Thatcher years and the even tougher one introduced subsequently by the Coalition government, very familiar themes emerged: the need for tougher measures to ensure that all who could work, did work. Focus on getting people into work shifted from just those registered as unemployed to all 'workless' households: the unemployed, lone parents, those who were registered as sick and disabled. Labour continued the 'scrounger' rhetoric and launched increasingly uncompromising advertising campaigns drawing attention on 'benefits thieves' on to whom, according to the menacing voice-over of the television advertisements, 'we're closing in'. The Coalition government has continued and intensified much of the Labour strategy, notably in the introduction of extremely tough assessment tests for those claiming as sick or disabled. Within months of becoming Prime Minister, David Cameron launched his 'war' on benefit scroungers. In justifying lower than inflation increases in benefits to those under retirement age, in his 2012 Autumn Statement, the Chancellor offered a new, even more derogatory term for those on benefit (which incidentally includes many in low-paid work), 'shirkers' rather than 'workers'. The whole of the Coalition's welfare reform programme has been based on the Centre for Social Justice's pathological analysis of the causes of poverty, and the need to change behaviour rather than provide extra money (Social Justice Policy Group, 2006). More recently, in another echo of the Thatcher strategy led by Cameron, the government has begun to question what we understand by poverty.

The 2012 British Social Attitudes (BSA) Survey found that 'negative perceptions of welfare recipients are a pretty constant strand in British public opinion' (see Farrall and Jennings, Chapter 7 in this collection) and 'an increasing belief that the welfare system encourages dependence': such findings are unsurprising given the negative coverage given to these issues by successive governments representing all three of the main political parties. It found also that public attitudes to welfare in this economic crisis are rather different to those expressed during the recessions of the 1980s and early 1990s when attitudes to the poor and those on welfare benefits tended to become more sympathetic (Taylor-Gooby, 2004). Previously, attitudes towards welfare tended to become more sympathetic in tough times. Clery (2012), attributes this shift, first, to 'the long-term influence of Labour's stance as well as that of the current coalition' which 'embraced a more tough minded view of welfare than it held in the past' and, second, to the debate around the Coalition government's welfare reforms which include 'claims that large numbers of welfare recipients do not really deserve their payments', which will have led people to be less supportive of benefits and those who receive them. For example, the proportion of people who said that the 'government should ensure that people have enough to live on when unemployed fell from 85 per cent in 1998 to 59 per cent in 2011; even support for adequate pensions fell from its peak of 62 per cent in 2001 to 52 per cent in 2011.

Thatcher's message stressing the primacy of individual responsibility is also alive and well. The 2012 BSA Survey (Clery, 2012) found that, whilst still in the minority, the number of people who did *not* think that the government should take the lead in providing welfare had increased over the previous decade. The proportion saying that individuals and their families should take the main responsibility for ensuring they have a sufficient retirement income rose to more than one in three (35 per cent), while around one in ten (11 per cent) thought it should be the person's employer. With regards to support for the unemployed, one in three (33 per cent) thought the individual or their family should be mainly responsible, compared with one in ten (10 per cent) who thought this in 1998. The report's author warns against taking this as an endorsement of the Coalition government's welfare reforms, which significantly reduce eligibility for, and levels of, benefits, given that it was also found that support remained strong for the government to provide for the long-term sick and disabled, a group which has been subject to highly negative media coverage since the Coalition launched radical changes to the way their benefits are assessed. However, support for extra spending on benefits for disabled people who cannot work fell by 21 per cent since 1998 and by 10 per cent in the last three years, which does fit with the adverse publicity they have received from the current and previous government. The proportion favouring an increase in taxation and spending at around 30 per cent was half what it had been 10 years ago and far lower than it had been in earlier recessions.

Conclusion

More than 30 years on, since Margaret Thatcher became prime minister, it is easy to overlook just what a radical impact she had on key aspects of social policy. She was the first post-Second World War prime minister to make a virtue of inequality and argue against measures to reduce it. She was the first to question the existence of poverty, to systematically question the deservedness of the poor, regardless of benefit status; the first to openly cut benefits and to insist that the poor, along with everyone else, had to take their share of cuts and the first to argue for means-tested rather than universal benefits. All of these approaches are now part of mainstream policy-making and debate. The Conservative-Liberal Democrat Coalition is returning to Thatcher's old themes and pursuing them even more rigorously leaving thousands of people at further risk of poverty, with the inevitable consequences for both physical and mental health, educational achievement, homelessness and crime. Both poverty and inequality are rising and are set to rise further.

First, Cameron has begun to question how poverty is measured. Second, as under Thatcher, one of the first changes in welfare reform was to introduce a less favourable method of benefit uprating; and the Chancellor then went far further by announcing that in April 2013 benefits for those under retirement age will be raised by only 1 per cent rather than in line with inflation. Third, contrary to Cameron's arguments against means testing in Opposition, the proposed new universal credit will be one super means test to replace seven other means tests. Fourth, the welfare benefits system is undergoing unprecedented cuts as it bears a disproportionate share of the public spending reductions: housing benefit has been capped and a financial penalty imposed on those with a spare bedroom. The overall benefit cap is likely to affect about 67,000 working-age households, reducing their benefit entitlement by an average of £83 per week (Joyce, 2012). As with Thatcher's little lamented poll tax the poorest will again have to pay some council tax, even though many local authorities maintain it will cost more to enforce than it will yield in revenue. The social fund has been abolished and local authorities, whose own budgets are under severe pressure, will decide how far they are willing, and able, to fill the gap.

Though, apparently at the behest of the Liberal Democrat coalition partners, many people have been taken out of tax by the significant increase in the personal allowance (though the greater advantage this brings to higher-paid workers, and its irrelevance to the very poorest, is conveniently overlooked) the highest rate of income tax paid on incomes over £150,000 belatedly introduced by Labour will fall from 50p to 45p, with a clear indication from the Chancellor of the Exchequer that he would like to reduce it further. There have been numerous cuts in corporation tax and legislation introduced to make it easier for employers to fire people. While the Liberal Democrat ministers have railed against excessive salaries of chief executives and others, nothing has been done to rein these in.

One area where there is a tantalizing glimpse of change concerns public attitudes to the rich. The economic crisis has finally led to questions being asked of the legitimacy of the excessive pay of senior executives, with a growing number of shareholder revolts against directors' remuneration packages, and on whether the rich are paying their fair share of tax. The rich are getting the merest taste of the public opprobrium, which has always been directed at the poor.

Thatcher left subsequent governments with the highest levels of poverty and inequality since the Second World War. The New Labour government tried to address the problem of poverty and had some success but the figures remained very significantly higher than when Thatcher came to office and they failed to reduce inequality. No government has been able to affect a steep drop in either poverty or inequality to match the sharp rises which occurred between 1979 and 1990. While the Coalition government makes constant allusions to 'fairness' and criticizes Labour for their record on inequality and social mobility, in reality their policies will only make poverty and inequality worse.

Tackling the problem of poverty has also become more difficult as Thatcher's anti-poor rhetoric has gained hold of the political and public imagination. The growing individualism of British society which her policies fostered has led to a growing concern for one's own economic security and a tendency to blame others for any insecurity. This has increased in recent years as austerity has started to bite and affected growing numbers of families on middle incomes. David Cameron attributed this increase in selfishness to the 'size, scope and role of government in Britain . . . [which] is now inhibiting, not advancing the progressive aims of reducing poverty, fighting inequality, and increasing general well-being. Indeed there is a worrying paradox that because of its effect on personal and social responsibility, the recent growth of the state has promoted not social solidarity, but selfishness and individualism' (Cameron, 2009). However, the main growth occurred while the Thatcher governments were pioneering severe cutbacks in welfare services and social security, both policies being pursued once more, and with increased vigour, by the Coalition government.

References

Abel-Smith, B. and Townsend, P. (1965) *The Poor and the Poorest: a New Analysis of the Ministry of Labour's Family Expenditure Surveys of 1953–4 and 1960*. London: Bell.

Atkinson, A.B. (1989) *Poverty and Social Security*. London: Harvester Wheatsheaf.

Atkinson, A.B., Rainwater, L. and Smeeding, T. (1996) *Income Distribution in OECD Countries*. Paris: OECD.

Atkinson A.B. (1996) 'Income Distribution in an International Context', 1996 Annual Lecture. London: South Bank University.

British Social Attitudes Survey 29th Report (2012), http://www.bsa-29.natcen. ac.uk/

Clark, T. and Goodman, A. (2001), *Living Standards under Labour*, IFS Election Briefing 2001. London: Institute for Fiscal Studies.

Cameron, D. (2009) *The Big Society*, Hugo Young Lecture, http://www.conservatives. com/News/Speeches/2009/11/David_Cameron_The_Big_Society.aspx

Clery, E. (2012) 'Welfare: Are Tough Times Affecting Attitudes to Welfare?', in A. Park, E. Clery, J. Curtice, M. Phillips and D. Utting (2012) *British Social Attitudes 29*. London: NatCen Social Research.

Cm 1264 (1990) *Children Come First: The Government's Proposals on the Maintenance of Children*. London: HMSO.

Crawford, R., Emmerson, C., Phillips, D. and Tetlow, G. (2011) 'Public Spending Cuts: Pain Shared?' in *IFS Green Budget 2011*. London: Institute for Fiscal Studies.

Dilnot, A. (ed.), *Election Briefing 2001*, Commentary no. 84. London: Institute for Fiscal Studies (www.ifs.org.uk/election/ebn4.pdf)

DHSS (1988) *Low Income Families*. London: HMSO.

Franey, R. (1983) *Poor Law: The Mass Arrest of Homeless claimants in Oxford*. London: CHAR/CPAG.

Giles, C. and Johnson, P. (1994) 'For Richer for Poorer: The Changing Distribution of Income in the UK, 1961–91', *Fiscal Studies*, 15(4): 29–63.

Goodman, A. and Shephard, A. (2002) *Great Britain: Some Facts*. London: Institute for Fiscal Studies.

Goodman, A. and Webb, S. (1995) *The Distribution of UK Household Expenditure 1979–1992*. London: Institute for Fiscal Studies.

Hills, J. (1995) *Income and Wealth: Report of the Inquiry Group*. York: Joseph Rowntree Foundation.

Hills, J. (1998) *Income and Wealth: The Latest Evidence*. York: Joseph Rowntree Foundation.

Hills, J., Sefton, T. and Stewart, K. (eds) *Towards A More Equal Society? Poverty, Inequality and Policy since 1997*. Bristol: The Policy Press.

Johnson, P. and Webb, S. (1990), *Poverty in Official Statistics*, IFS Commentary. London: Institute for Fiscal Studies.

Joseph Rowntree Foundation (1995) *Income and Wealth: Report of the JRF Inquiry Group: Summary*. York: Joseph Rowntree Foundation.

Joyce, R. (2012) *Thoughts on a Benefits Cap, IFS Observations*, http://www.ifs.org.uk/publications/6012 (accessed 24 January 2013).

Lamont, N. (1991) *Hansard*. House of Commons, Westminster. 'Hansard'. Publications.parliament.uk, cols 410–413, 16 May.

Mack, J. and Lansley, S. (1985) *Poor Britain*. London: Allen & Unwin.

Moore, J. (1987) *The Future of the Welfare State*. Mimeo, 26 September.

Moore, J. (1989) *The End of the Line for Poverty*. Conservative Political Centre, 11 May.

Murray, C. (1984) *Losing Ground: American Social Policy 1950–80*. New York: Basic Books.

Murray, C. (1996) *Charles Murray and the Underclass: The Developing Debate*. London: Institute for Economic Affairs.

OECD (2008) *Growing Unequal: Income Distribution and Poverty in OECD Countries*. Paris: OECD.

Oppenheim, C. (1997) 'The Growth of Poverty and Inequality', in A.Walker and C. Walker, *Britain Divided: The Growth of Social Exclusion in the 1980s and 1990s*. London: CPAG.

Pentazis, C., Gordon, D. and Levitas, R. (2006) *Poverty and Social Exclusion in Britain: The Millennium Survey*. Bristol: The Policy Press.

Pile, H. and O'Donnell, C. (1997) *Britain Divided: The Growth of Social Exclusion in the 1980s and 1990s*. London: CPAG.

Sefton, T. (1997) *The Changing Distribution of the Social Wage, Findings Social Policy Research 114* York: Joseph Rowntree Foundation.

Social Justice Policy Group (2006) *Breakdown Britain: Interim Report on the State of the Nation*. London: Centre for Social Justice, http://www.centreforsocialjustice.org.uk/client/downloads/CSJ%20FINAL%20(2).pdf

Social Services Select Committee (1988) *Fourth Report: Families on Low Incomes: Low Income Statistics*, Session 1987–88. London: HMSO.

Thatcher, M. (1990) Inaugural National Children's Home George Thomas Society Lecture, http://www.margaretthatcher.org/speeches/displaydocument.asp?docid=107992

Thatcher, M. (1979) 'Remarks on Becoming Prime Minister', Margaret Thatcher Foundation, 4 May http://www.margaretthatcher.org/document/104078 (accessed 13 August 2012).

Thatcher, M. (1975) 'Let Our Children Grow Tall', Speech to the Institute of SocioEconomic Studies, 15 September, http://www.margaretthatcher.org/document/102769 (accessed 13 August 2012).

Titmuss, R. (1987) 'Social Division of Welfare', in B. Abel-Smith and K. Titmuss (eds) *The Philosophy of Welfare*. London: Allen & Unwin.

Townsend, P. (1979) *Poverty in the UK*. Harmondsworth: Penguin.

Walker, A. and Walker, C. (1983) *The Growing Divide: A Social Audit 1979–1987*. London: CPAG.

Walker, A. and Walker, C. (1997) *Britain Divided: The Growth of Social Exclusion in the 1980s and 1990s*. London: CPAG.

Walker, A. (1997) 'Introduction: the Strategy of Inequality', in A. Walker and C. Walker, *Britain Divided: The Growth of Social Exclusion in the 1980s and 1990s.* London: CPAG.

Walker, C. (1993) *Managing Poverty: Limits of Social Assistance.* London: Routledge.

Commentary

Inequality, its persistence and its costs

ADRIAN SINFIELD

In June 1979 the first Thatcher government announced that it was abolishing the Royal Commission on the Distribution of Income and Wealth. This provided a clear and early indication of the 'strategy of inequality' that Carol Walker examines. The first post-war standing Royal Commission was set up to analyse and improve the indicators of the distribution and redistribution of resources across society and was beginning to reveal the fuller dimensions of inequality when it was terminated. The Conservative government's dismissal of the report, *Inequalities of Health*, two years later and its subsequent insistence on writing and speaking of 'variations', not 'inequalities', in health, underlined that government's strong commitment to making the market, and so society, work through the incentives of inequality (Townsend and Davidson, 1982).

Reading this chapter with its careful detailing of policies and their impact on inequality made me very aware of how much current discussion tends to be distorted by a foreshortened view of history where New Labour is seen as responsible for so many of the changes that were actually Thatcher's. The failure to understand how far the policy agenda was rewritten under the Conservatives encourages a mistaken view of what scale and type of changes are needed now. The chapter also made me more conscious of how closely the current Coalition government is following the spirit of Thatcherism. It is finding this all the easier because it is benefiting from the failure of intervening governments to tackle the scale of changes then. Carol Walker spells out the particular importance of the new dominant discourse where the poor and workless are presented as the problem that redistribution downwards only reinforces.

Governments before Thatcher were criticized for failing to identify and tackle inequality sufficiently, not for actively promoting it as a central part of their strategy. Abel-Smith and Townsend, for example, began *The Poor and the Poorest* by challenging 'two assumptions [that] have governed much economic thinking in Britain since the war . . . that we have 'abolished' poverty . . . that we are a much more equal society' (Abel-Smith and Townsend, 1965: 9). Those few who addressed these issues did not receive that much support among many in the social sciences. In his essay on 'the commitment to equality' in 1983, Atkinson noted the 'lack not only of political will but also of intellectual momentum behind principles such as equality' (Atkinson, 1983: 22–3).

By contrast, those who believed in the necessity of increasing inequality for driving growth and opportunity in a market society did so with vigour, as the chapter demonstrates. They lacked neither will nor momentum – nor institutional and media resources and support to back them up and disseminate their market messages. How the rhetoric of 'individual responsibility' as a policy principle with its rejection of redistribution was crafted over time and how it was established so successfully that it now appears ingrained in public and policy discussion deserve further research.

The Coalition's dominant strategy reflects the first sentence of the first Thatcher budget's *White Paper on Public Expenditure*: 'Public expenditure is at the heart of Britain's economic difficulties' (UK, 1979). The same paragraph stressed the particular problems caused by 'social spending'. Resources, it was constantly argued, must be targeted on 'those in greatest need' as opposed to the 'indiscriminate handing-out of benefits' that 'builds up pools of resentment among taxpayers who are footing the bill'.

The specific rejection of any scientific concept of poverty helped to shift concern to what the economy could afford and away from benefit adequacy, equity and take-up. Social rights were part of the problem, not the solution, asserted John Moore, Mrs Thatcher's most vigorous proponent of greater conditionality and insecurity as incentives to work (1987). Relative poverty he later condemned as a political construct to mask the success of capitalism (Moore, 1989) – and Moore was tipped at the time as a possible successor to Mrs Thatcher.

The chapter brings out particularly well the vigour of the attack on 'welfare dependency', supported by fraudulent myth-making on 'welfare abuse' (see also Walker, 1993). In her second volume of memoirs Mrs Thatcher devoted two sections to 'welfare dependency', on its growth and proposals 'to strengthen the family, curb welfare dependency and reduce crime' (Thatcher, 1995: 538). Re-reading her analysis today reveals how closely the present Coalition government is pursuing her policies of 'welfare reform' (see Iain Duncan-Smith's own speeches, particularly and appropriately his Keith Joseph Memorial Lecture, 2011).

Margaret Thatcher drew heavily upon American sources to discuss 'welfare dependency' as have so many others since. Many of the 'welfare' policy changes had close parallels in the USA, and some at least appeared to have been transported with little change (Levy, 1988; and 'welfare' to displace 'social security'). The ways in which the social insecurity policies of the 'Washington consensus' were put together and maintained by undermining preventive, protective and compensatory strategies by the 'individualisation of the social' (Ferge, 1997) deserve much more searching scrutiny than they have received from analysts.

The legacy of Thatcherism

In 2004, in *Who Runs this Place?*, Anthony Sampson reflected on the greatest change in the 42 years since the first edition of *The Anatomy of Britain*: 'Above all, the rich feel much less need than their predecessors to account for their wealth, whether to society, to governments or to God. Their attitudes and values are not seriously challenged by anyone. The respect now shown for wealth and money-making has been the most fundamental change in Britain over four decades' (Sampson's own summary in *The Observer*, 28 March 2004, based on p. 342). The parallels with Edwardian Britain a century earlier, recalling Masterman's *The Condition of England* with its criticism of 'public penury, private ostentation' (Masterman, 1908: 34), were largely the achievement of the first decade of Thatcherism. The legacy of increased inequality combined with deregulation also contributed to the credit crunch (Sinfield, 2011).

'Inequality has a dynamic of its own' in 'the irresponsible society' with its 'changing concentrations of economic and financial power' (Titmuss, in Alcock et al., 2001: 141). This is understood better today, but policy engagement with inequality was weak under New Labour and has largely been abandoned under the Coalition. As Carol Walker makes clear, who contributes to welfare, and how, are just as important questions as who benefits, and how, in getting to grips with the factors that maintain inequality and undermine attempts to restrain it (van Oorschot, 2008). Mrs Thatcher saw the social contribution of taxation very differently – for example, on the very last page of *The Path to Power*, 'all enjoyed the greater freedom and control over their own lives which cuts in income tax extended' (Thatcher, 1995: 606). This emphasis on the individual rejected any need for solidarity or a role for the common wealth in marked contrast to one earlier Conservative's *Middle Way*: 'freedom and poverty cannot live together. It is only in so far as poverty is abolished that freedom is increased' (Harold Macmillan, 1938: 372).

The pattern of contributions through taxation and other routes requires cross-disciplinary scrutiny that takes fuller account of the ways in which some, as individuals and through their families and, increasingly, by means of institutions, can insulate themselves both from the social costs of change and from contributing to their compensation. More study is needed of corporate welfare and the use of companies and tax havens to avoid both corporate and individual 'tax wastage' that leaves the rest of society lacking the resources to prevent poverty and restrain inequality (Farnsworth, 2012). Meanwhile, the price of Thatcherism and its social costs are still being paid, particularly in the areas still visibly scarred by its de-industrialization.

Post-mortems on Thatcherism have tended to be better at identifying the redistribution of resources individually than spelling out the extent of structural change and the reinforcement of anti-welfare institutions and groupings that support those at the top and even strengthen their privileged position. This facilitated 'the hardening of class inequality', as John Westergaard subtitled *Who Gets What?* (1995), widening the gaps between rungs of the social ladder with those higher up now much better provided and resourced to ensure their children's security (Goldthorpe, 2011).

'To recognise inequality as the problem' rather than poverty 'involves recognising the need for structural change, for sacrifices by the majority' and acknowledging 'the limits of conventional welfare' (Titmuss, 1965: 132, 131), 'The welfare state is only a way of redistributing *some* income without interfering with the causes of its maldistribution' (Cole, 1955: 88). While some measures under the last government started to alleviate elements of poverty, there has been less analysis of, let alone engagement with, 'the elaborate hierarchy of wealth and esteem, of which poverty is an integral part' (Townsend, 1979: 926). The power of those already in control continues to be little challenged – illustrated by the Governor of the Bank of England: 'I was surprised at the degree of access of bank executives to people at the very top, it was certainly easier access to people at the very top than the regulators had' (King, to the Banking Standards Commission, 6 March 2013). Regulating the poor (Piven and Cloward, 1972) continues while deregulating the rich and powerful neglects Tawney's advice of exactly one century ago: 'Improve the character of individuals by all means – if you feel competent to do so, especially of those whose excessive incomes expose them to peculiar temptations' (Tawney, 1913: 11–12).

The future of the Thatcherite regime

At the time of writing, early in 2013, as food banks grew more numerous and busier, there were some signs of wider and more determined concern over excessive pay, artificial tax avoidance and the use of tax havens to protect and even advance financial privilege and inequality. Outside the UK a financial transaction tax is being planned and a cap on bonuses imposed but inside media and political discussion remains largely dominated by opponents to such measures. However, market insistence that inequality is not only good for the economy but vital for society is being more trenchantly challenged by those who argue that more equality is better (Lansley, 2012; Wilkinson and Pickett, 2010).

'We must all be careful that we do not unthinkingly adopt the cynically divisive and cruelly humiliating words offered to us by those who regard inequality not as a problem but as a solution' (Donnison, 2013). Vigorous challenges to the Thatcher discourse are now coming from what Cameron might call 'the big society'. We have already seen two well-argued and well-documented reports denouncing the demonization of those in poverty and on benefit, *The Blame Game must Stop* (McCarron and Purcell, 2013) and *The Lies we Tell Ourselves* (Baptist Union et al., 2013). The Poverty Alliance's 'Stick your Labels' campaign, launched three years ago after all leaders of the political parties in Scotland signed a declaration against stigmatizing those in poverty and on benefits, continues to thrive and collect examples of political manipulations (Mooney and Wright, 2011: see also Baumberg et al., 2012).

The challenge to inequality is now coming from unexpected quarters. In January 2013 Christine Lagarde told the World Economic Forum of the rich and powerful at Davos: 'Excessive inequality is corrosive to growth; it is corrosive to society . . . the economics profession and the policy community have downplayed inequality for too long. Now all of us – including the IMF – have a better understanding that a more equal distribution of income allows for more economic stability, more sustained economic growth, and healthier societies with stronger bonds of cohesion and trust. The research reaffirms this finding' (Lagarde quoted in Weldon, 2013).

310

The quotation is long, but when else has a Managing Director of the International Monetary Fund presented the case for 'a more equal distribution of income' so clearly and cogently? It also reminds us of the strength of the anti-egalitarian consensus outside this country, as well as inside, that Thatcherism helped to establish and the need to better understand the institutions that maintain it, nationally and internationally. There has, of course, been no shortage this time too of indignantly confident 'never agains' in the erratic and spasmodic struggle against inequality. Maybe today there is more 'intellectual momentum behind principles such as equality' than under Thatcher (Atkinson, 1983: 22–3), but how strong is the political will? Will this time be different?

References

Abel-Smith, B. and Townsend, P. (1965) *The Poor and the Poorest*. London: Bell.

Atkinson, A.B. (1983) 'The Commitment to Equality', in J. Griffiths (ed.) *Socialism in a Cold Climate*. London: Unwin, pp. 22–36.

Baptist Union of Great Britain, Methodist Church, Church of Scotland and United Reformed Church (2013) *The Lies we Tell Ourselves*. London.

Baumberg, B., Bell, K. and Gaffney, D. (2012) *Benefits Stigma in Britain*. London: Turn2us.

Cole, G.D.H. (1955) 'Socialism and the Welfare State', *New Statesman and Nation*, 23 July, pp. 88–9.

Donnison, D. (2013) 'Some Ideas for Reversing Britain's Gross Inequality', *Scottish Review*, 31 January. At: http://www.scottishreview.net/DavidDonnison54.shtml?utm_source=Sign-Up.to&utm_medium=email&utm_campaign=287073-Prison+a+home+from+home?+Let's+see+how+she+likes+it+

Duncan Smith, I. (2011) 'Welfare Reform: The Wider Context', Keith Joseph Memorial Lecture. London: Centre for Policy Studies.

Farnsworth, K. (2012) *Social versus Corporate Welfare: Competing Needs and Interests within the Welfare State*. London: Palgrave.

Ferge, Z. (1997) 'The Changed Welfare Paradigm: The Individualisation of the Social', *Social Policy and Administration*, 31(1): 20–44.

Goldthorpe, J.H. (2012) *Understanding – and Misunderstanding – Social Mobility in Britain: The Entry of the Economists, the Confusion of Politicians and the Limits of Educational Policy*, Barnett Papers in Social Research, 1.

Lansley, S. (2011) *The Cost of Inequality*. London: Gibson Square.

Levy, D. (1988) 'Moore's American Cure for Britain's "Dependency" Habit', *The Listener*, 18 February, pp. 4–5.

Macmillan, H. (1978 [1938]) *The Middle Way*. Wakefield: EP Publishing.

Masterman, C.F.G. (1960 [1909]) *The Condition of England*. London: Methuen.

McCarron, A. and Purcell, L. (2013) *The Blame Game must Stop*. London: Church Action against Poverty.

Mooney, G. and Wright, S. (2011) 'Presenting and Representing Poverty', in J.H. McKendrick et al., *Poverty in Scotland 2011*. London: CPAG, pp 133–45, and at: http://www.facebook.com/StickYourLabels

Moore, J. (1987) *The Future of the Welfare State*. London: Conservative Party Office.

Moore, J. (1989) *The End of the Line for Poverty*. London: Conservative Party Office.

Piven, F.F. and Cloward, R. (1972) *Regulating the Poor: The Functions of Public Welfare*. London: Tavistock.

Sampson, A. (2004) *Who Runs this Place? The Anatomy of Britain in the 21st Century*. London: John Murray.

Sinfield, A. (2011) 'Credit Crunch, Inequality and Social Policy', in K. Farnsworth and Z. Irving (eds) *Social Policy in Challenging Times: Economic Crisis and Welfare systems*. Bristol: The Policy Press, pp. 65–81.

Tawney, R.H. (1913) *Poverty as an Industrial Problem*, Memoranda on Problems of Poverty, no. 2. London: Ratan Tata Foundation, LSE.

Thatcher, M. (1995) *The Path to Power*. London: HarperCollins.

Titmuss, R.M. (1965) 'Poverty vs. Inequality: Diagnosis', *Nation*, February: 130–3.

Titmuss, R M. (2001) 'The Irresponsible Society' in P. Alcock et al. (eds), *Welfare and Wellbeing: Richard Titmuss's Contribution to Social Policy*. Bristol: The Policy Press.

Townsend, P. (1979) *Poverty in the UK*. Harmondsworth: Penguin.

Townsend, P. and Davidson, N. (1982) *Inequalities in Health: The Black Report*, Harmondsworth: Penguin (only released in typescript by UK Department of Health in 1981).

UK (1979) *White Paper on Public Expenditure 1979*. London: HMSO.

van Oorschot, W. (2008) *The Social Legitimacy of the European Welfare State*. Edinburgh: Social Policy Association Annual Conference, plenary paper.

Walker, C. (1993) *Managing Poverty: Limits of Social Assistance*. London: Routledge.

Weldon, D. (2013) *Miliband, Obama and Lagarde on Reforming Capitalism*, ToUChstone Economics, 19 February. At: http://touchstoneblog.org.uk/2013/02/miliband-obama-and-lagarde-on-reforming-capitalism/

Westergaard, J. (1995) *Who gets What? The Hardening of Class Inequality in the Late Twentieth Century*. Cambridge: Polity Press.

Wilkinson, R. and Pickett, K. (2009) *The Spirit Level: Why More Equal Societies Almost Always Do Better*. London: Allen Lane.

312

PART III
CONCLUDING OBSERVATIONS

10
Locating 'Thatcherism' in the 'here and now'

STEPHEN FARRALL and COLIN HAY

> The perception of the Thatcher era as a significant period of transition in British politics is increasing rather than diminishing.
>
> (Gamble, 1996: 19)

Three and a half decades after Margaret Thatcher entered Downing Street and nearly 25 years after she left office, what are we to make of the legacy of the '-ism' that bears her name? In this final chapter we return to two influential earlier assessments, written whilst Thatcherism was very much still a work in progress, to re-assess and re-evaluate the legacy of Thatcherism in the terms they provided but with the benefit of the hindsight they did not enjoy. For whilst the evaluation of Thatcherism that these authors presented is in need of very significant revision in the light of the passing of time, the framework for the analysis of the legacy of Thatcherism that they presented continues to be extremely valuable.

Our inquiries into the impact of Thatcherite social and economic policies have drawn much inspiration from the earlier work of Rhodes and Marsh – and in particular their edited collection on *Implementing Thatcherite Policies* (1992). They pose three questions at the outset of their book (1992: 4):

1 How much change occurred in the Thatcher era?
2 To what extent did this policy change result from a distinct policy agenda and legislative programme which was pursued by the Thatcher government(s)?
3 Why did more change occur in some policy areas than in others and, in particular, why was there less change than might have been expected?

These are the questions posed to the contributors to their volume, each charged with assessing the implementation of Thatcherite policies in a distinct realm of public policy. In their integrative final chapter they seek to draw together the findings of their co-authors, much as we seek to do here, in providing more general answers to these questions (1992: 170–87). They argue that whilst a lot of the legislative changes were very radical, and whilst a lot of policy areas were characterized by significant change rather than continuity, the actual outcomes changed far less than one might have expected from the seeming radicalism of the administration (1992: 170). They go on to note that much of the change which took place was at the institutional level – that is, at the level of those bodies and government departments which implement policies. So, for example, whilst there was a high degree of change in the areas of local government finances and the privatizing of once-nationalized industries, they conclude that the reforms to social security did not produce much substantive change at the level of policy outcomes. Overall, writing in the very early 1990s, they remained sceptical of the claims of others that the Thatcher governments had achieved very much by way of lasting change – and certainly less than Thatcher and her supported may have hoped for or for which they were typically given credit). This, they argue was in part due to unintended consequences of one policy domain working against policy aspirations in another. The oft-cited example of this is the pursuit of economic policies which increased unemployment, and so put the social security spend up at a time when the government was trying to reduce it. Similarly, the privatizing of council housing led to an inflationary boom, which undermined the broader economic strategy (Marsh and Rhodes, 1992: 176–7).

Rhodes and Marsh account for what might now be seen as the relative lack of immediate impact (that is, an enduring legacy already in place by the early 1990s) from the Thatcher governments in terms of the problems of implementation faced by all governments (1992: 181–6). They argue that the observed level of impact was rather less than the anticipated impact due to a range of factors: (i) the absence of clear and consistent objectives; (ii) insufficient and/or inconsistent information about the issues at hand; (iii) lack of the appropriate tools and resources to implement the desired changes; (iv) insufficient control over the officials charged with implementing the policies; (v) the obduracy and capacity to derail reform strategies of key stakeholders; and (vi) the unstable socio-economic conditions in which Thatcherism came to be implemented (which meant that consecutive Thatcher governments had to shift the focus of their efforts in order to maintain political support amongst their supporters and voters). They conclude that one of the reasons why much of the previous literature on the impact of Thatcherism had (falsely) anticipated, presumed and in some cases even described what was characterized as radical change was because it had focused on legislative changes, rather than on policy outcomes (1992: 186–7).

Though we, too, have focused on the policy outcomes of Thatcherism, our aim in this collection has been somewhat different to that of Marsh and Rhodes; we asked our contributors to consider the ways in which the policies they have reviewed have created unintended consequences not just in their own areas of research, but also for other areas, and the ways in which even the intended effects produced outcomes further downstream than Rhodes and Marsh were able to consider. Our aim, therefore, has been to focus on the long-term impacts of the policies pursued between 1979 and 1990 (and, by extension, to 1997) in a way that was simply not possible for Marsh and Rhodes. In this respect our aim has been both more ambitious and much harder than that undertaken in *Implementing Thatcherite Policies*. Some of the matters which we (the chapter authors as well as the editors) have had to grapple with have included the discourses developed during this era (which may well have outlasted the individual policies themselves; see Phillips, 1998) and the shifts in social attitudes, which may be evolving in numerous ways themselves, unrelated to government action. We have also sought to consider some of the silences of the Rhodes and Marsh volume – such as economic and social inequality and the uneven spatial dimensions of change during this period.

The second key text on Thatcherism, to which we return, is that by Jessop et al. (1988). Although we take issue with some of the specifics of their periodization of the -ism they identify and seek to characterize (see Hay and Farrall, 2011), we nevertheless draw on some of the aspects of what they suggest about how to assess both what Thatcherism was (and, indeed, might still be), and about how to determine the long-term impacts of Thatcherism. We start by summarizing their contribution.

As they note from the very outset, most theories of Thatcherism up to the late 1980s had focused on either the economic, or the political or the ideological aspects of Thatcherism (Jessop et al., 1988: 154). Clearly theories must attend to all of these aspects of Thatcherism (as well as attending to the social bases of Thatcherism). They argue that their approach is an attempt to develop a range of concepts which identify the institutional forms through which civil society, the state and the economy are inter-linked. The questions which Jessop et al. and which Rhodes and Marsh raise are useful ways of thinking about the enduring legacy – if there can indeed be said to be one – of Thatcherism. Jessop et al. identify the following concepts as key to their approach.

Social base

This refers to 'a set of social forces which support – within an accepted institutional framework and policy paradigm – the basic structure, mode of operation and objectives of the state system in its role as the official representative of civil society' (1988: 156). Such support involves not merely values, beliefs and feelings, but also incorporates those 'institutional modes of mass social and political integration' (1988: 156) as well as the accepted ways of managing conflicting material demands. The situation is further complicated by their observation that 'lived experiences must be interpreted and organised through some ideological framework; and political forces in turn seek to rework such popular sentiments into their own distinctive ideologies' (1988: 157), or, in other words, politicians are able to assist social actors to understand their experiences and predica-ments via the deployment of their own analysis of popular sentiments. However, the structure of political systems and the state itself moulds the very social forces to which Jessop et al. refer. So whilst social structures play a major role in shaping political processes and outcomes, these very outcomes can, in turn, also shape the nature and character of the social bases too. Accordingly, whilst widespread experiences in the social realm (e.g. a growing dislike of state regulation of, for example housing) can be responded to and interpreted by politicians seeking to deregulate social housing (as the first Thatcher administration did), the resulting deregula-tion of access to social housing will have impacts on both material and belief structures (i.e., people will have changed access to housing as a resource and will also undergo a change in their beliefs about housing as a social and personal resource).

However, not all social groups have equal access to processes of political influence, nor are all groups equal in terms of their ability to mobilize support for the understanding (and 'naming') of their experiences. As Jessop et al. write (1988: 157), in this way 'a form of structural power is inscribed into institutional structures themselves through their differential impact on access to centres of power and their implications for different strategies'. In this respect, Jessop et al. argue, the creation and mobilization of power blocs should become a key aspect of our approach to phenomena like Thatcherism.

Accumulation strategy

This concept refers to 'a specific pattern, or model, of economic growth together with both its associated social framework of institutions (or "mode of regulation") and the range of government policies conducive to its stable reproduction' (1988: 158). Any accumulation strategy is, almost by definition, therefore a result of the extent and manner to which the state is prepared to intervene in the economy and the nature and balance of those forces operating in the economy and the organization of the economy itself. The state may, for example, try to promote the fortunes of specific sectors of the economy and withdraw or limit support for other sectors which it sees as moribund or associated with interests that it does not seek to advance. However, and drawing on the insights made above about the social bases of support, the state will need to attend to the interests of key power blocs and the extent to which it is able to carry with it the beliefs and values of key sections of civil society. Of course, some sections of civil society and some power blocs may, at times, attempt to secure or initiate radical change or be deliberately excluded from any consideration on the part of the state (an example being the desire during the early 1980s not to support the mining sector of the economy or to acknowledge the plight of those people who depended on mining for their livelihoods).

State strategy

The concept of state strategy refers to the nature and pattern of intervention by the state in the economic realm (1988: 159). A state strategy, one can expect, will follow what, from the perspective of the actors involved in its production and implementation, appear to be the most effective means of pursuing the state's accumulation strategy. (Of course, in some instances the chosen course of action may not be the most effective way of achieving the accumulation strategy, or may even produce outcomes which impede the accumulation strategy.) In this respect, one might expect that state strategies would favour the flow of material gains to specific social bases and power blocs and, furthermore, give preferential access to spaces of political and economic power to such actors. But, as Jessop et al. also argue, the state can be seen to have relative autonomy from social forces in that state actors are able to act independently of them (1988: 161). Although Jessop et al. do not cite examples of how state actors found their autonomy limited, examples from within the period they seek to theorize are not hard to identify. For example, despite their wish to curtail the extent of the NHS, ministers were deterred from challenging its legitimacy because of their awareness of the widespread affection and support for the NHS (as consistently demonstrated in the British Social Attitudes Survey). In this respect state actors are never free to act in accordance with their ideological dispositions in the absence of a consideration of the depth of popular support for specific policies. Arguing for a position between those who argue for strong state-centred approaches and those who claim that political outcomes are predetermined by the structures of the economy and civil society, Jessop et al. write that, 'we must pay attention not only to the social forces acting in and through the state but also to the ways in which the rules and resources of political action are altered by changes in the state system itself' (1988: 161).

Hegemonic project

A hegemonic project is, in Jessop et al.'s approach, 'a national–popular programme of political, intellectual and moral leadership which advances the long-term interests of the leading sectors in the accumulation strategy while granting economic concessions to the masses of the social base' (1988: 162). This clearly speaks to the extent to which political actors are able to mobilize and bring together their social base, accumulation strategy and state strategy into a coherent project that is widely accepted (or in the case of the UK electoral system, accepted widely enough to achieve a stable mandate in a first-past-the-post electoral system). This, they suggest, requires the creation of both historic and power blocs (united around a common political and economic programme) of key social forces in society along with the institutions of civil society, the polity and the economy. Historic blocs are made up of historically constituted and socially reproduced structures which unite the economic base with the institutions of political and ideological governance. Power blocs on the other hand are a stable, structurally determined and organized grouping of dominant social classes and social, economic and political actors. The historic bloc, as such, refers to the accepted ways and means of accomplishing things, handed down from generation to generation to varying degrees of stability but remaining largely unchanged (or experiencing only incremental changes) over time. Power blocs refer to key actors, groups, organizations and parts of the state itself which are broadly aligned behind a specific accumulation strategy, state strategy and hegemonic project (which itself may be defined to varying degrees of completeness or rigidity and which may, of course, change over time or unfold as it encounters new phenomena). Power blocs, however, as Jessop et al. note, are different from short-term and goal-specific alliances which come together for the accomplishment of a key task and then disband. The characteristic which binds together a power bloc is, in many respects, less instrumental and more organic than this, being the sharing of an ideological outlook (or at least, an ideologically inspired critique of an existing set of policies and procedures).

Assessing the legacy of Thatcherism

Applying this to the details surrounding the emergence of Thatcherism, Jessop et al. note that Thatcherism grew out of the continued decline of the British economy and the repercussions which this produced for British society, and in particular the support for the welfare state (1988: 163). They argue that the post-war commitment to the welfare state, international liberalization and Atlanticism ruled out any possibility of the British government being able to develop a strategy for wholesale industrial regeneration (1988: 164), since such a strategy would have required that interest rate policy be subordinated to the requirements of domestic investment and, in any case, the state had limited capacities to intervene in anything other than on an ad hoc basis (1988: 164–5). Coupled with poor balance of payments figures (exacerbated by the openness of the British economy) and the legacy of policing the world as an ex-colonial power (which merely added further costs on an already over-burdened state), this created continuing problems for the management and steering of the British economy. As the economic crisis progressed in the late 1960s the commitment to full employment, the welfare state and the willingness to work productively with trade unions all started to be called into question (1988: 165). As the global recession of 1974–75 started to emerge, so British trade unions started to flex their muscles, leading to a bout of prolonged and crippling strikes between 1972 and 1975, leading ultimately to the Winter of Discontent in late 1978 and early 1979. At this stage too, having lost power in 1974 and then failing to regain it later the same year, the Conservative party was facing its own crisis, revolving around the extent to which it commanded a sufficiently large social base to ensure re-election. These forces worked to encourage the production of an emerging power bloc who aligned themselves around a project of eroding the economic and

321

social gains of the working class. Thatcher eventually became the figure-head for an increasingly large section of the middle and skilled working classes.

For Jessop et al., Thatcherism was an attempt to halt the electoral decline of the Tory party through the mobilization of a new social base around popular capitalism (as opposed to the welfare state). The mobilizing of some sections of the working class (part of the new social base, along with the lower middle class) meant that what had previously been publicly owned needed to become available for private ownership (via sales of state-owned assets and the 'marketization' of services once provided by the state). At the same time, strongholds of Labour Party support (such as amongst trade unions and local governments) needed to be weakened or undermined. Whilst the old sectors of the economy which provided the backbone of the labour and union movement were closed or privatized (mining, shipbuilding and the steel production industries) new sectors of the economy were encouraged (financial and service sector economies), typically concentrated in the south and east of England. Such sectors were encouraged to develop an international outlook and their success served to consolidate a significant part of the social base of Conservative support in this period.

Jessop et al. (1988: 167–8) pose a series of questions designed to assess the extent to which Thatcherism had, by the late 1980s, created a new social base, encouraged a new model of economic growth, restructured the state system so as to solve the crisis of the state and, finally, created a new power and historic bloc which supports the Thatcherite project and secures its future. Here we summarize the results of their inquiry, updating it in the light of the evidence presented in the preceding chapters of this volume.

Is there a new social base for Thatcherism?

This question has four sub-questions to it (1988: 167–8):

1   Has the electoral decline of the Tory party been arrested and reversed? Jessop et al. claim that Thatcherism has arrested, but not reversed the long-term decline of Conservative electoral support. Had their research been conducted and their book published after the events of 'Black Wednesday' in September 1992 their answer may have been slightly different. The 1997 general election saw a haemorrhaging of support for the Tory Party, so much so that even at the 2001 general election

they were still unable to mount a serious challenge to the Labour Party. Even the 2010 general election saw the Tory Party struggling (and ultimately failing) to win a parliamentary majority. It is far from clear, therefore, that Thatcherism has helped to arrest or reverse the long-term decline in electoral support for the Tory Party. (Indeed, given that Thatcher herself was ditched as she became an electoral liability, it is far from clear that Thatcherism has assisted the Tory Party terribly much after the 1980s). Given also that she won a smaller share of the vote than any Tory government since 1922 and fewer actual votes than John Major (Jackson and Saunders, 2012: 1) her influence on the fortunes of her party may not have been as positive as appeared at the time. Some of the efforts to attract once-taken-for-granted Labour voters (such as those in council housing) do not appear to have lasted either; although much of the housing stock was sold (see Murie, Chapter 5 in this collection) this did not appear to have produced a new electoral base for the Conservatives.

2   Have other powerful institutions and/or social forces in civil society been won over to the Thatcherite agenda? The answer to this question is predicated on which institutions and social forces one wishes to consider. In many respects the generally lower levels of direct taxation would suggest that this element of the Thatcherite agenda has gained wider support. More widely, neo-liberal and neo-conservative thinking on specific topics (such as the creation of internal markets within public sector bodies) would appear to have also gained support. Similarly, some have suggested that the creation of New Labour in the mid-1990s was the result of the seeming success of Thatcherism (see Kavanagh, 1987). Richard Heffernan (2009: 9) notes that whilst the ideas promoted by Thatcher were initially seen as 'dangerous' and 'radical' these now 'reflect a dominant set of ideas which . . . still provide policy-makers with a compass, not a road map', and have, by and large, been accepted by the Labour Party (Jackson and Saunders, 2012: 16). He goes on to note that whilst Labour tried to tackle poverty whilst in office, they did little to tackle wider notions of social inequality. Gamble (1996: 34–5) also noted how Thatcherism altered the culture of the Labour Party – forcing it to embrace ideas around choice, individualism and anti-statism. Other powerful elements which support the Thatcherite agenda include employers' bodies. There is also the observation that more people now accept that they must be more self-reliant.

0

3   How far have the old social bases of social democracy been fatally weakened and/or displaced? As Jessop et al. argue (1988: 169) much of the work undertaken by the Thatcher administrations up to the late 1980s had taken the form of a 'ground clearing' operation, paving the way for a more ambitious Thatcherite project. In the period since, we have seen the erosion of power amongst trade unions (whose membership has declined from 13 million in 1979 (its peak) to 6.4 million in 2011), and which has resulted in a lower paid and more insecure workforce. Along with this one has seen the 'death' of the working class as a power bloc to which both Labour politicians and trade unions would appeal and/or defend the interests of. Similarly, the power of local governments has been eroded (they now own far less of the housing stock than they did in 1979), and their control and regulation of local schools has also been curtailed and challenged by the promotion of grant-maintained schools (by the like, foundation and community schools, after 1998). Indeed, Wilding suggests that there have been around 50 Acts which have, in various ways sought to reduce the power of local governments (1992: 206). The national state has also seen a whittling back of influence in a number of realms. These include, for example, transport (where private train companies now operate in place of the national operator).

4   As a consequence of the above, how far has the party system been recomposed around a Thatcherite agenda? Other than the Labour Party shifting rightwards towards a new political middle ground (and for some elections during the New Labour period, being considered to be to the right of the Liberal Democrats), there is little evidence that the party system has been recomposed around a Thatcherite agenda. Indeed, Jessop et al.'s concern with this issue at the time may well have been spurred by the growth of the Social Democratic Party (which merged with the Liberal Party in 1988). Thus, whilst noting that Blair accepted much of the immediate legacy of Thatcherism (1996: 19), Gamble goes on to note that Thatcher did little to alter the constitution – despite that fact that some of these changes (such as the creation of parliaments for Wales and Scotland) would have made it very hard for a Labour government to be elected (1996: 22). Devolution and the creation of elected assemblies in Cardiff and Edinburgh only came after Labour had been elected.

In the light of these questions, it appears that the social bases have changed dramatically (council housing, local governments and trade unions being the obvious policies responsible for this shift). However, it is far from clear that this represents the emergence of a new social base on which Thatcherism can be built. The terms 'Thatcherite' and 'Thatcherism' have more often than not taken on a pejorative sense over time (to the extent that Ken Clarke described his policies as 'Thatcherism with a human face'). As such, whilst Thatcher lost the support for the ideas she promoted whilst they were branded as 'Thatcherite', we have seen a shifting social base, which, by and large enables the sorts of policies she may have pursued to be articulated and remain largely unopposed.

The new model of economic growth

Writing in 1988 Jessop et al. suggest that the extent to which Thatcherism might be seen to have succeeded in establishing a new economic settlement rests on it having identified and successfully made the transition to a new model of economic growth or accumulation strategy. This was a crucial question in 1988 and no less important a question today at a time when the long period of steady if unremarkable economic growth ('the Great Moderation') has come to an end. The stability of an accumulation strategy, Jessop et al. contend, depends on the capacity to ensure an advance for the long-term (perceived) interest of capital (not necessarily British capital, but capital invested in Britain) and, at the same time, to consolidate a social base around the distribution of the proceeds of such growth. In exploring this at the time Jessop et al. focused on four subsidiary elements: (i) the overall pattern of growth within the economy; (ii) the sectors within it most likely to prosper; (iii) the geographical location of such leading sectors; and (iv) the kind of work provided by such sectors.

Their analysis of emergent neo-liberal accumulation strategy in such terms was innovative and important then – and it is remarkable how much of it continues to resonate today. The model of growth they identified contained four core elements: (i) privatization, deregulation and the introduction of market discipline into a residual public sector; (ii) the deregulation of financial markets and the attempt to establish the City as a global centre for finance capital; (iii) a weakly sponsored industrial renaissance around the small business sector, labour market flexibilization, the utilization of new technologies and the attraction of high levels of foreign direct investment; and (iv) a broader aim to transform the 'UK economy into a dynamic multinational space' by exploiting 'the synergic effects of a tri-continental multinational presence' (1988: 171). What is remarkable re-reading their analysis today, a quarter of a century on, is just how much of it continues to resonate. That is testament both to the prescience and insight of the account they offered at the time and to the legacy of Thatcherism. Thus understanding Thatcherism's economic legacy is very considerable indeed. It established the now long-standing neo-liberal disposition of consequent British governments (Conservative, Labour and Coalition alike) to privatization, deregulation and the intro-duction of market mechanisms and incentives in the provision of public goods. Similarly, its deregulation of financial markets has been crucial in establishing the UK's leading position in the international provision of financial services and, crucially, in generating a considerable exposure to the risks of financial interdependence. And whilst the mantra and consistent practice of labour-market deregulation and flexibilization has persistently failed to generate an export-oriented manufacturing renais-sance, it too has now been firmly established as an Anglo-liberal disposition – long post-dating the Thatcher administrations which first instituted it.

But, arguably, Jessop et al.'s analysis captures only one half of the legacy of Thatcherism – for, today, we must look at the economic legacy of Thatcherism just as much in terms of its unanticipated (and, in 1988, unanticipatable) consequences as in terms of those intended. Thus, whilst Jessop et al. are almost certainly right to detect in Thatcherism a nascent accumulation strategy and even a distinct model of growth for the British economy, Thatcherism was not responsible for the model of growth that would emerge in the years after Black Wednesday to deliver 15 years of consecutive growth before the credit crunch and the global financial crisis since 2008.

This growth model has been termed the Anglo-liberal growth model and, as shown elsewhere, it would not have been possible without Thatcherism (Hay, 2013). But its development was not in itself a direct product of Thatcherism. It was in fact stumbled across serendipitously. It was an unanticipated effect of a series of significant decisions – all of which were market-conforming or liberal in character. Thus, the key policy choices which led to a growth dynamic sustained by escalating consumer credit were consistently liberal or market-conforming. It is for precisely this reason that it is useful to label this an Anglo-liberal growth model. The key decisions were those relating to the austere and fiscally conservative spending plans of the incoming Labour administration in 1997, its orthodox neo-monetarist decision to cede operational independence to the Bank of

England to set interest rates (and the specific remit it gave to the Bank's Monetary Policy Committee) also in 1997 and, prior even to that, the decision to liberalize UK financial markets in the 1980s. What all of these decisions shared was a profound confidence in the superiority, all things being equal, of private, market or quasi-market mechanisms over collective, public or state action or intervention – they were all, in other words, profoundly market- or neo-liberal. They were, in other words, a product of the ideational legacy of Thatcherism, though other than the liberalization of financial markets, they were not themselves Thatcherite.

Resolving the crisis of the state

A further means of gauging the significance and character of Thatcherism, both at the time and now, more retrospectively, Jessop et al. suggest, is to consider whether the Thatcher governments resolved the state crisis which brought them to power (1988: 168). In posing this they ask themselves whether a clear Thatcherite state strategy can be identified. And here, again, there are a series of subsidiary questions: (i) what are the dominant forms of state intervention?; (ii) how have channels of political representation been restructured?; (iii) how has the internal structure of the state changed/; and (iv) what are the implications for the institutional biases (or, in Jessop et al.'s terms 'strategic selectivity') of the state?

These are interesting and important considerations and it is again helpful to assess how one might revise, update and extend the characterization of Thatcherism to which they led Jessop et al. in 1988 (174–7). At the time they identified a number of trends which, together, served to circumvent, outflank or even abolish any remaining 'social democratic apparatuses of intervention and representation' (1988: 175). These included: (i) the reorientation of both the management of public finances and macroeconomic policy so as to 'cut and restructure the state budget away from traditional social democratic and employment concerns' (1988: 175); (ii) the abolition of corporatist structures of interest intermediation and the emasculation of local democracy; and (iii) a turn to more authoritarian modes of policing and the rise in the use of societal surveillance combined with a greater resort to the populist politics of demonization of oppositional groups (like the miners, teachers and left-wing metropolitan local authorities). The result, they suggest, has been the development of an increasingly authoritarian-liberal state – a state whose economic policy disposition is resoundingly liberal and yet one also characterized by the strengthening of its capacity to deal in an authoritarian way with the opposition of those who have suffered from the distributional asymmetries such policies have exacerbated.

Again it is difficult not to be struck by how much of Jessop et al.'s analysis in 1988 resonates a quarter of a century later. Whether or not Thatcherism resolved the crisis of the state that brought it to power (as distinct from redefining the terms in and through which it came to be seen), it is difficult not to see it as having set the state on a rather different course. That course has, of course, been reaffirmed and consolidated by subsequent administrations and arguably, in the austerity agenda of the Cameron-Clegg Coalition, it has been radicalized anew. Jessop et al. perhaps make too much of state retrenchment and not enough of state restructuring – in particular the near wholesale attempt to treat the public sector as a laboratory for the development of new public management practice (see, especially, Le Gales and Scott, 2008). But they capture extremely well the tension between liberalism and authoritarianism which continues to characterize British politics and which is arguably one of the most potent and yet least acknowledged legacies of Thatcherism.

Towards a new historic bloc

This brings us to an overall assessment of the Thatcher years. Here, again, Jessop et al's approach – and the substantive analysis they offer within it – is instructive, even if the language within which it is couched might now appear a little arcane. Here Bob Jessop and his colleagues ask whether a new historic bloc can be said to have emerged capable of ensuring the reproduction of a Thatcherite agenda into the future. The three subsidiary questions they pose here are extremely valuable and there is much to be gained by reflecting on how they might be answered today, in the light of the preceding chapters. They are: (i) do the leading sectors in the economy support the Thatcherite accumulation strategy; (ii) were the state and intellectual elites won over to the Thatcherite state strategy; and (iii) have the key institutions of civil society been restructured to such an extent that they have come to promote the Thatcherite agenda (168-9)?

It is worth considering each in turn.

Do the leading sectors in the economy support the Thatcherite accumulation strategy?
Though an understandable way of framing the issue at the time, with the benefit of hindsight, this seems like a somewhat strange way of posing the question. For what is perhaps clear now is that Thatcherism was rather less an accumulation strategy or model of growth per se than it was a set of liberal/neo-liberal economic dispositions. These would, in turn, come to inform policy choices in an increasingly consistent way, sowing the seeds rather inadvertently for the Anglo-liberal growth model which started to implode so spectacularly in 2008. But, as this suggests, the issue was never so much the generation of active support for a clearly articulated growth model as it was the gradual and iterative erosion of the possibility of imaging an alternative to the liberalizing disposition. Thatcherism's economic legacy is, above all else, that disposition – a disposition that, it seems, is set to outlive the crisis – and the crisis itself.

Were the state and intellectual elites won over to the Thatcherite state strategy?
This question can be answered today in much the same way as the first. Thatcherism's success as a strategy for the transformation of the state, like its success in the economic realm, was that it did not demand the kind of active support that the question presumes. It was sufficient, for the reproduction and iterative institutional embedding of its state project, merely that no alternative was actively countenanced. That was true in 1988 and arguably it remains true today. Indeed the experiment in new public management that Thatcherism's state project represents is, today, a much more profound, wholesale and radical one than it was in 1988. Interestingly, however, it is an experiment which has not served to reduce the size of the state as a share of GDP; but it has nonetheless transformed the internal operation of each and every institution within the public sector in ways unimaginable in 1979. Needless to say it is a very significant legacy indeed.

Have the key institutions of civil society been restructured to such an extent that they have come to promote the Thatcherite agenda?
Jessop et al.'s third and final question, like the other two, reveals what might now be seen as something of a consistent false premise – that Thatcherism, in order for it to succeed and survive and in order for it to generate a legacy, needed to be actively accepted, embraced and promoted by the key institutions of civil society. In fact, the story of Thatcherism, one

actually described in an extraordinarily prescient way by both Jessop et al. and, before even them, Stuart Hall (1979), is less one of the mobilization of active support than it is one of the *silencing* of active resistance. Whether it be the trade unions or left-wing metropolitan local authorities, those who suffered the malign redistributive effects so graphically described by Danny Dorling in this volume, found the institutional resources on which they had relied to mobilize politically removed. It was this, far more than the mobilization of active support that led to the consolidation of the Thatcherite agenda and, in the process, its effective depoliticization – as its market liberal disposition became normalized and institutionalized.

Answering Rhodes and Marsh's questions

At the start of this chapter, we revisited the three questions which Rhodes and Marsh posed at the outset of their earlier book (1992). Here, by way of a preliminary conclusion, we reflect on these questions in the light of the passage of time since they were first posed. To what extent, then, can one discern a 'Thatcherite project' and a legacy arising from that project in and from the policy domains considered in the chapters of this collection? What is not difficult to identify is the existence of a certain Thatcherite instinct or disposition, albeit one unevenly implemented. Early efforts were undoubtedly aimed at 'unshackling' citizens from the influence of the state (with wage restraints removed, public housing made available for purchase, and expressions of greater choice for parents in terms of schooling, even if there was little direct action on this). In addition, there was also an attempt to reduce public spending (as evidenced in the open disavowal of industrial policy to 'prop up' manufacturing, efforts to cut, freeze the value, or limit the availability of social security, and the ending of support for new public housing). These policies were closely aligned to new right thinking (particularly neo-liberal elements within it) and also arose fairly directly out of the construction of the crisis of the late 1970s on which Thatcher's initial electoral appeal was predicated (Hay, 1996). Other early instinctual reflexes informing policy included the attempt to promote entrepreneurialism and innovation through a succession of tax cuts to high earners and incentives for both share and property ownership. Such policies created the processes associated with social and economic polarization and the 'residualization' of some forms of welfare provision. From the late 1980s, we see the rise of the extension of the choice agenda (especially as it applied to education); this was further radicalized in the early 1990s. Unlike the economy, housing, social security or education, however, criminal justice policies remained untouched by the radicalism which characterized this period. Indeed, it is not until the early to mid-1990s that we begin to see the development of a more obviously 'Thatcherite' angle on criminal justice, with an emphasis on 'just deserts', the removal of sentencing guidelines in 1991 and a politically stated desire for 'tougher' sentences on the basis that 'prison works' (under Howard).

The threads, then, which unite and characterize for us the 'Thatcherite project' are to be found in: 'rolling back' the state; 'liberating' citizens from the control of the state; the creation of a social order modelled on 'free market' thinking whereby social and economic inequalities were encouraged (and legitimated in terms of the entrepreneurialism they were seen to promote), and the chastisement of those unable to compete under such conditions. In terms of the *content* of Thatcherism, then, there is little here that challenges the established view of the Thatcher governments. It is when we move from content to implementation, however, that our analysis becomes more distinctive in the context of the existing literature.

In this it is important to distinguish between two levels of periodization – one at the level of the project as a whole; another at the level of each specific policy domain. Most periodizations tend to operate at the level of the first, but we need an account which can operate at both levels. At the macro-level there is often a notion of a sequencing which runs as follows: accumulation of contradictions; crisis; paradigm shift; consolidation and addressing unintended consequences. Yet the implication of the preceding analysis and the substantive analysis of key policy sectors presented in previous chapters is that such a periodization gets key elements of Thatcherism wrong – and, in the end, is too simplistic. It is far more credible, we suggest, to see this kind of sequentially unfolding process linked to crisis at work at the level of certain individual policy domains than it is at the level of the project as a whole.

This is the case, we would contend, in economic policy, industrial relations and education (and in some other areas of public sector reform). And in housing policy a very similar sequence is observed, though with one subtle difference. Here policy change does not arise in direct response to a crisis per se – with policy being driven, it seems, more by a sense of electoral expediency and/or ideological conviction than by the sense of a crisis in prior policy. But other policy domains exhibit a rather different sequencing and temporality.

The question is why this is so and what it says about the extent to which we can identify a (single) Thatcherite project unfolding across a series of policy fields. Economic policy was, of course, key to the very identity of the first Thatcher administration. For it was the basis of the critique of a nation in crisis. Similarly, as Alan Murie shows, housing policy was profoundly implicated in the Thatcherite claim to distinctiveness in 1979 – since it was crucial to the strategy for the mobilization of a cross-class electoral base. As such, it had key symbolic significance. The Thatcherite vision of a 'property (and in due course, share-owning) democracy' undoubtedly resonated with members of the upper working class who had come to share in middle-class aspirations (which the Tories' electoral strategy merely sought to accentuate and reinforce). These, then, were crucial domains to target for an incoming administration, since they were central to the claim that the Thatcherites offered a solution to the crisis that brought them to power, and crucial to the mobilization of an electoral base. As such, they were always most likely to be the focus of initial policy radicalism – for, in effect, they were a core part of the contract made with the electorate in 1979.

Social security and education were more complex beasts, and it took the Tories some time to work out what they wanted to achieve – and, longer still, *how* they wanted to achieve it (see Hill and Walker, Chapter 3; and Dorey, Chapter 4, both this collection). In this respect they were, we suggest, representative more generally of public sector reform. Both were left largely untouched until the mid-1980s as the Tories started to gear up for a 'radical' third term. Thus, it was not until 1986 that right-wing think tanks started to turn their attention in a concerted and coordinated way to education, culminating in the Education Act 1988. But in this respect, the reform of education exhibits a very similar temporality and sequencing to that of other core public services – notably the NHS and the system of local government finance. The Thatcher governments, it seems, responded first and quite radically in those policy fields most implicated in the crisis whose narration had brought them to power. It was only later that their attentions would turn to a working through, and then eventually a translation into policy, of the implications of the Thatcherite instinct for public sector reform.

Crime, as Farrall and Jennings (Chapter 7 in this collection) make clear, was left alone for even longer. Partly this was due to the home secretaries being of a distinctly 'one nation' approach, but partly this was also due to 'the party of law and order' feeling that their own and the police's value were sufficiently in line for the police to be left alone to get on with the job, by and large unhindered. However, this started to change in the very late 1980s when the Tories became increasingly aware of what they perceived as the failings of the criminal justice system and when a succession of more 'tough-minded' politicians took control at the Home Office and started to voice their concerns about earlier legislation. However, this is only part of the story; crime is the result of numerous processes (individual motivation, structural disadvantage and opportunity, not least of all), and some of these processes were precisely those processes which had been altered by changes in legislation in other policy fields. In effect, legislation on criminal justice was necessitated by the cumulative consequences of Thatcherite radicalism in other issue domains. For example, there is a strong relationship between unemployment and crime (Wells, 1993). Similarly, the 1980s housing policies have been associated with increases in some forms of crime (Murie, 1997 and Chapter 5 in this collection), School league tables introduced in 1992 had the unfortunate side effect of encouraging schools to exclude unruly children (school exclusions rose throughout the 1990s, reaching a peak of 12,668 in 1996–97, DfES, 2001), who, dumped on the streets, only served to cause further problems for local residents and the police (Timmins, 2001: 566). One of the additional reasons why crime came so late as a concern for the Tories was that the need for reform was itself the consequence of the 'spill over' from policy radicalism elsewhere (see Farrall and Jennings, Chapter 7 in this collection).

What emerges, then, is a complex and uneven picture of public policy radicalism. The Thatcher administrations were radical from their first election, but they were cautiously radical – confining their initial radicalism to policy domains integral to resolution of the state crisis whose narration brought them to power and/or to the consolidation of a social base (housing is the clearest example). This initial burst of radicalism subsided and it was only really in the latter half of the second term and into the third that radicalism returned again – this time as the Thatcher administrations started to take on core elements of the public sector. Finally we see late, but again targeted, radicalism in issue domains (such as criminal justice) that had remained largely untouched by Thatcherism, despite (or perhaps even because of) rhetoric to the contrary. Such late radicalism, we contend, is better seen as a consequence of the need to respond to the unintended spill-over effects of earlier radicalism in other policy areas rather than the product of a more consistently strategic project unfolding over time in distinct waves.

Beyond Rhodes and Marsh and Jessop et al.: missing considerations

Whilst the questions posed by Jessop et al. and Rhodes and Marsh are very wide ranging, they do not – for no fault of their own – touch on some issues which we feel are crucial to any long-term assessment of Thatcherism and the policies pursued under this banner. These include:

- *Rises in economic and social inequality*: The rise in economic inequality was only starting to be detected at the time when these authors were writing (in the mid- to late 1980s and early 1990s). Clearly, and as we summarize below, this trend continued throughout much of the period since (with Brown's administration trying to make some efforts to reverse it) and were to have very great implications for the lives of many of those living in the UK. Yet inequalities do not feature in the assessments made by Rhodes and Marsh or Jessop et al. This now seems like a strange omission, given that levels of economic inequality have grown hugely during this period, and become entrenched along geographical lines also.
- *The outcomes for policy areas which were not focused on*: No collection can consider all topics (we, for example, have not focused on foreign policy or relations with the EEC, EC and then EU). Similarly, there were key areas of social policy which Jessop et al. and Rhodes and Marsh neglected. Foremost amongst these are the issues of crime (which grew dramatically throughout the 1980s and 1990s and which became a source of much public concern and the geographical implications of the shift in inequalities; see respectively Farrall and Jennings, Chapter 7; and Dorling, Chapter 8, above). Similarly, each study gives little attention to families, the position of females in society and the economy, or education, despite the evidence that all of these were undergoing dramatic shifts or being targeted for policy intervention at the time.
- *Direct and systemic models of causation*: One issue which is also neglected is that of *how* causal processes unfolded. The obvious ways in which policy changes led to changes in experiences was via changes within that policy arena. For example, there can be little doubting that the changes in housing policy initiated from 1980s onwards dramatically changed many people's experiences of housing. This direct causation we contrast with streams of indirect causation, such as Farrall and

Jennings describe in Chapter 7. There were few changes in crime policies that were either designed to, or which led directly to, changes in crime levels in the UK during this period. Yet crime went up quite dramatically. The indirect causal chain worked through changes in the economy and shifts in housing, education and social welfare policies which preceded the dramatic rise of crime. Crime, and other indicators associated with it, such as the fear of crime (on this see Farrall, Jackson and Gray, 2009) might therefore be considered as a social barometer of the state of a society as it experiences and adjusts to rapid and far-reaching social and economic change. But beyond this, there is also the issue not just of causation but also of failures to effect change (attitudes towards the NHS remained solid) or to prevent change (female engagement in the labour force continued regardless of any of the social policies pursued). As such, thinking through the causal path-ways and influences of the changes initiated (and of a whole lot of other changes which were in train before 1979) is not a straightforward matter (but then, we did not embark on this project because we thought it would be an easy one!). Yet clearly there is a lot to be gained from attempting to synthesize what took place between 1979 and 1997 (and since). It is to a consideration of this matter which we now turn.

Conclusion: summarizing the long-term impacts of Thatcherite social and economic policies

In this closing section we wish to reflect on what we have learnt about the long-term impacts of Thatcherite social and economic policies, both as a result of editing this book, but also as a result of a wider engagement with these matters. We structure this section along two lines of thought; first there are those things which need or ought to be said about this period of history; second, there are those things which we would say, to varying degrees, have been the outcomes of the policies enacted and enabled by the Thatcher governments and the consequences of these.

First, it is important to remember that some areas of policy were 'touchstones' for the radical right, and hence when both neo-liberal and neo-conservative instincts coalesced around these issues and policy implications, one could expect to see more change. Similarly, some areas did not rank highly amongst the things the Thatcher governments felt needed tackling, or for which no immediate policy could be decided upon. In some cases it proved hard for policies to be implemented. In other cases, as our contributors have documented, some policy areas were clearly out of the immediate control of the government (such as the shifting position of females in the labour market). In other instances the outcomes took several years to start to come to fruition and were the results of changes in other policy domains (crime and the geographical shifts in inequalities for example). Other policy concerns only emerged after Thatcher had left office and were essentially part of a binge of privatizing various sections of the state which had thus far escaped privatization (such as the railways).

Second, it is important to note that the Thatcher governments pushed radical changes faster and further than anywhere else (a point made most forcefully by Thompson, Chapter 2; and by Hill and Walker, Chapter 3). Change was at the heart of what these governments were about. There was, of course, no one-to-one correspondence between the aims of the Thatcher government and the outcomes of the policies they pursued; but this should not lead us to overlook or mischaracterize the radicalism in thinking that Thatcherism represented. Implementation gaps were always likely to be considerable – arguably all the more so because of the radicalism of core parts of the ideology informing the policy disposition. Nevertheless, as Heffernan notes, most of the Thatcherite economic prescriptions reflect a dominant set of ideas which help to structure policy in a variety of ways (2009: 9). Third, and as we have noted above, any legacy will have been shaped by factors beyond the immediate (or even wider control) of government. As Murie shows with regards to housing, the impact of housing policies was affected by changes that had been working their way through the housing system, coupled with rises in income inequality, increases in unemployment and immigration and the demand for housing from a growing student population. Fourth, and as Taylor-Goobey notes, there was a strong moralistic tone to much of what the Thatcher governments tried to do, and this extended to cover both people (the 'poor', the 'work-shy', 'the unemployed' and so on) and organizations and institutions (nationalization and the industries associated with it become seen as 'unproductive'). Hence the nation-state became something from which individuals needed to be de-coupled. This extended to, and found popular expression in, television programmes such as 'That's Life!' which regularly lampooned companies and authorities for their employment of obscure procedures and poor administrative systems. Such sentiments helped to create a reservoir of attitudes against the state and bureaucratic organizations, and which helped to legitimize attitudes which were dismissive of corporate endeavours – core parts of the Thatcherite disposition became normalized in this way. Finally, there is the observation which needs to be made that so deep-seated were these changes felt to be that the Labour Party was forced to shift to the right in order to embrace key aspects of the supporting rhetoric of Thatcherism (such as the central importance of choice and quasi-market mechanisms in the provision of collective public goods such as welfare). In so doing, it helped further to consolidate key aspects of the new right agenda and the thinking that underpinned it – as New Labour came in effect to embrace more enthusiastically than its Conservative predecessors the new public management revolution in the provision of public services.

Let us turn now to consider the long-term consequences of Thatcherism. Our review is necessarily brief. As several of our contributors have highlighted, high levels of unemployment became socially and electorally acceptable. In 1979 the unemployment rate was just over 4 per cent, and never fell below that level in the period to 2010 (see Thompson, Chapter 2). The cause was, amongst other things, a decline in the manufacturing base which, although already in evidence, was not helped by the early economic policies of the Thatcher government (see Thompson, Chapter 2). The consequence of this has been both a lessening of the political problem of unemployment, but also the rise in poverty (see Walker, who also points to changes in the tax system away from direct to indirect forms of taxation, Chapter 9) and the attendant acceptance of poverty too (see Hill and Walker, Chapter 3). These rises in unemployment (which were often concentrated in sectors of the economy dominated by men) and poverty encouraged more females into the labour market (see David, Chapter 6). The consequences of the rise in unemployment was an increase in economic inequality (Thompson – Dorling describes inequality as being 'defended', Walker describes it has being a strategy). Both Murie and Dorling point to the increasing social and spatial concentration of poverty and social polarization. Of course, such spatial concentration actually made it harder for the Conservatives to win in 2010, since the additional votes that they attracted were concentrated in existing 'safe' Tory seats. Following on from these processes which spatially and socially concentrated poverty, crime, amongst other social problems, rose (Farrall and Jennings, Chapter 7) and started to exert an influence on the policy agenda in ways it had not done so previously. As such, one of the consequences of Thatcherite social and economic policy changes was to create new 'problems' which needed to be 'solved'. Those people unfortunate not to be able to retrain or find new employment and who relied on the welfare state were accordingly stigmatized (Hill and Walker, Chapter 3), as social security, housing and welfare generally became to be seen as 'charity' rather than as 'a right', Dorling). There was a return to means testing and a shift in attitudes towards welfare recipients (Walker, Chapter 9).

One of the unintended consequences of the loss of the manufacturing and mining bases in the English north midlands, north of Britain and Wales was the shift of large numbers of people south (towards London, Dorling, Chapter 8) and the consequent change in household formation (David, Chapter 6). In part this encouraged (or required) more women to enter the labour market, but the rise in home ownership also played its part; as interest rates rose and as male breadwinners lost their jobs, so women of working age needed to enter the labour market. The changes in housing policies and the rise in levels of poverty meant that homelessness rose (Murie, Chapter 5). Indeed, houses, like education too (Dorey, Chapter 4), became fetishized. With regards to education, the increased use of league tables has meant not only that pupils are taught to the test (Dorey), but also excludes poorly performing pupils (Farrall and Jennings, Chapter 7).

For what is clear from the preceding analysis and the chapters we have brought together in this volume is that whilst Thatcherism may or may not 'be with us' today, the effects of the shifts in social and economic policies initiated by her governments will continue to work their way through the UK at a number of different levels and in a number of different ways. In this respect, and often in ways which go unrecognized or are obscured by more immediate concerns, the legacies of Thatcherism can be distilled along economic, political, social and cultural lines. That not all of these consequences were intended – and that a number of the unintended consequences may appear more dramatic than some of the intended ones – does not make these legacies any the less important.

References

DfES (2001) *Permanent Exclusions from Maintained Schools in England*, Issue 10/01, November.

Farrall, S., Jackson, J. and Gray, E. (2009) *Social Order and the Fear of Crime in Contemporary Times*, Clarendon Studies in Criminology. Oxford: Oxford University Press.

Gamble, A. (1996) 'The Legacy of Thatcherism', in M. Perryman (ed.) *The Blair Agenda*. London: Lawrence & Wishart.

Hall, S. (1979) 'The Great Moving Right Show', *Marxism Today* (Jan.): 14–20.

Hay, C. and Farrall, S. (2011) 'Establishing the Ontological Status of Thatcherism by Gauging its 'Periodisability': Towards a "Cascade Theory" of Public Policy Radicalism', *British Journal of Politics and International Relations*, 13(4): 439–58.

Heffernan, R. (2009) 'The Continuing Shadow of the Thatcher Governments', *British Politics Review*, 4(1): 8–9.

Jackson, B. and Saunders, R. (2012) 'Introduction: Varieties of Thatcherism', in B. Jackson and R. Saunders, (eds) *Making Thatcher's Britain*. Cambridge: Cambridge University Press.

Jessop, B., Bonnett, K., Bromley, S. and Ling, T. (1988) *Thatcherism*. Cambridge: Polity Press.

Kavanagh, D. (1987) *Thatcherism and British Politics: The End of Consensus?* Oxford: Oxford University Press.

Le Gales, P. and Scott, A (2008) 'Une revolution bureaucratique brittanique? Autonomie sans controle ou freer markets, more rules', *Revue francaise de sociologie*, 49(2): 301–30.

Marsh, D. and Rhodes, R.A.W. (eds) (1992) *Implementing Thatcherite Policies*. Buckingham: Open University Press.

Phillips, L. (1998) 'Hegemony and Political Discourse: The Lasting Impact of Thatcherism', *Sociology*, 32(4): 847–67.

Rhodes, R.A.W. and Marsh, D. (1992) 'Thatcherism: an Implementation Perspective', in D. Marsh and R.A.W. Rhodes (eds) *Implementing Thatcherite Policies*. Buckingham: Open University Press.

Timmins, N. (2001) *The Five Giants*. London: HarperCollins.

Wells, J. (1994) *Mitigating the Social Effects of Unemployment: Crime and Unemployment*, Report for the House of Commons Select Committee on Employment. Cambridge: Cambridge University, Faculty of Economics and Politics.

Wilding, P. (1992) 'The British Welfare State: Thatcher's Enduring Legacy', *Policy and Politics*, 20(3): 201–12.

339

Index

82, 86, 87, 93, 100; structure of the
economy 35; tax cuts 293; tax revenue
49; unemployment under 215
Malpass, P. 148
managerialism 75, 109, 117, 121, 126–8,
131–2, 137, 139–41
Manchester 124, 261
Mandelson, Peter 119–20
Mansell, Warwick 119, 128
manufacturing 37–9, 42–3, 58, 65–6, 337,
338
marketization: education 109, 113, 117,
121, 124, 126, 129, 132, 137; New
Labour 191; social welfare 189, 284;
state services 322
markets 9, 101, 112, 126, 326, 327;
education 132, 137; housing 144, 171
Marquand, David 76
marriage 86, 180, 199–200, 204, 205
Marsh, David 3, 10, 12, 14, 16–17, 22,
315–17, 330, 334
Marwick, Arthur 5, 7, 211
Massey, Doreen 276
Masterman, C.F.G. 308
maternity benefits 84
means testing 80, 83, 89–90, 92, 94,
100–1, 290, 301, 338; child benefit 205;
Heath government 78; housing
benefits 85, 163, 169; inequality 292;
Jobseeker's Allowance 220; New
Labour 296, 297; pensions 103;
'poverty trap' 85–6; unemployment
benefits 82; Universal Credit 102
Medium Term Financial Strategy
(MTFS) 57, 59, 73
Merkel, Angela 137
micro-economics 70, 75
middle class 103, 194–5, 322
'Middle England' 78
Milburn, Alan 192
Miliband, David 130
miners' strike 70, 242–4
Minimum Lending Rate 57
minimum wage 101, 106, 296
Ministry of Justice (MoJ) 227
Mitterand, François 59

monetarism 10, 13, 214–15, 230, 295, 296;
'monetarist turn' 72–5
monetary policy 35n1, 38–9, 57–62, 66–7,
71, 72–5
Monetary Policy Committee 61, 327
money supply 35n1, 57–9, 67, 73, 74, 215
Moore, John 286, 307
morality/moralism 103, 105, 106, 110,
115–16, 178, 336
Morgan, Patricia 189
Mount, Ferdinand 130, 178–9
multiculturalism 137, 138, 189
Murray, Charles 87, 97, 188, 194, 285

National Curriculum 113, 114, 117, 122,
141
National Endowment for Science,
Technology and the Arts (NESTA) 66
National Equality Panel (NEP) 297
National Health Service (NHS) 94, 114,
116, 129, 332; attitudes towards the
320, 335; Health and Social Care Act
241; marketization 131; privatization
265
National Insurance 81, 82–3, 181, 293,
294, 298
National Union of Mineworkers (NUM)
63
National Union of Teachers (NUT) 111
negative equity 161
neo-conservatism 5, 9–10, 97, 207, 226–7;
crime 21, 208, 227, 228, 229, 234;
education 110, 114–15, 117, 122; family
policy 176, 282; housing 144–5, 162;
'instincts' 211; social policy 236;
Thatcher's legacy 323; 'touchstones' 335
neo-liberalism 4–5, 9, 97, 187–8, 226–7,
229, 236; accumulation strategy 325;
crime 207–8, 227, 228, 230, 234;
education 108–11, 113–14, 122, 126, 131,
136, 138–9, 141; family policy 176;
Foucault on 141; inequality 282, 284;
New Labour 191, 193; spending cuts
295; tenets of 208–11; Thatcher's legacy
33, 34, 323, 326, 327; 'touchstones' 335;
'watchman' state 237

347